The Greenwood Encyclopedia of
Homes through American History

The Greenwood Encyclopedia of Homes through American History

Volume 3
1901–1945

1901–1920, Leslie Humm Cormier

1921–1945, Neal V. Hitch

Thomas W. Paradis, General Editor

GREENWOOD PUBLISHING
Westport, Connecticut • London

Library of Congress Cataloging-in-Publication Data

The Greenwood encyclopedia of homes through American history.
   v. cm.
   Includes bibliographical references and index.
   Contents: v. 1. 1492–1820/Melissa Wells Duffes, William Burns, and Olivia Graf; 1781–1820/
Melissa Wells Duffes; Thomas W. Paradis, general editor—v. 2. 1821–1900—v. 3. 1901–1945—
v. 4. 1946–present.
   ISBN 978–0–313–33496–2 (set : alk. paper)—ISBN 978–0–313–33747–5 (v. 1 : alk. paper)—
ISBN 978–0–313–33694–2 (v. 2 : alk. paper)—ISBN 978–0–313–33748–2 (v. 3 : alk. paper)—
ISBN 978–0–313–33604–1 (v. 4 : alk. paper)
   1. Architecture, Domestic—United States—Encyclopedias.   2. Decorative arts—
United States—Encyclopedias.   3. Dwellings—United States—Encyclopedias.
I. Greenwood Press (Westport, Conn.)   II. Title: Encyclopedia of homes through
American history.
   NA7205.G745   2008
   728.0973'03—dc22   2008002946

British Library Cataloguing in Publication Data is available.

Library of Congress Catalog Card Number: 2008002946
ISBN-13: 978–0–313–33496–2 (set)
        978-0-313-33747-5 (vol. 1)
        978-0-313-33694-2 (vol. 2)
        978-0-313-33748-2 (vol. 3)
        978-0-313-33604-1 (vol. 4)

First published in 2008

Greenwood Press, 88 Post Road West, Westport, CT 06881
An imprint of Greenwood Publishing Group, Inc.
www.greenwood.com

Printed in the United States of America

The paper used in this book complies with the
Permanent Paper Standard issued by the National
Information Standards Organization (Z39.48–1984).

10 9 8 7 6 5 4 3 2 1

I wish to dedicate my book on American homes to the many children in orphanages around the globe who may never have a book or a home.

—Leslie Humm Cormier

Contents

HOMES IN THE DEPRESSION AND
WORLD WAR II ERA, 1921–1945

Foreword

What if the walls of our homes could talk? Though perhaps a frightening thought for some, our walls would certainly relate countless happy memories and events throughout our lives and past generations. They might also tell us of their own origins—their own past explaining their history of construction; materials; positioning within the home their relationship to doors, windows, rooflines, and basements; and all the special ways in which they have been decorated or altered by their owners. In a sense, this unprecedented series of volumes on the history of the American home will allow our walls to talk to the extent possible through the written word. The physical structures of our homes today—whether condominium, townhouse, farmhouse, apartment house, free-standing house, mansion, or log cabin—all have a story to tell, and the authors of this set have been determined to tell it.

It is easy to take our homes for granted; we do not often recognize the decades and centuries of historical development that have shaped and informed the construction of our own walls that shelter us. Our homes' room layouts, construction materials, interior furnishings, outdoor landscaping, and exterior styles are all contingent upon the past—a past comprising individual innovators, large and small companies, cultural influences from far-away places, political and economic decisions, inspirational writers, technological inventions, and generations of American families of diverse backgrounds who have all contributed to how our homes look and function. This set, titled *The Greenwood Encyclopedia of Homes through American History,* treats the American home as a symbolic portal to a historical account rarely viewed from this perspective.

This set focuses just as much on the interrelated past of American culture, politics, economy, geography, transportation, technology, and demographics as on the home itself. By twisting the title a bit, we could easily justify renaming it to *American History through the Home*. Given that most of us find history more meaningful if connected tangibly to our own lives, the American home perhaps serves as the ideal vehicle for relating the fascinating and engaging aspects of American history to students of any age and educational background. Our homes today are in large part a product of our past, and what better way than to use our own dwellings as veritable gateways to understanding American history—and for better understanding ourselves?

The volumes herein take us on an introductory though comprehensive tour through the dynamic developmental process of the American home, from the earliest colonial cabins and Native American precedents to present-day suburbs and downtown loft condominiums. Though treated as a historical account, this collection constitutes a multidisciplinary approach that weaves together the influences of geography, urban and rural development, cultural studies, demographics, politics, and national and global economy. Each book in the set considers regional developments, relevant historical issues, and multicultural perspectives throughout the current-day contiguous 48 states. Further, because most of us do not live in grand, *high-style* estates or mansions designed by professional architects, our authors devote more than the typical amount of space on common, or *vernacular*, architecture of the home. It is nonetheless vital to recognize the vast amount of past and contemporary research from which this set has borrowed and showcased. More than the latest write-up on architectural history, these volumes also provide an extensive overview of the more significant resources on this topic that will lead enthusiasts well beyond these specific pages. This set is perhaps best interpreted as a beginning to the journey of life-long learning.

Those interested in the American home—whether student, professional, layperson, or a combination—can approach *The Greenwood Encyclopedia of Homes through American History* in various ways. The set is divided into parts, or time periods, each written by a different scholar. Thus, each volume is divided into two or more chronological segments, and each can be read as a narrative, moving in the order presented by the sequence of chapters. Others will find an encyclopedic approach to be useful, allowing those searching for specific information to quickly access the volume and topic of choice through the volumes' contents pages and through the comprehensive index. Every chronological part of each volume includes a glossary and lengthy recommended list of resources to enhance the reader's search for clarity and to provide further sources of information. While impossible to scour the Internet for all relevant resources on the topic, this set has included a commendable listing of reliable and informative Web resources, all of which can potentially lead in new directions.

Like scaffolding that enables a building's construction, the sequence of chapters found in each chronological segment of the volumes progresses logically through major topics relevant to the home. With a few exceptions, each part takes us on a veritable tour, beginning first with a chapter devoted to relevant history and contextual background. From there, we tour the American home's exterior treatments, referred to as architectural styling, perhaps the most visible and public feature of our dwellings. The tour then continues to the inner workings and construction of the home, highlighting the important building materials and manufacturing techniques available during that period of time. The home's interior serves as the next stop on the tour, with two successive chapters devoted to floor plans; room layouts and uses; topics on lighting, heating, and ventilation; and a full chapter devoted to furniture and interior design.

Completing most segment's tour is a final chapter taking us back outside to consider the approaches to landscaping around the home, its site on the lot, its situation in the local or regional environment, its relationship to the streets and neighborhood, and any outbuildings that may have contributed to the homestead.

Organized a bit differently from the rest, the final segment, from 1986 to the present, provides a sort of conclusion to the entire set, interpreting the most current trends in contemporary housing and society, with which we can all directly relate as we progress through the early part of the twenty-first century. As the series editor, I speak for all of our authors by inviting you to explore the endless fascination provided by our cherished American home through history, and to discover for yourself how, indeed, our walls can talk to us.

Thomas W. Paradis
General Editor

PART ONE

Homes in the Early Modern Architectural Era: 1901–1920

Leslie Humm Cormier

Introductory Note

History is only 100 years long; that is to say, living modern history. The fleeting, first-person event as lived, lasts only three lifetimes, three generations, 100 years, and then the relevance and perhaps poignancy of the first-person account of the moment is lost. Families of a century ago are gone, but their homes—mansions, tenements, suburban Tudors—stand amidst our cities and towns. This first section of the volume is a contemplation of the architecture of the home in the period of 1901 through 1920 and also of the idea and ideal of "home," and of history as a living subject of lives lived in rooms under roofs. Time passes into history, lives are lost to epidemics, and machinery, and old age, but architecture endures.

Writing critical modern architectural history for me is a manifold process of voices and sites. I wish to clarify that I have said *critical* history because for me, that is the truth of my teaching and my writing. Modern critical history is an analytical and a creative act. A critical history is not a compilation of facts, but of fact considered, understood, and interpreted within a wider context. Critical history, therefore, is not afraid of considered opinion; indeed, such a study is obligated intellectually and emotionally to offer an interpretation of the meaning of lives lived in the near past. If one does not imbue the societal actions and concrete creations of the past with authentic emotion and meaning, history devolves into lives lived in vain and vacant monuments.

A HIERARCHY OF MODERN HISTORY

Sources of modern historical writing are hierarchical, based first in primary sources to ground the work in authenticity. Therefore, the first priority for me is always the architectural site visit, for we cannot truly know a building or a landscape except in the space of three dimensions. This can mean standing on a street corner in a new city and staring upward at a seemingly unimportant building (architectural historians must accept, even embrace, being seen as eccentric in public places occasionally). On the subject of staring upward—every American, not only writers, should make the trek to look upward toward the Empire State Building or Yosemite Falls at least once—to grasp the sublime in American architecture and landscape. There is no more profound event in architectural research than the site visit to a place not yet seen.

Next are the voices, voices of those who were there at the time of the event, to bear witness to the moment being studied, and so I, whenever possible, write from first-person accounts, here in many cases from memories of my grandfathers who were born with the twentieth century. Where we cannot find sites or first-person accounts, as modern historians we must look to original artifacts and documents of the day; to museum exhibitions of contemporary objects; and to historical sources of journalism, such as *The Architectural Record,* the *New York Times,* the *Chicago Tribune* and the *Los Angeles Times.* Researching this period, I read about certain well-known disasters, for example, the 1906 San Francisco Earthquake and the 1912 sinking of the Titanic, in order to compare commentaries of the time. I found it quite poignant to experience history in retrospect, reading the great optimism of the day before the ship's maiden voyage, but knowing the end of the story as the reporter did not.

When the newspapers have crumbled, there is the near-contemporary book, such as Frederick Lewis Allen's *The Big Change,* or classic monographs by ground-breaking theorists such as Henry-Russell Hitchcock's *In the Nature of Materials, The Architecture of Frank Lloyd Wright.* The books most valuable to me were these historical and architectural commentaries written mid-twentieth century, when memories of the early modern era were still fresh and first person. The books of modern architectural historian William H. Jordy, *American Architects and their Buildings,* are invaluable sources. More recently, the excellent specialized architectural encyclopedias in the library reference section introduce new subjects coherently to the reader. There are many current illustrated books on American domestic and landscape architecture and home styles, though fewer on this quiet American period of 1901–1920. A number of these recent compilations were valuable to me in writing on landscape, in particular.

It is crucial for modern history to distinguish itself as the only history that can be written from a living perspective. Therefore, the hierarchy I have observed for authenticity of this history of the American home of the early modern era has been as follows: architectural and landscape site visits, first-person accounts, original documents, museum objects and exhibitions, newspapers and periodicals of the early modern era in the United States, 1901–1920, books written within 50 years of these dates, recent architectural encyclopedias and scholarship, and perhaps most obvious of all, personal observation, memory, and interpretation. While early modern history is still directly within my reach, I will write it as I see it.

SOCIAL HISTORY OF THE EARLY MODERN ERA

History, architectural style, and landscape define America. Therefore, to my mind, the chapters "History of the Early Modern Era, 1901–1920," "Styles of

Domestic Architecture around the Country, 1901–1920," and "Landscaping and Outbuildings, 1901–1920" are the most significant commentaries in Part 1 of this volume, for they interpret important technological and societal acceleration, architectural stylistic advances, and the integration of architecture with nature during the early modern era. I note that an American, such as my grandfather, born at the turn of the century and dying in the 1960s, underwent the most accelerated period of change in human history, from horse to Apollo mission. Great technological advances were made during 1901–1920, yet simultaneously, aspects of American culture remained astoundingly retrograde, especially before 1913. Writing about both Fifth Avenue mansions and philanthropic housing for the poor, I note the extremes of class divisions I encountered. As a person who has lived her life in the late twentieth and twenty-first centuries, I was amazed while reading newspapers by the structurally ingrained stratification of society of this period, particularly by the open callousness to the poor to the point of cruelty.

Callous, too, was the exploitation of the masses, forced by the aristocracy, to engage in World War I. I have written from my early childhood memories told to me by survivors of early twentieth-century immigration and World War I. Even as I share their stories of the trauma of that time, I question, as I did even as a school kid, whether we must define history by violence and war dates. Did not people in the past live outside of wartime? Do civilizations not only destroy, but build? *The Greenwood Encyclopedia of Homes through American History,* I hope, will answer my childhood question by acknowledging that Americans have lived productive lives, in spite of work and pain and conflict, within the structure of a social compact, moving toward democratization of their society. They have planned communities; they have planted trees; and their homes are the architectural testaments to these peaceful pursuits. During the early modern era of the United States, there were thoughtful voices for social justice and peace. Freud was writing on "Work and Love," and later he attempted to answer Einstein's eternal question, "Why War?"

EARLY MODERN ARCHITECTURAL STYLE

Style is for me the definition of the home, for my passion is modern architecture, and herein I explore the factors that created the stylistic streams of early twentieth-century American culture. Eventually, those streams would feed into the ocean of the International Style, my specialty in the modern visual arts, as émigrés synthesized American styles with their European modernism. Indigenous American modernism is a somewhat new focus for me, as in my career I have explored America primarily from the viewpoint of émigré artists and architects. Material on style in "Styles of Domestic Architecture around the Country, 1901–1920" is drawn from my lectures at Radcliffe on "American Architecture In Situ." I have categorized the homes I have observed of 1901–1920 as *Traditional Styles, Emerging Modern Styles,* and *Modern Styles.* Architecture experienced in situ allows us to read buildings for motifs and historical links within context, fully experiencing the visual cacophony of the streetscape, for then the entire city stands out in higher relief.

"Styles of Domestic Architecture around the Country, 1901–1920" allowed me to look at architect Frank Lloyd Wright, about whom so much has been said. Just when it seemed that every bit of minutiae had been stated, I noted something strange in an old document that might (or might not) solve a mystery about this famous man (though certainly that is a tale for another book), but I note this as an illustration of just how history becomes exciting, a trail of clues to a surprise ending. Another trail I followed gave me the privilege to have access to original photographs of early twentieth-century California, to Irving Gill's work, and to the buildings and documents of a number of important scientific observatories and their "monasteries" of the early modern era. Combining architectural site visits with specific documents related to the construction of that site imparts historical authenticity and excitement to discovered places. Thus, paradoxically, buildings and their stories allow us to feel an enthusiastic anticipation of the past.

MATERIALS, DESIGN, AND DECORATION

The chapters in this volume are like a framed house, from outside to inside: The first chapter, "History of the Early Modern Era, 1901–1920," is the foundation; the second chapter, "Styles of Domestic Architecture around the Country, 1901–1920," represents the facade; and the sixth chapter, "Landscaping and Outbuildings, 1901–1920," becomes the acreage about the house. The interior chapters, "Building Materials and Manufacturing, 1901–1920," "Home Layout and Design, 1901–1920," and "Furniture and Decoration, 1901–1920" are the rooms inside that house. These chapters are observational and empirical, based on looking at the American vernacular home in its various iterations. Many generations have lived in the old house in which I am writing this manuscript; your home, too, is your piece of history. If you have lived in a vernacular American home, you, too, can note materials, layout, and furnishings within, but you may not be aware that 1901–1920 was the last era in which all building materials were natural, and that the movement toward democratization of the American home can be understood as expressed through the simplified open plan.

Sources of materials, design, and decoration can be found in building and construction manuals, and because much of the information in the interior chapters is common knowledge within the public domain, I also used reprints of house plans and furniture catalogues found in the library. I offer this caveat on the authenticity of reprints and particularly of Internet sources: Part of the strength of the Internet is that it is immediate and unvetted; the weakness of the Internet is that it is unedited and unvetted. Currently, the Internet is valuable as a tool for some creative visual artists and writers, and reputable material is beginning to become accessible online. For the purposes of scholarship, however, it is rife with third-hand, sometimes public domain, but often-plagiarized sources. It is a handy place to check a date (and even in that instance you have to be careful), but for serious research, students are advised to confine themselves, as this book does, only to Web sites specifically written and authorized by authoritative organizations and publishers, such as the National Park Service, Craftsman Farms Foundation, and the Metropolitan Museum of Art.

LANDSCAPE, PLANNING, AND PRESERVATION

The sixth chapter, "Landscaping and Outbuildings, 1901–1920," was a serendipitous study, a chance to research in books and paintings the most dramatic American landscapes I have previously explored on foot: Yellowstone, Yosemite, Big Sur, Long Island's North Shore estates, and New York's Central Park. The salvation of American landscape during the period 1901–1920, both Western wilderness and Eastern park land, is to me the greatest gift that we have inherited as Americans from the prescient thinkers and preservationists of the early modern era. The classic view I see as defining the early modern American landscape is found in Manhattan, looking toward Fifth Avenue or Central Park West, as seen from a clearing in Central Park or from the roof of the Metropolitan Museum of Art. This vista encompasses at once the artistic apex and the oppositions of American aesthetics: ancient wilderness below and modern skyscraper above.

One thematic interest to which I return in many chapters is the meaning of the city and of urban planning in the early modern era. The history of the home of the early modern era occurred in conjunction with the growth of the city and the invention of the suburb. Urban planning thus created the skeletons of the bodies of our communities, positively or negatively. Therefore, I write on early modern planning within the contexts of the first chapter, "History of the Early Modern Era, 1901–1920"; the fourth chapter, "Home Layout and Design, 1901–1920"; and the sixth chapter, "Landscaping and Outbuildings, 1901–1920" in the hope that the reader will begin to look, and to feel responsible for, the built and the landscape environment, beyond one's own home, moving with society toward enlightened awareness of the city and open space beyond the property line.

I have also included a number of helpful features for readers: a timeline to put prominent events of this period into a chronological context; a glossary, for terms that may be unfamiliar; and a resource guide, which provides information for readers from a wide variety of resources, including archives, books and journals, and Web sites. Note that though the term "modern" is sometimes used in a general historical sense, it is employed very specifically in the architecture and design of the 20th century, and I have applied the more specific stylistic use often in this book. "Modern" here refers to the creative visual design motifs of 1901–1920 and beyond, defined by the simplification of design, the clean lines, the geometric forms, and the unornamented surfaces, that spoke symbolically to a fresh vision of a new world.

Architecture and nature are long-lived, and domestic architecture, in particular, represents the changing aspirations, the social and aesthetic values, the actual lives of a civilization. The simple architecture of the home in the city may therefore be the most moving and authentic form of history we can know.

Acknowledgments

No architect works alone. Many craftsmen are needed to build a house; so, too, is the building of a book. For this reason, I would like to acknowledge and to thank the many persons who have helped me to craft this text. Among scholars, I owe the greatest debt to my former advisor, historian of modern architecture, Professor William H. Jordy, Department of History of Art and Architecture, Brown University. I am particularly indebted in this book to his writings on Wright's Robie House. I also recall an informative walk through Gill's architecture with Professor David Gebhard. Through elegant lectures at Brown, I learned the significance of architectural form and the meaning of modernism.

I have been fortunate in this project to have open-minded, encouraging editors, concerned not only with writing, but with writers. Special thanks are due to Tom Paradis, for his insight into architecture and planning, and to Anne Thompson for her publication professionalism. Thanks also to Debra Adams and Greenwood Press. This historical homes project has provided an excuse for me to make site visits from Manhattan to Tucson to Pasadena, and thanks Roberta, Denise, Annette, and Pam for sharing your homes while I looked at buildings. Back in Boston, I have enjoyed the good humor of my many Emerson College students.

Thanks to the librarians and staffs of the following architectural libraries and archives: Rotch Library, Architecture and Planning, and the Humanities Library, Massachusetts Institute of Technology; Scripps Institution of Oceanography Library; Huntington Library, Museum, and Botanical Gardens; Carnegie Observatory; and Houghton Library, Harvard University, for specialized papers and architectural books. For architecture and memories, I thank people for their personal gifts, especially Ati Gropius Forberg. For listening, thank you WMK, JMcD, MAG, et merci, DPA, vous etes vraiment penseur de la vie. I have been sustained during my modern inquiries by many persons who have generously shared their time and expertise.

Godspeed, grandfathers Hans and George, this study has let me know you as I could not in your lifetimes. To my family, we had fun in the sun those days in our La Jolla home, didn't we?! And to my husband, Vernon, scientist and fellow traveler, without whom there would be no home away from home, nor architecture of life, may we keep our passports always current.

Leslie Humm Cormier
Department of Visual and Media Arts
Emerson College, Boston

Timeline

1901	The twentieth century begins on January 1. It is interesting that though the early modern era considered the new century to begin in 1901, we have celebrated the new millennium beginning in the year 2000; therefore, the 20th century was historically a rather short century, only 99 years long.
1901–1920	Millions of European immigrants continue to stream into Ellis Island in New York Harbor throughout the early modern era. Most move into urban tenement slums, while the wealthy inhabit Beaux-Arts townhouses and estates. Particularly during the first half of this time, until 1913, America was a land of extremes of poverty versus wealth, with little in between.
1902	Theodore Roosevelt becomes President of the United States and makes tenement housing standards in eastern slums an American issue. He is further committed to saving western American landscape.
	Louis Comfort Tiffany designs his avant-garde estate, Laurelton Hall, on the Long Island's North Shore.
	Frank Lloyd Wright designs the modern Heurtley House in suburban Oak Park, Illinois.
1903	The Wright Brothers make their first successful flight.
	In May, Gustav Stickley publishes his first volume of *The Craftsman* magazine, featuring his Craftsman Style homes and Mission furniture designs.

1904   The New York City subway is constructed as urban infrastructure advances. Thomas Edison makes his first film with sound.

1905   Vernacular housing styles now include the bungalow, the colonial, the foursquare, the triple-decker, and the rowhouse.

1906   The Great San Francisco Earthquake devastates the city on April 18. Thousands of wooden rowhouses fall from the shaking or are burned by the fire.

1907   The Gamble House, a landmark in American Arts and Crafts, is designed in Pasadena, California, by architects Greene & Greene.

1908   Forest Hills Gardens, New York City, is designed by architect Grosvenor Atterbury and landscape architect Frederick Law Olmsted in Traditional Tudor style for the Russell Sage Foundation. As an example of middle-class suburban housing, this plan of enlightened urban design was intended to serve as a housing model for the emerging middle class.

Architect Irving Gill designs the Director's House and Laboratory, Scripps Institution of Oceanography, La Jolla, California, in his abstract modern style.

1909   The popular Model T automobile is introduced by Ford Motor Company. Automobiles lead to the suburbanization of America.

Beaux-Arts architect Charles McKim of McKim, Mead & White is awarded the Gold Medal of the American Institute of Architects for his traditional designs.

Kykuit, The Rockefeller Estate, is designed along the Hudson River by traditional architects Delano & Aldrich.

Frank Lloyd Wright builds his early modern masterpiece, the Robie House, in Chicago.

1910   Taylorization brings time and motion efficiency studies to the home, especially to the kitchen.

1911   American Modernism and modern homes gain international recognition with the publication of the works of Frank Lloyd Wright in Germany, as aesthetic debates rage in avant-garde European circles, and the modern theories and forms that will become the Bauhaus and the International Style are conceived.

1912   April 14, the *Titanic* sinks. Americans read newspaper headlines of tragedy.

Stickley designs and constructs his Craftsman Farms communal home in New Jersey.

1913   Graduated Income Tax is at last introduced by the 16th Amendment, leading to a decline in the construction of private estates and landscapes for the wealthy. Income tax represented the change in American consciousness toward a more even distribution of wealth and the development of a middle class, and therefore led to the construction of the middle-class home and the rise of sub-urbanization.

Asilomar, and its cottages and landscape, is designed for the YWCA by Julia Morgan on the Monterey peninsula in California.

1914   The Great War breaks out in Europe. President Woodrow Wilson encourages America to stay out of the conflict.

1915   The Panama Pacific and Pacific California Expositions introduce the Beaux-Arts and the Spanish Colonial Revival styles to the West.

1916   The New York City Skyscraper Set-Back Law shapes the tower architecture of Manhattan.

The National Parks are established in the West, including Yellowstone and Yosemite, by the National Park Service Organic Act.

1917   American Doughboys ship out to France as America enters WWI.

America is unprepared for the needs of workers' housing; housing shortages plague America, as few homes are constructed.

1918   November 11, WWI ends with the Armistice.

Influenza epidemic kills 20 million people worldwide.

Coe Hall, Planting Fields, private estate and arboretum, is constructed on Long Island.

1919   Women's Suffrage begins with passage of the 19th Amendment.

The public becomes the beneficiary of the previously private Beaux-Arts Frick mansion, art collection, and garden on Fifth Avenue.

1920   National optimism is high as the economy grows rapidly. Urban infrastructure improves as cities modernize, and middle-class American suburban homes are developed in the East and Midwest, in traditional revivalist or more modern styles. A land and housing boom begins in Florida and California, where bungalows and modern styles prevail.

History of the Early Modern Era, 1901–1920

The Century is dead: long live the Century! Yesterday was the Nineteenth, today the Twentieth. Some time last night the one died and the other was born . . . the event took place at midnight . . . a moment of darkness . . . a hush among the crowd—and the Old Century was buried. The lights flashed . . . bells peeled, bombs thundered, rockets blasted skyward, and the new Century made its triumphant entry . . . It was distinctly an electric celebration . . . Everywhere the shimmerring gleam of electric lights shot their effulgence out over city and river and harbor . . . throwing the deep reflection against the overhanging sky, making the darkness radiant.

—*New York Times,* "Twentieth Century's Triumphant Entry," 1901

THE TURN OF THE TWENTIETH CENTURY

This ecstatic New Year's "electric celebration" commenced the modern world we inhabit today in our contemporary homes. To begin a century with the aspiration to make "the darkness radiant" and "triumphant" was an optimistic goal for America, in an era precariously poised on the cusp between diurnal darkness of the historical past and utopian dreams of a brightly lit future. At its inception, the twentieth century was understood to be both a technological breakthrough, and, simultaneously, a continuity with a late millennial revival of thought, a reinvigoration of the national consciousness of America. Following a period of intellectual and aesthetic development sometimes referred to as the American Renaissance, the worldview of the early modern era reflected a period half a millennium earlier, the fifteenth-century Italian Renaissance. In its breadth, from the sciences to the arts, the early modern era of America reminds one of enlightened Renaissance thought, based in scientific observation of the natural world infused with ancient classical learning.

The early twentieth century became at once the birth of a modern electric lighted world, and in some cases, the rebirth of much earlier ideas. The Wright Brothers astounded the nation with flight in 1903, at last realizing Leonardo da Vinci's predictions of human flight from 500 years before. Freud's theories of the mind, based in metaphors of classical mythology, brought Americans the Oedipus complex when he visited in 1909. Even Americans who could not understand Euclid's mathematics were awed by Einstein's 1905 Theory of Special Relativity and his visit to the United States. America was a world moving forward, ever faster in science and technology, with seemingly endless curiosity, invention, and aspiration. Major changes in thought and daily life were occurring with increasing frequency in the early modern era. The electric light, the telephone, the automobile, the airplane, to name the most obvious, were all invented in America during the period 1901–1920. This century literally took flight.

Yet, in retrospect, as we observe the homes and social conditions of the early modern period, we find that the utopian aspirations of the beginning of the twentieth century perplex the reader at the beginning of the twenty-first. For, as we consider the cities and domestic architecture of the early modern period, we encounter a world of major contradictions and a reality of extremes: new versus old, beauty versus decay, wealth versus poverty, townhouse versus tenement. Such social oppositions resulted in striking visual contrasts in living conditions for Americans and the homes they inhabited. Socially, extravagant mansions coexisted with seedy slums in our cities. Visually, simple vernacular building contrasted with high architectural style. America of the early modern era was

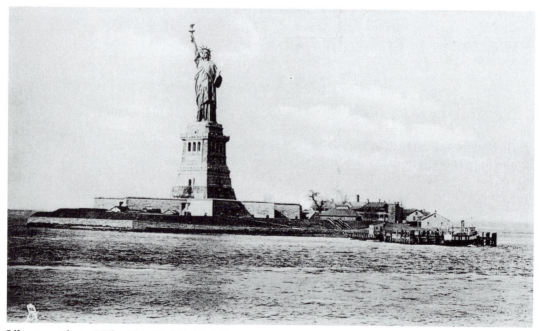

Liberty, at last. © The New York Public Library.

in essence two societies, divided by a chasm of class, made most apparent by the home that one inhabited. One wonders, in retrospect, whether this utopian new "electric century" would truly be so "radiant" for all Americans and their homes. Within the context of social contradictions and visual dichotomies, we will search the American landscape for the fundamental meaning of *home* in a time "triumphant," the dawn of the twentieth century and the early modern architectural era.

THE MEANING OF HOME IN EARLY TWENTIETH-CENTURY AMERICA

The concept of *home* in America, particularly in the early modern era, bears the sometimes contradictory burdens of form and function, emotion and mythology. Whereas Americans have always desired to come home to a place of modern comfort and convenience, home is, by definition, a nostalgic place. While electric light, streetcars, and automobiles might light the worker's factory and transport him home at night, he longed to come home, physically and emotionally, to an old-fashioned looking house, in which, in the early modern period, a traditional family was expected to be waiting at home for the breadwinner; this was a conservative, traditional, and sentimental time in our country. Americans have long resisted modern aesthetic style in the home, even as they seek modern labor-saving devices of industrialization. Thus, the basic concept of the American home, by nature, tends to be *retarditaire,* or out-of-date even in its own time. Housing always seems to be just a step behind so-called progress, as even today, Americans maintain an odd ambivalence concerning technology versus housing style.

The House In Situ

Therefore, amidst all the change, electrification, and modernization of 1901–1920, the only major industry not to be invested intensively in industrialization, or even in the idea of the future, was housing. Housing, just as today, seemed in the early modern era to be the laggard in adventurous new movements, perhaps due to the emotional composition of housing, but economically explained by the fact that housing alone as an industry is produced in situ. Except in very rare exceptions, there is no house factory. By its nature, housing is the one industry that consistently stays tied to its site, is predominantly hand-built, is often nonstandardized, and is very rarely mass-produced.

For the most part, from 1901–1920, the American home was in a period of quietude. During this period, a relatively small amount of housing was built, especially considering the increase in the population of cities due to immigration. This is the period just before the advent of the housing boom and before the housing tract development. During this period, housing construction was still primarily the province of the individual builder–laborer. Advances were more prevalent in transportation, industry, and private enterprise because the forward-looking electric century simply did not consider housing a major American problem, and certainly not a government concern. Even in the housing built, homes that may have been modern and electrified usually continued to look backward aesthetically, sheathing themselves in the nostalgia of historical motifs. Only very rare, forward-thinking architects understood that the new home of the new era demanded new forms.

Change and Acceleration in Early Twentieth-Century America

The early modern era must have been a difficult and fleeting era to grasp for Americans actually living through it, that is, if they had the luxury of time to reflect upon their age, and most workers never did. After a long period of stability, the world suddenly began to change so fast that this must have been both a wonder and a disorienting experience. Not only was technological change pervasive, but the acceleration of change during this period surely exceeded any in the history of mankind. So much change occurred in the first two decades of the twentieth century in America that a man born at the turn of the century, living to the age of 65, would recall childhood in an era of the horse and carriage, adulthood during a time of the automobile and airplane, and perhaps even personally experience the beginnings of the jet and space age. If this person lived to age 70, he might have watched America land a man on the moon on a television in the living room of his home. All the technology of his world, from airplane to television, would be new, but his house and its living room would be much the same as the house of his childhood. For as American modernism led the world of the early twentieth century in the fields of science and technology, American homes, with rare exceptions, remained relatively stable environments.

Despite the sameness of the living room, however, America outside the house was undergoing significant transformations that would eventually affect life in the modern home. There are so many things in the city and the American home of 100 years later that we must erase from our minds to understand the early modern period. In *The Big Change, America Transforms Itself 1900–1950*, social historian Frederick Lewis Allen discussed how in many ways, American cities and towns in 1901–1920 were just as amazing for what they did not yet have as for what they were. Streets were quiet and darker; automotive engines were rarely heard; horses were common. Gas streetlights, not yet completely replaced with electric, were dimmer than today's electrified streets; immigrants from European cities were surprised to find that the United States was not yet fully electrified. As the telephone was newly invented, and very few telephones had yet to be installed in private homes, one wonders to whom the caller might actually expect to be connected.

American urban and rural life was far more regional than today, with population in the United States concentrated in the northeastern and midwestern cities. New York and Chicago were the prime cities, the economic, financial, and architectural engines of this era. Farms were beginning to mechanize, but ranch and farm life were very isolated from the population centers. California and the far West were still nearly frontier, quite sparsely populated, except for post-gold rush San Francisco. The southern region, still recovering economically from the Civil War, only 35 years before and still within memory, was barely in touch with the rest of America. Except for the rare settlement, Florida remained gators and glades; land booms were still in the future.

People knew only their extended family and neighbors within their town or urban neighborhood and had little contact with outsiders; life was local. Children, when not working, ran after their rolling wooden hoops, and boys played stickball in car-free streets. Daughter's dolls had porcelain faces, and teddy bears were all the rage. Daily life was circumscribed and predictable, as choices and amusements were much more limited than we expect today, perhaps board games and cards filled an evening. New visual media, such as nickelodeons and flickering moving picture shows, were introduced to the amazement of the public. An exciting adventure awaited, perhaps once in a lifetime, if you were fortunate enough to attend a fair, such as the Chicago World's Fair of 1893, the St. Louis Exposition of 1904, or the Panama-Pacific Exposition in San Diego of 1915.

Conversation would have been more limited to local information, for though early crystal sets were popular, surprisingly, there was no radio until the 1920s, no less more advanced forms of audio-visual communication or programmed entertainment. Important national and international information could travel almost instantaneously now via telephone, telegraph, and wireless, but then had to be widely dispersed via print journalism. Competition among daily newspapers was cutthroat, and newspapers sometimes exaggerated stories to increase circulation; however, newspapers and magazines were the primary connections to current events and to the wider world for those who could read. Three major metropolitan newspapers of this time remain the strongest sources of documentation of early modern American life and housing information, led by the *New York Times,* the *Chicago Tribune,* and later, the *Los Angeles Times.*

Light, Speed, and Front Porch

Even as the world sped up, personal relationships and communication remained more direct, and friendships longer, perhaps, than today. Thomas Edison, of the light bulb, and Henry Ford, of the automobile, were friends over many years, and their neighboring winter homes reflected their personal and professional associations. They vacationed for years on the Gulf coast of Florida, a very undeveloped region at that time, their families wintering in simple wooden houses with verandas, laboratory facilities, experimental tropical botanical gardens, garages, and even an early swimming pool steps away. Together, the synergy of these two figures drove the engine that became modern America, eventually bringing electrical light, appliances, and automobiles to all classes of American homes. Yet, here in Florida they spent hours chatting in wicker chairs on the front porch, just American folks who happened to invent things.

The early modern era invention and dispersal of electricity by Edison, and the production of the automobile by Ford, together transformed the physical conditions of the American home and city more than any other latter-day inventions have done. The light bulb meant human life and work were for the first time in history not tied to the rhythms of sunlight. Cities no longer needed to move to the demands of diurnal time. Edison personally electrified a sector of Manhattan near City Hall just to demonstrate the wonders of the electric light as streetlight. Shrewdly introducing his invention for free, he managed to create in the public the demand for electricity that became so intrinsic to the future of the American city and home. Ford likewise put cheap cars on the American road, and in the process, actually created the conditions that would redraw the map of America as a land of highways, to suit his invention.

Transportation and Infrastructure

Automobiles were an expensive anomaly until 1913, when the first assembly lines sent affordable Ford Model Ts to farmers. Before then, without cars, there were no high-speed paved roads as we know them now; there were certainly no interstate highways. Asphalt roads were rare outside cities, dirt being the most common turn-of-the-century country road, with concrete just beginning to enter the picture. Even urban streets were neither divided nor lined, and cars shared the roads with horses and horse-drawn carriages. Rural communities were virtually unconnected with the wider world, unless they were on train lines. Transit, like life in general, tended to be local. The common forms of town transportation were walking and bicycling, riding old-fashioned wagons and carriages and horse-drawn and later electrified streetcars, or the very occasional car. More modern local streetcars and elevated trains were being introduced and covered extensive routes within and between cities and towns. Larger urban areas were served by intercity trains. Early subways were under construction in New York and Boston. Electrified trains and streetcars, through the addition of the third rail, allowed cleaner electric powered trains to replace smoky stream engines within the confines of the city.

Cars did not rule America before the 1920s. As late as the mid-teens, city plans assumed that automobiles would co-exist with horse-drawn vehicles indefinitely. Only the richest man in the neighborhood could brag about his Model A, and he generally cranked it up and drove it only for Sunday motoring in the country, rather than for commuting. A family without a car, however, could sometimes take a Sunday outing, too, because the streetcar companies invented entertaining weekend excursions for the working class, such as Coney Island. A Sunday excursion might bring the worker out of the inner city for relief from the summer heat, but more important, it was intended to provide fares for the private streetcar company. This is an illustration of the synergy of private invention and public life common in the early modern era: successful invention supplied by private capital created its own demand.

City and Suburb in the Early Modern Era

Advances in transportation became a major catalyst giving rise to new architectural forms in early twentieth-century America, as streetcar lines and urban roadways both followed and dictated the forms of cities and their housing agglomerations. The invention and dispersal of electric trains and automobiles influenced urban configurations, as a newly growing middle class chose not just excursions, but permanent flight from the inner city. In a rare early warning concerning the changes to be wrought by the automobile, the Russell Sage Foundation noted foresightedly, "The coming into almost universal use of the automobile has brought with it very difficult problems radically affecting property subdivision" (Veiller 1920). Planned developments of housing, even entire towns on the outskirts of older cities, were designed and built in the early modern era, the so-called streetcar suburbs.

The countryside was also transformed by invention in the early modern era, as open land contiguous to cities became satellite communities reached via

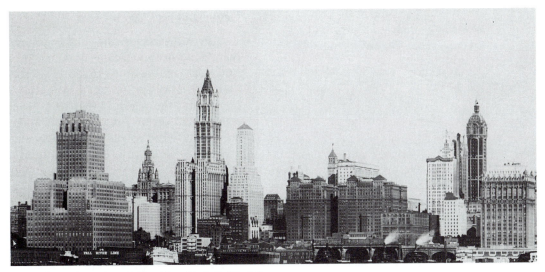

First view, America. © The New York Public Library.

urban transportation, the public streetcars and the new automobile. A major shift in modern urban life occurred as America's earliest suburbs were developed during this period: Forest Hills, New York; Brookline, Massachusetts; and Oak Park, Illinois, for example. The transformations of land use brought about by the close-in streetcar suburbs of the early century within decades spread outward to encompass the suburban commuter town, served by local train lines and eventually automobile routes: Garden City, New York; Radburn, New Jersey; Wellesley, Massachusetts; and Riverside, Illinois, for example. Suburbs, opened as extensions of the city and alternatives to either urban crowding or country isolation, thus created a completely new and original concept of the American home.

The suburb would have been an amazing and unexpected environment for the immigrant of the 1910s to envy, riding along on the streetcar on Sunday afternoon. Even the well-off in Europe tended to live in urban environments, as land outside the Old World city needed to be given over to cows or cultivated; only Americans could afford to throw arable land away on subdivided lots and lawns. It is important to grasp the value of land to understand the American dwelling of 1901–1920. Scarcity and urban accessibility were driving up the price of land, but Americans still aspired then, and always, to occupy their own land.

Though America may have appeared as an expansive new frontier, its cities by the early twentieth century were over crowded. Therefore, land beyond cities was increasingly inviting for new development; the spacious American suburban form has remained to this day a defining characteristic of our land-consuming nation. Americans, becoming less class-restricted and dreaming of homes, demanded a new form of home that synthesized urban amenity within country-like space. Thus, during the early modern era, the concept of the suburb was invented, refined, and replicated. Since this time, the American suburban single family dwelling within landscape has become both the paradigm of home and the American dream.

From Row House to No House: The Great San Francisco Earthquake and Fire of 1906

Among a population of 400,000 residents of San Francisco at the turn of the century, more than half, approximately 225,000, became homeless within three days of shaking and burning that began April 18, 1906 at 5:12 A.M. One might even say that all these people lost their homes within 60 seconds, for that was how briefly the initial event of the San Francisco Earthquake lasted; long for an earthquake, but short for the near total destruction of a city. Ruptured gas lines, dynamiting of the city, and lack of water supply fed the fire that destroyed much of what was left after the shaking. This disaster has been measured after the fact by seismologists, according to the U.S. Geological Survey, with estimates from 7.7 to 8.3 on the Richter Scale (USGS 2006).

Most of the housing in San Francisco during the early days of the twentieth century consisted of wooden attached row houses. Thus, the massive destruction of at least 24,000 wooden structures, in retrospect, is less than surprising, considering the dangerous combination of seismic waves followed by flames, as attached houses collapsed against one another, or fire jumped through common walls. Another four thousand brick buildings were destroyed. A rare Victorian home that survived the Great Quake, the Haas-Lilienthal House (1886), may be visited.

Earthquake resistant structures, fireproofing, and consistent public water supply were unknown or inadequate features of seismically active San Francisco. Seismographs, too, were rare in 1906. Current concepts of engineering, architecture, and urban planning went virtually unconsidered in this boomtown gold rush city. Public buildings, commercial structures, houses, apartments, and hotels all fell en masse.

The great leveler of San Francisco's frontier society, therefore, was to be a natural catastrophe totally unexpected and unprecedented, for now homeless men, women, and children of all classes, by necessity, lived side-by-side in tents, their temporary homes. Traumatized as the city was, however, refugee tent camps were established by the city and the Army in Golden Gate Park and the Presidio quickly and efficiently. One cannot help but compare and contrast the urban emergency response and home rebuilding after the 1906 San Francisco Earthquake to the aftermath of the 2005 Hurricane Katrina in

Urban Lot and Open Land

The American dream of home, entwined with the dream of land, is a universal and defining feature of this country. Though America was moving during the period 1901–1920 from an agrarian to an industrialized nation, land continued to be a primary consideration, if not anymore a farm, then at least a subdivided lot. Americans understood that the one intrinsically valuable resource, the one commodity that can never be increased even by invention, and the one thing they could never have owned in Europe, was land. Thus, land is inextricably linked with the meaning of the home, and the ideal home began to come to fruition for the new middle class during the early modern period. Though only the wealthy could afford a true picturesque melding of country home with landscape, the suburban home allowed the middle class the illusion of open space within the confines of the 40' × 100' subdivision lot.

The American land dream was personified in the early twentieth century by one maverick figure, President Theodore Roosevelt, who can be judged either as a crazy cowboy or an early conservationist for his interests in American wilderness and in his own home. Born in urban New York City, the country estate home he built for himself, Sagamore Hill (1885), really represents the values of Roosevelt most incisively. Atop a treed and grassy hill, he built his own White House, with its porches and pergolas overlooking the waters of the Long Island Sound. Though the house is filled to bursting with the mounted heads of trophy animals he bagged in Africa and the American west, contemporary readers must understand that Roosevelt was a figure epitomizing the contradictions of his period. A wealthy man might have servants, yet consider himself a social liberal. He might amuse himself on a shooting safari, yet still consider himself a serious conservationist, and this is Theodore Roosevelt, father of American National Parks. Thanks to Roosevelt and successor President Woodrow Wilson, we have preserved and inherited, as protected landscape and architecture, the Grand Canyon, the waterfalls of Yosemite, the geysers of Yel-

> *(continued)*
> New Orleans. Soon after the 1906 disaster, the City of San Francisco valiantly and rapidly was reconstructing its streets, infrastructure, and hillside homes.

lowstone, and the forests of Sequoia as National Parks. Significantly, Theodore Roosevelt initiated not only the preservation of pristine American open space, but also initiated some of the first federal laws, passed under President Taft, defining housing standards for tenements in teeming urban space.

American Disasters: Sunk, Shaken, and Sick

American dreams were conceived, but just as often shattered, during this precarious period. There were many serious disasters in early modern America, both due to human error and natural disasters. Newspapers were rife with tragedy. Housing laws were virtually nonexistent. Worker safety laws had not yet been enacted. Fire was particularly destructive before the implementation of modern fireproofing.

The 1906 San Francisco earthquake destroyed thousands of homes through shaking and subsequent fire within three days. In a city composed of attached wooden row houses running up and down hills, fire was paramount, more lethal than the earthquake itself. One might run from home if stairs remained intact, even as the earth shook, but fire would block escape. Spring certainly did seem to be the cruelest time in the early twentieth century, with disasters and wars coincidentally traumatizing the nation so often just as hope might have been reawakened. After the April 15, 1906 earthquake, the sinking of the "unsinkable" *Titanic* followed in April 1912. The modern immediacy of information transition via the wireless ship to shore, the telegraph, and the newspaper meant that the terrible nightmare of the last minutes of the maiden voyage of the ocean liner came to the public within a day via the *New York Times* and the main other extant papers of the day.

The sinking of another American ocean liner, the *Lusitania,* spurred America to declare war on Germany and its allies, and the United States entered the international conflict in May 1917. Time was beginning to speed up as America awoke this spring, against its will, from its hibernation of the early modern period. World War I (1914–1918) had awaited America's entrance for three of its four violent years. The United States eventually agreed to send troops to a pointless war that would kill both Americans, 50,000 of them, and Europeans, totaling approximately 7 million internationally. Unfortunately, war-borne disease approached America with great alacrity as the war ended. Following soldiers home, the deadly flu epidemic of 1918 spread quickly and grimly through the crowded streets of American cities. Houses were quarantined, but more than half a million Americans and at least 20 million people worldwide died within the years 1918–1919. Mothers in tenement homes were said to have exposed siblings to each others' infections, hoping futilely to move the household through the influenza epidemic as quickly as possible, seemingly inviting inevitable death into their homes. Influenza was just one of the surprises that America would receive from its move out of dormancy in the early years of the twentieth century.

The Great War: Life and Death in the Trenches

> Oh, how maddening are these horrible bloody sights! Can it be possible to reap such wholesale destruction and butchery in these few hours of conflict?
>
> —*New York Times,* "A Doughboy Killed in Action Is Home At Last," 2006

During the first years of the twentieth century, modern America had matured in innocent and ignorant isolation from Europe. This changed irreparably, however, as Americans were pulled into international conflict across the Atlantic, then called The Great War or The War to End All Wars, now referred to as World War I. Destined to become neither "great" nor the "end" of warfare, this destructive American intervention, horribly fought as trench warfare, in retrospect was meaningless, lacking the moral justifications of World War II. Even attempts by President Woodrow Wilson to make a moral example of the futility of the war were thwarted, as his peaceful concept of a League of Nations was defeated in the United States. Unlike the coming Second World War, the First World War had little effect on the growth of the contemporary American post-war economy and was not a major catalyst in the production of American housing.

As Doughboys, or infantry, shipped out to Europe from 1917–1918, young Americans were displaced from their homes in a kind of reverse immigration back to Europe, and many would never return home, except for burial on American soil. Boys who had never left their tiny midwestern village or Brooklyn neighborhood now fought a war in France they did not understand, as sons of immigrants left home to fight their own former homelands. The historical past of Caesar's "pitched battle" met the industrialized future on the bloody battlefields of World War I, as lines of infantry charged canons and the newly invented machine gun. In the words of poet Matthew Arnold's "Dover Beach," trench warfare existed "where ignorant armies clash by night."

An army recruit recalled forever the trauma of a troop ship, shelled, exploding at sea. At his feet fell mules' heads and hoofs, for America had moved into global warfare on the backs of the pack animals that predated jeeps. Sadly, the same boy who had witnessed this event, on his way home from France, arrived exhausted late one night to his parents' home, only to find an unrecognized family inhabiting his house. His parents and brothers had moved while he was in the trenches, so he walked the streets of Brooklyn while he searched all night for the family he had left behind (personal communication with the author). Wartime communications and housing shortages made early modern life so erratic that while the son had never received news of their move, his parents likewise had had no idea he was alive and coming home.

Class Divisions in America: Posh or Not

Like the Titanic, America was a ship strictly divided by class in the early modern era: P.O.S.H. ("Port Out, Starboard Home") for the rich, steerage for the poor, with no decks in common . . . and without a change of course, a ship headed for disaster. The early modern period, at first, feels deceptively like a part of the past, but fortunately fundamental cha nges were being fomented during this period such that America post–World War I would be quite a different place, perhaps more tragic and traumatized, certainly less isolated and innocent, and clearly less class divided, from America of 1901. The years of 1901–1920 reflected an America that was on the edge of the past and the cusp of the future. Anachronistic class divisions of rich versus poor still held fast, even as forces were beginning to create a new middle class. Long stagnant social and economic forces were rupturing, as the United States entered the international political scene via the Great War, while simultaneously coping with the chaos of immigration and social crisis on our home front.

America in the early twentieth century was a divided, two-class, polarized society, and the American home was the clearest illustration of the inequities. In the words of insightful social critic Frederick Lewis Allen, "Of all the contrast between American life in 1900 and half a century or more later, perhaps the most significant is in the distance between rich and poor—in income, the way of living, and status in the community. At the turn of the century the gulf between wealth and poverty was immense" (Allen 1954). In early twentieth-century America, democracy and community implied an ideal of opportunity and equality, within a reality of overworked immigrants and over-capitalized industrialists.

The rich were getting richer at incredible rates, while the poor were sucked deeper into inescapable debt and poverty. For the wealthy and the small but growing middle class, health, education, transportation, urban amenity, and especially housing, were improving. You were either upper class or under class; middle class was a newly developing concept that would not take hold until after the initiation of income taxes; significantly, there was no federal income tax, even for millionaires, until 1913. Prior to that time, socioeconomic classes were impassable and cruel. What housing was built in the 1910s was generally either tenement slums or high falutin' homes for "the four hundred" society swells of the day, with relatively few homes in between. As Allen pointed out, Andrew Carnegie is estimated to have had an income 22 thousand times the average American income of $400 a year at the turn of the century (Allen 1954). An untaxed multimillionaire like Carnegie lived the life of a modern emperor, and in terms of his home, "the first thing these princes did was build themselves palaces" (Allen 1954).

HOMES FOR THE POOR: TENEMENTS AND TRENCHES

Immigration and Urban Conditions

The shocking social conditions were long-standing, unacknowledged problems of urban squalor, immigrant crowding, and lack of decent housing and welfare for the poor in America. Extremes and contradictions of the early modern American city and society astound us today, yet were the rule from 1901–1920. Laissez-faire capitalism ruled work and home in early modern America, Horatio Alger myths notwithstanding. The strictures of class, ethnicity, race, religion, and country of origin controlled one's life from birth to death, especially for immigrants. Masses of immigrant poor had been arriving before 1900 daily via eastern ports, Ellis Island, New York City (now Ellis Island National Monument); Hoboken, New Jersey; Boston, Massachusetts;

Bridgeport, Connecticut, for example. Millions arrived during the first years of the twentieth century. The Statue of Liberty may have lighted their passage, yet for most immigrants, dark urban slums awaited.

Slums were growing without planning during the first two decades of the twentieth century. Sanitation was deplorable even by the standards of the time. Infectious diseases, such as tuberculosis, became epidemic and could not yet be effectively treated, for antibiotics had not yet been invented. Health and human welfare were cruelly class-dependent. Unemployment was high, and factory and sweatshop work was hazardous. Education was limited, and child labor had not yet been eliminated. Factory workers, farm laborers, or household servants could never hope to escape their plight, and they were ripe for exploitation. Racial, religious, and ethnic prejudices were open and endemic. The average American standard of living stayed low as literally boatloads of immigrants flooded the cities looking for work in the promised land, competing with each other for jobs and homes, thereby driving down their own wages and raising rents. Crowded substandard housing reflected their plight.

Slum Tenements

> Housing evils as we know them today are to be found in dangerous and disease-breeding privy vaults, in lack of water supply, in dark rooms, in filthy and foul alleys, in damp cellars, in basement living rooms, in conditions of filth, in inadequate methods of disposal of waste, in fly-borne disease, in cramped and crowded quarters, in promiscuity, in lack of privacy, in buildings of undue height, in inadequate fire protection, in the crowding of buildings, in the too intensive use of land.
>
> —Lawrence Veiller, *A Model Tenement Housing Law,* 1920

Though the nineteenth-century word *tenement* has a critical and pejorative sound to today's audience, at the beginning of the twentieth century it was a standard urban vernacular housing type, fulfilling its intended purpose of housing new immigrants in high-density cities. A tenement was defined as a 6–8-story walk-up apartment house, attached to others like it, in a populous urban environment. Tenements were almost consistently built to eight stories, this height being considered the upper limit of an average person's ability to climb stairs, and elevators were certainly not found in tenements. The serious problems of tenements were not due to the concept of the structures per se, but to the lack of amenities they provided per unit. For example, today one will be shocked to learn that a nineteenth-century tenement of 6 stories housing 12 families in railroad apartments might have only one toilet to share, and that would be downstairs in the back alley. By the early twentieth century, crowding had not been alleviated in the tenements; however, some effort was being made in sanitation and fire safety. Toilets and cold water were being installed indoors, as well as improved access to light and ventilation.

"How to Build Tenements"

An interesting survey of urban leaders, architects, housing developers, and city officials conducted by the Municipal housing authority in 1900, produced an article in the *New York Times* titled "How to Build Tenements . . . 5 Stories for Non-fire-Proof Houses—Baths, Elevators Discussed." The cost-effectiveness ratio of amenity versus rent was a serious consideration, for tenement housing was a private enterprise, neither government financed nor barely regulated. Interestingly, most experts queried wanted fire safety and sanitation, but realized that demanding these extras could cause rents to rise, driving the price too high for immigrants, or the profit too marginal for developers and landlords. Land developers at the time felt a 7 to 12 percent profit, actually quite a good investment for the money, to be

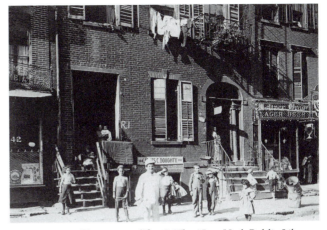

Downtown: Tenement life. © The New York Public Library.

the breakeven point for operating tenement housing. In light of this balancing act between housing amenity for tenants and housing profit for developers and landlords, some comments were recorded in the survey that sound strange and callous to our ears a century later. One respondent commented on how to improve health and sanitation by "teaching the poor to make the most of what they have," and another on fire safety by stating, "It is better to sacrifice a life now and then than to increase rents all around."

Unfortunately, housing regulations only began to afford better access to health and safety long after the crowded tenements had already filled to capacity with immigrants. The first federal investigation and regulation of housing was made in 1909 under former President Roosevelt's housing commission. Significantly, the first comments on housing were titled "Slums." Because tenements were built before federal housing regulations, natural light, air, and ventilation were nearly impossible to find after a day in the sweatshop, except on the rooftop. Children, when they were not working, played in the street. Ironically, in the same issue of the *New York Times* as the article on slums was another article on society titled, "The News of Newport."

"Moral Dangers"

The problem of the tenement and slum continued into the 1920s, even as immigration eased. In 1920, the Russell Sage Foundation published *A Model Tenement Housing Law,* by Lawrence Veiller, and the *Architectural Record* argued the pros and cons of demolition versus reconstruction of tenements asking, "Is It Advisable to Remodel Slum Tenements?" It is wise to remember the rule of urban planning that one should never build a "temporary" building thoughtlessly, for it is likely to be there permanently, as were these crowded, unventilated buildings. The once-controversial question of remodeling or remediation of tenement housing is moot, for currently lower Manhattan still has rows of these century-old low-rent buildings standing basically unchanged. Some are even on their way to gentrification, again pushing out the poor. The Tenement Museum today tells the story of these buildings and their immigrant occupants.

Not until the 1920s did the architectural profession take an in-depth look at the problems of mass housing that had plagued America for more than 50 years. Finally, after decades of overlooking substandard housing for immigrants, laborers, and the poor, the *Architectural Record* in 1921 published "A Short Bibliography and Analysis of Housing," detailing topics such as "bad housing," "moral dangers," and "prevention" (Boyd 1921). The high-profit motive, coupled with blaming condescension to the poor (note "promiscuity" and "moral dangers" as the downfall of good housing) were certainly stumbling blocks to housing improvement in American cities of the early modern era.

HOMES FOR WAR WORKERS

World War I and Workers' Housing

We build munitions but not housing, workers are overlooked.

—Claude Bragdon, "Architecture and Democracy Before,
During and After the War," 1918

The *Architectural Record* published a series of articles in 1918 titled, "Architecture and Democracy Before, During and After the War." The author, Claude Bragdon, commented, "For wage earners housing problem is not solved . . . he is caught between the Devil of speculative builder and deep sea of predatory landlord . . . [or] homelessness" (Bragdon 1918). The effects of a great war and a not-so-great economy meant that in America, home building had been stagnant for some time; therefore, one finds that surprisingly little housing, and particularly little government-sponsored housing, was built during 1901–1920. There simply was no real sense within the government of an imminent need for working-class housing or for government interference in private housing enterprise. When skilled armaments workers of the First World War required housing at shipyards, however, America finally woke up too late to the fact that it had neglected for decades to build basic workers' housing, or any housing at all, for the low wage earner or the poor.

There was very little public, or even private, housing development during the earlier years of the twentieth century. The nation's urban infrastructure was fairly undeveloped. Railroads and ships served intercity travel, but between major cities, few roads and little housing existed. By the time of the American entry into World War I, it was finally noted, actually too late to be effective, that there was a severe shortage of housing for skilled workers in the American urban shipyards, who were to build the materiel to win the war in Europe. For this reason, the American government for the first time entered into the housing business, a reluctant and half-hearted precursor to the later government building projects the Works Progress Administration (WPA), the Tennessee Valley Authority, and the World War II housing projects of the 1930s and 1940s. A handful of new towns and developments were built for workers during the early modern era: a workers' housing development within the existing city of Bridgeport, Connecticut, and two completely new towns for shipyard workers in Virginia. Therefore, considering our late entry into World War I, the United States eventually did make at stab at the controversial idea of federal housing.

Government-Planned New Towns

"Uncle Sam, Landlord, He Built and Owns Town of Cradock, VA for Navy Yard Employees, Has 550 Contented Families on Hand," declared the *New York Times* in 1919. Cradock and Truxton, Virginia, by architect and builder George B. Post, were designed as complete new towns with housing, factories, schools, parks, and recreation. There was very little media commentary at the time on these new developments, for although little was built in the United States in general during this time, even less was built in the South. Newspapers of the day did not even think to comment on the fact that these new government-built towns were intentionally segregated: Cradock for white workers, Truxton for African Americans. To our contemporary minds, such federal institutionalizing of segregation is both shocking and abhorrent, yet it is an honest reflection of early twentieth-century America, post–Civil War and pre–Civil Rights. Today such segregation would be considered profoundly un-American. Yet, of greater concern during these early decades was the taint of a different kind of un-Americanism, Bolshevism, attached to publicly planned and financed housing. Public housing, even when sorely needed, seemed somewhat Leftist, or radical, to the government and the public in the early modern era. In contrast, America seemed to accept private industry funded company towns, such as Pullman, Illinois, and Gary, Indiana. With private housing stagnant and government efforts both suspect and lagging, little housing at all was constructed for the working class beyond the Cradock and Truxton experiments.

Architect–planner Post, with federal approval, chose the ultimate American patriotic style for public housing at Cradock and Truxton, the "Colonial Style of a New England Village." Thus, American architectural style declared to the world that a development that might be considered un-American was rather a highly patriotic symbol. Cradock and Truxton, aesthetically conservative but socially liberal, must be noted as isolated but progressive precedents for opening the doors to government-sponsored urban planning in America. Though they represent a successful experiment in workers' housing, these few projects, built expressly for supporting the World War I effort, were an example rarely to be followed until the advent of another war. America had found itself desperately unprepared to gear up industrially for World War I, but it would not make the same omissions of workers' housing again during World War II.

Progressive Post-War Housing Proposals

A sad commentary on the meaning of World War I housing was published in the *Architectural Record* in 1918 when the Secretary of the National Housing Association anticipated that America would soon be in need of housing for "disabled soldiers." Strongly advocating for constructing veterans' housing, not in isolation from society, but within real new towns, the writer advanced consciousness both of housing and of disability. In "Housing After the War, What of America?" he wrote, "We need garden cities, 'New Towns' " (Roosevelt 1918). The housing secretary sought models for American housing, looking at British new towns and garden cities, but also certainly to the American model communities of Cradock and Truxton.

The enormous oversight in the lack of production of public housing during World War I was an extension of the pervasive laissez-faire attitude toward the welfare of the lower classes in general. Housing shortages forced American families to double and triple up, resulting in generations of working class and their relations sharing a home. There were tenements constructed for profit in industrialized cities by private developers with little government regulation, but certainly not sufficient in number of housing units or sanitation in comparison to the number of immigrants arriving daily. The poor and the low-paid war factory worker were just assumed to get along, as they always had, sharing the rent in speculators' tenements or crowding triple-deckers with extended family. The era echoes with Dickensian attitudes toward the poor and their homes. In early modern America, only a few truly progressive, compassionate minds were looking beyond laissez-faire capitalism toward the future of housing for the poor, the disabled, and the disenfranchised. President Theodore Roosevelt, who had initiated the first American Federal Housing legislation, a decade later poignantly stated the case for postwar public housing, "When we have closed the giant war, we must then prepare for the giant tasks of peace" (Roosevelt 1918).

HOMES FOR THE WEALTHY

Urban Mansions and Luxury Apartment House Flats

As the poor had their tenement problems, so, too, did the rich suffer, plagued by The Servant Problem and The Empty Too Large Country House Problem. As immigration slowed, the economy of the early part of the twentieth century stagnated, and war intervened, the mansions of 5th Avenue and their country cousins, the elegant houses of Long Island and Connecticut, fell into disuse. With fewer boatloads of potential servants to clean their kitchens and hand wash their laundry, the rich found they simply could not keep up their lifestyle, to which cheap labor had so generously contributed. Because the supply of land in Manhattan was by nature so limited, the land-owning rich did well financially by selling their urban mansions for the development of luxury apartment houses on 5th Avenue, where their private 2-story mansions gave way for new 20-story elevator apartment house flats; but woe to the antiquated country house, dysfunctional without a full complement of immigrant servants.

Outside the city, country estates with their labor-intensive houses became a so-called drug on the market by 1919. Their owners were forced out of their comfortable homes and private landscaped grounds to make do within the confines of 14-room flats, built on the very sites of their former urban mansions. The country houses, however, stood idle, as land and households were broken up, someday perhaps to become suburban development. Urban land, when used for single-family dwellings as it was in the early part of the twentieth century, had truly been an extravagance of the upper, upper class. As urban land became increasingly valuable, density had to increase on the limited land, and thus stories were added to the city's best neighborhoods as the invention of the elevator allowed land to be developed to its greatest capacity. Hence, the high-rise urban apartment house took the place formerly occupied by the urban mansion. The *silk stocking* east side of Manhattan, with its upscale white limestone Renaissance Revival apartment houses, thus, actually reflects the downfall of the upper, upper class. By 1907 the development of flats on Park Avenue led to the loss of single family houses in the city. Today, these early modern urban apartment house flats for the wealthy, with their epaulet-uniformed doormen, are aligned along Manhattan's 5th Avenue and Park Avenue; Chicago's Lakeshore Drive; and atop San Francisco's Nob Hill and Pacific Heights. The facades of these buildings form a monumental, contiguous, perhaps uninviting but not unattractive, streetscape for the urban pedestrian.

The Fifth Avenue Mansion and Garden

The urban mansion as home could be the finest illustration of what wealth and beauty, private capital, and a Beaux-Arts trained architect together might create. Architecture critic Russell Sturgis, in 1901, called this phenomenon "the art gallery of the New York streets." The restrained elegance of many east side townhouses or 5th Avenue mansions of Manhattan, including among others, the Frick mansion, the Duke mansion, and the Cooper-Hewitt mansion, attest to this concept, proving that money could indeed buy good taste if the right architect and landscape designer were found. The formality of the Beaux-Arts encouraged a hierarchy of forms, and appropriateness of architectural style to function was emphasized. Note, for example, the calm, ordered rows of Beaux-Arts townhouses on the east side of Manhattan with their limestone facades and black iron fencing, which together complement the more elaborate facades of the museums.

One of the last extant free-standing mansions of 5th Avenue, the Frick Museum and Library, opens the urban mansion form and its gated gardens to the public, encompassing a full city block

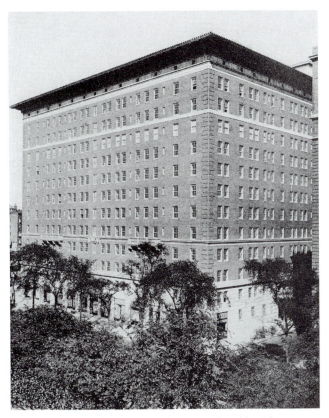

Uptown: Astor Court. © The New York Public Library.

Beaux-Arts Mansions as Museums

"Museum mile" forms for the walker a memorable Beaux-Arts architectural processional along Fifth Avenue and Central Park in Manhattan. On the park side of the street is found the grand portal of limestone steps leading to the Metropolitan Museum of Art, by architects Richard Morris Hunt (1902) and McKim, Mead, and White (1911). Opposite this signature structure, lining the most famous avenue in America, one can discover myriad Beaux-Arts mansions of the early modern era of 1901–1920. Today, many of these mansions function as public and private art museums.

Presenting a continuity of finely delineated limestone facades in counterpoint to the naturalistic design of Central Park, the Beaux-Arts style gracefully lines Fifth Avenue. Beginning at Fifth Avenue and 89th Street, the Cooper-Hewitt mansion houses the Smithsonian National Design Museum, formerly the Carnegie mansion (1898), across the

(continued)

street from which one may view an important Renaissance Revival palazzo, the former Otto Kahn mansion (private). Striking visual features of the Cooper-Hewitt include an iron and glass portico above the entrance, a glass conservatory, and a walled formal garden into which the conservatory projects. The Neue Galerie at 86th Street is a Carrere & Hastings mansion (1914) with a classic black and white theme and sweeping interior staircase. At 79th Street the Institute of Fine Arts of New York University is housed in the former Doris Duke mansion (private), designed by Horace Trumbauer. Downtown, at 36th Street, McKim, Mead, and White designed the Beaux-Arts Pierpont Morgan Library (1906) for rare books and manuscripts.

Most aesthetically significant of all the mansions, however, is the Frick Collection at Fifth Avenue and 71st Street, once the city home of Henry Clay Frick and his daughter, Helen Clay Frick. This gracefully restrained Beaux-Arts mansion, by Carrere & Hastings (1904), faces a formal Italian garden and houses one of the finest art collections and art reference libraries in America, a gift that Frick dictated should be shared with the public. A rarely seen treetop view from the terrace of the library above Central Park is nothing short of inspiring, for it articulates the aesthetic counterpoint of the Frick's restrained formal architecture and garden with the Olmsted designed metaphorical wilderness of Central Park across Fifth Avenue.

More romanticized and less restrained by Beaux-Arts formality than its sophisticated New York contemporaries, the Isabella Stewart Gardner Museum in Boston is a Venetian palazzo revival (architect Willard Sears, 1901). Originally an eccentric art collector's private home shared only with her Botticelli, it is now open to the public. An explosion of flowers in a central courtyard is surrounded by interior balconies and an arched loggia. The Gardner is an unusual atrium mansion, looking inward toward art, rather than outward toward its urban park setting along Olmsted's Emerald Necklace.

The West Coast counterpart of the East Coast "mansion as museum" is the Huntington Library, Collections, and Botanical Gardens in San Marino, California (architect Myron Hunt, 1911), open to the public. The mansion and estate include British art collections, an art library, and an unexpected early modern Greene and Greene series of architectural rooms. Extensively landscaped grounds surrounding

between 71st and 72nd Street fronting Central Park. The Frick, designed by Carrere and Hastings, presents a formal, symmetrical, limestone facade with Palladian windows to Olmsted and Vaux's Central Park. Like much of the upscale architecture of its day, the elegance of the mansion spoke more to the restrained image that the owner wished to project than to the struggles of the great robber barons to amass their pre-income tax fortunes. A visit to any of the Beaux-Arts museum–mansions in America today allows us a better visual understanding of the domestic life of an early twentieth-century industrialist. Fortunately, a number of these persons remembered their roots and gave generously to the public; Henry Clay Frick's art philanthropy after his death was attested to by his will read in 1919.

The Frick mansion's penthouse opens via French doors to the city, overlooking the treetops of Central Park and the private garden below. The gardens of the Frick mansion are formal, in the French style, composed of boxwoods and cast iron gate running along the street. As such, the Frick garden provided a private urban sanctuary and a contrast   to the rugged informality of Central Park across the street. Formal and informal, private and public, have never been so clearly demarcated in America as in the Fifth Avenue landscape. The ability to maintain open land within the high urban density of expensive Manhattan's most exclusive neighborhood remains one of the greatest status symbols ever achieved in American culture.

The Weekend Country Estate

Weekend retreat to the cool fresh air of open land outside the confines of the city has always been the province of the truly fortunate, from antiquity until contemporary times. Of Roman villas, particularly Hadrian's Villa at Tivoli, outside Rome, was a prime example. Tivoli was followed in the Renaissance by the Medici villas in the environs of Florence in Fiesole. In this tradition, the rich of 1901–1920 built weekend estates, often set within elaborate gardens with water, within commuting distance of New York City, in prime locations such as the North Shore of Long Island, the Connecticut shore of the Long Island Sound, or along the Palisades on the Hudson River. A handful of the gold coast estates and gardens of this period are now open

(continued)

the mansion include specimen collections of palms, cacti, and Asian gardens. Also in California, the most avant-garde of these mansion museums is in San Diego, the La Jolla Museum of Contemporary Art, formerly the Ellen Browning Scripps House (1906), by architectural innovator Irving Gill. This house is an early study in twentieth-century architectural simplicity and a model of the aesthetic restraint of early modernism.

to the public and university communities. Included among these estates are Kykuit, the Rockefeller Estate (Delano and Aldrich, 1909, gardens by Welles Bosworth), overlooking the Hudson River in Pocantico Hills; the more modest Lamont estate across the river owned by Columbia University, operated as the Lamont Earth Observatory; Old Westbury Gardens; and Planting Fields, the Coe Estate, both on Long Island's North Shore. With the grace and beauty that great wealth could procure, these estates represent the exquisite possibilities of the picturesque American home within landscape.

ART AND ARCHITECTURE OF THE EARLY MODERN ERA

Art, Tragedy, and Social Realism

Through their creative lenses, the arts throughout history have provided observational insight into, and critical commentary upon, society. Fortunately, the visual and literary arts held fast to this ancient role in early twentieth-century America, acting as the Greek chorus to the drama of American societal tragedies. Indeed, art has never been so powerful a social engine in America as it was from 1901–1920. The arts, by definition more reticent and reflective than science and enterprise, stood back, commenting with insight during the early modern era of America, like Socrates' Athenian "gadfly" before them, choosing to critique this new America and its attendant class divide.

While elaborate architecture within landscape was designed during the first decades of the twentieth century, paintings and books of the period narrated a vividly different and more tragic picture of human conditions prevalent during the period of industrialization, immigration, and modernization. Social realist painting and muck-raking literature proved that illustration or fiction can be more convincing and engaging to the public conscience than dry fact. Popular film, on the other hand, embodied a strange irony, for even as Chaplin's *Little Tramp* wrung empathy from America, the actor himself was living in luxury, earning one of the highest incomes ever paid for the time. *Agents provocateurs* or *enfants terribles,* the creative arts in the early modern era entertained while inciting class ire and social consciousness.

Muckraking and Murder

Literature has told the story of early twentieth-century America poignantly. Books abound of the muckraking, or expose, genre, narrating the cruel social, factory, and housing inequities of the time. Most infamous is *The Jungle* of 1906 by Upton Sinclair (1878–1968), on the horrors of Chicago industry in the early modern period. More subtle and personal was *An American Tragedy,* written by Theodore Dreiser (1871–1945) in 1906. Dreiser's fictionalized story of a true but sensationalized murder of 1906 was a humane study of class struggle, and as such became a highly compelling story to the American public of the time. It illustrated the significance of class in America in a highly personal narrative with which so many Americans of the time might identify.

As the main character, Clyde Griffith, rises from factory worker to supervisor; the reader sees Griffith's life physically change, as illustrated by his homes. Moving from seducer of working-class mill girl to her murderer, he literally moves between workers' housing and girls' dormitory, toward mill owner's country estate, and eventually, on to prison cell. The perpetrator thus becomes a symbol of unbridled capitalism and the victim a symbol of abused proletariat, as Griffith trades the life of mill girl for the country club life of the rich mill owner's daughter. So pathologically motivated is he by upward class mobility and its attendant milieu that Griffith is literally willing to kill, and eventually to die, for his environment and his status. In the title, *An American Tragedy,* Dreiser reminds us that class is not just a personal struggle to the death, but a metaphor for the tragic national callousness inherent in early twentieth-century America.

Ash Cans and Alleys

As early modern literature explored the unacknowledged world of the working class, so, too, did the social realist artists of the Ash Can School look unflinchingly at the unseen habitations of the working class: streetscapes, tenements, rooftops, alleys, ash cans, and all. A visual picture of American life in the early twentieth century thus emerged, painted by the early New York Bohemian painters, originally known as Robert Henri and The Eight. These artists were the first to enframe the urban life they saw through their Greenwich Village studio windows, painting houses and the housed as observed unsentimentally, inventing the backyard view as an art form.

The Ash Can School found contemporary Greenwich Village alleys and street life full of color and vitality. The unadorned city that The Eight painted was home to immigrant crowds and congested streets. American artistic eyes before Henri had been carefully averted from the poor, but like their literary contemporaries Sinclair and Dreiser, artists Henri and The Eight demonstrated the tragic nobility of the unseen of society, the proletariat. These early modern artists revolutionized American visual art, making the ugly beautiful, the unseen visible, the world of the poor apparent, dignifying and validating the home life of the poor. In the long tradition of bohemianism in the arts, the Ash Can School identified with the proletariat as the outcast. As avant-garde art at its most profound level can, the Ash Can painters anticipated and precipitated truthful observation of class struggle in American art and society.

In their naive zeal to modernize American art, the Ash Can painters curated, or brought together the art, of one of the watersheds of American modern art, the Armory Show of 1913, a major exhibition displaying works by American and European modernists side by side. Much to the shock of The Eight, Americans learned that the naturalistic depiction of a backyard view was hardly revolutionary in comparison to its European counterpart, cubist abstraction, whose adherents were dubbed "the wildmen of Paris" by the American architectural critics in 1910. Artistic isolation reflected American isolation of the times. Though social realism was artistically revolutionary for America in the early twentieth century, it appeared quite timid in the face of European modernism of the time. The Armory Show was therefore an intimidating event for American artists who had heretofore considered their realism avant-garde. It demonstrated both the gulf in sophistication between early modern America and contemporary Europe, and further, that America would need to enter the modern world bravely or be left behind.

Artists' Studios and Homes

Artistic figures of the early modern era were often perceived by society as avant-gardes, outside or beyond the strictures of class, and their bohemian studios homes reflected this eccentricity. The outsider status of artists' lives and housing was often somewhat ironic, however, for artists have coveted their exclusion from society as creative exclusivity, and in the early twentieth century it was an inverted luxury to live among and pity the poor without truly enduring their pain. The communal home and work environments of artists' studios became clubby, sophisticated variations on the flat. As in the case of the Ash Can painters and their 8th Street digs, artists might paint, sleep, and hang out all in one space with inspiration available, not to mention critique and cigars, down the hall.

Artists' studios and homes represented some of the most creatively designed arts and crafts types of homes in America. Their decorative programs varied considerably from one another; however, studios consistently followed specific rules of layout and are therefore a simple architectural form to discover walking about an older city. Studio windows always face north, for northern light is considered to be the most steady, unvarying sunlight, and thus the most reliable for painting. Even in tight urban areas, these buildings were designed to be drenched in light, thanks to double-height working spaces with high glass fenestration that was almost factory-like in its functional aesthetic. Studios were quite a modern form in their embrace of expanses of glass, a forerunner of the International Style glass curtain wall of the 1920s–1950s.

Though it appears that early painting and writing studios were the origin of the current usage of the word *studio* to name a more mundane one-room apartment, historical artists' studios can still be found in New York City's Greenwich Village and Central Park South, in Chicago's Tree Studios, and in Boston's Riverway and Fenway Studios. Original artists' studio homes of the early modern period may now be anachronistic—a twentieth-century American revival of a nineteenth-century Parisian form, a pre-electric era environment—but they recall in brick and mortar the days when natural light and a once-authentic avant-garde came together to paint significant scenes.

Art and Architecture that Reflect American Society

> The habits and customs of people are more clearly portrayed in the architecture of their houses than through their literature, their music, their government, or any other medium.

> —*New York Times,* "Town Plan Helps Future Land Value," 1924

The artistic milieu of early modern America, like the time and country it represented, was defined by its strong visual contrasts and blatant societal contradictions. At the same time that the social realists were in their downtown studios painting their gutsy American ash canned street scenes, uptown industrialists were amassing important collections of European Renaissance and Baroque paintings and sculpture. Mansions to house growing art collections were rising for the wealthy—the Fricks, the Carnegies, and the Morgans, to name a few—Baroque palaces built on the backs of cheap immigrant labor. Yet, ironically many of these robber barons in time became the great American patrons of the arts who have now shared their European art collections and neoclassical mansions, through generous bequests, with the American public. Industrialist Henry Clay Frick may have seen labor-management violence in his lifetime, yet his living legacy to America is the serene architecture of his home, housing his perfect and peaceful Vermeer.

The art of architecture clearly expressed the dichotomies of early modern America. Aesthetic response to societal and technological change exhibited great ambivalence. Schisms of social class were gaining notoriety. Technology advanced so rapidly that style had difficulty keeping apace. Architecture strove to respond to change in modern America, to find appropriate motifs for modern times, yet this was artistically very difficult. The structural technology of the skyscraper, for example, progressed in New York and Chicago while the Beaux-Arts style brought Old World architectural orders to clothe contemporary New World architecture. Renaissance ideals of the city as the center of civilization influenced modern American urban planning during the City Beautiful movement, while prosaic subway tunnels were dug by hand and dynamited through major cities. The city itself was exploding exponentially, sharply declining and yet advancing simultaneously. Beaux-Arts ballrooms were built in private mansions for the rich, while mere blocks away, bathrooms were overlooked in homes for the poor.

Thus, as we today examine the architecture of the American homes of the early twentieth century, we must always ask not only about the physical structure of the house, but also about the societal conditions and technological advances that are the foundations of these early modern homes. As compromises between poverty and wealth were with great difficulty negotiated during the early modern architectural period, the middle class home at last became a reality. Simple vernacular houses to high style domestic architecture, city to suburb, saw the transformation of the new American middle class. Optimistically noting a glimmer of developing social and aesthetic consciousness, early modern critic Russell Sturgis presciently observed in 1901, "Architecture is slowly taking more of a place in the general culture."

PLANNED HOMES AND IMPROVING HOUSING CONDITIONS

Philanthropic Housing: Forest Hills Gardens

An enlightened example of model middle-class housing was created in 1909, not by government or private development, but by a philanthropic foundation. Forest Hills Gardens, Queens, New York City, was brought to fruition by the Russell Sage Foundation, a research and service charity in New York City. Based on existing English models of town planning, Forest Hills Gardens' American architect and site planners were Grosvenor Atterbury and Frederick Law Olmsted (Brush 1911). Station Square and the surrounding housing remain today a beautifully designed urban place of Medieval and Tudor Revival housing across the East River from Manhattan, connected by railroad to the city. As such, this planned community invented the first important model of suburban design in America.

Forest Hills Gardens was planned "to create on the site a suburban community that would exemplify some of the possibilities of intelligent town planning, with the hope of encouraging similar ventures elsewhere. The specific aims were to provide healthful, attractive, and solidly built homes, and to demonstrate that convenient thoroughfares, quiet domestic streets, and ample public open spaces are economically practical as well as beneficial features in a suburban development" (Glenn 1946).

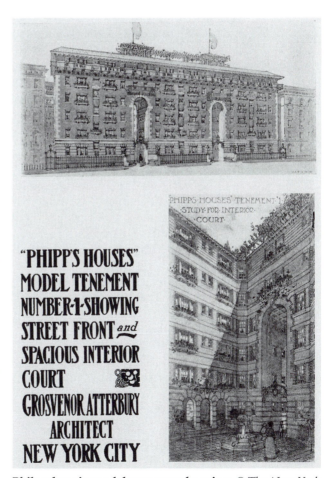

Model Town Planning

There is an overall unity to the design to Forest Hills Gardens, within variations of housing styles and densities, from apartment houses to single family residences, all with a communal design theme of Tudor architecture. The community buildings, shops, housing, and street patterns are focused on the transportation connector to Manhattan, the Long Island Rail Road, with Station Square as the physical node and aesthetic heart of the Forest Hills. Local and urban amenities are accessible via pedestrian and train connections, and housing logically increases in density with nearness to the commuter

Philanthropic model tenement housing. © The New York Public Library.

line. Forest Hills predates the automobile; however, it is wise to consider that housing within walking distance of public transit should remain a coveted and copied American precedent if we are to maintain the physical integrity of our urban environments.

The internal logic of this planned community is coupled with its livability and embrace of gracefully treed streets and park-like grounds, proving that fairly high housing density and open space can complement each other. It is not surprising, therefore, to note that the father of American landscape architecture, Frederick Law Olmsted, drew the master plan for Forest Hills Gardens. In this urbane design upon previously open land within easy commuting distance of a major city, Olmsted and the Russell Sage Foundation provided a model for an American garden city, a landmark creation, one of the finest early modern contributions to American urban planning: the planned suburb (Brush 1911).

The economics of this planned community were as well thought out as the physical design. The Russell Sage Foundation was committed to creating a decent and livable community for the working class, expecting only a modest rental return of 4 percent on its investment, at the same time that slumlords were demanding 12 percent. Ironically, the success of the Russell Sage strategy, coupled with its excellent design concept and convenient rail connection to Manhattan, has meant that most of this originally philanthropic housing venture is now well beyond the financial reach of its targeted housing population. Such unintended up-scaling of thoughtful architectural planning, and the subsequent loss of affordability to the working class, is one of the sad ironies of good design, yet Forest Hills Gardens remains as a viable model for American middle-class home and community.

Garden Apartments in Cities

Other early modern communities looking for well-considered alternatives to the tenement or apartment building question arrived at the urban garden apartment, literally, a series of apartment buildings within landscaped gardens. In seeking garden apartments in cities, early modern architectural theorists advocated for urban agglomerations of high-density but mid-rise multi-unit apartment structures. With open space between repeated buildings, light, air, and social interaction and play would enter the family living environment. Based on such precedents as the English Garden Cities Movement, the Russell Sage Foundation's model town planning, and the German modern *existenzminimum,* or minimum living standard movement, this was an innovative concept for the early modern home.

Considered as amelioration for high-density urban walk-up tenements, or later for high-rise apartment buildings, garden apartments were more theory than practice in the early modern city. The economics of scarcity of land, demolition costs, and floor area ratios to rent generally prohibited garden apartment development in major urban areas for most of this early period. Although garden apartments did not replace downtown tenements in older American cities, the garden apartment did take hold later as a design concept in newly developed, close-in suburban areas, especially in post–World War II housing projects. The later dissemination of the early modern garden apartment concept has made this model an important precedent in middle-density cities and in late-developing low-density southern and western cities. If configured for social interaction and safety, well-landscaped, and served by public transit, the garden apartment within the city can be a good American urban alternative to the tenement or the high-rise housing project.

Many beautiful suburban towns and satellite cities—Garden City, New York; Brookline and Wellesley, Massachusetts; Radburn, New Jersey; and Oak Park and Riverside, Illinois—to name a few, would also partake of some of the excellent early modern concepts of the planned suburb. Newly designed or maturing older towns, these suburban places offered homes within open space, in towns focused on public transportation nodes, as alternatives to the congestion of the city or the isolation of the country. The development of the planned town or garden suburb closely mirrors the rise of the middle class in early modern America.

THE EMERGENCE OF THE MIDDLE CLASS

The Advent of the Middle-Class Home

Despite the dichotomies of robber baron palaces and immigrant slums and the extremes of class they illustrated, during the early modern architectural era income and housing began to display some hope for the common man. With income tax instituted in 1913 and the war won in 1918, American federal and municipal governments for the first time began to take an interest in domestic issues, regulating laissez-faire capitalism and the abuses in standard of living and housing it had engendered. Graduated federal income tax initiated the process of leveling out income and social extremes, and the new national income tax, coupled with a resultant growing mercantile class, together spurred a new demand for a decent home for the common family; hence, the advent of the middle-class home in America. American housing at last, by the end of the early modern era, began to reflect the first inklings of the more even status and quality of life that defines the middle class of America today.

A small number of newly middle class, more-educated Americans could now feel secure for their families' futures, living in a modern mortgaged, electrified, plumbed, and landscaped home of their own. The future and the past were both apparent to the new middle class of early twentieth-century America. Sentimentality and nostalgia for the past led to homes that were middle class and modern, yet stylistically disguised houses of the early American settlements. Thus, one sees the continuity in the early twentieth century of a historicizing and nostalgic view of the American past embodied in the eighteenth-century Cape Cod and Colonial houses. In the words of social critic Allen:

> [O]ne must admit that there is a basis for the [middle class] nostalgia. Space and service [in the middle class house] add up to a good deal. Yet we must remember that the [well-off] family's ample life in the big house was made possible by the meager wages of the maids who lived in narrow rooms at the very top of the house, four flights above the level on which they did of their interminable work; by the meager wages of . . . the carpenters and masons who had built the house, of the workers in factories . . . who produced . . . the goods they used; and that the

space and service which were at the disposal of even the [middle class] family were likewise made possible by low wages. (Allen 1954)

The American Dream Achieved

The American home of the early modern architectural era tells a story of modern class struggle: American house as domestic dream and democratic manifesto. Against great social and economic odds, many American families from 1901–1920 did manage to move from coldwater flats in urban tenements to simple, single-family houses in streetcar suburbs within two generations post-immigration. The American dream could be achieved as the middle class became a reality. The American dream, which had been promised nationally at the time of the Civil War, had now in 1901–1920, become an international dream. A European immigrant coal miner could live to see his son graduate from a state college in America. If this worker saved his factory wages, and his wife perhaps took in piece work sewing or hand laundering, he could aspire to owning his own house; certainly his son and grandchildren could.

At worst, the cities and homes of the early modern architectural era celebrated the rich and degraded the poor. At best, the American home of this era expressed the emerging middle-class qualities of stability and decency for all that define the American ideal. The concrete *reality* of American homes, from slum to palace, farm to city, had too long spoken to cruel inequalities, even as the *concept* of the American home strove toward a more modern democratic ideal. To

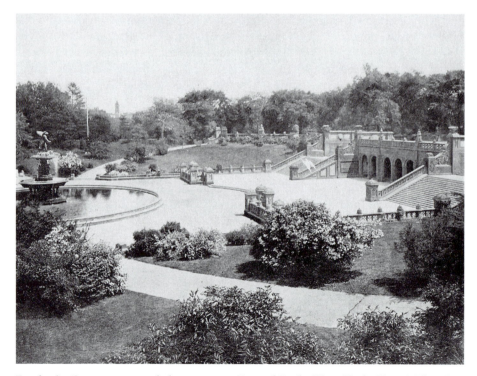

Fresh air. Open space and skyscrapers. Central Park, New York City. © The New York Public Library.

comprehend the architecture of the home within the prevalent polemical culture of the early modern architectural era, it is important to define the types of extant homes one would have observed or inhabited in America at this time, whether built during 1901–1920 or before it. The simple American house, the dream, the vernacular house—bungalow, foursquare, two-family, triple-decker—for Americans of the early modern era, and for generations to come, would lead the way out of the squalid slum and into the comforts of home.

VERNACULAR ARCHITECTURE IN EARLY TWENTIETH-CENTURY AMERICA

Vernacular Homes: Architecture Without Architects

The spoken vernacular is the language of the common man; the visual vernacular is the background architecture of the community. The *vernacular house* is the term applied to the common American home, the anonymous house, architecture without architects. The vast majority of houses in America fall into this generalized category, including the house or apartment building in which the reader and writer of this book are most likely to live.

Most American architecture was not, and is not, made by architects. It is most often builders and housing developers, rather than architects, who make domestic buildings, for it is actually rare to be able to seek out or to afford the services of a trained architect. Thus, the vernacular house is the product of aesthetic informality, sometimes unschooled, often built more for bucks than for beauty. Avoiding sophisticated high-style and high-cost architecture, the vernacular is targeted to satisfy the tastes of both the working and middle classes and the capitalist speculators who are ready to rent or sell the home to them. Unpedigreed, but certainly not unappealing, the American environment of background vernacular homes reflects the diverse melting pot atmosphere of American democracy.

Vernacular Architectural Typeforms

The key to appreciating the vernacular lies in observing the vast variety of homes in America, all arrived at via simple transformations of a limited number of basic normative forms, *prototypes* or *typeforms*. Structurally and aesthetically, the American house tends toward a simple box standing on land, very much like the drawing a child would paint to depict a house, or construct of big wooden kindergarten blocks. In terms of geometry, the vernacular American house is a cube topped with a triangle set in space. How this normative cubic box is transformed within simple constraints into so many variations is the wonder of the American vernacular.

A typeform or simply type, is the basic, repeatable architectural model of the simplest built form evolved to satisfy the functional needs of its day. In the early modern architectural era, most builders in America were concerned with continuing to construct basic vernacular homes in established normative types, while a few forward-thinking modernists sought to create new architecture. Thus, the basic box of American architecture during this period both stayed the same and underwent the most significant transformations of any period in American housing history.

Still-functional vernacular types with historical references persisted into the early modern period. Yet, a few insightful avant-garde architects, primary among them Frank Lloyd Wright and Irving Gill, were creating new forms from the box appropriate to a new century. Form and function, in modern architectural theory, must be simplified and synthesized in the aesthetics of the modern house, and the house must have a natural relationship to the land. Even as the bravest creative architects pushed the American house stylistically into the modern era, the All-American typeform homes of the past persisted. A historical typology of the housing extant, or still present in original form, in the early modern era of 1901–1920, therefore must examine both domestic vernacular and architect-designed homes.

Vernacular Middle-Class Styles

The Box: The Cape Cod House and the Colonial House

The Cape Cod house has continued as a vernacular form and aesthetic prototype for homey suburban cottages and country estates alike into the present day. To make a Cape, add a heavy roof and central chimney to the box. This very basic American antique gained renewed popularity during the early modern period of the Colonial Revival, as nostalgia gripped America, and the style spread about the nation, especially in the Northeast. Though now found everywhere, this house was built for cruel climates. Its powerfully sloped roofline, allowing New England winds to pass over it like a wave from front to back, was an innovation and an aesthetic, fusing form with function. The sheltering sloped roof carried heavy snow loads and shed icy water efficiently, seeming to prefigure known principles of aerodynamics. In fact, the three little pigs probably could have built their own Cape house of any material at all, if the roof were heavy enough and the slope steep enough to withstand the wolf's huffing and puffing.

Evolved for its lonely seaside beginnings, the antique Cape Cod house was like a strong boat sailing through northern winter landscapes. Contemporary students of home design, like the early modern architects of the best Colonial Revival, should study authentic Cape Cod houses, such as the Jared Coffin house in Nantucket, Massachusetts or the Fairbank house in Dedham, Massachusetts, for inspiration and understanding of this form. The Cape, from the original of the seventeenth century into the twentieth-century revival, has consistently done the job it was built to do. Thus, it has persisted as a most sensible and serviceable, perhaps even boring and ubiquitous, box upon the American landscape.

A transformation of the Cape involved enlarging its low proportions into a more formal and sophisticated Colonial. By adding a full second floor, thus increasing the height of the front elevation, and thereby raising the roofline, builders created the more graceful and roomy American Colonial type. The front facade could face either direction in relation to the street. An unadorned, historically inaccurate version of the Colonial house was built during 1901–1920 as a common vernacular house, without the sophistication of a trained revival designer. This tall angular house may be visually enhanced by the strong silhouette of a blue spruce, elm tree, or other significant planting.

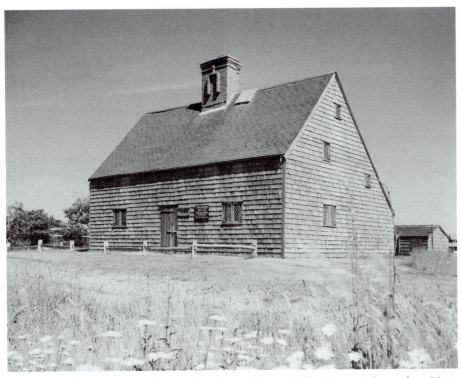

Vernacular American typeform: The Cape. Jethro Coffin House, Nantucket, Massachusetts. Courtesy of the Library of Congress.

The Curve: The Queen Anne House

To the geometric regularity of the basic box of the Cape and the Colonial house, the Queen Anne adds asymmetry in the form of an appended cylinder and sweeping lines, often a fenestrated tower on the corner of the house and a front porch. The curvilinearity of the Queen Anne and its graceful proportions are enhanced by respect for overall surface continuity, usually shingling. Americans living during the early modern architectural era would certainly have seen extant historical styles all about them; revival house types supplied conscious and unconscious inspiration, the background canvas against which new American homes were to be drawn. Aesthetically, the modernized Queen Anne house type was a major advance in the history of the American home that was to be inspirational to early modern architects, particularly H. H. Richardson.

The Porch: The Bungalow

Unlike the antique forms of the Cape and the Colonial, the bungalow was a new American invention of the early modern architectural era, a modern typeform and a new American icon. Though we may not be able to define it, we know the bungalow when we see it by its inviting porch and roofline. Not much more complicated than a Cape Cod, it might also generically be called a cottage. The primary identifying features of the bungalow are its sheltering, umbrella-like shed or hip roofline and its deep, shading front porch. The innovative indoor–outdoor aesthetic of the bungalow became a landmark in the design of the American home.

The bungalow type home enwrapped American nostalgia for a pre-industrial world within a machine-made form for the masses. The concept of a bungalow was a simple framed box with roof, with the appearance, though not necessarily the reality, of being hand-made. Because of its comforting commonness, this tiny cheaply constructed home has, in the late twentieth and early twenty-first centuries, enjoyed a retro-popularity that belies its humble beginnings in the early twentieth century. A bungalow is complemented equally by a palm or a spreading deciduous tree, depending on locale. Variations within this building have been infinite, and like the Cape, the bungalow exudes a simple homey American presence.

One would never expect that this normative American house actually derived from an ancient thatched Hindu hut, but surprisingly, the origin of the common American bungalow and its odd name were derived from colonial India, where it served as shelter along tropical routes for foreign travelers. Its origins and first mentions in America can be specifically traced to an engaging series of articles published in the *Chicago Tribune,* chronicled by an itinerant American professor then exploring the Indian subcontinent, in 1901, an amazing feat, called "Professor D's Travels." Considering the Chicago newspaper as its American source, this type of home became pervasive in the Midwest, spreading like prairie wildfire with land development booms to the hotter parts of the United States. The bungalow, though, as an unassuming, "ah shucks," American vernacular, fits comfortably anywhere in the United States.

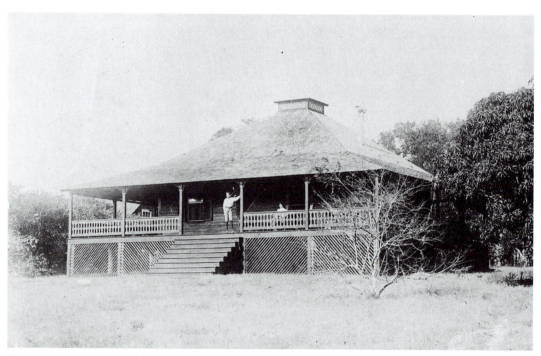

Early bungalow type with sheltering roof. Courtesy of the Library of Congress.

Though a bungalow was proud to be anonymous and humble, the finest architect-designed bungalows have taken their place within the cannon of great American architecture. The best bungalows joined outside with inside, creating a complete and integrated, fully designed home environment for the developing middle classes of the early modern era. Sophisticated variations on the bungalow were created within the aesthetics of the Craftsman style, further inspiring early modern architects in the Midwest and particularly southern California. The hand-made quality of a Stickley or a Greene and Greene bungalow melded American Arts and Crafts aesthetics with increasing material luxury, and thus the early modern architectural era raised this simple normative home type, the American bungalow, to an individual work of art.

Summer Cottages and Speculative Bungalows

The simplicity and low cost of the bungalow type made it a natural choice for summer stays. Individual bungalows at the beach or mountains, as well as picturesque ensembles of bungalows, can be found wherever Americans vacationed in the early modern era. The concepts of respite and vacation, obviously, were only now becoming more democratized as the middle class developed, and a place to stay was the first necessity of leisure. An excellent example of an active summer bungalow community of this era can today be found preserved at the Colorado Chautauqua Association in Boulder, Colorado (open to the public). The informal collection of varied bungalows, spread about a lawn, look up from grassy slopes to the towering Flatiron and Rocky Mountains. Each bungalow is fronted by an American front porch, the transition from out to in. The porches and light-weight board and batten framing of the cottages ensured that music from the Chautauqua performers in the large, bungalow-like auditorium could be heard by residents all about the bungalow colony.

The Foursquare

So common and conventional is this vernacular typeform house that we barely notice it; the foursquare is the generic American house. A foursquare house is just as it is named: a square box of a house, square in all elevations and dimensions, square in ground plan, and square in interior spaces. Most often the foursquare is two or two and a half stories, with a symmetrical front facade and a four-sided hip roof, sometimes a shed roof. A defining feature of the foursquare house, and the only addition to its box, is the protruding front porch with its centered steps and front door, a fairly consistent feature that makes these houses inviting. The foursquare is a true American typeform, comfortably and comfortingly found in nearly every region—rural, urban, or suburban—of the United States.

The original foursquare, though its neighborhoods may by now be upgraded by gentrification, was never intended to be a fashionable residence; rather it was a good, solid, unassuming house, and therefore, a real American specialty. Only in America could the middle class, indeed even the working class, aspire to single-family housing. Foursquares were equally built in the country or the city, in the East, the West and the Midwest. As a farmhouse, the foursquare could be ordered from a catalogue and delivered by train to the site. As a city house, it could be elongated, lined up, and repeated along narrow, deep city lots by a housing developer. In the new streetcar suburbs of the early twentieth century, the easily reproduced foursquare could provide the amenity of the single-family residence within a relatively dense, repetitive landscape. The foursquare remains the workhorse of the American domestic dream.

Multiple Family Dwellings: Two-Family and Triple Decker Houses

The foursquare house, generally so symmetrical, was also amenable to transformation into a two-family or three-family home. In this case, the symmetry of the front facade was sacrificed to necessity: The central doorway and inside staircase are relocated to one side, so that side-by-side access to divided spaces was created. Efficient and economical, the common American foursquare model could be divided into next-door adjoining units, or upstairs–downstairs units. Its combination of neighborliness and privacy allowed related families to cohabit, especially important at the turn of the century when extended families remained in the same location for generations. It also made good financial sense, providing entry-level into the housing market for the working class as the mortgage of one household was paid by the attached rental unit. Thus, the two family foursquare house has proven itself, physically and economically, the portal into American domestic ownership. Endless examples of the single-family and the two-family foursquare can be found regionally in older middle- and working-class sectors of such cities as Boston, Providence, Chicago, Seattle, and Denver, appropriately known there as the Denver square.

The foursquare has its higher-density variation. In more thickly populated urban centers of the Northeast, such as working-class sections of Boston, the foursquare is stacked into its apartment equivalent, the triple-decker. These boxy, top-heavy, highly serviceable constructions still line streetcar sections of many older cities. Here, instead of two families inhabiting two floors, three families, often related immigrants in the early twentieth century, share the house in three equal, stacked apartments, each with a covered front porch and rear service porch that provide secondary egress in case of fire. This very economical housing stock can be stretched out of its square configuration, elongated back from the street, to fill narrow urban lots.

Multifamily housing based on the foursquare came to fill whole neighborhoods of American cities. This was intended as working-class housing, never housing for the wealthy. It remained economical due to its excellent usage of land, its lack of necessity for an elevator, and its basically human, neighborly scale. In Boston and Providence, as in other eastern cities, the triple-decker was an especially functional housing arrangement for immigrant families, allowing new arrivals homes within the safe haven of their extended family. The triple-decker was, and remains, the New England alternative to the New York City tenement, the urban typeform home for diverse neighborhoods in ports of entry.

The Streetscape: The Urban Row House

The verticality and repetition of the row house was its dominant motif. With front facades flush to the street, shared outer walls, and rear service yards or small gardens, row houses made good use of urban land. The type can be produced either as a flat facade or a curvilinear bowfront. This form of home was usually a four to five story narrow building, but unlike the triple-decker, all floors of the row house were originally intended for one family, with servants' quarters upstairs. In the early twentieth century, many of these middle- to upper–middle-class homes were, by economic necessity, subdivided into single-story apartments.

In the East, most row house neighborhoods were based on European models: Boston's eighteenth-century Beacon Hill and nineteenth-century Back Bay, for example. In the many early row houses of Boston, Philadelphia, and Washington, D.C., brick and mortar predominated, and street and row house scale was intimate. In the later nineteenth- and early twentieth-century New York or Washington row house, however, large blocks of hewn stone gave the name to the larger scale row house type generically now called brownstones. To illustrate the changes in scale and materials between the eighteenth- versus the nineteenth- and early twentieth-century row house, compare, for example, Boston's Beacon Hill with the same city's Back Bay; or Georgetown with Washington's Dupont Circle neighborhood. In the late nineteenth and early twentieth centuries, the late and

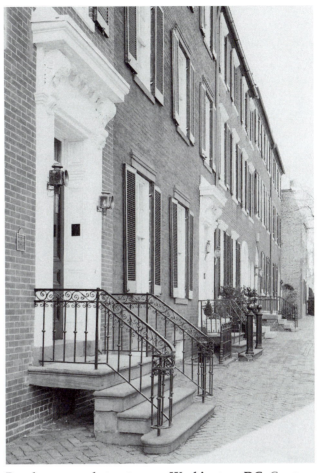

Rowhouses and streetscape. Washington, DC. Courtesy of the Library of Congress.

fast-developing city of San Francisco built its own version of the urban row house. Painted row houses, forming interconnected wooden structures, were fanciful but fateful. Building a high-density city of wooden homes proved, during the Great San Francisco Earthquake of 1906, to have dire consequences.

Forming an even street set back along the sidewalk, row houses in their multiplicity create a monolithic yet humanely scaled composition along the city street. Consistency of scale in fenestration, doorways and doorknockers, shutters, limited ornament, and especially street trees, lend the row house street an urbane quality as it composes the city. Some of the finest streetscapes in America have resulted from the rhythmic, undulating repetition of row houses.

VERNACULAR VERSUS STYLE IN EARLY TWENTIETH-CENTURY AMERICA

Revivalism or Modernism in Domestic Architecture

A great conundrum plagued the early modern architectural era: how to rectify technological invention in modern America with architectural form and style; or how to create an architecture that spoke expressively to the new world of technology. In the early twentieth century, Janus-like, American architecture looked backward and forward simultaneously, referencing colonial or even classical motifs, while simultaneously creating new forms. The average American home continued to be constructed within the well-known parameters and vernacular conventions previously defined, but high-style architect-designed homes of the early modern period, as discussed in the next chapter, were caught up by the historicist motifs of a passing world, or conversely, by the sweeping *tabula rasa* of modernism. The early modern era was a complex time of great technological change and social struggle, and the architecture of the American home reflected these contradictions. Early modern domestic architecture thus responded to change with opposing views: unconscious continuity of vernacular form; consciously conservative revivalist styles; or progressive pure modernism.

Reference List

Allen, Frederick Lewis. 1954. *The Big Change, America Transforms Itself 1900–1950.* New York: Harper & Row, 27–28, 48.

Boyd, John Taylor. 1921. "A Short Bibliography and Analysis of Housing." *Architectural Record* (February): 180–185.

Bragdon, Claude. 1918. "Architecture and Democracy Before, During and After the War." *Architectural Record* (July): 75–84.

Brush, Edward Hale. 1911. "A Garden City for the Man of Moderate Means." *The Craftsman* xix(5): 445–451 (pen and ink illustrations of Forest Hills).

Desmond, Henry W., and Herbert Crowley. 1906. "The Work of McKim, Mead & White." *Architectural Record* (September): 207–216.

"A Doughboy Killed in Action Is Home at Last." 2006. *New York Times* (24 September): section 1, 29.

Dreiser, Theodore. 1925. *An American Tragedy.* New York: Boni and Liveright.

Glenn, John. 1946. *Forest Hills Gardens,* vol. 1. New York: The Russell Sage Foundation, 1907–1946.

"How to Build Tenements." 1900. *New York Times* (12 October): 11.

"The News of Newport." 1900. *New York Times* (12 October): 7

Roosevelt, Theodore. 1918. "Housing After the War." *Architectural Record* (July): 151.

Sinclair, Upton. 1906. *The Jungle.* Cambridge, MA: R. Bentley, 1971.

Sturgis, Russell. 1901. "The Art Gallery of the Streets." *Architectural Record* (July): 92–112.

"Town Plan Helps Future Land Value." 1924. *New York Times* (18 May): RE2.

"Twentieth Century's Triumphant Entry." 1901. *New York Times* (1 January): 1.

"Uncle Sam, Landlord." 1919. *New York Times* (29 June): 82.

United States Geological Survey. 2006. "The Great 1906 San Francisco Earthquake, Earthquake Hazards Program." Available at: www.usgs.gov.

Veiller, Lawrence. 1918. "Housing After the War." *Architectural Record* (July): 140–151.

Veiller, Lawrence. 1920. *A Model Tenement Housing Law.* New York: The Russell Sage Foundation, 40–41.

Styles of Domestic Architecture around the Country

TRADITIONAL HOME STYLES, EMERGENT MODERN HOME STYLES, AND MODERN HOME STYLES

What is the meaning of modernism? How is the home emblematic of the modern world? Modernism was one of the most profound social and aesthetic transformations in history, as the western world offered new visions of living environments for the common person and sought to create architectural aesthetics appropriate to the social, cultural, technological, and scientific revolutions of 1901–1920. Until the early modern era at the beginning of the twentieth century, scientific knowledge and artistic motifs were generally thought to exist within a continuum from classical times, through the Renaissance, into eternity. Modernism, a wholly new stream of early twentieth-century thought, meant that assumptions of historical continuity were forever shattered, for modern thought and aesthetics reveled in abruptly questioning and disrupting long-held beliefs.

The architecture of the early twentieth century grappled with the theoretical questions of finding aesthetic form that was both appropriate to the modern technological and scientific era, and structurally truthful. Yet, even as the early modern era in America represented a period of intense change, traditional aesthetics continued to exist parallel to developing modern styles. Many of the major changes of modernism were embraced at home with immediacy by Americans because, as seen in the previous chapter, the concept of home had been moving, particularly after 1913, slowly but surely toward democratization during this period, in economic availability, physical comfort, and technological advance. Not only was the American home at last becoming a more optimistic environment for the common

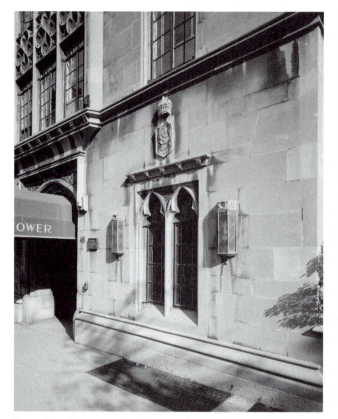

Entering history: Architectural revivals in the urban environment. The traditional home. Courtesy of the Library of Congress.

person, but improvements in social conditions and status of the growing middle class were expressed via the varying styles of homes within the growing suburban neighborhood configurations. Thus, the prevalent contrasts of historical and new home styles during 1901–1920, and the transformations from traditional domestic building to modern architectural style, truly represented the deeper intellectual challenges of the early modern era. The early modern era, as a period of transition from the nineteenth-century past into the twentieth-century future, partook simultaneously of stylistic continuity and revolt. The American home as visual artifact reflected these conflicting extremes and the transitions between them.

Throughout history, whenever the concept of *style* in architecture has had real significance, it has meant that the visual aesthetic, or style, displayed on the facade of the house has articulated the true meaning of the underlying physical and social structure of the domestic building within its social milieu.

One expected, rightly or wrongly, in 1901–1920, to gain some insight into other people by knowing their home neighborhoods—social class, economics, ethnicity, education, traditional or progressive values, housing choice, or lack thereof. A beautiful facade was not just a pretty face, but an honest communicator of meaning, for the American home could be deciphered socially and stylistically, and thus cultural meaning was symbolically transmitted by the prevalent housing styles.

During the early modern era of 1901–1920, the myriad architectural styles of aesthetic import, reflecting the internally diverse spirit of the age, can be understood as: traditional revivalism, based in historical motifs; emergent modernism, based in Arts and Crafts materials; and modernism, uniquely created of forms expressive of the twentieth century. The home functioned stylistically as an authentic and meaningful cultural emblem in early modern America.

TRADITIONAL REVIVALISM

The Reign of the Period House in the Older Cities and Suburbs of the East, Midwest, and West Coast

At once traditional and new, the so-called period houses of the early modern era ruled America in their time. This all-encompassing term, used primarily by nonprofessionals as opposed to architects, in the early twentieth century was meant to evoke an American striver's romantic dreams of a French Provincial house, an English Tudor house, an American Colonial house, or any other apparently high-class, olden-days architectural "period" to be relived. Period homes were more accurately described by their specific revivalist styles, as will follow in this book, or more simply referred to as the traditional homes of the early modern era. The rather pretentious Anglophone title "period" has often, like the term High Tea, been class elevated, in the case of the house, to describe fanciful, traditional upper middle-class homes of 1901–1920. The all-encompassing nature of the term renders it meaningless; for does not every year, even every day, belong to a period? After acknowledging the absurdity of this nomenclature, however, one is free to enjoy the encyclopedic nature of the traditional period domestic architecture of the first quarter of the twentieth century, particularly of the 1910s into the 1920s.

Traditional homes are the landmarks of every American town. We see these homes everywhere, yet we just assume that, like the oaks that surround them, they were just always there, though both the placement of the trees and the slope of the slate roof were actually produced quite consciously, exemplifying the educated aesthetics of the early modern architectural period. These sublimely emotive homes and estates with their accompanying landscapes were designed throughout America's cities and early suburbs, together evolving an overall aesthetic unity to American domestic architecture. One can find revival houses and estates of the early modern era in leafy suburbs in Tarrytown and Tuxedo Park, New York and Greenwich and Westport, Connecticut; in Wellesley and Lincoln, Massachusetts; in Oyster Bay and Glen Cove on Long Island's North Shore; in Bloomfield Hills, Michigan, and St. Louis, Missouri; in Riverside and Oak Park, Illinois; and in Hancock Park and Pasadena, California, to name but a few locales.

These homes were built of the highest quality materials, by the most skilled craftsmen, from plans by architects thoroughly versed in historic architecture. Architects of this period understood the aesthetics of the past; they had traveled in European cities and countryside; and they could really draw, thereby transmuting all their traditional skills into a traditional but new American domestic style. Free-hand drawing skills are rare today in architecture, fine materials are prohibitively expensive, and craftsmen, fortunately, are now far more fairly paid. We will therefore never again be able to reclaim the standard of architectural excellence in American domestic building we have inherited from the well-built, romantic traditional homes of the early modern period.

Tradition, Architects, and Architectural Education

Who designed the fine homes of the early modern period? American architecture of the last decades of the nineteenth and first decades of the twentieth century was delineated by pedigree: A home was either architecture by architect or simply a building. Likewise an American architect was either formally educated in the Neoclassical Revival styles and methodologies or not, and if he were not, he was hardly considered qualified to design the mansion of an American parvenu. Thus, a rigid hierarchy was maintained for American architecture, built upon the American architect as professional; the required professional teaching and accreditation were clearly defined by the diploma, methods, and aesthetics of the Parisian École des Beaux-Arts (literally, the School of the Beautiful Arts, as opposed to the technical school, the École Technique). The famous French architectural academy emphasized drawing and drafting skills, design of formal facades, the imposition of formal axial planning, and especially knowledge of the Classical Orders.

The Orders of architecture, proportional and decorative systems developed in Greco-Roman antiquity, were known as the Doric, Ionic, and Corinthian Orders, and could be found both on the facade and in the interior of a building. These decorative systems were not arbitrary decorations; they could be read to understand the building, for the Classical Orders were actually symbols referring to the meaning and function of the building they adorned. For example, the simple but strong Doric Order was considered appropriate for a bank or a fortress. The Ionic Order, refined and elegant, might be symbolic of scholarship, and therefore was appropriate for a campus lecture hall or a library. The ornate Corinthian Order was emotive and rich, and thus would be favored in a ballroom. École-trained architects understood and appreciated the connotations of the Classical Orders and employed their aesthetics with finesse.

Rigorous classical principles were taught at École-influenced schools of architecture in America, including Columbia University and Massachusetts Institute of Technology, each on a Beaux-Arts campus, and at Harvard University and Boston Architectural Center. Because the system was based on merit, it represented one of the first examples of diversity: an African American architect, Horace Trumbauer, and one of the first female architects, Julia Morgan, were products of the American École system. The most successful student might advance to Paris to study European buildings in situ. Exposure to European aesthetics could be a blessing or a curse to a potential American architect, for whereas it encouraged excellence in formal design, it no doubt excluded American personality and originality. Note that whereas proto-modernist H.H. Richardson was École trained, modernist Frank Lloyd Wright declined. The rise of modern corporate multipartner firms grew out of this movement, including prolific partnerships Adler and Sullivan, Carrere and Hastings, Delano and Aldrich, and McKim, Mead, and White. The most talented American students to be École-educated synthesized historic European formality with incipient American modernism.

French Neoclassical Beaux-Arts: City and Country Homes

The Neoclassical styles were formal, and thus, in addition to private mansions and townhouses, were often found in public edifices. Government offices, diplomatic embassies, and libraries were considered commissions of appropriate gravitas to warrant Beaux-Arts formality. From the large cities of Boston to New York to San Francisco, to small towns, neoclassical facades front American libraries. Many of the small ones were the beneficiaries of Carnegie Foundation-sponsored libraries. A simple, dignified classical facade beautifully decorates the Morgan Library in Manhattan (1906) by Charles McKim. For finesse in Beaux-Arts design, the pinnacle of American neoclassicism can be found in Boston's historic Copley Square, McKim, Mead, and White's design for the Boston Public Library (1895), based on Bibliotheque Sainte-Genevieve (library) in Paris. In the spirit of American democracy, Charles McKim called his American library masterpiece the Palace for the People. Of particular interest for early modern architectural figures were two commissions: Horace Trumbauer's design for Widener Library at Harvard, commissioned to honor a victim of the sinking of the Titanic; and McKim, Mead, and White's reconstruction of the White House for President Theodore Roosevelt.

The greatest of the American Beaux-Arts architects managed to design neoclassical palaces for the rich that were stately without being ostentatious, French without being foreign, and contextual in both city and country setting. Basing their designs on the classical École principles of symmetry and proportion in which they were immersed, traditional architects produced the townhouses or country estates famous today. Formal French and Italian gardens often surrounded these homes. Among these beautiful private urban or rural homes, a number are open to the public as museums, others are private residences, and others are in reuse. A French-inspired townhouse by Carrere and Hastings (1914) now houses the modernist collections of the Neue Galerie on Fifth Avenue. Various New York mansions and Long Island country houses for the Astors and Whitneys were the product of McKim, Mead, and White; Delano and Aldrich designed Kykuit for the Rockefellers; and Carrere and Hastings for the Fricks. With its French facade by Charles McKim and interiors by his partner, the notorious Stanford White of McKim, Mead, and White designed the neoclassical Villard Houses in New York City (1885), currently incorporated into a hotel. Like other large American firms of the turn of the century, however, McKim, Mead, and White eventually branched out, becoming more eclectic, developing expertise not only in the French Neoclassical style, but also in the newly developing American Colonial Revival and even into the more modern Shingle Style. Thus, one firm could create contrasting home styles of European historical revivals or progressive protomodern American architecture.

Eclectic Styles in Eastern Cities and Suburbs

Within the eastern urban and suburban context, other revivals included French Chateaux or Mansard, British Tudor, American Colonial Revival, and Spanish revivals. The commonness of style and significance varied for the myriad eclectic styles. Some were pure fantasy, others led toward a considered new American modern idiom. Chateaux style, for example, was a rare remnant of the Gilded Age, occasionally constructed during early modern times, but not truly modern or even traditional. Relying primarily on its seventeenth-century silhouette, turrets, and the storybook romanticism of castles and kings, Chateaux style offered enjoyable escapism to the street, but was not expressive of the modern truthfulness. Faux castle styles were seen in flamboyant New York townhouse facades or full-blown chateaux that stood like crenellated stone castles in early suburbs, or were hidden behind winding driveways in the Hudson River Valley.

Critiques of Eclecticism

Eclecticism, historicism, and the Beaux-Arts styles, however successful, did have critics in America who felt they were both retrograde and too foreign to ever represent America truthfully, viewing the style and theory in opposition to the creation of a purely American modernism. Commenting on the eclecticism of American architecture of the early twentieth century, the critic Ernest Flagg, in the *Architectural Record* (1900) wrote, "American Architecture as Opposed to Architecture in America," seeking "the evolution of a National Style" (Flagg 1900). A critic in the *Architectural Record* commented, "the modern French school . . . [represents] the importation of an idea . . . We are unduly magnifying [the École's] importance and are even insisting that they are the foundation and reality of architecture. We should glory in our freedom and strive to solve our problems in a truthful and vigorous way" (Barney 1907). As these early critics of the revivalist styles so presciently pointed out, the operative words of the developing American architectural style would one day soon, but not quite yet, be truth, vigor, and freedom.

Architecture and Clients for Traditional Homes

Who lived in these traditional revival homes? Who commissioned American domestic architecture in the early modern period? The American home had become much more than a shelter by this time; it was a statement, a sign of success. Success for the arriving middle class and upper middle class was now set in stone, brick, and shingles. A growing mercantile class demanded the comforts and class of "Stockbroker Tudor," and we see that often it really was financial managers, brokers, and bankers, or successful self-employed businessmen, entrepreneurs, manufacturers, inventive innovators, and various small town titans who were the upper middle-class architectural clients of 1901–1920. The story of traditional revivalist form reads as an architectural and historical continuity, from the eighteenth to the twenty-first century, from Old to New World, embodying a visual narrative of what it is to be American and how we define American form.

The health and distribution of the American economy and the creation of high-style architecture for the home have been inextricably synergistic since the early modern period. In the East, the financial sector demanded urban work-week and country weekend homes. In the booming industrial cities of Chicago and Detroit, manufacturing, industry, and transportation were closely tied to architectural development. Economics and business co-existed with consumer demand—entrepreneurs sold products, products made wealth, wealth created domestic demand, demand made for clients, clients paid for significant homes, and homes in turn increased demand for products. The Gamble House, for example, floated on the soap bubbles of Proctor and Gamble; the Robie House rolled in on two wheels, commissioned by a bicycle manufacturer. Later, as the automobile drove over the transportation industry, suburban Bloomfield Hills, Michigan, grew up as home to automotive executives and an architectural enclave. Here, Frank Lloyd Wright would build his very American "Usonian" homes, and the Cranbrook Academy of Art, an early modern landscaped campus with faculty homes and student dormitories amid sculpture and landscape, was designed by architect Eliel Saarinen, recent European émigré (Anderson et al. 1986).

Émigrés and the American Home as a Symbol of Success

The home was the most powerful material proof of the transformation and success of a newly arrived American in the early modern era, and either architect or client was likely to be a recent immigrant or émigré (Hans Otto Humm, personal communication with the author, October 1987). One true example of an émigré's journey will here illustrate the meaning of home for a new class of American: the self-employed, home-owning entrepreneur. Son of a Swiss schoolmaster, scorning an apprenticeship to a pastry baker, Hans ran off from Alps to sea as a cabin boy at age 16. In 1913, returning home but still seeing little opportunity for economic or social advancement in his native Switzerland, he relocated his young family to America. His wife and infants faced a freezing ship across the Atlantic, only upon disembarking to catch a train as he moved his family cross-country. Arriving on the freezing Colorado plain, they learned their journey was based on mistaken promises of sharing a family farm or ranch. Out West, Hans and his family were to endure months of unexpected and unrequited pioneer existence, primitive indeed compared to the life they had left in Basel. This man, however, inspired by the myths of the American West, remained undaunted and unbeaten by circumstance. Focusing again on sustenance for his family and success as an American, he invented and patented a machined mechanism for the most popular contemporary pistol then used in the West, subsequently selling the patent to the major American firearms manufacturer of the day. The patent money paid his family's train fare back to New York City, where he started his own manufacturing business with no formal training in engineering, not for dangerous weapons, but for safety equipment for heavy machinery. Note that his factory produced goods not for the consumer, but rather manufactured parts for manufacturing, illustrating the multiplier effect of one entrepreneur upon a growing modern economy. Thus, with no resources but his ingenuity, from failed farm to firearms to factory, literally Deus ex Machina, Hans had valiantly created his own little military/industrial complex.

The factory in Brooklyn paid for Hans' Tudor house in suburban New York. His substantial brick home of sweeping slate roofline both acknowledged its European architectural sources and left Europe behind, looking forward to an American life for Hans and his family, its owner having truly arrived in the land of opportunity that had at last rewarded his gutsy inventiveness. Hans' traditional home represented the end of his early turmoil in Europe and his hard times in the American West, and became the concrete architectural symbol of his urban American success. Hans died prematurely in the big Tudor house, no doubt worked to death, but like so many émigrés of the early modern era, given the choice, rather than living long enough to become an aging baker in Basel, surely he would have chosen to be successful but short-lived in America. This house and others like it of 1901–1920 have become emblems of the daring entrepreneurial spirit of the early modern era, and the refuge that America represented to so many European émigrés.

English Tudor Revival: Appropriate to Urban and Suburban Life

English Tudor Revival, defined by its dark wooden half-timbering, patterned brick, and white stucco, gave great gravitas to traditional American homes. Its sixteenth-century British royal associations and medieval heraldic character made Tudor popular in new money commuter suburbs in Westchester and Connecticut, which were springing up from 1901–1920. Sometimes facetiously referred to as Stockbroker Tudor, the style reflected the upward aspirations and mobility of the growing middle and upper middle classes in America. The powerful dark and light facades gave this British-derived style an aesthetic solidity complementary to comfort and wealth and avoided the flamboyant fakery of French chateaux. Towers and turrets associated with Tudor architecture allowed it to serve well in country and suburb silhouette, and even in urban high-rise settings. Tudor City, a major early modern apartment development of the 1920s on Manhattan's East River (East 42–44 Streets), was the high-rise and urban garden ensemble that enshrined this eccentric but refined English style in the urban consciousness. One of the most important Tudor Revivals, and the predecessor to Tudor City, was Forest Hills Gardens.

American Colonial Revival: Appropriate to Suburban and Country Life

Some early modern architects and clients were looking not to European roots, but closer to home for inspiration, within America's own history. They sought to return from historical flights of foreign fancy to the pressing question of appropriateness of form for the new century in America. McKim, Mead, and White, when not working in the "Frenchified" classical style, often found inspiration here within American historical architecture in the Colonial Revival, inventing early modern America as a kind of 14th original colony. Americans were looking both forward into the new twentieth century and backward to the eighteenth century, as they strove to create a truly American architecture. Important American domestic monuments, such as George Washington's Mount Vernon, Thomas Jefferson's Monticello, and Theodore Roosevelt's Sagamore Hill, were being preserved for posterity and opened to the public during the years of the Colonial Revival, and philanthropies such as the Daughters of the American Revolution were in their heyday. A pervasive appreciation of all things American was an aesthetic underpinning of Colonial Revival domestic architecture.

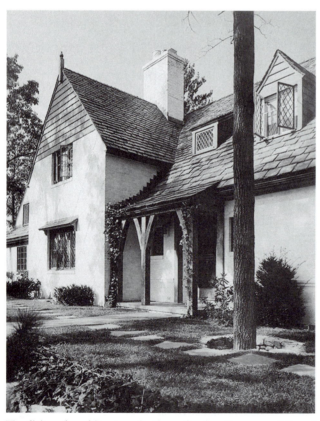

Traditional architecture in the suburbs. Courtesy of Royal Barry Wills Architects.

In the historicizing design of the early twentieth century, the Colonial Revival was a modern look at our original American roots. The term *Colonial Revival* tended to take in all motifs of an earlier America, so-called Early American architecture, from early settlers' capes, to simple

Federal farmhouses, to fancy Georgian townhouses and estates; it was not until the late 1920s that historical accuracy became significant in Colonial Revival architecture. The generic "Colonial" was used more often to refer to vernacular rural houses and farms, but Americans thought of anything Ye Olde American as Colonial. Georgian architecture versus Federal versus Colonial was a fine distinction, particularly in revivalism. Georgian referred to Tory architecture based on aristocratic models of George III, bane of American rebels. Anyone today, by the way, who paints a black rim around the white brick chimney of their Colonial home is inadvertently telling the world they are British sympathizers, for this was a secret Tory symbol. Just as rebels were less likely to wear the English powdered wigs, they were less likely to powder their houses with swags and decorations. The simple, undecorative Federal style home reflected the simple, straight-forwardness and democratizing ideals of the American colonies.

At the beginning of the Colonial Revival in the early modern architectural era, the spirit of the past trumped accurate recreations of the past. The mixed motifs of historical eclecticism actually allowed for greater creativity in revival architecture in the hands of a creative architect, such as Charles McKim, who had early on made the case for American study of colonial architecture (Roth 1983). McKim, Mead, and White's early twentieth-century works and influence may be found in domestic architecture all over America. Excellent Colonial Revival architecture covers eastern sectors of America from Massachusetts to Virginia, from city to suburb to farm and often to campus. Good urban examples of twentieth-century American Colonial Revival in Cambridge, Massachusetts, include the brick walls and dormitory buildings of Radcliffe College and Harvard University. Brown University exhibits one of the most complete architectural ensembles of authentic early Federal and Greek Revival architecture with Colonial Revival additions atop College Hill in Providence, Rhode Island. Neighborhoods of urban town houses in Boston and New York, and embassies and diplomatic residences in Washington, D.C., exemplify the Colonial Revival of the early modern architectural period.

Spanish Revivals in the West

> Spain offers us an architecture the versatility of which is perhaps matched in no other European country.
>
> —Rexford Newcomb, *The Spanish House for America,* 1927

Whereas French and English Revivals influenced Eastern architecture where these European countries had established colonies, Spanish styles were inspirational wherever Spanish colonies or missions had been established in America. Transported Spanish motifs of the Old World were so pervasive in the American West, Southwest, and Florida as to define the character of entire regions of the New World. In the hot climatic regions of America, Spanish revivals bloomed like cacti in the desert, as Moorish-derived architecture mixed with indigenous New World traditions to form the melanges known as Spanish Colonial, Mission, and Pueblo styles.

Spanish architecture of the early modern architectural era exhibited regional variations, and was composed both of original buildings of Spanish settlers and of Spanish-influenced early modern designs, which together illustrated "the

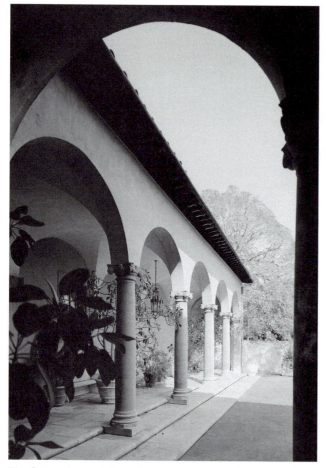

Traditional Spanish revival architecture. Courtesy of the Library of Congress.

fundamental simplicity and well-proportioned masses of the old houses" (Newcomb 1927). Simplicity and sun spoke to Spanish Revival architecture. Simple geometric solids defined a Spanish house. It was not the decoration so much as the materials and massing that truly defined a Spanish home. Colors reflected the contrasts of the bleak with the bright; earth toned stucco walls supported bright red tile roofs. Aesthetic characteristics of Spanish architecture were ornate decoration set against the simple adobe surfaces and mass; a highly decorative window or door cut into a smooth stucco wall. A plain flat *fachada,* or facade, was ornamented with elaborate picturesque patterns of tiling.

Traditional Spanish architecture, with its heat deflecting adobe forms and cooling atrium garden, responded to the Mediterranean-like climate of the western desert and southern subtropical sectors of the United States. Though early modern Spanish homes in America ranged from simple bungalow types to suburban revival homes to elaborate mansions, thoughtful design for sun and shade, as well as spatial flow from interior to exterior, were the hallmarks of all Spanish architecture, adding to the American house the atrium, the arch, the colonnade, the loggia, and the pergola. The Spanish styles, with central courtyard and fountain, were the most beautifully integrated with the outdoors compared to any other traditional architecture. In the words of early modern architect Rexford Newcomb in his seminal study of the 1920s, *The Spanish House for America,* "The salient message of all Mediterranean architecture is its reaction to climate, its essential sunniness, its emphasis on light and shade. This quality is apparent in its every line, be it plan, elevation, roof, or decorations" (Newcomb 1927).

Spanish Revival architecture, during the early modern architectural era, was suddenly advanced, though with controversy, by the 1915 Panama Pacific Exposition in Balboa Park, San Diego, designed by architects Bertram Goodhue and Irving Gill. Their stylistic argument pitted Goodhue's decorative Spanish revivalism against Gill's simple modernism, and Goodhue won. The formal yet exotic buildings of this exposition still stand as testaments to the originality and great joy of Spanish Revival styles that spread throughout the warm climatic regions of the United States.

Tropical Spanish Revivals in Florida

Spanish Revival architectural home aesthetics exploded in Florida in the first decades of the twentieth century under the Spanish moss, due not only to Florida's ancient lineage to Spain via St. Augustine, but also due to the modern land boom. Playful fantasy motifs of fast-developing Florida home subdivisions, with their "fanciful bungalows" (see "History of the Early Modern Era, 1901–1920"), still recall the joys of tropical Spanish architecture. Contrasting with the simplicity of the western Mission style, Spanish architecture in Florida was lighter and more island-like in its use of balconies, awnings, shutters, spouting water features, often lushly planted with palms, hibiscus, and vines growing within interior courtyards.

Excellent Florida Spanish Revival homes can be found in Miami's Coral Gables and Coconut Grove, and in Boca Raton and Palm Beach. Architect Abner Mizner developed the elaborated style for the newly rich entrepreneurs arriving in the sunny climes for second homes, who had become accustomed to the style while visiting his Boca Raton Hotel and Cottages. Many tropical Spanish Revival homes in Florida were privately hidden behind manicured hedges; however, the public may visit the extravagant Villa Vizcaya, commissioned by a successful tractor manufacturer (architect Paul Claflin, 1916) and owned by the city of Miami on Biscayne Bay. Vizcaya is the pinnacle of crazy tropical beauty among American homes—a fanciful melange of Spanish, French, and Italian motifs, of villa, gardens, and visual dramatics.

Mission and Pueblo Revivals in the Southwest

More naturalistic Spanish architecture is found in the American southwest, particularly in New Mexico and Arizona, where architecture was more desert-like in character, finding its inspiration in the thick walls of the missions and pueblos. Desert domestic featured flat expanses of stucco or adobe walls, sometimes articulated with wood projecting beams called *vigas,* either rough or painted. Windows, doors, and even fireplaces were literally cut from the very walls of the house. The houses laid low against the flat expanses of the desert landscape, saguaro cactus, cottonwood, and tumbleweed forming the natural vegetation about the desert and its dry washes.

The best of Spanish Revival mission and pueblo adobe homes respected the desert and, like the native rattlesnake, made the most of the sun and rocks. In such towns as Santa Fe, New Mexico, and Monterey, California, both old territorial towns, the styles live, not only historically, but also by local taste and building ordinances. Ironically, consistency of historical style has led to historically correct latter-day structures such as gas stations. Still, the pervasive adobe of mission and pueblo aesthetics at their finest have lent an overall integration to the organic, geometric forms of American towns and individual homes within the desert environment.

Native American Revivals in the Southwest

Before the Spanish settlers in the desert Southwest there were the Native Americans. Tribal motifs that would have been read generically as Indian or at best Anasazi between 1901–1920 were mined for architectural inspiration in the West during the early modern architectural era. The living pueblos of New Mexico and Arizona, for the few outsiders who found them, represented an ideal but unknown form of domestic architecture that successfully integrated the private family home with the communal place, and the communal home with the natural environment.

Some of the most unique architecture of the Southwest, indeed of the entire United States, is the architecture of the American National Parks inspired by the Native Americans. At Grand Canyon National Park, in northern Arizona, Mary Colter (1869–1958, sometimes spelled Coulter), a maverick early modern architect, spent 30 years of her life studying and recreating the archeological sites of the Southwest within the dramatic American landscapes of the National Park. In these works, she developed a completely unique style of architecture, reviving Native American pueblo motifs that blended seamlessly into the rugged landscape. Colter's cabins and hotels at the Grand Canyon's Rim and Bright Angel Trail have been the temporary homes of travelers and hikers for a century. Complementing the vernacular Phantom Ranch cottage styles below were her dramatic Anasazi-inspired ruin-like park buildings that seemed to grow as geologic outcroppings along the rim. Colter's Native American–inspired works represent some of the most powerful edifices and evocative American imagery ever created in historical revival architecture. Though we may not technically consider the hotels and cottages of our National Parks our individual homes, in a deeper sense of belonging, they are the inherited home of every American and Native American.

EMERGENT MODERN STYLES

Arts and Crafts–Influenced Homes in the East and Midwest

> There can be no doubt in my mind that a native type of architecture is growing up in America . . . It is my own wish, my own final ideal, that the Craftsman house may so far as possible meet this demand and be instrumental in helping to establish in America a higher ideal, not only of beautiful architecture, but of home life.
>
> —Gustav Stickley, *The Best of Craftsman Homes,* 1912

Craftsman denoted far more than a style of architecture; it was an ideal style of life. As a prescribed domestic lifestyle, Craftsman implied a utopian, back-to-the-land reform of contemporary modern life within the context of the industrialization and the increasing social complexity of the country during the early modern period. Craftsman style, sometimes referred to as Mission style though it is fully American and not Spanish in origin, created an internally and externally integrated home and landscape. The Craftsman way of life found its inspiration within reform and within a mythic medieval past, projecting these concepts into the American future. Reflecting its social philosophy in aesthetic simplification (Stickley 1912), the visual design was reductivist, geometric, rectilinear, functional, and constructed of natural, unadorned materials. The ideal was far broader in its aesthetic and concomitant social implications than the word *style* often implies.

The Craftsman home varied in style and size, as well as in sophistication, from log cabin to bungalow to suburban house, but materials and structure

truthfully expressed function and origins in all Craftsman homes. The Craftsman style took hold not only in the new eastern suburbs, but very significantly
in the urban and suburban Midwest, and seemed to have the landscape covered: the farm, the city, and the suburb were all equally considered by Gustav
Stickley (1858–1942) to be good locations for his newly reformed architecture.
Stickley was also a vocal proponent and publisher of home design. Examples
of Stickley homes featured in his own magazine, not surprisingly called *The
Craftsman,* included: A Small Cottage that is Comfortable, Attractive, and Inexpensive; A Craftsman Farmhouse that is Comfortable, Homelike, and Beautiful;
A Craftsman House for City or Suburban Lot; Little Wood Cottage Arranged
for Simple Country Living; and A Bungalow of Irregular Form and Unusually
Interesting Construction. Descriptive words in the names of Stickley's house
plans appear repeatedly—simple, comfortable, inexpensive, homelike—and
speak to his vision of the early modern home. (For more on Stickley's philosophy and design, see the appendix.)

Gustav Stickley at Craftsman Farms

Lyf so short craft so long to Lerne.

—Old English quotation over Stickley fireplace that appears
also in his publication, *The Craftsman*

In its utopian vision of the world, one might say Craftsman or Mission
style approached a religion, or at least a cult, in its missionary fervor: perhaps
"Craftsman Reformed" or "Ascetic Aesthetic" would be appropriate. Stickley
himself lived the Craftsman reformed life within his fully designed communal
environment, appropriately named Craftsman Farms, now a historic landmark
in New Jersey. As an early modern American social-aesthetic reformer, Stickley
created a communal home at Craftsman Farms, a kind of faux medieval or
perhaps protohippie, retreat from the modern industrial world. The Craftsman ideal may therefore be read either as regressive, running from contemporary life to an illusionary past, or forward-looking, moving toward enlightened
emergent modernism.

An artistic community of homes and studios, in the form of related Craftsman bungalows, cottages, and log cabins within woods only miles from urban
Manhattan, Craftsman Farms today attests to a life of Craftsman ideals (Stickley
1912, see illustrations). Here, Stickley endeavored to build a community of
woodworkers and craftsmen living off the land. Though he is celebrated today
as a great American innovator of the home, it was really in furniture, rather
than house building, that Stickley excelled (see "Furniture and Decoration, 1901–1920"). Unlike his furniture and philosophy, Stickley's architecture
tended to be inconsistent. His lack of architectural education was both a detriment and an advantage, allowing him to work in natural materials and design forms dictated by the land without the constraints of architectural rules.
Stickley's own house at Craftsman Farms was therefore an interesting though
not wholly successful experiment. Perhaps not so sophisticated aesthetically,
the social intentions of this home were significant. The massive log and bungalow house that dominated the farms was meant to represent not only a family

home, but a communal clubhouse for friends and fellow workers at Craftsman Farms, and eventually a school of handcrafts.

Nature permeated Stickley's earthy home. His design was not of one flowing aesthetic, but was instead engaged in the process of defining Stickley's design ideas through experimentation. Multiple stone chimneys and fireplaces warmed the house. Running from the rustic first floor upward through the second story shingles, the chimneys integrated the exterior design with the interior, as well as the upper and lower floors. All throughout Craftsman Farms, workers' homes of natural wood logs, shingles, and stone were scattered. (Some homes are part of the historic site, others are private.) A number of small common bungalows, typical of Stickley's own published house plans, were dispersed about the site, as well as larger Craftsman homes, among them Alpine chalet and Shingle Style influenced homes. The many stone hearths gave meaning to the Craftsman homes and would become a major motif of organic architecture in the future. Handcrafted copper plates with engraved aphorisms applied to these fireplaces have left us a distinctive, didactic Stickley touch of Craftsman Lyf.

The Shingle Style: Emergent Modern Architecture in the East

> [A] free shingle style had developed: it moved more and more toward cohesion and order in design. It sought for basic forms, for the essential elements of architectural expression.
>
> —Vincent J. Scully Jr., *The Shingle Style and the Stick Style,* 1979

The Shingle Style represented one of the most cohesive, sophisticated, totally indigenous architectural movements ever originated on American soil. Shingle Style homes can be read as the precursors of modern architecture, pointing the way toward the simplified aesthetics of the distinctly modern American home of the twentieth and twenty-first century. The Shingle Style, first identified by architectural historian Vincent Scully in his book by the same name, bracketed both the turn of the century and the map of the United States, appearing circa 1880 in New England, 1900 in the San Francisco Bay Area, and influencing home design from east to midwest to west as late as the 1920s. "The shingle style . . . continued for some time much as it had developed . . . Many excellent houses were built . . . in the early 20th century" (Scully 1979). Though often the province of the wealthy country or suburban home, the Shingle Style denied the overt pretensions of its contemporaries, such as the Beaux-Arts estate, bringing the image, if not the economic reality, of a more democratic home to the American street and suburban enclave. Noting that many of the most advanced works of this style were completed more than a decade before the turn of the century, one is amazed to see how advanced were certain architects, and how modern, long before modernism.

Surface Continuity in the Shingle Style

The Shingle Style was a modern take on the indigenous American style of wood-sheathed building. An overall visual and tactile surface continuity provided by the shingling unified the picturesque, asymmetrical, counterbalancing parts of a Shingle Style house, giving "cohesion" and "order" in place of the strict symmetry of previous house designs. Also unprecedented were the

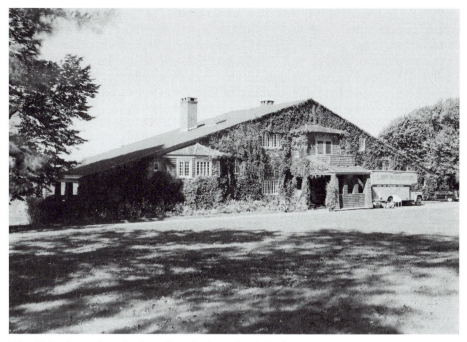

The Shingle Style: The last days before the fall of the Low House. McKim, Mead and White, Bristol, Rhode Island, 1887. Courtesy of the Library of Congress.

relationships of solids to voids, for fenestration was often composed of tightly grouped windows to avoid interruption of the facade and to give continuity to the surface, and doors were suppressed under heavy porches. The natural wooden shingles emotively imparted inviting warmth and rugged yet refined character to the modern American home. Like a woody vine, a shingled house grew outward from the earth. Aesthetic characteristics thus defined the Shingle Style as a clean suave break with a Victorian past and a harbinger of American modernism of the 1930s–1970s.

Geometric Form in the Shingle Style

Scully's words "basic forms" and "essential elements" articulate the Shingle Style at its deepest level. The Shingle Style partook of a new but eternal architectural vocabulary. An asymmetrical, flowing architecture of space and grace, the Shingle Style was composed of integrated, counterbalancing, volumetric forms. The volumetric solids of geometry, the cube and the cylinder, were held in opposition to one another: an extruded, turreted stair was often appended to a shingled box. The whole composition was greater than its individual geometric parts. One notes in this style a return of architecture to the eternal, simplest elemental forms of geometry: the square, the circle, the triangle, the cube, and the cylinder as the basis of American proto-modernism and, eventually, of modernism.

Regional Expressions of the Shingle Style

After its invention in New England by architects H. H. Richardson and McKim, Mead, and White, the Shingle Style was disseminated by regional architects, such as Peabody and Stearns, about the Northeast and Midwest, as well as in northern California. The Shingle Style was often a coastal style in the East, ranging from the Hamptons of Long Island and Newport, Rhode Island, to the environs of Boston and Cambridge, as far north as Bar Harbor, Maine. In the West, the Bay Area Shingle Style enveloped the coast from Carmel to San Francisco and Berkeley, California. The style has recently influenced a twentieth- and twenty-first-century regeneration in American home design, led by contemporary revivalist architects Robert A. M. Stern, and with some stylistic transformations, by Robert Venturi and Denise Scott Brown.

Significant Shingle Style Homes in the East

H. H. Richardson, Stoughton House, Cambridge, Massachusetts. Among the most influential American architects ever to design a home or a public building was H. H. Richardson. École-educated, Richardson invented new motifs expressive of the emergence of modernism, Shingle Style, and so-called Richardsonian romanesque. The premier extant example of the Shingle Style was Richardson's Stoughton House (1883), still clearly visible (but private) on historic Brattle Street, Cambridge, Massachusetts. In nearby Harvard Yard, the reader should also note Richardson's Sever Hall (1888), perhaps the most important protomodern building in America. Comparing Sever Hall, a brick academic building, with Stoughton House, a wooden domestic design, one notes Richardson's intense comprehension of the overall integration of the geometry, the sublimation of parts to the whole, the new concept of surface continuity, and the materiality of both buildings. Richardson constructed Stoughton House of parts: basic cubic pieces arranged perpendicular to each other about a projecting turret, opposing an inset porch, all under a heavy roofline, with tightly grouped fenestration. The overall aesthetic was quite horizontal and managed to integrate modern curvilinear lines with the rectangular shapes by suppressing each element to the overall mass, then sheathing that entire mass with one surface material: soft wooden shingles, from ground to roof.

A breakthrough house in American protomodernism, Stoughton House preceded early modernism by two decades. The overall integration of form was so suave that the multitude of asymmetrical elements and complex silhouette were drawn together into one unified object that typified Renaissance theorist Alberti's comment on perfection of architecture that is complete such that nothing can be added or removed except to the detriment. The unifying factor of the complex massing of Richardson's masterpiece was the surface continuity provided by the shingling of the walls, roof, and turret. This attention to surface continuity prefigured American high mid-twentieth-century high modernism, becoming the so-called stretched skin of the International Style.

McKim, Mead, and White, Low House, Bristol, Rhode Island. Had it not been demolished in the 1960s, another shingled house, McKim, Mead, and White's Low House (1887), would be visited today as another landmark in American protomodernism. This home amazed in its modern simplicity, based on McKim's adherence to the strictures of geometry, for the overall massing was subsumed into one giant form, a gentle sheltering triangular, shingled silhouette. Like the early Cape Cod houses, the Low House understood and responded to the sea, settling into its natural hillside above a rocky coast. A giant obtuse triangle, this home featured a continuous sweeping shingled roofline overhanging and dominating the design. The whole of the Low House was covered in the soft natural wooden shingles of this emotionally evocative style. The loss of this private home, like the destruction of McKim, Mead, and White's greatest public masterpiece, Pennsylvania Station, perversely had a positive long-term effect on the preservation of architecture, for these tragic losses spurred the movement to save significant early modern structures that were fast disappearing from America during the middle of the twentieth century. With more appreciation today, Rhode Island has preserved the Newport Casino of McKim, Mead, and White (1881), which may be visited by the public, as well as a number of other important Shingle Style homes along Newport's Cliff Walk.

Bay Area Shingle Style

Many . . . practices came from the indigenous house, whose virtues of plan, orientation . . . and direct use of materials were later to influence a whole California school of architecture.

—Esther McCoy, *Five California Architects,* 1960

The naturalism and aesthetic appeal of the Shingle Style allowed it to spread from its roots in the East across the country, via Chicago, to flower again in the West, in the Bay Area Shingle Style. The style, in northern California, was integrated in a unique way that could only have happened outside the strictures of the East. Architects of the Bay Area style looked to Richardson's work, to the Beaux-Arts, to medieval architecture, to English Arts and Crafts, to Asian architecture, and especially, to the indigenous California coastal cottage. Bernard Maybeck and Julia Morgan were leaders of this protomodern movement in San Francisco and Berkeley. The lively range of style, from historical revivals to more modern Shingle Style, may be observed via the Powell and Mason Cable Car line; throughout the hills of Pacific Heights; and across the bay via ferry to Sausalito.

Maybeck and Morgan in the Bay Area. The most original architect associated with the Bay Area Shingle Style was Bernard Maybeck (1862–1957), best known for the creativity of his romantic churches and his historicist Palace of the Fine Arts in San Francisco. In domestic architecture, Maybeck managed to blend the simple redwood shingles already present in San Francisco, Berkeley, Belvedere, and Carmel cottages with his romantic, École-trained bent,

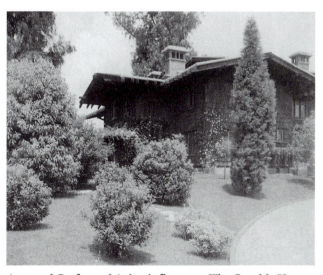

Arts and Crafts and Asian influences. The Gamble House, Greene and Greene, Pasadena, California, 1907. © Greene and Greene Archives, Huntington Library, USC.

creating a quirky domestic style unseen except in his work. Maybeck, however, was not only a designer and draftsman, he was a good builder, as well, investigating the early use of wood and concrete trussing in his houses.

Also active in the western United States, École-trained Julia Morgan was a pioneer architect of the early twentieth century, known to have an amazing range of abilities in terms of design, from Beaux-Arts formality to Bay Area Shingle Style informality, freely appropriating, reconfiguring, and recombining motifs of many eras and locales. She made her name as the architect of the Hearst family, for whom her wide-ranging designs were reflective of their eclectic taste, as Hearst roamed Europe bringing back disparate artifacts to his California domestic castle. It is astonishing that the same hand that had designed Hearst Castle, as well as Hearst's whole hilltop complex of Spanish Colonial inspired cottages and pools, likewise designed simple Shingle Style row houses and cottages.

The most beautiful and restrained work of Morgan was Asilomar, on the rugged coast of California on the Monterey peninsula. In the Asilomar project (1913) for the YWCA, she created a retreat and cottage homes for women. Here, Morgan cast off the indulgent pretenses of Hearst Castle to create one of the most gently sensitive total architectural and landscape ensembles in America. Asilomar, meaning "land and sea" is a quiet, poignant statement in architecture, in which the cottages can be forgotten, as the natural beauty of the coast and the stars above it at night still inspire awe. In timeless Asilomar, Morgan was so far behind modern times, and so far ahead of them, that she sensitively prefigured by a century today's interest in architecture in relation to the environment.

The Hand-Crafted Homes of Greene and Greene

It is the intimate quality of Greene & Greene's architecture which so moves us in the presence of their buildings.

—William H. Jordy, *American Buildings and Their Architects,* 1972

The ideal of the total environment within a hand-crafted home reached its epiphany in the work of Greene and Greene, architect brothers of the early modern architectural era. These homes were not only integrated with nature within their California arroyo sites, they were one with it. The aesthetic concept of a Greene and Greene home elevated the design of the rustic, humble American bungalow and the simple ancient concept of hand-craft to high art. Structure was articulated and celebrated in a Greene and Greene home, as in the traditional Japanese houses that inspired their work. These homes were textural masterpieces, outside and inside. Every join, grain, hand-rubbed polish, together transformed a Greene and Greene home into a sensual wooden sculpture. Covered in hand-cut shingles, rising from boulders, with deep overhanging eaves and articulated wooden framing, the southern California homes of Greene and Greene were highly individualized, yet totally recognizable stylistically. The Greenes offered the kind of luxury home that only the most sophisticated client would appreciate—the Arts and Crafts, Asian-influenced hand-made house of exquisite design and craftsmanship—the home as art form.

Greene and Greene, The Gamble House, Pasadena, California. Pasadena is rich in hand-crafted Greene and Greene homes: the Gamble house; the elegant Blacker house with its diagonal porte-cochere; the many houses under live oaks on some of the most beautiful streets in the West; and an eclectic collection of bungalows of wood and boulders in the Arroyo. One might note that the Pasadena Gamble House was green in many ways: subtle arts and crafts green in color, green in its of embrace of nature, green in terms of money, and of course, Greene and Greene created. The David B. Gamble House (1907–1908) was the consummate Greene and Greene home and one of the most important homes in America, and now, fortunately, open to the public. This home was at once simple but highly sophisticated, giant but graceful, costly but unpretentious. The Gamble House is a serene combination of horizontally oriented, Asian-influenced American bungalow with projecting sleeping porches and heavy, overhanging eaves. The totality of the design from overall concept, to varied but complementary facades, to interior finish and detail, to furniture, to integration with landscape, to disparate influences, has made this home one of the most complete works of art or architecture ever created in America. A home defining the spirit of early modern California, the Gamble House was the original Zen-like modernist American retreat.

MODERN ARCHITECTURE: ORGANIC AND GEOMETRIC AESTHETICS

Frank Lloyd Wright: Modern Architecture in the Midwest

It is impossible to overestimate the creative contribution of Frank Lloyd Wright to the development of the modern American home. The profound stylistic influence of his Prairie style houses,

---

Frank Lloyd Wright, American Architect

His modern homes reflected the low horizontal line of the prairie, but Frank Lloyd Wright (1867–1959), the man, has stood like a skyscraper towering over American architecture. He was without doubt the most influential American architect of the twentieth century and very well aware of this distinction himself. Wearing a plumed hat and cape, individualistic to the point of arrogance, theatrical, but likewise articulate, talented, and undaunted, Wright invented not only the forms of modern domestic architecture in America, but the mythic persona of the architect as creative artist and societal soothsayer. Despite some of his social pronouncements, one can concur that his mythic artistic status is deserved, for America is a different place visually because of this individual, and his influence reached beyond this country into Germany and Japan; by 1911 he would become highly influential to important European modernists.

A myth must have a "how it came to be story," and so it has been said that Wright was formed as an architect by the German Froebel wooden kindergarten blocks with which he played as a child, and this certainly appears possible. He never did study architecture formally, rather, he took a year in engineering studies and famously turned down an opportunity to study at a traditional European academic architectural institution. Instead, Wright decided to apprentice in Chicago, at a time when great breakthroughs in the Chicago style and its simplified, integrated ornament were being made by his mentor, Louis Sullivan, of the firm Adler and Sullivan. Wright's choice, was prescient, for it meant that his innate abilities and rugged American midwestern character would have the chance to grow uninhibited by the more sophisticated strictures and traditions of European architecture. Thus, his internal creativity, the architectural mentors he selected, and his refusal of foreign training and tradition, together created one of the greatest, and certainly the most American, architects of all times here within the artistic isolation of the United States of the early twentieth century. A continuation of his ideas exists today in the Taliesin Fellowship created to perpetuate his work. Wright has been celebrated for a century both by his profession and by the public, rare for architects.

Wright's architectural oeuvre was very focused on the home, as concept and design. Thus, he was able to advance the most intimate form of architecture

(continued)

in which we all participate, imbuing domestic architecture with universal aesthetic meaning, via his spreading architectural forms and emotive theories of the family. His designs of 1901–1920 were truly revolutionary, offering a newly developed style to a new kind of world, the early twentieth-century American suburb. Extending design throughout the home via furniture and window patterns, Wright was conscious of the integration of the home's interior with its exterior, giving America a fresh vision of "total" architecture. Even more importantly, he considered the integration of the architectural object with landscape paramount. His constant theme, though never as clearly defined as one might expect, was to advance the modern home toward an organic ideal, in which the house, the materials, the interior design, the landscape, and the humanity of the family would be mutually enhancing and embracing.

and his emphasis on the home as both a physical and social basis of human interaction, defined the meaning of the single family home for the early modern era into the mid-century. His intense focus on the house as architectural form allowed Wright to explore fully the significance of the typology of the house; to consider all aspects, interior and exterior, as an integrated whole; to write a personal theory of the meaning of the house; and then to combine his theory with his building.

Unlike many important architects of early modernism, Wright's focus was overwhelmingly on domestic architecture, for the most part eschewing developments such as the verticality of the urban high-rise skyscraper. Aesthetically obsessed with the horizontal line, he permanently changed the proportions of the modern American house from a vertical to a horizontal box. Designing for the suburban lot rather than for the city street, Wright contributed (rightly or wrongly) to the defining configuration of modern American housing of the first half of the twentieth century: the single family, low-density home within the spread out, trolley, or automobile suburb (inadvertently presaging suburban sprawl). Wright's houses were ground-hugging and low-slung (presaging boring suburban ranch houses to come), for the fundamental look of the American prairie that influenced his design was surely open, flat, and horizontal. Observing just a few houses he built within the decade of 1899 to 1909, one is astounded not only by Wright's prolific ability to build his houses, but by the stylistic advances he could make of such a simple proposition as the American home.

Wright's Organic Architecture: The Prairie Style

Wright defined aesthetic rules for the American house, applicable to all of his works: A house should express simplicity and repose. The hearth is the center of the house. The house should display a simplified plan and a minimal number of rooms. Openings and ornamentation should be an integral part of the structure, and the house should be of natural colors and textures. There should be "as many kinds of houses as kinds of people." The house should grow naturally from the site (Jordy 1972). The American prairie, Japanese architecture, and the Shingle Style all influenced Frank Lloyd Wright's sensitive incorporation of nature and natural materials. As Scully points out, "Wright, at the beginning of his career, was thus seeking direct inspiration from the masters of the developed shingle style . . . He seems to have seized especially upon the essential forms . . . Wright's tie with the shingle style is thus well established" (Scully 1979). Together, these earthy influences and personal design tenets would produce what Wright termed "organic architecture." The low, horizontal, fully integrated Wrightian house of the early modern architectural era would henceforth be called the Prairie Style.

Wright's Dissolution of the Box

As previously noted, the American house is basically a box. Though Wright began with the same box as other American architects, he saw this simple cubic form as one that begged for manipulation. Thus, he deconstructed the cube into its primary planes and spaces, paradoxically, working toward a complex, yet simplified, process in which the dissolution of the basic box of the house became a series of creative dissolutions and reconfigurations of the cube of architecture. In his most advanced and modern designs, Wright changed the basic boxy proportions of the American house in a very fundamental way, designing, for the first time in American architecture, a house whose overall creative and functional concept was horizontality.

Wright further broke apart the solid geometry of the house, pulling the house into horizontal versus contrasting vertical planes. A floor became an extended horizontal plane, heavily emphasized in the elevation of the design. What we call a "wall" might be now just an upright plane in front of another vertical plane. A strong counterpoint vertical, in the form of a chimney, sliced though the layers of horizontal floors. Wright pulled apart and redefined the integrity of the box, so that outside and inside spaces interwove. In Wright's hands, like the kindergarten blocks he so loved, parts of the house were thus taken apart, examined, knocked down, built up, and reconfigured. Emphasizing individual

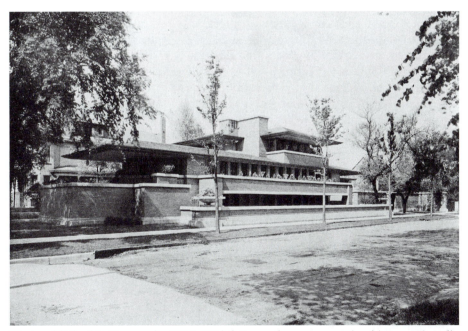

First published in Europe in 1911, Wright's work was recognized internationally for its revolutionary modernity. The Robie House, Frank Lloyd Wright, Chicago, Illinois, 1909. Courtesy of the Library of Congress.

geometric parts within the whole, Wright exploded the box and with it American architectural assumptions of the home.

What Hath Wright Wrought? Landmark Modern Homes of Frank Lloyd Wright

Frank Lloyd Wright Home and Studio, Oak Park, Illinois. The Frank Lloyd Wright home and studio (1889–1909) in Oak Park, Illinois, spoke powerfully to the use of geometry in architecture. For his own family home, the architect designed a home that, while referencing elements of traditional style, reconfigured them into a new and unexpected composition. A steep, equilateral triangle was the primary motif facing the street; the dominant triangular roof and square elevation defined the very geometric silhouette of the house. Employing a more complex geometric form, he added an attached hexagonal studio for his work. Windows were drawn tightly together to form compact groups, sometimes topped with a half-circle window, and the surface of the house and studio was shingled. Thus, all geometric forms, the triangle, the square, the circle, even the hexagon, spoke within the facade of the house and studio complex. As in the Shingle Style, wooden shingles were the unifying surfacing material of the Wright home and studio and an organic reference to nature.

The home and studio complex would become increasingly intricate as Wright added to the ensemble over a decade, using his own house for experimentation. An overall respect for geometry, and a relationship with the forms of nature, however, continued to impose order on this early yet highly innovative design. Many of the concepts expressed in Wright's Oak Park home and studio would later inform the inventions of his fully developed Prairie style, as he sought to fuse the concepts of architecture and nature. A complex breaking up of the front facade created a richer, more complex environment of light and shade, an important Wrightian trick. Low brick walls were implied, but not constructed, by a series of planes that illustrated Wright's ability to break the geometry of the box. Expecting a full front wall, one instead found a low stone wall that metamorphosed into balustrades, at once walls, but not walls. These balustrades and planters fused the house to the ground, integrating it with nature and illustrating how Wright meant his architecture "to grow naturally from the site." The classical urn-shaped stone planters seemed to bear plant gifts to the gods of architecture.

Winslow House, River Forest, Illinois. In the early Winslow House (1893), Wright used the basic symmetrical box of the American house under the standard midwestern hip roof, but he changed the proportions of the expected composition by greatly exaggerating the roof into metaphor for shelter, a motif he would develop more fully in his coming Prairie houses. The Winslow House was a contemporary of the eastern Shingle Style built in midwestern masonry, and it worked within conventions of its time, while simultaneously making subtle breaks with the past. Wright used symmetry in tact on the front facade and answered it with asymmetry in the rear facade, anticipating the suburban American lifestyle of backyard informality. The house looks both backward to the box of the historical house, and forward toward the exploded box of modernism that Wright was soon to invent.

Heurtley House, Oak Park, Illinois. Just down the block from the Frank Lloyd Wright home and studio was built the urbane Arthur Heurtley House (1902), stunning not only for the sophistication of the Roman brick composition, but for the very early date. This house was at last a fully integrated Prairie composition, a horizontally extended box under a sheltering hip roof, perfectly expressing Wright's ideal of the home as shelter, illustrative of Wright's concepts of organic architecture. The overall cubic symmetry of the Heurtley house was enhanced by the asymmetry of the front doorway inset under a curvilinear Richardsonian arch. Wright's subtle displacement of the front door was a masterful touch, transforming our expectations of the standard central entrance American home. Further, Wright's addition of the stone arch to the box of the house added a powerful counterpoint to the traditional American brick house. The Heurtley House was perhaps Wright's finest home of the early modern architectural era: a strong, straight-forward, yet subtle design that was at once traditionally American and yet wholly new. The Heurtley House was a premier example of the restrained creativity of the finest early modern American homes.

Gale House, Oak Park, Illinois. The Laura Gale House (1909) exhibited the house so fully deconstructed that it appeared to be simply a series of horizontal planes, stacked atop one another like a modern sculpture, rather than a domestic dwelling. In its pure sculptural abstraction, the Gale House was revolutionary and was a contemporary of Wright's early masterwork, the Robie House, but lesser-known. The Gale House was the exploded box of Frank Lloyd Wright taken to its conclusion at an amazingly early date and prefigures his own later sculptural high modernist masterpiece, Fallingwater, of 1937. Further, the Gale House anticipated advances in international modern architecture, including Constructivism and Cubism. So extreme a home for its time and place, the Gale House would be more influential in European modern design than in American.

Robie House, Chicago, Illinois: The Home as Art Form

On looking at the major elevation . . . it is the "exploded" quality of the structure which immediately attracts attention.

—Jordy 1972

The Robie House (1909) was the mature summation of all the creative invention of Wright's early modern period of design, and as such was not just a private home, but has become one of the major works within the canon of American art and architectural history. In creating the Robie House as an illustration of his rules of domestic architecture, Wright forever marked the concept of the modern American home as his own. If he had made no other house than this one, his reputation as premier American domestic architect would be deserved; however, this home is so much more interesting when understood within the chronology of Wright's own domestic development, from the roof line of the Winslow house, to the asymmetry of the Heurtley house, to the exploded box of the Gale house.

To the planes and exploded box of the house, in the Robie House, Wright added a heavy projecting cantilevered roof and strong central Roman brick chimney, working with subtle transformations in materials and proportion. A *cantilever* is an architectural element that projects without supports. The unprecedented deeply cantilevered roofline and horizontal planes of the Robie House elevation were held together in a constructivist aesthetic developed by Wright via the strong vertical of the central counterpoint, the upward thrusting chimney cutting through the planes of the house. The hearth, as visual, metaphorical, and structural center of the home, spoke to the historical memory of the fireplace as a symbol of family gathering. Continuing his affinity for the sheltering roof as a metaphor for shelter, and the hearth as the heart of the home, Wright displayed his signature elements.

By this very early date, only nine years into the twentieth century, Wright had designed in the Robie House a work that both reflected his previous explorations and prefigured many of his later compositions, those he called his contemporary "Prairie" houses, and others that he would later name his "Usonian" houses. Fortunately, this landmark modern home, architecture within its original urban setting, can be visited, thanks to the University of Chicago, allowing the public to witness the finesse that an artist develops only after years of rehearsal for a breakthrough performance. Wright's own future, and the future of the modern American house, can be traced to this bold design. In the Robie House, Wright synthesized his abstract sculpture of horizontal planes within an integrated, livable, and urbane composition, wholly modern yet uniquely referential to the traditional idea of the American house on a city street. Perfect architecture of the home can only result when function, aesthetic form, and domestic symbol are synthesized, as in the Robie House. Here, in a startlingly modern artistic composition, Wright melded the *organic* reality of the home as a modern place for living with the eternal abstract ideal of shelter.

The Geometric Style of Irving Gill: Modern Architecture in Southern California

> In Gill's elevation, as in modern European architecture typical for the twenties, we feel an equilibrium on the very brink of disintegration, which yet retains a taut stability.
>
> —William H. Jordy, *American Buildings and Their Architects,* 1972

Abstraction and Cubism in Gill's Architecture

As America searched for shelter that could express its new spirit of artistic openness and scientific exploration, a starkly International Style and abstract architectural aesthetic, the white Cubic style of Irving Gill, debuted to fill this visual void in the early days of the twentieth century. Gill (1870–1936) never enjoyed the recognition of Wright, yet he was equally innovative and prescient for his early time and was more structurally truthful than Wright. He developed his unprecedented, deceptively simplified concrete architecture in near total isolation from other architects and stylistic influences, both American and European, working primarily in California. At the turn of the century, the West Coast was surprisingly remote, and thus southern California became a clean canvas for advances in both art forms and scientific investigations and a magnet for a young architect with a creative new vision. The abstraction of Gill's facades spoke prophetically to the nature of the coming International Style: Gill's white cubic, asymmetrical facades prefigured the European modernism of a decade later.

Early Modern Homes of La Jolla

Away from the strictures of neoclassical New York and Arts and Crafts Chicago taste, San Diego and environs of Coronado and La Jolla (pronounced La Hoya), in particular, grew rich with the legacy of Irving Gill, as first noted by architectural historians William H. Jordy and David Gebhard (personal conversation and walking tour, La Jolla, California, May 1994). This region today retains the primary enclave of this architect's work. There were Gill houses all about San Diego, some more mission influenced and others purely modern, many built with his choice of innovative tilt-up concrete construction. In addition to homes for well-off clients, Irving Gill also designed a number of socially progressive housing complexes in southern California: prototype workers' cottages (1908) and a children's home (1907) for the less fortunate of society. Examples of Gill's California designs accessible to view (though private property) include the Marston House, San Diego (1904–1905) and

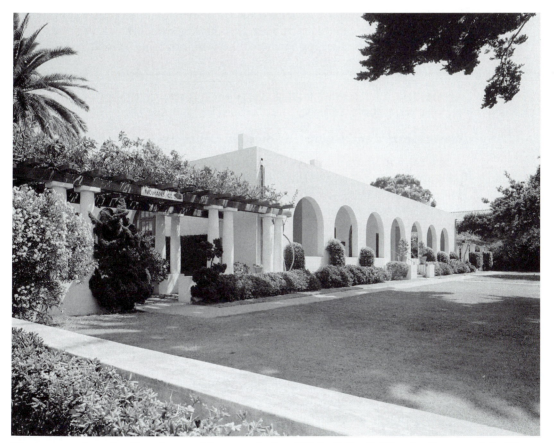

The geometric style of modern architecture. Irving Gill, La Jolla, California. Courtesy of the Library of Congress.

the Bailey House, La Jolla (1907; Hines 2000). The important Dodge House (1914–1916), Los Angeles, was thoughtlessly razed in the 1960s (Jordy 1972). Some of the most striking ensembles of early modern philanthropy and modern architecture extant in America, Gill's La Jolla Women's Club (1912–1914), Scripps Recreation Center (1913–1914), and the Bishop's School (1909), were all built within walking distance of the cliff-side home Gill designed for his patron, Ellen Browning Scripps, currently open to the public as a museum. Overlooking La Jolla cove, the former home, now an art museum, has since been restored to a style similar to Gill's original arcaded plans by postmodernist architect Robert Venturi.

The facade of this modern concrete home, now the La Jolla Museum of Contemporary Art, was reminiscent of the Spanish arcaded hacienda architecture of early San Diego without being specifically historicist. A flat stucco facade fronted a white cube articulated with curvilinear arches, giving the house a subtle reference to the locale while simultaneously redefining the regional aesthetics. Composed of the geometric solids and planar lines of modernism, it played cubic modernism in counterpoint to the dramatic natural environment of southern California. Gill's sophisticated hand was able to extract the simplicity of antique arched forms in their essence, making them the basis of a wholly new, simplified American modernism. Another of Gill's creative concrete homes in La Jolla epitomized his own stylistic development and that of cubic early modernism itself at its inception: the Director's House and Laboratory (1908) of the Scripps Biological Station, now the Scripps Institution of Oceanography of the University of California, San Diego.

MODERN ARCHITECTURE AND MODERN SCIENCE: HOMES IN ISOLATION

Observatories and Homes in Southern California

An early modern intellectual community was evolving in the art, architecture, and science of San Diego, a tabula rasa during 1901–1920. Irving Gill was often called upon to give form and style to artistic and scientific visions. The growing modern scientific establishment created a unique demand for contemporary housing at the myriad modern research observatories being endowed and founded in America during this time. In these newly emerging institutions, America was proving itself to be in the forefront of scientific advancement, a position it has held since. Newspaperman E. W. Scripps supported investigations of the Pacific coast and ocean, engaging Irving Gill to design architecture and site plans for his coastal observatory. Gill thus had the unique opportunity to take complete charge of one of the most significant early modern campuses in America, the Scripps Institution of Oceanography. An amalgam of architecture, science, landscape, and homes, this campus, on a cliff overhanging the Pacific, was representative of the exploratory environment of the modern scientific community, in which laboratory and home, like work and life, were inextricable. Science, in a great triumverate with technology and the arts, was in the forefront of defining the world of the early modern era, and innovative architects and builders were needed to rise to the challenges of housing modern scientific inquiry, indeed scientists themselves, within modern forms.

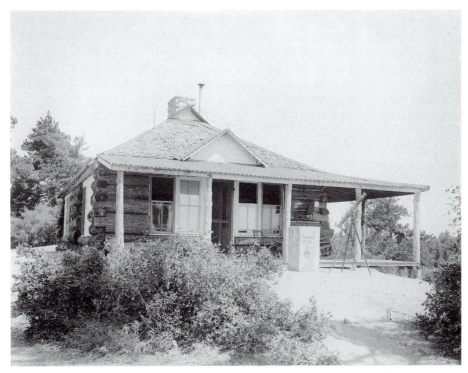

Isolation observed. Homes for science in the early modern era. © The Huntington Library.

Homes for Early Modern Scientific Observatories

Though the scientific community may be highly collegial, science by nature, paradoxically, is a pursuit of solitude, and early modern homes for scientists reflected this. Scientists' new laboratory homes were needed at this time not in established city campuses, but more often in isolated California coastal regions or even more remote rural mountaintop locales. Housing for scientists, therefore, presented unexpected problems to early modern architecture, of both style and construction. This was particularly true for earth, planetary, and marine sciences, such as astronomy and oceanography, with their unusual functional programs and base camp locations. In undeveloped and even dangerously inaccessible sites, homes for researchers were constructed during 1901–1920 in conjunction with observatories under very adverse conditions. Interesting examples of housing for science included the lonely homes for staff and visiting scientists atop the new telescope facilities of Mount Wilson above Pasadena and Mount Palomar above Los Angeles (Carnegie Observatories Photograph Collection 1907); and the homes of the director and students of the then very isolated Scripps Institution of Oceanography (1908).

Homes in the Sky: Telescopes and "Monasteries"

Major telescope projects, feats of both engineering and science, in the early years of the twentieth century brought the largest glass objects ever cast in history into focus on Mt. Wilson and Mt. Palomar to search the then pristine skies above southern California. All the fragile parts of the 50″ and 100″ telescopes, observatory structures, and affiliated housing had to be hauled up Mt. Wilson and Mt. Palomar. The Mt. Wilson 100-inch glass mirror, for example, cast in Corning, New York, was taken cross country by train to Pasadena, California, and then carried by horse and wagon and early truck, in a precarious, death and glass-defying climb up a wild, rutted, switch-back road. One slip could destroy the carefully ground object and set astronomy back for years. This is still an isolated place, though on a clear day, the telescopes are within view of Los Angeles far below. Even in southern California, due to elevation, the only road up or down could be closed for snow.

It is stunning to see how primitive California was in the early days of the new century, yet how gutsy were its scientific builders. Once arrived at the telescope, there was reason to settle in for the long haul and the dark nights and to call this place home. Even a husky pup grew up in his doghouse atop the mountain, a mascot for lonely researchers. Trees were felled by hand for the Mt. Wilson summit roadway, their logs fashioned into traditional bungalows and log cabins on site. Architectural style was less significant than simple shelter. Dormitory housing for visiting scientists and students, a house for the director, a half-way station cabin, and even a hotel all had to be included in the Mt. Wilson building plans, because the road up was so treacherously impassable. Most importantly, homes were needed to support scientific research: Summit homes were necessitated because astronomers must by the nature of their research work through the night. It is no wonder that these early modern homes in the sky were referred to by their ascetic scientists and architects as monasteries: Mt. Wilson Monastery and Mt. Palomar Monastery.

Homes By the Sea: Oceanography

Irving Gill, Director's House, Scripps Biological Station

Within the context of science at the turn of the century, scientist and architect together displayed a spirit of pioneering to create original forms to enhance new discoveries. Along the Pacific coastal cliffs, architect Irving Gill designed the original laboratories and housing of the Scripps Biological Station, now called the Scripps Institution of Oceanography of the University of California, San Diego. One of Gill's first significant buildings, the Director's House and Laboratory (1908), was a startling home for its time, for Gill essentially designed a modern factory style home for an open site amid dramatic landscape. The Scripps Director's House, a white, cubic building with its accompanying concrete water tower, stood in stark industrial contrast to its scenic but lonely coastal location. These two simplified structures were so far ahead of their time aesthetically, that this complex should be considered one of the first truly modern buildings in America.

Within this small but multipurpose concrete construction, the lower floors housed a laboratory and aquarium, faculty offices, and classrooms, with a home for the director and his wife on the upper floor. The domestic home upstairs was almost as spartan as the laboratories, with large industrial windows and modest mission style furnishings. From this isolated home at the oceanographic station, the director viewed only the sea, no neighbors or structures were in sight; faculty and students were provided bicycles to pedal to the laboratory from the village along rutted roads. The hills heading to the cliffs over the sea were barren, for the eucalyptus and palm trees of California had yet to be imported and planted. Shingled bungalows were later added by the architect for faculty and students, and these extant examples of early California homes remain amid mature subtropical trees and landscape. Today, the original Scripps Director's Home, called Old Scripps, still stands on the campus above the cliffs, though it does not house anyone, and its domestic past, as the past of many scientific institutions, could be easily forgotten, for modern science moves ever forward without nostalgia.

This must have been a lonely, contemplative place to live, and it leads to contemplation of the aesthetic meaning of modernism. In the Scripps Director's House, Gill created a concrete cubic counterpoint to the landscape of beach and cliff, and thus he invented an aesthetic in which the man-made stood in stark counterpoint to organic form. In a polemic with Wright's sense of organic growth of architecture, Gill celebrated the man-made in opposition to nature. Either position, however, heightens the meaning of nature and the significance of form within early modernism. Dramatic aesthetic contrasts were designed by Gill as he boldly explored the new world of the modern, where abstract geometry played in opposition to nature.

ORGANIC AND GEOMETRIC STYLES OF THE MODERN HOME

Wright's Prairie style and Gill's Geometric style, though opposed in aesthetics, epitomized and anticipated the totality of the American modern home and

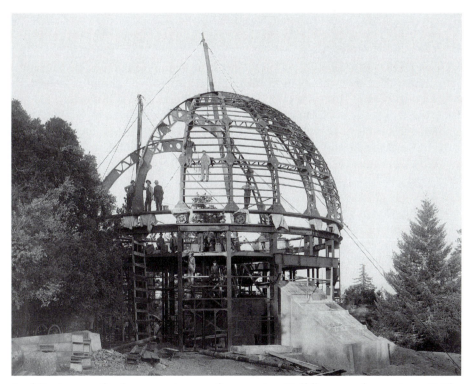

Architecture and science, nature and geometry. Building an observatory. © The Huntington Library.

together are astonishingly prescient of the future of both American and European modernism. In pointing the way during the early modern architectural era of 1901–1920 toward the high modernism of the 1920s–1970s, Wright and Gill defined the aesthetic oppositions—the parameters and possibilities—of a new domestic architecture of the twentieth century.

Wright and Modern Aesthetics

Frank Lloyd Wright reconstituted the aesthetics of the early modern American home in its relation to nature, as the *organic* houses he made "grew naturally from the site." Wright anticipated simplicity in design and naturalism in materials that, though highly original, displayed an understandable evolution from indigenous American housing stock. In his most sophisticated designs, Wright invented the extended planarity and horizontality of constructivism in American architecture. Wright's lasting appeal was that while he was both simple and traditional in domestic values, he was complex and modern in architectural style. The greatest exponent of Wright's early modernism would be his modern classic home, Fallingwater, Bear Run, Pennsylvania (1937; open to the public). Every low slung, glass and redwood, ground-hugging suburban American ranch home of the 1940s–1960s in addition to his own Usonian homes, would become pale reminders of Wright's bellwether early modern Prairie style. Wrightian aesthetics have endured in America, for even as Wright invented forward-looking forms for the home, he simultaneously looked back symbolically to recall the fundamental meaning of hearth and home in America.

Gill and Modern Aesthetics

Irving Gill was unusually prophetic for European architecture, developing a personal Cubist style in isolation in America, anticipating the pure geometric abstraction of early International Style architecture and high modernism. He built these abstract art forms amid arid landscape. In this sense, Gill independently arrived at the aesthetic theories of Europe of the 1920s and 1930s: the directness of the Factory style of Walter Gropius and the Bauhaus; the simplicity and structural truthfulness of Mies van der Rohe; and the juxtapositions of French architect Le Corbusier's "Machine in the Garden." Gill's designs reflected the modern spirit of technology and science and worked in an articulate counterpoint to nature. Creating an aesthetic bridge between American and European early and high modernism, Gill's pure, white geometric forms prefigured modern art and architecture by decades and were early antecedents of the sophistication of the International Style in America.

The Aesthetic Foundations of the Modern Home

The International Style in America

With the oeuvres of Wright and Gill in mind, one can conceptualize virtually all the stylistic directions the modern home will take in the next 50 years in Europe and America, for their contrasting styles will form the aesthetic foundations of modernism. There is one modern home in America that synthesized all the aesthetic elements that Wright and Gill had explored for the first time in American architecture: Nature and Geometry, Constructivism and Cubism, architectural high style and indigenous domesticity, European and American modernism. This is the 1937 home of Walter Gropius, refugee and founder of the Bauhaus. In the Gropius House, Lincoln, Massachusetts (open via Historic New England), the émigré architect integrated his European International Style, in aesthetics anticipated by Americans Wright and Gill, with American indigenous domestic form. Though the dates of this house are beyond the scope of this study, it is fitting to note, for tracing the diverse meanings of the early modern era in America, that it was an émigré—a refugee from Germany, disembarking in New York Harbor via London, teaching architecture in New England, riding horses out West—who would design the house that has synthesized the modern meaning and form of the American home (Cormier 2004a). This landmark modern home of European International Style exterior, Bauhaus interior, set amidst antique New England architecture and stony landscape, has stylistically defined the American home of the twentieth century as a new integration of abstract aesthetic object with emotive natural environment.

The International Style and Émigré Architects

The International Style of modernism transformed America in the 1920s and 1930s, as many of the most important European émigré architects of the day sought refuge here, in the turbulent period between the two world wars (Cormier 2004b). Most influential of these émigrés were Germans Walter Gropius, founder of the Bauhaus, and Mies van der Rohe, modern architect. With them these architects brought the reductivist aesthetic style and philosophical tenets of the Bauhaus, the important German design school of the early modern period. Bauhaus design was based on Gropius' philosophy of "unity in diversity" wherein all the visual arts—fine art, architecture, and industrial design—together created a modern, machined synthesis of simplified and socially conscious "Total Architecture" for the modern world.

The fusion of European modernism, in Gropius' case with American vernacular style and in Mies' case with classicism, produced some of the most significant homes in the history of American architecture. Primary among their domestic works were the Gropius House, Lincoln, Massachusetts (1937) in a village outside Boston (Cormier 1993); and the Farnsworth House by Mies, in Plano, Illinois (1951). Fortunately, both of these once private landmark modern homes may now be visited and studied by the public. The Gropius House and the Farnsworth House illustrated to the art world that American early modernism had at last joined the International Style. Together these two very different, but very white, very abstract, and very simplified residences set a new standard for design creativity for the modern home in America.

Reference List

Anderson, Stanford, Leslie Cormier, Jacqueline Gargus, Felipe J. Prestamo, Charles Rusch, and Lydia Soo. 1986. "Architectural Design as Research Programs: The Schools at Cranbrook by Eliel Saarinen." *Places* 3(2): 59–69.

Barney, J. Stewart. 1907. "The Ecole des Beaux Arts: Its Influence on our Architecture." *Architectural Record* xxii (November): 333.

Carnegie Observatories' Photograph Collection. 1907. Archives and Special Collections, Huntington Library, Pasadena, California.

Cormier, Leslie Humm. 2004a. "Walter Gropius." *Encyclopedia of 20th-Century Architecture,* vol. 2. New York: Fitzroy Dearborn, 563.

Cormier, Leslie Humm. 2004b. "International Style." *Encyclopedia of 20th-Century Architecture,* vol. 2. New York: Fitzroy Dearborn, 681–685.

Cormier, Leslie Humm. 1993. "Gropius House, Lincoln, Massachusetts." *International Dictionary of Architects and Architecture,* vol. 2. Detroit: St. James Press, 947–949.

Flagg, Ernest. 1900. "American Architecture as Opposed to Architecture in America." *Architectural Record* x (October): 178–190.

Hines, Thomas S. 2000. *Irving Gill and the Architecture of Reform.* New York: Monacelli Press.

Jordy, William H. 1972. *American Buildings and Their Architects, Progressive and Academic Ideals at the Turn of the Twentieth Century,* vol. 3. New York: Doubleday and Company, 195, 198, 261.

McCoy, Esther. 1960. *Five California Architects.* New York: Reinhold Publishing Corporation, 5.

Newcomb, Rexford. 1927. *The Spanish House for America.* Philadelphia: J.B. Lippincott Company, 2, 13–14, 20, 48.

Roth, Leland M. 1983. *McKim, Mead & White, Architects.* New York: Harper & Row, 44.

Scripps Institution of Oceanography. 1908. University of California San Diego, Archives and Special Collections, La Jolla, California.

Scully, Vincent J., Jr. 1979. *The Shingle Style and the Stick Style.* New Haven: Yale University Press, 155–156, 159.

Stickley, Gustav. 1912. *The Best of Craftsman Homes.* Reprinted 1979. Santa Barbara: Peregrine Smith, 6, 9, 83–89.

Building Materials and Manufacturing

Happily, our present day architects and dealers in building materials, realizing that architecture is ever the index of a nation's civilization and that a people's environment has a strong influence upon their lives, have in recent years, taken a keener interest in the problem of domestic architecture as applied to moderate priced houses.

—*Chicago Tribune,* "The Harmonious Home," 1920

STANDARDIZATION OF HOME BUILDING

The movement in the early modern home was toward democratization through simplification and standardization. As society changed significantly from 1901–1920, so did the house, as mansion and tenement gave way to a middle road of suburbanization. The private railroad cars and endless rooms of the rich, versus the cold-water railroad tenement flats of the poor, were being replaced by a more even distribution of lodgings and a more logical number of multipurpose rooms in the more standardized suburban home. This newly standardized, middle-class home was the product not only of architecture and style, but also of twentieth-century materials and manufacturing. The builders and contractors who used those materials were becoming increasingly independent and professional. In the early modern architectural era, the standardized home might be in one of four common categories: a home within a suburb of preplanned, similar homes; a home based on mail order plans sold by an architect or craftsman to be built by individual carpenters hired by the home owner; a kit home put together of pre-cut parts ready to be assembled on site; or an actual prefabricated or manufactured home sold via catalogue dealer. Standardization rather than total manufacturing was key to the common homes of this period.

Mail-Order House Plans

Far more house plans were sold than manufactured houses, and still are. Though the mail-order home was a good invention for some limited isolated areas and would eventually become a more popular option with the coming of the cheap land and cheap bungalow days of the 1920s, the delivered mail-order home was not the most significant form of home during 1901–1920. Companies that sold mail-order manufactured or kit houses included Sears, Roebuck & Company and Montgomery Ward. Pattern books and mail-order house plans were available from design firms such as Henry L. Wilson, Gordon-Van Tine Co., Henry Atterbury Smith, Royal Barry Wills Architects (who sold plans primarily during the Depression), and of course, Gustav Stickley's Craftsman homes. It was true that a farmer could order his plow, a washer for his wife, a big pre-cut farmhouse for his family, and a tiny bungalow to boot for his married daughter, from Sears, Roebuck & Company, but except in remote farm and ranch areas with good railroad access, this was a less common alternative to in situ, or built on the site, housing. Though we want to believe in the Sears Roebuck "wishing book" storybook home and the concomitant futurist myth of the manufactured house in America, these concepts tended to be

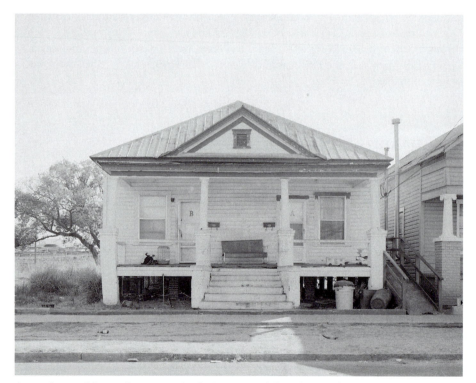

A good wood bungalow gone bad. Courtesy of the Library of Congress.

overemphasized in American lore, actually representing a limited percentage of homes in the early modern era of 1901–1920.

Even in an era of progress in manufacturing, the housing industry had always been among the most economically regressive, hands-on, nonstandardized industries in America—the antithesis of the newly developing manufacturing sectors of the auto industry, for example. The realities of building in situ, first with cheap labor, and then with more expensive unionized labor, have both helped to minimize manufactured housing in the United States. One major exception to the common home construction techniques of 1901–1920 was the innovation of the patented method of Tilt-Up Concrete construction, used solely in California, a combination of in situ and manufacturing methods. True manufactured housing in America has been more of an anecdote than a major impact on housing stock. Local contractors, however, have often relied on purchased plans and then built and rebuilt the same plans, so that an overall regional repetition has occurred in America, even in the absence of a factory mentality for housing. Further, and still true today, complex and conflicting local building codes have made the "machine for living in" nearly an American pipedream.

HOME CONSTRUCTION AND METHODS

Because building was basically hand-made, though more standardized, in the early modern era, and because housing was made by highly skilled craftsmen moving from job to job, housing of 1901–1920 tended to be well-built sturdy housing. These homes were lasting investments, and from mansion to multifamily suburban development house, there was not a decline in the physical act of construction partly because the skilled laborers—carpenters, framers, plumbers, electricians—maintained high standards. Further, materials, such as lumber without knots, were of very high quality, and homes of this era were generally overbuilt by today's standards, that is to say, stronger, more enduring structures than they actually needed to be. Structurally, the 1915 middle-class developer-made house in Queens was the work of the same crew and nearly as well built as its 1905 architect-designed Long Island mansion predecessor. Savings to developers were in the lower price of more open land of the time and the economies of scale that accrued through repetition of housing models.

By 1903, *Architectural Record* was publishing columns on the general contractor and other information on home construction, the kind of information that would not have been considered significant by previous architectural editors before the expansion of middle-class housing. Early modern middle-class homes were not compromised in materials, labor, and quality; rather, size, ornament, and fittings were less generous. Expensive kitchen and bathroom fittings were limited or omitted, the number of rooms was significantly downsized, as was the overall square footage, but the walls and roof were strong. The middle-class family shared a single indoor bath, neither luxurious mirrored room nor communal privy. There might be one fireplace, not six, but there was also coal-fired central heat.

Construction Solidity

The early twentieth-century Cape Cod and Colonial homes were built to last of durable materials, of solid wood frame and planks, and brick, rather than of veneers. Their solidity meant that these houses were internally quiet enclosures, even in urban environments. Though the bungalow building boom of the 1920s brought lighter, faster construction, the real compromise in construction methods and materials would not occur until after the Second World War, when dry wall, hollow core doors (note the rising interior noise levels of later modern houses), and other short-hand materials and methods were introduced during the housing boom of the 1950s. American homes of the first quarter of the twentieth century were some of the most solidly built domestic structures in this country. So many of these homes remain extant in America a century later due to the solidity of their initial construction. Indeed, an American home built pre-World War I is likely to outlast its younger post–World War II neighbor. Much to the detriment of suburban housing stock, many of these quality early twentieth-century homes in the early twenty-first century are currently being demolished thoughtlessly for their prime lots in suburbs, only to be replaced with nightmarish mansionettes. The materials, labor, and level of architectural design of early modern homes are irreplaceable today, and thus this practice is damaging to the overall aesthetics of the American homescape.

In Situ Housing

In situ housing, or built on the site homes, of the early modern architectural era were constructed by skilled carpenters using long practiced, repeatable methods. The logic of the box of the house is clear when one notes the lumber parts involved. The sill was the bottom horizontal timber, attached to the foundation. Perpendicular to the sill and standing straight up, the studs were nailed upright to create the frame of the outside walls. Joists made the horizontal floor surfaces. The plate was nailed to the top of the studs to create a horizontal surface to hold the rafters. The rafters were the strong diagonal timbers that created the sloped roof, and roof boards were attached to the rafters. Finally, horizontal boards were nailed to the vertical studs to complete the wooden box of the house. Inside the walls and ceilings were finished in plaster. In situ housing continued to be the most prevalent housing built in the East during the early modern architectural era. An even more modern frame, particularly popular in the West and other warm climates, simplified and sped up this process and allowed for even unskilled labor to cheapen housing construction costs: the American balloon frame.

The Balloon Frame

In his seminal modern treatise, *Space, Time and Architecture, The Growth of a New Tradition,* Sigfried Giedion pointed to the great American invention in building—the wooden balloon frame—stating, "The balloon frame marks the point at which industrialization began to penetrate housing" (Giedion 1978, 349). It was the simplicity of the balloon frame that allowed early modern American building to boom in the West and Florida. Balloon framing meant that no heavy supporting posts had to be set in the ground. The walls of the home were built of light lumber as panels on the ground. The completed flat surface wall panels were then raised upward, perpendicular to the ground, in a single motion. The basic box of a house could be built like a cardboard box being assembled from a flat surface. Each complete wall was nailed flat and raised to its position, as simply as the sides of a soapbox.

The balloon frame, as its name implied, meant that walls ballooned around space and volume, and were therefore both surface and structure. The house was now conceived of as a volumetric space. This was an extremely simple yet effective standardized building method, allowing cheaper unskilled labor to be hired. As the common building method for the western bungalow home, the balloon frame allowed the extremely swift reconstruction of San Francisco after the 1906 earthquake, as well as the beach bungalow building boom in California and Florida during the 1920s. This innovation in the wooden house was truly American: fast, efficient, cheap, and effective.

All Natural Materials

> The plane surface—the flat wall of wood, brick, or stone—has always been a basic element in American architecture.
>
> —Sigfried Giedion, *Space, Time and Architecture,* 1978

The early modern architectural era was the last period in American history to partake only of natural materials, that is to say, wood, brick, stone, and slate. Modern inventions, such as plastic, post-date this time. Homes and interior objects were made of organic or inorganic materials, but only those found in nature, not of invented materials. For example, the modern flooring called linoleum that predated vinyl was man-made but composed of organic resins and natural felt. Even organic but manufactured plywood was not yet in common use, so wood of this era was always solid wood. There was a kind of historical truth in materials of 1901–1920 that has been lost to later invention.

Sticks and Stones: Homes of Natural Materials

Sticks and stones as materials of architecture inspire a primitive architectural connection of humans to our past, for the stone cave was perhaps mankind's first home, and the earliest temples were believed to have been built of fallen tree trunks. Eventually, these found materials were replaced by the more permanent structures of hewn logs and stones, rough cut or elegantly fashioned into posts and lintels by ancestors of the Greeks. We humans have therefore enjoyed continuous relationships with the building blocks of architecture and the geology of our environment, and thus we respond intuitively to the materials of nature.

The regional usage of materials can be historically informative to the observer and rich in architectural metaphor. The rock walls of the rugged New England landscape, for example, speak to a pragmatic yet emotive relationship of colonists to the New World. Born of necessity, these stone walls have become an aesthetically defining line upon the northeastern landscape. Fine examples of classic New England uses of natural materials may be found in Wellesley and Weston, Massachusetts, in stone, and on Nantucket Island, in wood. The wood and stone buildings and streets we see everyday in New England—the fieldstone fireplaces, the cobblestone streets, the clapboard colonials, the capes with shakes, the sticks and stones of New England—are part of a larger environmental structure we think of as America.

Regional variations in the built environment define America. From rural fields to urban streets, from prairie to skyscraper, from wooden bungalow to brownstone apartment building, differences in architecture are most clearly visible in the local use of common materials. Observing the use of natural materials in the physical structures of the houses of the United States encourages an appreciation of the breadth of the functional beauty of the American home within its unique regional setting. Built infrastructure, such as civic, streetscape architecture, train stations, as well as the residential homes we have constructed, continues to reflect our lasting human affinity for the most basic materials of nature: the sticks and stones of architecture.

Materials of American houses, like styles, reflected their regions of origin in the early modern architectural era. In the forested East, either wood frame construction, or brick masonry, was the rule. In the Midwest, where lumber was less available, brick masonry or cement pier construction were common. In the South and West, where lightweight construction reflected the warm climate, wooden balloon framing was common. In the Southwest and Florida, stucco, sometimes over brick and occasionally over real adobe, reflected a regional idiom. To see a town returning from mistakes of materials of mid-twentieth century to original, natural materials, one might visit San Juan Capistrano, near the California Newport coast. Here not only the adobe is authentic at the Mission, but early California wooden and adobe shacks along the railroad are being brought to life again as vibrant artists' studios and homes.

Wood in Woods Hole

Some towns that have been thoughtfully conserved provide excellent examples of American natural materials. In the East, one might consider a visit to the tiny, pristine seaside hamlet of Woods Hole, on Cape Cod, Massachusetts, to see the natural use of wood shingling and stone construction. The main buildings of the Woods Hole Oceanographic Institute, including Fenno House (1908) and its contemporary Carriage House, speak to the material relationship of the early modern home to materials and to landscape. (Visit the campus information center in town.) Shingle Style Fenno House overlooks Nantucket Sound. The building was sensitively renovated (in 1997), continuing the traditional style of white, wooden Doric columns, set against a natural wood shingled facade and shingled roof with eyebrow windows in dormers. Balconies, stone patios, and steps look toward views of the water. A more sophisticated, early modern waterside (private) Shingle Style home, influenced by Wright's horizontal style, can be viewed from a distance, jutting out above a private peninsula just beyond the Woods Hole Ferry to Martha's Vineyard Island. The town of Woods Hole and the dominant presence of the Woods Hole Oceanographic Institute (WHOI), together have created an outstanding environment respectful of nature and the natural materials complementary to the early modern architectural era.

Wood and Wood Framing

Whereas European ancestors had built in heavy half-timbers and stone for the ages and the aristocracy, Americans built in lightweight wood, readily available from seemingly endless forests, most usually in this era for the new, middle-class homeowner. Democratization of the home necessitated less lumber and less labor. For centuries, wood framing had necessitated individualized mortise and tenon construction; however, by the early modern period mass production of manufactured nails allowed framed houses to be much more simply and lightly built. Older wooden homes were built in an ancient post-and-lintel form: vertical posts supporting horizontal lintels. Post-and-lintel architecture had meant that the house was composed of point supports holding up the roof, with the material between the beams simply infill. The beauty of post-and-lintel construction was its structural truth and logic; however, for housing, it was lumber and labor intensive. In lighter wood frame construction, the frame became the structural skeleton of the home. A timber frame for a house was built by a carpenter from foundation upward in a logical, traditional manner; particular pieces of lumber had standardized names and size specifications. Simplification, standardization, manufactured parts, and repetition made wood framing economically feasible for more middle-class homes.

Wood Siding and Shingles

As nineteenth-century board and batten siding, composed of wide vertical boards with battens along the joints, took on an old-fashioned look in the new century, it was replaced with tongued and grooved siding, wide lapped boards, and clapboards. Depending on the location of the home, siding and shingles of the time were cut from cedar, pine, redwood, and cypress. In the East and Northwest, where lumber was plentiful, wooden houses were commonly built with planks, sheathed in either clapboards or shingles. By the twentieth century, shingles and clapboards were machine cut, so they were fairly regular, though hand-split shakes could be called for by architects trying to recreate the softness of earlier Colonial homes. Both shingles and clapboards were very functional in weather, for their horizontal overlapping application meant that the house could shed rainwater and snow efficiently. Cedar shingles could be left to weather naturally, especially near the sea where they turned silver gray, or painted. The material that truly spoke to the era was weathered wooden shingling, and homes of the Shingle Style were the consummate expression of wood as material in American architecture. Clapboards were commonly painted, usually white. Fences, too, were white, but they were more cheaply maintained with "white wash," an old-fashioned water and lime mixture. Wood was everywhere in the early modern architectural era, for wood was simple and simplicity was modern.

Roofs and Roofing Materials

The American roof was generally canted to shed water and heavily built to support snow loads; the flat roof had yet to make its appearance in America, except in very rare cases. In a well-built house of this era, the roof could last half a century with simple patching. Roof shingles were either of expensive slate, of more common wood, or of economical cement, and were laid over roofing felt and planks. Roofs were also shingled in this period, with an underlying roof felt for waterproofing. Asphalt or composition shingles with asbestos illustrated that a modern concern for finding waterproof and fireproof materials for the roof was becoming a factor in home building. Though it was not universally used, architectural publications sold simple ways of fireproofing to home architects and contractors, for there was at last beginning a growing concern in the early twentieth century for safety.

Bricks and Mortar

The beauty of brick was found in its material honesty, warm textural quality, and the geometric regularity it contributed to an early modern home. Brick houses were constructed either of planks over wood frame with a single row of brick masonry, or more rarely of double rows of brick. (At this time, a single row of bricks was called brick veneer, though today we have a cheaper interpretation of "veneer" as something much thinner, or material imitating brick.) It was possible, though costly even by this era, to construct housing with brick walls that were load-bearing, in which the thick wall was strong enough to support both itself and the roof. Brick construction, of double rows of brick, was the rare but most solidly built domestic architecture. This technique was really overbuilding for a domestic house, and actually belonged in the factory loft where heavy machinery, rather than dining room chairs, would be the load.

Various styles of homes demanded variant brickwork, including: running bond, Flemish bond, or herringbone. Brick masonry allowed for great variation in the home facade. Evenly laid brick masonry with white mortar, using soft fired red brick in regular or common running bond was popular for Colonial Revival styles, sometimes painted white. More attractive homes of the time were built in Flemish bond, an alternating pattern of headers and stretchers, or short and long ends of brick, making very textural walls. Tudor homes often included herringbone patterned brick between the half-timbers. Attention to detail can reveal interesting new designs in early modern brickwork. Creatively, some early modern architects, led by Greene and Greene in Pasadena, introduced the use of clinker brick: irregular, broken, fire-darkened material that had always been considered discardable. This irregularity of form was popularized in the picturesque Craftsman style. Even the thickness and projection of the mortar may create varying looks for the facade. Inset mortar will create a shadowed brick wall; smooth mortar will create a monolithic wall. Frank Lloyd Wright

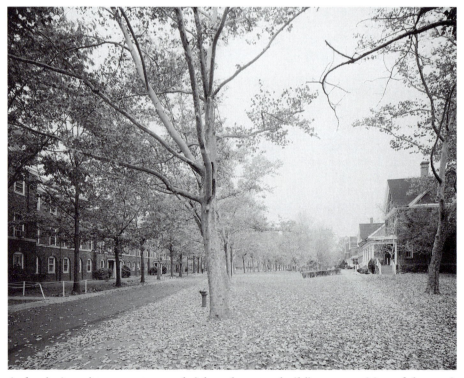

A classic American streetscape: brick and mortar buildings, repetition of decoratiive motifs, even set backs, walking paths and street trees. Courtesy of the Library of Congress.

used these subtleties effectively in the Robie House, varying the relationship of brick to mortar to create varying wall surfaces. Such extreme attention to detail, however, was generally out of line with the suburban home and difficult to achieve even for the skilled mason.

Masonry

In the Midwest, economical, durable masonry was created through the use of cement and concrete. These foursquare or bungalow homes tended to look exceedingly solid, and often their facades emphasized the strength of the structure by articulating the masonry piers at the corners of the house. The piers, or square columns, display and comment upon the concrete construction materials chosen. A building is good when materials and forms are truthful and complementary. Cement block, an economical but not necessarily a visually attractive alternative to masonry, was just coming into common usage at the end of the first quarter of the twentieth century. It was seen in houses most often in American tropical climates, such as in Florida and in Puerto Rico, but it was beginning to be seen in suburbs of the Northeast and Midwest, as well, often made to be disguised as ashlar rock masonry. These rough-sided cement blocks appeared in the modern garages that were trying to fit into their suburban landscapes in the 1910s and 1920s. The common labor and material saving cement block is one of the best examples of the economical standardization of housing of the early modern architectural period, for it was as strong as concrete piers, but hollow, and thus structures could be built without skilled labor.

Adobe and Stucco

Wood and adobe were the two most natural, indigenous American building materials, wood in the East and adobe in the West. Adobe was the original building material of the Southwest—composed of mud with straw that was dried into bricks within wooden forms left out in the sun—and it was an ancient material much copied, but not commonly produced, in the early modern architectural era. In the Southwest and Florida, Spanish or Mediterranean styles dictated a smooth sun-reflective facade, and thus adobe blocks, now replaced with formed concrete or later concrete block, were often stuccoed white. Stucco, previously called cement plaster, was not a true building material, rather it was a facing material, troweled onto a built structure. It could be smooth finished or rough cast, depending on the amount of crushed stone mixed into the material. Stucco was composed of cement, lime, water, cattle hair, or other fiber; white or tinted; and applied like icing to a cake. Like icing, it was malleable, turned corners, outlined windows, and could be made to conform either to a rectangular or a curvilinear form, allowing for endless variation within the simple cubic styles of the American Southwest and Florida.

THE IMPROVED HOME ENVIRONMENT

Innovation in Materials and Manufacturing: The Tilt-Up Concrete House

The most innovative building method of the early modern architectural period combined the logic of the balloon frame with the sculptural possibilities of concrete. This method, combining modern materials with manufacturing, was so simple yet so creative that it was patented. Concrete was poured into the forms of walls, flat on the ground, and tilted-up by heavy machinery when dry. The process is well illustrated by construction photographs taken on site by modern architect Irving Gill's crew (Hines 2000). This method was popularized in southern California by Gill as early as the teens, and although Gill is known for this method and concrete material, surprisingly, it appears that inventor Thomas Edison held a patent on just such a construction technique. Making flat walls with forms on the ground, and raising, or "tilting" them onto prepared concrete floors, Gill was able to create highly original, simple modern geometric forms with arches for modern homes in San Diego and Los Angeles. The beauty of this method is that it allowed sculptural elements such as curvilinear arches to be cut into the wall design. Thus, materials and manufacturing came together in the tilt-up concrete house: modern forms and modern mechanics together making architecture.

Manufacturing, Efficiency, and Taylorism

The American drive toward more homes for more people meant that principles of efficiency and manufacturing must be introduced into the housing industry just to keep the market viable. Taylorism, the contemporary time-and-motion theories of the new efficiency experts, was developing in the early modern architectural era. Applied manufacturing principles brought the logic of Taylorism, and industrial efficiency came to the home. Further, manufacturing meant that multiple standardized homes consisting of standardized parts could offer the economies of scale, at last, to the housing industry. Manufacturing could do nothing at this time for cooling, except the simple electric fan, but the heating of homes was by now a fairly advanced product of manufacturing. Central heating in homes was provided by cast iron coal-fired burners, much larger than today's home heating plant, and the heat could be steam, hot water, or forced hot air. Sometimes lower cost homes could only afford heat on the first floor, with open brass or iron grates in the floors above to allow heat to rise naturally into the bedrooms.

Manufacturing Convenience: Kitchens and Bathrooms

Most affected by manufacturing were the kitchen and bathroom and the general sense of convenience in the workings of the early modern home. According to an exhaustive study of kitchens and bathrooms in the American home, in 1902 only 8 percent of American homes had electricity; by 1918, 25 percent were electrified; and by 1925, more than 50 percent had electricity (Lupton and Miller 1992). Further, though electric kitchen appliances such as toasters and electric stoves were available

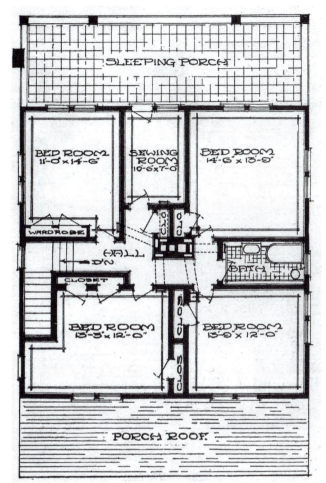

The simple modern home: balloon framed bungalow with sleeping porch. The Craftsman, 1911.

by 1910, they only become popular additions to the home in the 1920s. Thus, the period of 1901–1920 was a period of major change within the kitchen and the home in general. There was a consensus that the new century was bringing new light to the home. Literally, the wonders of electricity were invading even the home environment, in interior lighting and in time-saving appliances such as the plug-in hot plate. The darkness of the past was replaced by the light of electricity, and the home reflected this "enlightenment."

The Joy of Kitchens

In place of large retinues of retainers [servants] modern equipment such as electric washing machines, dish washers, vacuum cleaners, gas rangers, steam heaters, etc., are provided in the establishment of today.

—*New York Times,* "In the Real Estate Field," 1908

The overall democratization of America, brought about economically by the graduated income tax in 1913, meant that homes would reflect this big societal change. No longer was one either master or serf in the home. Specifically, this meant that the American home was both the place of toil and the place of living. Fewer and fewer people were employed as house workers, and the American wife became a "homemaker," actually a complementary term when one considers the credit the woman is being given as a *maker* or creator of her family's life. The mother now, at least within the home, could be head of household. In recognition of the mother's new role, classic cookbooks such as the *Fannie Farmer Cookbook* (first published in 1906), and later *The Joy of Cooking* (1931), detailed for women, especially women of recently reduced circumstances, how to feed a family and how to run a modern kitchen. These early texts even told one how to make skunk palatable for dinner by soaking it in milk before cooking.

The home was becoming an increasingly efficient and optimistic environment for the growing middle class, and visual design had barely begun to attempt to catch up with function. The kitchen, in particular, was transformed during this era from the dank space of bead board walls and zinc washstand to the new era of built-in cabinetry and appliances. White, rather than dark wood, became the new kitchen choice, for white surfaces and appliances were considered sanitary, just as creamy, white food was considered healthy in the early twentieth century. Walls that had been plaster were tiled in white. Dark wood was painted white in the new modern kitchen, and free-standing furniture pieces gave way for white wood and glass built-ins. Linoleum flooring was popularized during this era in the middle-class home, replacing less hygienic, porous wooden floors in the kitchen and bathroom.

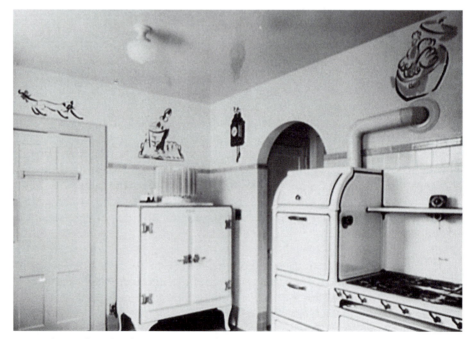

An early modern kitchen. Courtesy of the Library of Congress.

The electric kitchen appliances that were replacing handwork were white, built-in, and efficiently arranged. Even ironing boards were folded into wall cabinets, like Murphy beds, modern inventions that expanded space by disappearing into the wall when not in use. Appliances eventually became more integrated as objects. In this way, one can see an analogy to the early automobile of this era. The auto was an assemblage of working parts, each part distinct: chassis, fenders, windscreen. So, too, with early modern appliances: the electric refrigerator was composed of an old-fashioned ice box, on legs, with a separate motor atop. There was little thought to any overall visual sense of design of functional objects at this time in America, though glimmers of integrated design would appear by the 1920s and streamlining appeared in the 1930s.

Health and Hygiene, Baths and Bathrooms

Some Don'ts for Homes Builders: Don't invest in cheap plumbing and lavatory fittings.

—*Architectural Record,* "The General Contractor," 1903

Operative words for the early twentieth century were hygiene and sanitation. Cities were insisting through laws, such as the 1901 Model Tenement Reform Law, and through sewer construction, that sanitation at last be built into urban infrastructure. Hygiene began to be associated with public health. Before the reforms, multifamily tenements shared a single outdoor privy, and public bathhouses were the only real washing places for the urban poor. Consequently, water-borne diseases such as typhoid and dysentery, which we now consider problems only of the developing third world, were still being fought in American cities in the early twentieth century. Urban sewers, indoor plumbing for toilets, and washing facilities in the home would become the tanks of the early modern war on germs.

The bathroom as we know it evolved as a sanitary improvement, even more than as a convenience, within homes, ranging from the toughest tenement to the urban mansion. Simultaneous with interest in sanitation, standardization of parts and fixture manufacturing industries were revolutionizing the modern home. Sanitation and standardization were keys to the new home. Standard even became the name of major plumbing manufacturers, for example, Crane and Kohler being others. The original indoor bathrooms, or "water closets" of the early twentieth century, were still similar to other furnished rooms of the house, with toilet cabinets built of wood, for example, until it was understood that hygiene could be improved with impervious surfaces, such as porcelain. Shining white appliances became both the reality and the symbol of the new clean home. It was assumed by the homemaker that if it looked clean, it was clean, and white looks clean. The toilet was usually white porcelain, with black top and separate wall-attached tank above, chain controlled. Eventually, the one-piece attached tank toilet came to dominate the bathroom, as appliances were simplified and improved in design.

The early modern sink was similar to its predecessor, the washstand, a simple basin for hand washing, but as such, a major advance in American hygiene. The modern bathroom sink was composed of a white porcelain basin with exposed iron plumbing and two copper faucets that did not mix hot and cold; that had to be done within the sink basin. The sink of this time was the freestanding pedestal sink, one of the visually more integrated designs of the period. The walls of the bathroom began to be tiled in four by six horizontal ceramic tiles, white with white grout, of course. Bathrooms were designed to take up as little space as possible and were often underneath or at the top of the staircase, for day and night access. Floors were tiled with the distinctive black and white patterns still found in many older homes. The bidet has never had much appeal for Americans, as they have always preferred the bathtub or shower. In the early modern period, separate zinc tubs had been replaced by the late nineteenth-century claw foot. By the middle of this period, the smoothly integrated design of the built-in bathtub had appeared, sometimes with combined shower, quite similar to today's common fixtures.

Americans in the new century appreciated their kitchens and bathrooms as signs of necessary hygienic improvement, rather than of visual design. The recent American obsession with kitchens and bathrooms would have been considered unseemly in 1901–1920, for appliances were still looked at as conveniences, labor saving, quality of life additions to the work of the home, rather than status symbols.

Women, Homemaking, and "Labor Saving Devices" of the Early Modern Architectural Era

> Mechanical slaves, many of them powered by electricity, it was proposed, could replace servants in the home.
>
> —Arthur J. Pulos, *American Design Ethic,* 1983

One of the oddities of the advances in design of the modern kitchen and bathroom and the concomitant rise in efficiency and hygiene was that these advances did not necessarily free the American woman in the home. Although the 19th Amendment on women's suffrage was passed by Congress in 1919, women continued to be indentured to their homes, in spite of indoor plumbing and electrical appliances. It seems that women remained trapped in a cycle created by the improved home, for as the efficiency and acquisition of so-called labor-saving appliances rose, so, too, increased the expected standards of cleanliness and care and the expectations of labor devoted to home making.

Rising standards of living and comfort in the home implied rising standards of home making. Thus, before the vacuum cleaner appeared in 1907, the rugs were beaten twice a year in the back yard (in some cases by servants), but with the electric vacuum cleaner, those same rugs had to be cleaned once a week. Everyone expected the outdoor privy to be infectious and to smell bad, but the indoor bathroom had to glisten to justify its own cost. As families began to wash more often, and the homemaker acquired the electric iron and washing machine, dirty sheets and towels underwent spontaneous generation. More frequent labor to maintain higher standards of home hygiene and family cleanliness substituted for less frequent, heavier chores, but either way, women worked relentlessly at home and for the home. The early modern woman was given the vote and the vacuum, simultaneously.

Reference List

"The General Contractor." 1903. *Architectural Record* xiii (January): 120.

Giedion, Sigfried. 1978. *Space, Time and Architecture: The Growth of a New Tradition.* Cambridge, MA: Harvard University Press, 1941, 356.

"The Harmonious Home." 1920. *Chicago Tribune,* D8.

Hines, Thomas S. 2000. *Irving Gill and the Architecture of Reform: A Study in Modernist Architectural Culture.* New York: The Monacelli Press.

"In the Real Estate Field." 1908. *New York Times* (5 January): 15.

Lupton, Ellen, and J. Abbott Miller. 1992. *The Bathroom, the Kitchen and the Aesthetics of Waste, A Process of Elimination.* M.I.T. List Visual Arts Center and Princeton Architectural Press. Exhibition, May 9–June 28, p. 23.

Pulos, Arthur J. 1983. *American Design Ethic A History of Industrial Design to 1940.* Cambridge: The MIT Press, 228.

Home Layout and Design

DESIGN OF THE VERNACULAR AMERICAN HOME

A box of four wooden walls and a roof: This is the simplest and most persistent form of the American vernacular home, the longest lasting, and the earliest to evolve. The first American homes, the Cape and the Colonial, were created in early houses of the seventeenth and eighteenth centuries. By the early modern era, weighty and expensive post-and-lintel beams had been replaced by the great American building innovation of balloon framing, making the home more flexible as a form. This simplification of home building led to more flexibility in interior layout and design and to more flow in interior space.

Through nineteenth- and twentieth-century revivals of these styles, and via simple transformations of their normative types of layout and design, endless variations of American homes were created in the early modern period of the early twentieth century. The reader should note that when we discuss layout and design, specific architectural vocabulary is involved. Design consists of elevation and facade, or the views that we have from the street or yard. Layout implies plan: the footprint of the house and internal arrangement of rooms, windows, and doors. Additionally, layout can also mean site plan of the house on the lot and can further be interpreted as the relationship of the building to the street. The concepts of design and layout can even be extended into the meaning of the home within the community, as in the larger context of the home in urban planning.

Design of the Cape and the Colonial Home

Real Colonial architecture is a thing of beauty in house construction. It can withstand the scrutiny of time and is not affected by "vogue" in building.

—Ross G. Montgomery, "Colonial Home at Moderate Cost," 1919

Because the Cape is so deceivingly simple, it can be difficult to design well; therefore, it is crucial that correct proportions be observed for this house to have any visual appeal. A humble house, the Cape is not the most graceful of forms, one to one and one half stories, low-ceilinged, ground-hugging, with the roof extensively exposed on front elevation. In terms of fenestration, a minimal number of small window openings, usually of six over six panes, are cut into walls, increasing the house's ability to stand up to cold and treacherous weather, as well as creating cross ventilation in summer. The Cape was invented as a functional form and should be respected as such. The Colonial house is a mature version of the earlier Cape, and both designs are graceful only when integrated and simplified. In the Cape and Colonial house, the front door is found on the long elevation, and proper proportions are dictated by the relationship of parts—the door, the fenestration—to the front elevation and the roof. A very simple but significant transformation of this type was made by moving the front door to the side elevation, turning the house perpendicular to the street, thus emphasizing the triangular shape of the roofline, prevalent during the Greek Revival. These houses would have been part of the town of the early modern period, though even then seeming out of date.

Too often, twentieth-century builders have cheapened this antique type by flattening the pitch of the roof, omitting the heavy roof overhang, appending too tiny or too heavy dormers, or

Perspective and the Picturesque: Homes in Space

Practices of the visual arts may be applied to domestic architecture. Two concepts, in particular, have relevance to home design: the use of perspective and the picturesque. Illusions of perspectival depth and picturesque placement of objects together can improve the spatial design and layout of home and surrounding landscape. We by nature inhabit a three-dimensional spatial environment; therefore, if we increase the visual depth of home spaces through simple tricks of the eye, we will intuitively respond to the design.

In art, a convincing illusion of three-dimensional space or depth can be created on a flat two-dimensional mural surface, as seen in the historical painting techniques of one-point perspective, developed during the Renaissance. A horizontal line with a vanishing point delineated along it draws the eye into an illusion of infinite space beyond the horizon. A later technique, developed during the nineteenth century, called the picturesque, creates natural, irregular counterbalance among elements arranged in three-dimensions. In place of rigid symmetry, natural, informal lines and silhouettes are visually employed for spatial effect.

To increase space via perspective and picturesqueness in domestic architecture and landscape, consider simple transformations in design and layout. For example, in the suburban house, include a single tree with a soft silhouette in the front yard, planting it in an off-center middle space, rather than putting hedges in rigid lines parallel to the house. The tree not only opens space into nature, but emphasizes three-dimensionality, as the sidewalk becomes foreground, the tree middle ground, and the house facade background as if in a painting. In the limited space of an apartment, a palm on the balcony or a lone cactus outside the window draws the eye outward beyond the interior of the home, creating a surprising increase in depth of space. Visually interesting views and processionals, or paths of movement within space are thereby created within the home and landscape, enlivening the space. These simple tricks of visual design are analogous in the house to the focused spatial interest that a single sailboat creates, as observed from the shore tacking freely upon open water toward the vast horizon.

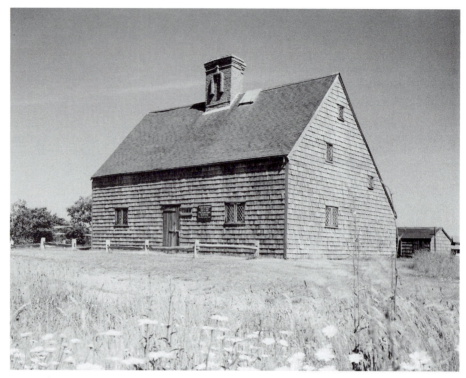

A timeless Colonial Revival. Courtesy of Royal Barry Will Architects.

mislocating the central chimney, thus destroying balance and symmetry. Windows and added dormers should be minimized and false shutters (non-functional) omitted. Tired clichés of Americana, such as patriotic eagle décor, are best avoided. Simplicity is the key. Softly weathered wooden shingling or clapboards should cover this house. Maintaining overall surface continuity is the key to this simple form, meaning that materials and colors of the facade and roof should be natural and neutral with very little contrast. A tall decidu-ous tree, such as a sugar maple, adds beauty and authenticity to this rugged American house.

Queen Anne Home Design

Queen Anne home design adds curves and porches to the early modern house. The concept of the deep front porch, often a wrap-around element, de-fines the innovation of a new interrelationship of outside with inside, of street to house, of yard to home. This home exudes openness and generosity to the streetscape, as no other early form can. American revivals of antique home styles before the Queen Anne—the Cape, the Colonial, and variations—predate the American front porch and the informal American lifestyle this addition sig-nified. The interrelationship of interior to exterior space was a later American home invention and will become one of the hallmarks of some of the finest architecture of the early modern architectural era.

Design and Development of the Bungalow Type

> Are you planning to build a House of Your Own? Couples bent on house build-
> ing can be spotted . . . if there's a vacant lot anywhere in the vicinity.
>
> —*Chicago Tribune,* "Are You Planning to Build a House
> of Your Own This Year?" 1910

The bungalow type home enwrapped American nostalgia for a preindustrial world within a machine-made form for the masses. Its fortuitive timing as a design coincided with the early modern architectural era, just as the American home began to be within grasp of the new middle class. The early concept of a bungalow was a simple framed box with roof, with the appearance, though not necessarily the reality, of being hand-made. Eventually, the bungalow was so standardized an American typeform that it could be carpenter built from plans or machine replicated and distributed by railroad. Humbly described as a "Little Wood Cottage Arranged for Simple Country Living" or "A Bungalow of Irregular Form and Unusually Interesting Construction" by *The Craftsman* magazine, a publication that informed both the vernacular builder and the more sophisticated architect, the bungalow was especially suited to fast construction and easy living. Therefore, it would soon become the perfect prototype for the developers of the Florida and southern California land booms of the 1920s.

An American bungalow was most often a one-story to one and one-half story house of low, horizontal proportions. Heavy columns support the downward sweeping roof physically and visually create functional porch space that is a transition between outside and inside. The roof may be interrupted by dormer or eyebrow windows. Fairly symmetrical, it was usually built of board and batten wood, clapboards or shingles, balloon-framed, but occasionally, depending on climate, of brick or even concrete. Often raised on a base, with wide steps leading to a central front door, it makes an informal and welcoming cottage. The house was carefully cross-ventilated and well-shaded to remain cool before the advent of air conditioning. Associated with the hot climates of the rural American South and California, balloon-framing made the construction of bungalow homes fast, feasible, and affordable, and the style advanced into the big cities of the Midwest, into the Pacific Northwest, the tropical Southeast and desert Southwest, and even occasionally onto the eastern seaboard.

Once humble cottages colonies, complete bungalow communities are today prized and preserved. In California, Pasadena's Bungalow Heaven historic neighborhood and La Jolla's seaside bungalows are excellent extant examples of the success of this repeatable house type. Serious, expensive bungalow type homes were also built in Pasadena by the architect brothers Greene and Greene. Bungalows constitute neighborhoods from Portland, Oregon, to border towns as far north as Bellingham, Washington (Roeder House, 1909), and as far south as the historic barrios of Tucson, Arizona. Board and batten bungalows are hidden amid tropical vegetation on every Hawaiian island and in coastal cities of Florida. In midwestern cities, brick and mortar bungalows compose comfortable urban neighborhoods of Chicago, St. Louis, and Denver. On the East Coast, the bungalow can be found from the rural south into the rural north, on the old farms of eastern Connecticut.

The *Architectural Record* commented rather snidely on the public's facile acceptance of speculative bungalows on tiny lots and the publicity that fed the bungalow boom. "A whole state is being sold to the American people by national advertising . . . social custom will eventually react in an interesting way on domestic architecture. We should expect to see the seasonal commuter between Florida and the north develop a gay, highly colored, amusing and somewhat frivolous type of bungalow-villa . . . The kind of bungalow . . . now being built is stereotyped, but . . . simple in design" (*Architectural Record,* 1925). The "amusing and somewhat frivolous" early twentieth-century bungalow has had such persistence in the American imagination that in the late twentieth century, this simple "stereotyped" form has been extensively copied and reproduced in contemporary bungalow revival communities in Florida, such as Celebration and Seaside, by architect-planners of the postmodern new urbanism movement. We have not seen the last iteration of this great American invention—the modern bungalow.

Foursquare House Design

The foursquare has always been far more successful in terms of function than of form. These boxy, top heavy vernacular houses were very plainly built things (Gowans 1986). Painted wood shingles, clapboards, stucco, brick, or a combination thereof cover these big-framed boxes. A variation on the symmetry of the foursquare facade was made by splitting the facade of the house visually at horizontal midpoint, with shingling for the top half of the house, and clapboards for the porch and first story, with the two stories painted contrasting colors. Unlike a Cape or smaller house, this simple house can handle strong visual contrasts because it presents such a simple large front elevation. Basically a blank canvas, the foursquare does not visually need the surface continuity of a smaller house. One awkward problem to be addressed in the foursquare is the relationship of this top heavy, overtly symmetrical house to its site. To tie the unadorned foursquare to its site, to relieve the monotony of the foursquare's blank facade, and the repetition of these common houses, and thus to improve its urban or suburban streetscape (see "Landscaping and Outbuildings, 1901–1920") it is advisable to soften this style with some asymmetrically arranged elements, such as informally planted shrubbery and one dominant shade tree in the front yard.

LAYOUT OF THE VERNACULAR AMERICAN HOME
"Flexible and Informal"

The flexible treatment of the house which has been common practice in since colonial days is one of the keys to its domestic architecture. The flexible and informal ground plan . . . remained strictly anonymous. It is the outgrowth both of the urge for comfort in the dwelling and the American tendency to tackle problems directly.

—Sigfried Giedion, *Space, Time and Architecture,* 1978

The layout and design of the American house of the early modern architectural period moved toward flexibility, just as Americans were becoming more middle class and more able to extend themselves into a home of their own. It was a phenomenon of 1901–1920 that at last there was a true American house, a house to which any American might aspire. The American dream of home ownership, which had been long been with its citizens, came to fruition during this period, and simplified house design was the thing that made this dream a reality. No longer are we talking about mansions and tenements, though of course they continued to stand. By 1920, we are seeing the prototypical American freestanding, single family, suburban house with yard, with which we are familiar today. An illustrated resource for homes of this period is *The Comfortable House, North American Suburban Architecture 1890–1930,* by Alan Gowans, in which the author discusses a "confident belief that within the American system a Comfortable House for all was a realistic goal" (Gowans 1986).

In terms of layout and design, it is important to note that the average American of 1901–1920 was burdened with far fewer objects and electrical appliances than today. The houses that were wired for electricity could not have borne today's extravagant needs. No television, no sound systems, no computers, no air conditioning, and usually no car existed. People even had less clothing. This meant that storage was not so important, and people had home-based interests other than the size of their closets, status of their kitchen appliances, and number of bathrooms. Basements, not finished rumpus rooms, were still simply cellars with coal bins and spider webs. The reader should keep in mind simplicity, democratizing design, and the family-oriented thrust of 1901–1920 when picturing the design of these homes. Life was harder than today, but time was slower.

The aim of layout and design of the first quarter of the twentieth century was toward enlightened simplification and integration of the yard with the house. Though interior design detailing continued to be primarily of Classical or Colonial Revival motifs, interior layout was undergoing a process of simplification. The myriad rooms of the Victorian house (i.e., the breakfast room, the butler's pantry, the sewing room, the dressing room, the billiards room) gave way to far fewer but more versatile multiuse rooms, with comfortable spatial flow, minimal hallways, and an overall efficient use of space. Is it really not possible to sew in the same room in which you ate breakfast? During this great era of the democratization of the American home, the trend was toward more and simpler homes, for a greater number of less affluent homeowners. The small American house for the working and growing middle class was a proud product of this period.

The Cape Layout

The very simplest layout for a house included four rooms, a central entrance, a few small windows and hearth, and thus the Cape Cod house was born in America. The central fireplace was the cornerstone of this design, for the hearth provided both the physical warmth and the emotional heart of the house and allowed heat to be transferred evenly throughout the house before central heating. Surrounding the hearth with four simple, adjoining rooms, with no hallway save a tiny one at the entrance, not only conserved heat and space but drew together family functions. In more modern, elaborated Cape models, a central staircase was added next to the central hearth. It led up to two or three bedrooms under the low-pitched roof, with dormers thrust outward for extra storage space and ventilation. Variations of the Cape included the modern invention of moving the fireplace and chimney to the side of the house to open up the interior space, adding more windows and modern amenities such as the bathroom at the top of the central staircase, between the bedrooms.

Commonly, later builders have lowered the pitch of the roofline, a postwar aberration, and frequently added awkwardly proportioned dormers that break the surface continuity of the Cape's strong sheltering roof, making the dormers both unattractive and useless as added space. It is common to add a nonconforming front entrance and to raise ceiling heights in Cape houses to appeal to taste and contemporary heating plants; however, the embrace of low ceilings is metaphorically more authentic to the original vernacular. To refuse to honor the simplicity of the Cape Cod house is to misunderstand willfully the meaning of an American idiom. The Cape was not in itself a beautiful style, but it was a design of rationally evolved proportions and economical layout. In both form and function, the Cape harkened back to a simpler day and thus was appealing to the American democratization of the early modern architectural era.

Layout Walkabout

Walk into any Cape house in America (after knocking!), from eighteenth-century antique to early twentieth-century revival. Enter via the central front door. You are standing in a minimal hallway that may or may not continue to the back door of the house. Directly in front of you is likely to be a straight central staircase, the older the house, the steeper the stairs. To your right is a low-ceilinged living room with central fireplace or one suppressed against the outer wall. Windows are somewhat small, six over six double-hung, and distributed symmetrically. Connected to this main room, now through a more modern archway, to the rear is a keeping room. Standing again at the front door, to your left is a dining room, connected to a rear kitchen. The kitchen again opens into the keeping room, so without hallways, the circulation of the layout downstairs in this house is elliptical. Now ascend the staircase. Directly in front of you is the wonder of the modern bathroom, if this is a twentieth-century Cape; closets are minimal. To your right, above the living room, is the master bedroom, where you will find the interior space of the dormer window pushed out into the roofline. The interior space of the bedroom will reflect the angles of the roof rafters. To your left are one or two bedrooms for children, into which colonials might have crowded eight children, early twentieth-century families three, and mid-twentieth-century five. Descend the stairs. Go out the door. You have now experienced the wonders of the modern American Cape Cod house.

The Colonial Layout

The Colonial of the early twentieth century is the graceful, respectable, middle and upper middle-class house, whose hallmark is its bourgeois yet beautiful symmetry. In plan, the Colonial was the enriched version of the Cape Cod house, allowing for the extra space of connecting hallways between rooms. It is an eastern suburban staple of two stories, with center entrance set importantly within a bilaterally balanced plan. The front hall became the defining feature of this layout, usually leading directly from the front door back to the kitchen in the rear for the convenience of the homeowner of the modern world who no longer had servants to carry groceries into the pantry, a room itself which may or may not have survived in these early modern houses. A full second floor of three to five bedrooms, with attic storage, made this home roomy. One might think of the Colonial as the upwardly mobile cousin of the Cape in historical, visual, and economic terms. In the suburban Colonial, there is no front porch relating the building to the street, for in this more sophisticated lifestyle, American life becomes more insularly lived in the back yard.

The Foursquare Layout

The plan and layout of the foursquare is emphatically that which it is called: it is square, there are four rooms per floor, and those rooms themselves are square. The addition of a high, defined second story sets the foursquare apart from the other vernacular American houses of this period, the Cape Cod and the bungalow. Because of the second story, the central or side staircase takes on importance in the plan of the foursquare. It both connects and dictates the plan of the interior of the first and second floors and demands the addition of a hallway both front and center of the first floor plan, and upstairs, as well. In the foursquare, rooms may be arranged either off the central hall, or they may be accessed via adjoining rooms. This leads to more doorways and broken up wall spaces, but it provides excellent cross-ventilation when windows, interior doorways, and halls are aligned so that breezes can blow freely through the house. The foursquare post-dates the Cape, and here central heating and cooling, too, became a factor. The world was somewhat less harsh by the time of the foursquare, and hiding from winter was not the only climatic design consideration. Even interior transom windows above doors help in the cooling of this house. If the Cape is the idiom of the northeastern winter, the foursquare is the house of the midwestern farm's summer on the plains. In an era of community spirit, the foursquare with its appended big front porch recalls neighbors sharing covered dishes.

Layout of an Atrium House

Mediterranean homes designed in the atrium style have always been rare in the United States. The layout has traditionally inverted the standard American plan of house on a lot with front and rear yards and grassy set backs from the street. Instead, the atrium plan set the house elevation flush with the street, configured its plan in a square with an empty center, and located the open space not around, but within, the home itself. This was referential to the standard Mediterranean home plan. In the words of Kevin Starr in his California History, "Already, from the 1910s onward, a formula was in place: the patio, a reversed floor plan, with the living area opening onto a rear garden or patio enclosure" (Starr 2002). The atrium house was unheard of in the East and Midwest, popular only in the far West, California, and Florida in the early modern architectural era, where Spanish styles were the heritage of the past. The atrium layout, however, was not only historically correct for these regions, but an excellent adaptation for the American hot climates. A central fountain could provide cool bubbling water to the house, and covered walkways around the atrium meant that each room, including bedrooms, could open directly onto fresh cooling breezes. A dramatic Spanish aesthetic of sunlight and shade were produced while the home, in plan and design, partook both of inside and out, of openness and closure, of architecture and landscape.

Bungalow Layout

[A]ll that bungles is not bungalow.

—Charles E. White Jr., *The Bungalow Book,* 1927

The layout of the bungalow popularized two major design elements in the American vernacular—the front porch and the sleeping porch—for the bungalow was a fair weather friend. The layout of the single story bungalow always seemed spatially larger in three dimensions than it appeared in plan, thanks to the convenient room layout and generous sheltering porch. "Open planning . . . is a product of the American development as a whole" (Giedion 1978, 364). The porch encouraged a welcome sense of transition from outside to inside from bright sunlight, through shade, to interior shadow. Thus, the generous porch and its addition of really livable outdoor space was the hallmark of the bungalow layout. The variations possible within a thematic small American house made the bungalow layout both interesting architecturally and a clean, well lighted place.

Interior plans of bungalows illustrated American economy and common sense within a process of industrialization and simplification applied to homes. For example, hallways and front halls are really a rather extravagant use of floor space in a home. Bungalows were simple, one floor affairs, designed with minimal or no hallways and doorways and with a minimum number of rooms, instead making simple interior spaces flow seamlessly into one another through large arched openings. Generally only one floor, but sometimes two, built on a concrete slab or no foundation at all, bungalows defied the traditional separation of downstairs living and dining areas from upstairs sleeping quarters. So simple was the bungalow layout that bedroom might be contiguous with living room or even kitchen, and the new "disappearing" beds and space-saving devices made this possible within limited space. Life on one floor omitted interior stairs, thus saving significant space within the layout.

The classless bungalow as home type and layout was so popular in California in the early modern architectural period that it ranged from light weight summer beach retreats, to cheap slapped up structures on tiny lots relentlessly repeated in prefabricated parts, to serious carpenter built suburban style via mail-order plans, to architecturally significant, upscale individually designed homes. This design diversity spoke in plain language to the versatility of the bungalow layout as a symbol of a new sense of democratization of housing and growing informality of lifestyle in modern America.

Craftsman Bungalow Design and Layout

Logic and simplicity were always applied to the Craftsman home in layout and design. A Craftsman home could also be constructed from a wide range of materials: wood beams, sheathing, and shingles, natural logs with bark, uncut stone, roof slate, and perhaps surprisingly, cement. Craftsman interiors articulated structure, just as exteriors did. This meant that wood and plaster were highlighted as artistic design, rather than hidden as building materials. Wooden beams were encased and exposed on the low ceilings. Walls were covered with wooden detailing, and cabinetry was built-in, inset against the wall. Importantly for Craftsman as well as for the Shingle Style design was the invention of the inglenook, a pleasantly confined space for cozy, informal sitting focused on the fireplace. The inglenook was an intimate space in an open plan home. The hearth, in brick or stone, was the physical and emotional center of the craftsman home.

The placement of doors and windows exemplified a conscious approach to the Craftsman bungalow home. The front door of this design in cold climates did not open directly into the house, rather into a small front vestibule with interior door, to provide an air lock to keep cold winter drafts at bay from the rest of the house. Windows, on the other hand, were usually placed in opposition of each other, to allow cross-ventilation and healthful breezes to flow through the house in summer. Though such simple design concepts may seem obvious, it is important to note the historical context of Craftsman homes and interiors: These designs were being created in a world ruled by the excesses of Victorian rooms and stiflingly over-elaborated, under-ventilated interiors. Quite literally, then, the simple, well-ventilated Craftsman layout was a breath of fresh air.

Stickley's Craftsman Farms: Home as Utopian Community

One often hears of any vernacular bungalow form referred to as a Craftsman bungalow whether or not the home was technically designed by Gustav Stickley, founder of the American Craftsman movement. The Craftsman style of Gustav Stickley is known not only from constructed homes, but also from extensive illustrated materials dispersed in the early modern architectural era, specifically by *The Craftsman* magazine, published by Stickley himself from 1903–1916. Craftsman style, the clearest American exponent of the European Arts and Crafts movement, though perhaps not wholly successful in Stickley's hands, was the first to seek to upgrade, to simplify, and to democratize the general concept of design for the American people in the early modern architectural era. Ironically, Stickley was also craftily mercantile, selling his back-to-nature goods in his urban shop.

The Craftsman magazine was an outlet for Stickley's idealistic social and aesthetic concepts, for his designs of furniture and functional objects, and for his architectural designs and layouts. Each issue contained an essay, often by Stickley, but also by other contemporary architects and designers, as well as illustrations of useful things, and most importantly, an illustrated home in which these things could be found, with complete plans for home design, layout, and construction. One such Stickley plan included, "A Plain House that Will Last for Generations and Need Few Repairs," the epitome of Stickley simplicity. (See the Appendix for excerpts from *The Craftsman*.)

Once a thriving communal home and landscape of 200 acres, the 26 acres of Gustav Stickley's home and utopian community, Craftsman Farms, buildings and landscape active from 1908–1915, are today being rescued. Even while the sounds of birds compete with the noise of New Jersey's major highways ringing the last rural property there within an hour of New York City, one can experience something of Stickley's original design vision. Homes at Craftsman Farms were at once modern design innovations and recalls of the past—logical extensions in design from the vernacular bungalow. A rustic though modern and clean-lined aesthetic rules the home. Stickley built himself a large log cabin in bungalow form (Stickley 1912), of which the public first floor is of one design aesthetic and the private second floor another. Intending his own home to be private and public space, Stickley made his massive log cabin home of rustic, Arts and Crafts, Asian, and medieval motifs.

The extensive first floor open plan layout included room for communal gatherings of other residents of Craftsman Farms. This story was designed to be both functional and emotive, with enclosed porch overlooking an orchard and supported by frost-heaved boulders found on the site. The natural material truthfulness of Stickley's log and shingle home was apparent on the ground floor, where a strong overall aesthetic of horizontality was dictated by dark stacked chestnut logs, interspersed with light infill. The downstairs public rooms were saved from being oppressively horizontal, low ceilinged, and dark by the natural light filtering in from the front porch. The warmth and meaning of the Craftsman home is conveyed in the inset inglenooks and many decorative fireplaces on the first floor. The upstairs of the home, in contrast, is shingled on the exterior and plastered and covered in grass cloth on the inside. With simple, screen-like walls, the private part of the home upstairs is a serene, and more conventional, contrast to the lower level. Stickley had traveled to the western United States to see other works by Craftsman-like architects for inspiration, including the hand-built homes of Greene and Greene in California. Their more advanced influence is obvious in his work, bringing the sophisticated Asian aesthetics of the western architects to the East. There is little internal continuity in Stickley's home, for the upstairs living quarters in design and layout do not reflect the rustic, robust, open plan aesthetic of the communal downstairs. One notes, however, that architects, including Frank Lloyd Wright, have often used their own homes for design experiments, and Stickley's Craftsman Farms was really all about his vision and spirit of social and aesthetic experimentation.

NECESSARY SPACES: KITCHENS, BATHROOMS, AND BEDROOMS

The Layout of the Early Modern Kitchen

This is what our inventive democracy has done for the world. We have made domestic service unpopular even for those who would be drawn to it . . . and have devised machinery to disperse with much of it.

—*Chicago Tribune,* "A Universal Cry for Smaller Houses," 1921

The "servant problem" begat the kitchen design problem of early modernism. For while there was sufficient cheap labor to go around, the kitchen was of little thought to the homeowner. The kitchen was simply a necessity and province of the low paid, a hidden place in the house from which heavy meals emerged into the family's formal dining room. In the early twentieth-century house of wealth, even of the early developing bourgeois household, the kitchen was a workroom for outsiders, detached from the family's interest. Heavy work it was: food preparation was done primarily by hand. Meat was sliced, ice was lugged, and pots were scrubbed by servants' hands. Before 1913, the wife as family meal-provider was a role only for the farm or urban lower class. Women of higher class would not conceive of handling raw chicken or of immersing their hands in dishwater. Later, due to democratic societal changes, as cooking and the kitchen were de-stigmatized, cookbooks and contemporary kitchens for the new woman as homemaker appeared.

The layout of the kitchen and its location within the house of the early twentieth century reflected the basically neglectful, class-oriented lifestyle of 1901–1913. Kitchens of this period were not yet designed for efficiency, for a servant's time and comfort were of little consequence, and the lower classes could simply make do. Thus, kitchens were large, inefficient spaces, with many steps between food storage, preparation, and service areas. Even the improved homemaker's kitchen after 1913 would still be just a square room with table in the center, cabinets along the walls, and major appliances pushed without planning into corners. Dinnerware, silver, and glassware were stored separately in the butler's pantry off the dining room. In a wealthy household, meals were taken in the first floor dining room, but the kitchen was located in the basement, thus requiring the carrying of heavy trays of food and dishes up and down staircases. The need to segregate on-going house labors from the eyes of the homeowner necessitated that domestic architecture include back staircases for servants. A useful tool sometimes built into the architecture of the house was the dumb waiter, an open shaft with a shelf on pulleys, enclosed by paneled doors, through which food from the basement could be unobtrusively raised to the pantry for service.

The kitchen was recognized by all as cruelly hot in summer. Thus, as in the nineteenth century, the kitchen was often found at the rear of the house, sometimes even in the back yard, such as a southern summer kitchen. Servants' quarters were naturally most likely to be near to the kitchen, both for the convenience of the worker who had to rise early and unseen to prepare the morning meal and for the repose of the homeowner. Servants could live in the heat they generated by their incessant baking and cooking. It was also of note that servants in urban townhouses usually lived on the upper floors, the hottest floors in summer and the coldest in winter, and the longest climb to bed. For the tenement class, seven flights of stairs home were common, and cooking was done in cramped, inefficient, unventilated spaces.

Not only was the kitchen of the early twentieth century inefficient, it was not particularly hygienic (Lupton and Miller 1992). Early twentieth-century kitchens, like those of the previous century, were assembled of detached, dark wooden furniture and storage units, sometimes with a preparation area and sink surfaced in zinc. Wood, as is now known, is quite difficult to keep sanitary, so even with the constant physical scrubbing of the scullery maid, bacteria must have enjoyed the good life in the early twentieth-century kitchen. The American household obsession with the sanitary kitchen was a later invention, just beginning to take hold before 1920. Efficiency and sanitation emerged in the American kitchen as the housewife entered it. With the decline in the number of immigrants for service, women of the growing middle class found that by the early modern period, they, too, were going to have to learn something about the kitchen. Thus, kitchens gained recognition in the American house as they became part of the family, as work and lifestyle.

The Layout of the Early Modern Bathroom

While the kitchen had always been part of the home, the early modern indoor bathroom was either an afterthought added to a house that had previously had an outhouse, or a minimal necessity of new construction. Older homes sometimes retrofitted a small former bedroom as the new bathroom; thus, surprisingly spacious, inefficient but very large bathrooms existed in older homes. A great deal of wasted space existed between the tub, the sink, and the toilet. These bathrooms were rarely tiled and had the look and permeable surfaces of wood and plaster of early kitchens. More modern homes were planned with a bathroom, usually found at the top of the stairs, but it was downplayed in the design and much more cramped for space, or perhaps efficiently arranged, more so than the big, inefficient bathrooms in older homes. Now the sink and toilet were closely aligned against one wall and the built-in tub was directly opposite. The big difference in the more modern, planned bathroom was in attempts to create hygienic conditions through the use of impermeable surfaces, such as tile walls and floors and porcelain and stainless metal fixtures. By the 1920s, most bathrooms had tightly arranged layouts, toilets, sinks, and tubs closely configured. These more modern bathrooms were often designed with white tiling with black tile borders, and checked tile floors, though marble was used in the wealthiest homes' bathrooms, an indulgence nearly Roman in extravagance.

The Disappearing Room: Smaller Families, Smaller Homes

If one were to compare design and layout of the average, middle-class bungalow or suburban home of 1905 with the design and layout of a similar residence of 1925, one would notice some subtle shifts in home priorities. Of course, the most obvious change would be in the modernization of the kitchen and bathroom. The most significant change, however, reflecting societal change, would be in size and efficiency. The housing trend was moving toward smaller homes with fewer rooms; however, these newer homes had more spatial flow and more efficient use of space, and were therefore more comfortable. A major difference was the declining number of bedrooms, and this must represent an important social condition: family size. It would be interesting to find the exact correlation between number of bedrooms and population trends; however, that is not within the scope of this book, but one might note that activist Margaret Sanger was advocating for female birth control during the Post World War I period. Birthrates declined as income and industrialization in America were advancing in the early modern era, only to rise again in the post–World War II population boom, when even tract houses added multiple cramped bedrooms to the American house. Four or more large bedrooms early in the century, allowing for multiple children per room, gave way to one or two medium bedrooms and perhaps a small nursery by the mid-1920s. It appears that the old adage held that children were an advantage on the farm feeding the stock, but themselves became mouths to feed in the town or city.

"THE GOOD PLANNER": EARLY MODERN CITY AND REGIONAL PLANNING IN AMERICA

That is . . . what the good planner does. He creates a setting in which people . . . will fit, where they will live a varied life, a convenient life, a beautiful life; where they will grow and change . . . The planner's subject, then, is man. It is his fellows and their reaction to their environment which he must study and understand.

—Clarence S. Stein, *Toward New Towns for America,* 1978

Urban planning was one of the great advances of the early modern architectural era. The most profound issues of layout and design were then, and now, within the large-scale realm of urban planning. Though modern advances within the individual home had diurnal effects on people's lives, the modern revolution in urban and suburban planning was far more meaningful on a civic level, for it established the permanent urban configurations, or community layouts, of American towns, cities, and suburbs. Urban design was not simply about how one lived in one's living room, but how one interacted with the larger society, and this was the

---

Urban Planning: Homes on Streets

To walk down a street in America we must be alert, not to chaos, but to beauty and order. For it is the ordered layout and design of the street that is the real foundation of our communities, and only through vigilant visual consciousness of our surroundings will we be able to improve our cities. Observe and question, for example, certain fundamental aspects of urban layout and design as you walk down a city street. Layout: Have the planners provided sidewalks so that pedestrians are given equal importance to cars? Is public transit accessible? We must no longer allow development to give precedence to cars over humans. Are individual houses or row houses set back uniformly from the street or flush with the sidewalk? Design: Are interesting breaks in urban uniformity created to deter monotony? Is there design repetition, not necessarily sameness, but uniformity in scale among the buildings? Is there coherence in the signs, street furniture, and lamp posts? Are there positive visual breaks, such as specimen trees, sculpture, or wrought iron fencing to encourage focus and processional through the streetscape? Or are there gaping holes of empty lots that could be improved with a simple fence at the set-back line? Most important of all, are shade trees planted and maintained?

Where architecture is juxtaposed creatively with urban amenity and the forms of nature, cities and towns become authentic homes. This is an achievable and economically feasible goal of urban planning. Simple factors of urban design and layout, such as those listed here, are enjoyed everyday by families strolling the many fake Main Streets of American theme parks. Yet so often we fail to demand the same level of design creativity and coherence in our real towns and cities that we seek and pay for in our faux environments.

---

sector of life that was changing most profoundly from 1901–1920. These are the places we inhabit today, for although an individual house may be torn down, a town's patterns of streets and spaces rarely deviate completely over time.

Therefore, land use decisions, and the layout and design of towns, are critical long-term commitments that should be made with social and aesthetic forethought, never left to chance. Early modern housing developments, for example, were generally either laid out on purchased former farms erratically at the fringes of cities by developers for maximum profit, or by planners in an organized fashion, sponsored by nonprofit philanthropic or government agencies for social motivations. "The transition to modern planning and housing

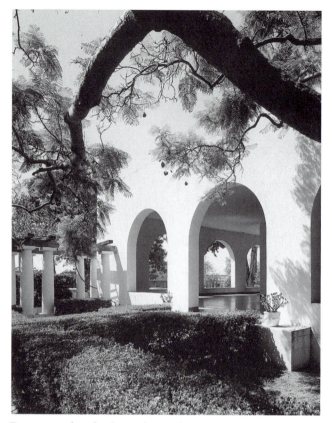

Beauty and order in early modern American urban design. Courtesy of the Library of Congress.

in America did not take place on any scale until the First World War," stated urban theorist Lewis Mumford, yet America had a history of planning communities and communal spaces, from Thomas Jefferson to Frederick Law Olmsted (Stein 1978).

Many excellent planned communities were designed during the early modern architectural era. The design of towns from the time included Olmsted's plan for Riverside, Illinois, outside Chicago (1880s), a suburb where Frank Lloyd Wright would later design homes. Decisions to exploit or to plan the layout of the land dictated both the housing of the early modern architectural era and the lives we lead today through nearly irreversible consequences. Urban planner Clarence Stein designed the communities of Sunnyside Gardens, New York and Radburn, New Jersey (1920s), as well Greenbelt, Maryland (1930s), based on theories he had worked on in the years between the wars. Stein's book, *Toward New Towns for America,* published in the post–World War II period (Stein 1978), reflected decades of societal change beginning at the time of World War I. However, the design factors Stein and his fellow town planners in this book, including Lewis Mumford, considered, are on-going, continuing into the twenty-first century, giving us hope for design. In their optimistic words, "After the First World War there was a strong surge of enthusiasm for a better world" (Stein 1978, 11).

Although it is beyond the purview of this book, the reader should become aware of the most fundamental factors in urban planning and design to understand one's home within its context. The relationship of the home to the central node or core of the town or city, the density of the housing stock, the relationship of the home to other buildings, the importance of urban transportation access, the relationship of building to open space, the incorporation of green space into the built environment of the town, and the inclusion of urban amenities are important factors to consider in the layout of the town and design of the home one chooses, indeed in the understanding of all human settlements (Cormier 2004). Urban planning teaches us that when we make our home, we are embracing at once our town, our city, our prairie, mountain range, or desert. Even in Hawaii, no home is an island.

Reference List

"Are You Planning to Build a House of Your Own This Year?" 1910. *Chicago Tribune* (13 March): G4.

Cormier, Leslie Humm. 2004. "Urban Planning." *Encyclopedia of 20th-Century Architecture,* vol. 3. New York: Fitzroy Dearborn, 1379–1382.

Croly, Herbert. "A National Winter Suburb." *The Architectural Record,* vol. 58. 1925. (December): 605–606.

Giedion, Sigfried. 1978. *Space, Time and Architecture: The Growth of a New Tradition.* Cambridge, MA: Harvard University Press, 1941, 363–368.

Gowans, Alan. 1986. *The Comfortable House, North American Suburban Architecture 1890–1930.* Cambridge, MA: M.I.T. Press, 84–86.

Lupton, Ellen, and J. Abbott Miller. 1992. "The Bathroom, the Kitchen and the Aesthetics of Waste, A Process of Elimination." M.I.T. List Visual Arts Center and Princeton Architectural Press. Exhibition, May 9–June 28.

Montgomery, Ross G. 1919. "Colonial Home at Moderate Cost." *Los Angeles Times* (27 July): V13.

Starr, Kevin. 2002. *The Dream Endures, California Enters the 1940s.* New York: Oxford University Press, 20.

Stein, Clarence S. 1978. *Toward New Towns for America.* With an introduction by Lewis Mumford. Cambridge, MA: M.I.T. Press, 1957, 11, 19, 226.

Stickley, Gustav. 1912. *The Best of Craftsman Homes.* Reprint of 1906 and 1912, *Craftsman Homes* and *More Craftsman Homes.* Santa Barbara: Peregrine Smith, 1979, 6, 9, 83–89.

"A Universal Cry for Smaller Houses." 1921. *Chicago Tribune* (21 July): 62.

White, Charles E., Jr. 1927. *The Bungalow Book.* New York: MacMillan Company, 1.

Furniture and Decoration

TRADITIONAL HOME DECORATION

Colonial Revival in the East

> "Rooms finished with straight lines with plain wood stained a harmonious color are . . . practical and artistic as well as economical." This and other sage advice from "The Harmonious Home" column in the *Chicago Tribune* will guide our way through the décor of the rooms of yesteryear.
>
> —*Chicago Tribune,* "The Harmonious Home," 1920

As the early modern architectural era represented a transition in style from the traditional into the modern, so, too, did interior home design recall the decorative past, while simultaneously moving toward a sleeker twentieth-century future. Simple décor, decorative objects, and the open plan made their debut during this era. "Don't forget that rooms designed after simple straight lines lend themselves more easily to decoration, prove more sanitary, and are less tiresome to live in than badly arranged rooms." The aim was toward a comfortable house of spatial flow from room to room, and interior decoration and furniture followed this pattern of simplification. An overall integration of architectural space and interior objects and simplicity of design were the hallmarks and high points of the emerging modernism of 1901–1920. Design dissonance, however, between the modern interior plan versus the facade and the furnishings, existed within the homes of the 1920s, as Americans nostalgically sought homes that fit into Colonial Revival suburban contexts, yet chose to live amidst the comfort of the modern open plan layout, newly designed fixtures, and more comfortable furnishings.

As one might expect, traditional styles, such as the Cape and the Colonial, in particular, continued with great popularity from 1901–1920, even well into the 1930s. These were excellent homes adorned with traditional detailing, such as working fireplaces with wooden mantels; rooms with cove, dental, or crown moldings; solid wood exterior and interior doors with paneling; and built-in china cabinets. Double hung six over six pane glass windows, glass door knobs set in brass hardware, and a decorative brass front door knocker adorned the traditional home. Wood paneled libraries were installed in more expensive homes. Stairways became significant as an architectural feature in a middle-class home and were wide, with oak treads and white risers and traditional wood banisters. Many of these features have either disappeared from homes or would be considered extras today.

Ceilings and walls were plastered by hand, smooth or in swirling patterns; there was not yet any plasterboard. Floors were uniformly wood, usually hard wood such as oak throughout, though sometimes builders compromised lower priced homes upstairs with cheaper soft woods such as pine. Wood floors were displayed waxed with decorative rugs; broadloom carpeting was not part of this era. Widely available, newly invented linoleum made its checkerboard patterns in the kitchen. Consistent use of a simple color combination gives a pleasing and decorative result, as "The Harmonious Home" reminded the reader. Interior rooms were usually painted a harmonious neutral or pastel by the builder, though often changed with color or flowered wallpaper for the worse by the buyer. Interesting details, such as arched doorways, made even the middle-class

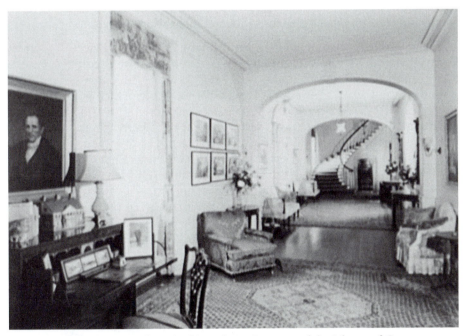

The comforts of Colonial Revival interiors. Courtesy of the Library of Congress.

house seem more spacious and light-filled. Though the movement in the early modern architectural era was toward simplicity, most of the earlier traditional detailing was retained, even in modern houses of the day.

Hideaways in Home Decoration

Even as trends were toward simplified house plans, architects and designers still were bringing more picturesque elements into the home. The intimacy of the *inglenook,* or tiny paneled seating space under the stairs, was perhaps the most beloved design of this period. The inglenook, fireplace, and staircase combination was an inviting feature of the Shingle Style and the Craftsman style, creating an unexpected reading corner or fireplace bench for quiet contemplation within the flow of the larger rooms. Open air sleeping porches attached to bedrooms became a cooling feature in pre–air conditioning California bungalows, especially in the larger Greene and Greene homes. Sleeping porches were the rich suburban homeowner's equivalent of the poor tenement tenant's "fire escape for sleeping" in the early twentieth century.

New-fangled appliances had their hideaways in the home that spanned the old and the new: arches were carved into plaster walls for the black stand-up telephone in the front hall for proud display. The ironing board was enclosed in a cabinet, and the refrigerator had its own arched niche in some really modern kitchens of the 1910s and 1920s. Front porches were certainly the most generous hideaway spaces of this period, a place to observe the street without being fully observable oneself, in the manner of the French cafe. Porches also functioned as usable space within the Queen Anne and bungalow layouts, creating an excellent transition from outside to inside, and thus were real American social spaces that integrated the individual home with the social environment of the street.

Traditional Influences on Early Modern Decoration

It is interesting how similar in form many authentic eighteenth-century early American or nineteenth-century Colonial Revival decorative objects were to modern design to come. Note, for example, the classics, the Windsor chair and the silver or pewter Revere bowl, both of which continue to be reproduced today. These indigenous American designs were so simple yet fully functional, made with such restraint, that the beauty of each object was its unornamented simplicity of form. The smooth, unornamented bowl was the vessel in its most perfect evolved form, and therefore may be read as one of our earliest American typeforms. The Paul Revere Silver Collection at the Museum of Fine Arts Boston remains a testament to the American tradition of pure form of eighteenth-century colonies, nineteenth-century Colonial Revival, and early twentieth-century emerging modernism. Often, however, modernist impulses were disguised within traditional decoration, revivalist facades, and interior decoration.

An example of early modern design masquerading as antique Americana can be found just outside of Boston in the Lawrence Estates section of Medford, Massachusetts (1920s), in which very spacious, modern plan homes were hidden within traditional motifs and decoration on streets lined with Colonial Revival, Dutch Colonial, and Garrison Colonial homes. This type of home development was common in the early modern architectural era and can be found all over America today. A modern, open floor plan was often shoved into a traditional neo-Colonial shell, and thus the flowing layout of a fairly modern house could appear from the street to be a very old-fashioned and traditionally decorated home. Upwardly striving but insecure homeowners of the era, instructed by conservative ladies' home magazines, felt that the interior decoration of their houses had to match the revivalist designs of the facades. Even today, people believe incorrectly that exposed beams were Colonial, though a well-off colonist would shudder at this rusticity, much preferring an enclosed ceiling. Thus, the early modern architectural era was disingenuously filled with retrograde colonial reproductions of faux French provincial and fake English pub furniture and decorative arts. Tiny brass eagles, various spinning wheels, and Martha Washington portraits adorned simplified modern homes, yet this naivete itself is an expression of American enthusiasm for having one's own home.

Traditional Homes in the Northeast Today

Later exponents of the Colonial Revival carried the American spirit and consciousness of domestic democracy that Boston architects McKim, Mead, and White had invented forward through the twentieth century. Architect Royal Barry Wills trained in Boston during the early twentieth century, and his family firm continues with the express aim of creating American Colonial Revival domestic architecture; many of the finest Colonial Revivals in the Northeast are attributable to this partnership's trendless adherence to premodern motifs (Richard Wills, interview with the author, December 1999). Americans like traditional forms, but architectural critics correctly find nothing cutting edge, so it has been through regional architects that the Colonial Revival has been widely disseminated and remains a major aesthetic force in America (see Appendix).

Spanish Revivals in the West

A very literal faux influence on early modern furniture and decoration was provided by the Mediterranean and Spanish styles in California and the West, including heavy wooden furniture in simple forms, with leather or brocade, brass nails, iron candelabras, and hanging tapestries. Spanish exoticism was to become all the rage in western houses. Spanish 'Valentino' exoticism was to become all the rage in prosperous places in America, especially during the 1920s.

Spanish Revival homes of the early modern era were categorized as Spanish Colonial, Mission, or Pueblo style. Mission homes tended to be simple, flat-roofed, horizontal, and geometric; while Spanish Colonial homes exhibited elements that were decorative, curvilinear, and ornately Baroque, decorated with painted tiles and red tile roofs. Gradations of Spanish-influenced styles fell somewhere between Mission and Spanish Colonial, and the mixtures of motifs in California reflected the social and cultural collisions of Spanish missionaries, colonists, conquistadors, Anglos, and Native Americans. The contrasting influences in California were made clear within the mission complex and can be observed today, for many missions are open to the public while still active religious institutions. The plain monks' homes

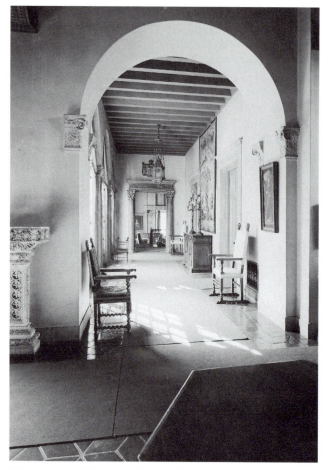

The drama of Spanish Revival interiors. Courtesy of the Library of Congress.

were indigenous Native American built adobe, stuccoed white. Rustic adobe was complemented by Baroque decoration, imported or copied from Spain. Furniture was almost painfully plain, reflecting the monks' denial of the feelings of the flesh.

Numerous excellent Spanish Colonial Revival homes of the early modern period can be found today in Los Angeles, Santa Monica, Pasadena, and San Marino, California, much of the best by revivalist designer Wallace Neff. Also in southern California, Spanish architecture prevailed in Santa Barbara, San Juan Capistrano, Monterey, and many mission towns, where original historical Spanish settlements have been preserved, to which early modern architects added revival homes. Similarly Santa Fe and Albuquerque, New Mexico; Tucson, Arizona; and San Antonio, Texas, were also noted for authentic Spanish Mission and Pueblo decoration as well as for revivals. In Florida, Spanish Colonial Revival modern houses were prevalent in Miami's old sections of Coral Gables and Coconut Grove, and Palm Beach has always been rich in Spanish Colonial Revival homes. The old towns from which Spanish-influenced modernists drew their motifs were extant in the New World in St. Augustine, Florida, and Old San Juan, Puerto Rico, the oldest cities in America, founded in the seventeenth century by Spain.

Homes, Horses, and Hospitality: Spanish Revival Decoration Today

California architects and decorators of the early modern architectural era traveled and seriously studied Spanish motifs and the integration of architecture with landscape features. Sadly today's mission revival developments may have taken visual inspiration from the monasteries along El Camino Real, but not the spirit or serious intent of these ancient buildings to heart. Current "mission" malls, often lining a highway strip that is no Camino Real, create the danger of diluting the authentic meaning and motifs of Spanish architecture. Pretentious and misappropriated motifs and the excessive size of homes (and certainly this is true for all the "traditional" suburban house styles about

America) are driving out good simple, ecologically sound homes and paving the natural woodland and desert landscapes.

Fortunately, authentic traces of an environment of adobe homes and roping horses expressive of the American West can still be found in Arizona in some of the last remaining early twentieth-century dude ranches: the Westward Look Resort (Tucson, 1912) and the Kay El Bar Historic Guest Ranch (Wickenburg, 1926)—well preserved, living American artifacts, each of which began as a private ranch home. In the early twentieth century, when passenger trains still ran cross-country, the American institution of the dude ranch introduced many easterners to western ways, open skies and Pueblo-styled homes. The oldest domestic buildings of these current tourist spots continue the hominess of a giant adobe fireplace with its mesquite aroma, amid ceilings of vigas and walls of Navaho rugs.

Among the most sophisticated guests to indulge his love of the American West by roping a dawgie was émigré architect Walter Gropius, founder of the Bauhaus, the influential German modern design academy. He was also a horseman and formerly a German cavalry officer who loved American western stories and films. Surely Gropius would have found the simplicity of American desert architecture, resort furnishings, functional objects, and abstract Native American motifs complementary to his European modernist roots and Bauhaus design forms (Beate Gropius, daughter of Walter Gropius, personal interview with the author, 1986).

EMERGING MODERNISM IN HOME DECORATION

"Exotic" Influences in the Early Modern Decorative Arts

Progressive architects and interior designers of the early modern architectural period looked for new sources of inspiration in the decorative arts. Nonwestern visual arts, in particular, interested the more avant-garde designers, particularly artists of the international Art Nouveau movement. Mediterranean and Asian motifs were considered exotic in early modern America. These smotifs were often employed in a highly sophisticated abstract, as opposed to literally copied, fashion by forward-looking creative designers. Modern architects Wright and Greene and Greene, and modern designer Tiffany, were strongly influenced by the Japanese house with its flat, apparently lightweight construction, and by the Japanese interiors of simple, hand-notched wooden construction and translucent shoji screens. Japanese prints were fashionable among early modern artists and designers for their recollection of nature, for their flat abstraction, and for their intense use of primary colors. All of these Asian influences came together with the English Arts and Crafts style to move American aesthetics toward greater simplicity and sophistication during 1901–1920.

> **Tiffany Design and Decorative Arts**
>
> The word "Tiffany" has always had a distinctive ring to it in America, for it embodies the fantasies of high living in grand mansions or glass houses. The Tiffany name has long associations with jewelry and the decorative arts, in particular with art glass. This name can be confusing, however, for it is part of a family tradition, of which Tiffany, the father, was the jeweler, and Tiffany, the son, was the designer of decorative objects. The name has also been part of various design business ventures in gems and glass, including Tiffany & Company, Tiffany Glass Company, Tiffany Studios, and Tiffany Furnaces.
>
> Louis Comfort Tiffany, the son, was the designer of luxury decorative arts, including the uniquely iridescent colors of Tiffany favrile glass popular

(continued)

in the early twentieth-century home. His patterns were sinuous and stylized, often drawn from nature, including colored glass representations of wisteria, lilies, and dragonflies. Tiffany balanced nature with modern abstraction, as well as function with decoration. Avant-garde, well traveled, and of great repute during the early modern era, Lewis Comfort Tiffany brought a new level of international sophistication to American design, introducing the exotica of the modern French Art Nouveau, as well as the ancient forms of Islamic motifs and Japanese aesthetic influences, to New York. Tiffany stained glass windows, lamps, and iridescent colored glass art objects were prized during this period in homes for the wealthy, as well as in the private, modern yet antiquated, estate retreat Tiffany built for himself in 1902 on Long Island Sound, Laurelton Hall, in Cold Spring Harbor, New York. Like Tiffany Furnaces, Laurelton Hall burned brightly for a time and then actually burned to the ground. The decorative arts of Louis Comfort Tiffany, and the design of his own home, illustrate that the gifts of old fashioned indulgence can be beautifully rewrapped in a modern, avant-garde package.

Tiffany Decoration and Laurelton Hall, the Tiffany Home

Tiffany glass and objects of art had an affinity to Arts and Crafts, as well as Asian influences, that dictated the design of decorative objects with forms in flat, sinuous lines, rich textures, and luminescent surfaces. Tiffany objects were considered excellent examples of the great early modern architectural era's visual advance away from the Victorian era and the excesses of the Gilded Age toward modern, but high end, simplicity in decoration—simplified, yet luxurious and exotic. One might consider Louis Comfort Tiffany's own home, Laurelton Hall, as partially recreated at the Metropolitan Museum of Art New York in a temporary exhibition (Louis Comfort Tiffany and Laurelton Hall, 2007), as well as permanently installed within the American Wing of the Metropolitan, to be the quintessential example of the fully integrated early modern, avant-garde upper-crust home, synthesizing architecture, interior design, and objects of art, furniture, and landscape into a unique, rather bohemian, masterpiece. This quixotic Long Island estate home burned to the ground, though within the museum setting at the Metropolitan's American Wing, one can again observe Tiffany's European and Asian-influenced architectural columns and pergolas, wall fountains, furnishings, pottery and metal work, and especially the famous Tiffany glass, in a rich home-like setting illustrative of an extinct early modern architectural era.

The Influence of the European Arts and Crafts Movement on American Design

The apparent contradiction of the modern machine with ancient handcraft had become a major conundrum of the early modern architectural period, particularly for architects and designers with a theoretical bent. The British Arts and Crafts movement of the late nineteenth century was a reaction to the decline of furniture design and decorative arts during the Industrial Revolution, as the machine cranked out tasteless English Victorian excesses: massive, irrationally laid-out Victorian houses; fussy furniture with machine-stamped imitations of hand-carved ornament; garish painted gilt pottery; carpets with ugly cabbage roses galore; and a general vulgarity of style. William Morris (1834–1896), aesthetic reformer and founder of the Arts and Crafts movement in England, was appalled by the effects of the machine and machine reproduction on the general level of taste and life

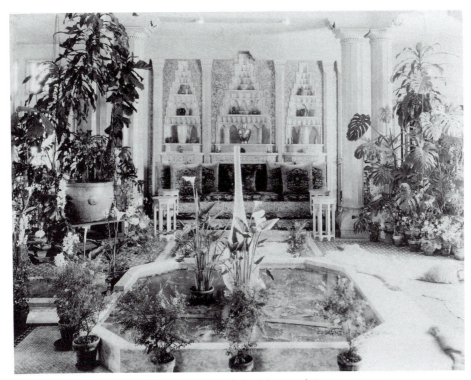

Breakfast at Tiffany's house. Courtesy of the Library of Congress.

in England and set out to reform design. From his famous Red House at Bexley Heath, Morris led the progressive design movement that initiated international advances in the next generation of reform-minded English and American designers, including Gustav Stickley. His approach, later appropriated by Stickley, was to form a group of handcrafters and woodworkers into a kind of post-medieval guild. This attitude was actually retrograde, for it denied the realities of the modern world, looking back nostalgically to a mythic past. Stickley's adherence to handcraft was both his strength and his undoing. Craftsman style of the early twentieth-century America, although appearing totally indigenous and modern, had its origins in late nineteenth-century European utopian design reform movements.

"Arts and Crafts" Versus "Craftsman"

The theory of the British Arts and Crafts movement was the foundation from which all simplified European and American styles of the early modern era were derived, including the German Werkbund, the Wiener Werkstatte, and especially the American Craftsman style. British founder William Morris, and American exponent Gustav Stickley, advanced similar ideals of hand work: exquisite craftsmanship, simplification of design, anti-Victorian decorative styles, and anti-industrial beliefs.

The similar and overlapping terms, Arts and Crafts versus Craftsman, tend to agree with the generalizations we make, right or wrong, almost unconsciously about the English character versus the American, and Americans have suffered for the comparison. British melodramas are suitable for educational "telly"; American TV is sponsored by car commercials. British Arts and Crafts writer Morris was intellectual and theoretical; American Craftsman publisher Stickley was pragmatic and commercial.

(continued)

The British Arts and Crafts movement was somewhat upper class-oriented; American Craftsman was a very middle-class style. British Arts and Crafts objects and furniture had finesse and detail; American Craftsman furniture was blunt and straightforward in comparison. British Arts and Crafts architecture produced the suave lines of modern medieval manors by Voysey; the landmark modern home of the American Craftsman style was a rough-hewn Stickley log cabin bungalow in New Jersey. The British style encompasses the "arts"; the American style omits the word, if not the concept.

Early Modern Design Theory and Debates

Theoretical denial of the physical realities of the machine could not be supported for long, however, for design debates, such as those of the Deutsche Werkbund, followed all over Europe in the early twentieth century. It was in those debates that the idea that handcraft must be the master of the machine were developed. The consensus of modernism would be that the designer's contribution was in creating *prototypes*, or originals, replicable designs for the machine, and this would become the basis of the Bauhaus, as movements such as Stickley's declined. Recognition of the European and American roles in design reform can be traced through Sir Nicolas Pevsner's seminal text, *Pioneers of Modern Design*, from William Morris to Walter Gropius. In a more aesthetically sophisticated but perhaps less utopian manner than Stickley, American architects Greene and Greene and Frank Lloyd Wright, extending Arts and Crafts principles into modernism, would also grapple with the problems of the Arts and Crafts in their progressive home and interior designs of 1901–1920.

Craftsman Style Home Decoration

Simplicity of form and solidity of materials were the hallmarks of Craftsman interiors and furnishings. This home decoration, though seemingly simple, was complex in theory and metaphor, for it represented a wholly new way of thinking in early twentieth-century America, a visual protomodern motif reflecting a new approach to home and to life as lived in the home. The interior forms of the Craftsman home décor and furniture reflected the simple rectilinear exterior of Craftsman style proponent Gustav Stickley's architecture. Craftsman style can be found from the macro scale of the house to the micro scale of the easy chair and dining fork, and further, his style was integrated beyond the confines of the house out into the flowering Craftsman garden (Stickley 1906).

Simplified ornament was an integral part of Craftsman architecture, reflecting the honesty of the house construction and function. Often, flat plaster walls were articulated with wooden beams and linear wooden ornament. A living room ceiling displayed crossbeams, a dining room its functional chair rail as ornament, and the china collection within the attached glass and wooden cabinets. These cabinets would be built-in, for Craftsman interiors were rich in built-in furnishings of beauty and function. Paneling, cabinetry, bookshelves, window seats, and fireplace mantels defined the interior space of the Craftsman home, and to some extent, so, too, did the arrangement of the presence of the very heavy wooden Craftsman furniture define interior space. Most important of all, perhaps, was the use of the inglenook, a pleasantly confined space for cozy, informal sitting. The hearth, in brick or stone, was the physical and emotional center of the Craftsman home. Interior plans of Craftsman homes showed common sense and a process of simplifying applied to homes.

Logic was consistently applied to the Craftsman home, in specifics such as the placement of windows and doors. For example, Craftsman homes were designed with fewer disparate hallways, rooms, and doorways, instead making simple interior spaces flow into one another through arched openings. The front door never opened directly into the house, always into the only important hallway, the front hall, to provide an air lock to keep cold winter drafts at bay in the rest of the house. Windows, on the other hand, are usually placed in opposition to each other to allow cross-ventilation and healthful breezes to flow through the house. Though such concepts may seem obvious today, it is always important to note the historical context of Craftsman homes and interiors: These designs were being created in a world ruled by the excesses of Victorian architecture and its stiflingly over-elaborated interiors. Thus, quite literally, the simple, well-ventilated Craftsman home was a breath of fresh air.

The Meaning of Mission Style

The common name of simplified wooden furniture of the early modern architectural era, Mission, was most likely derived from the simple wooden furniture of the Franciscan missionaries, though some sources argue rightly that Stickley himself was on a reform mission. A very similar confusion will later arise concerning the origins of the name Parson's table: Is it named after a person, a pastor, or a design school? Strongly influenced by Stickley's design principles were other protomodern furniture companies who called, and still call, their furniture Mission, Craftsman, or Bungalow style. The many early twentieth-century furniture manufacturers calling their furniture Mission style had certain things in common: solid oak materials, preferably quarter sawn and fumed to display the grain; natural, mostly unpainted wood finishes; simplicity and function; rectilinear design; and often with an appeal to economy, though not always. Mission furniture became trendy from 1901–1920, but the middle-class fad was fading toward the end of this period, for although this furniture was strong, durable, democratic, and of excellent design, in multiples it could become rather boring and lugubrious; the 1920s were looking for something less didactic and just more fun.

Craftsman Furniture

The simplified home of 1901–1920 demanded simplified furniture. Solid wood complemented with leather detailing was the predominant material, cut into straight lines intersecting at right angles, making for very rectilinear pieces. Little or no complicated ornament was applied to Craftsman furniture. The integrity of the simple design and the beauty of the wood itself were the ornament. This was well-built furniture, a great deal of which has lasted in excellent and useable condition into the twenty-first century and is now enjoying a new appreciation. Though one might appreciate these works for their abstract sculptural qualities, it is probably most popular simply because it fits well into so many styles of American homes. Simple and sophisticated, old-fashioned and protomodern, Craftsman furnishings are very American because they reflect the straightforward character of this country. Though certainly English Arts and Crafts influenced, this wooden furniture is also expressive of the American forest.

Stickley furniture extended the rectilinearity of the Craftsman room and, therefore, was successful as pieces that needed to be strong, rigid, and geometric, for example, bookcases, desks, dining room china cabinets, dining tables (though not necessarily its chairs), table lamps, wall sconces, and library tables. Mission furniture was not as successful in holding the human form, and this design problem would persist into the work of many modern architects of the early twentieth century, though the ideas of ergonomics, or human comfort design, had yet to be invented. Craftsman chairs and settees were exceedingly upright and hard surfaced, rather unsuited to human motion or repose. The ever-popular though ugly Morris chair, unfortunate precursor to the living room recliner and perhaps ironically named with William Morris in mind, was in truth one of the most Victorian, retrograde pieces in the mission furniture oeuvre. Just because mission furniture was plain, planer, and moralizing does not imply that it was all equally inventive or attractive.

Craftsman Furniture by Ellis

Fortunately, as a simple woodworker by training who grew up to be the leading furniture maker of the era, Stickley understood his own limits and smartly hired a better designer than himself in 1903, architect Harvey Ellis (1852–1904). The few but distinctive pieces of Stickley furniture designed by Ellis in 1903–1904 were the finest and most creative of the entire Stickley line of 1901–1909. To the Stickley simplicity and functionality of design, Ellis added fine linear wood inlay and gracefully cut curves in modern, almost Asian, motifs. Like its architectural setting in a Craftsman home, Stickley furniture was frank, direct, and honest in its expression of its function and materials, but architect Ellis raised furniture to the level of art through simple transformations of Stickley's more primitive style. It is helpful to recall that unlike more educated architects and designers of his time, Gustav Stickley actually worked with his hands, primarily as a woodworker, and had grown up within the tradition of labor, for his father was a stone mason (Stickley, 1906). Though less sophisticated than some figures of his era, Stickley had to work harder for his success and, ultimately, his failures. The lasting consistency of his work, and its current revival in popularity, are a tribute to one man's utopian vision.

Stickley Furniture Imitators

It was ironic that Stickley was undone by his own imitators, some of whom even advertised in Stickley's own magazine. These manufacturers cheapened Stickley's original democratizing theories and compositions and sold them to the public at lower prices. The contradiction of economic necessity with craftsmanship was both Stickley's strength and his financial undoing. He was on a mission to improve the modern home, but he also wanted to live comfortably off his mission. One notes that even as an idealistic leader of a reformed design flock, Stickley always intended to make a buck off his wares. He was also a businessman, and he sold his vision to the public in a showroom just off 5th Avenue. The public is still buying, collecting, and living his vision a century later. His competitors, however, lowered overhead by omitting the shop and selling mail order. Just as some entire homes were sold via mail order, furniture for these homes could also be available in catalogues. One of the most convenient was the Come-Packt Furniture Company (Linoff 1991), which sold its line of Mission furniture unconstructed, ready to be assembled with screws. The homeowner would receive a compact package by rail to save shipping costs, thereby making modern furniture affordable all over the country. The very simplicity of Stickley's own design vision, easily copied by others, ultimately put his business in jeopardy and closed his New York City showroom. Stickley was so clear on his concept of the fully integrated life that he had reached far in his enterprises. Unlike his imitators with their appropriated designs and simplistic mail-order catalogs, he published a journal of essays on Craftsman style and meaning, including not only his house drawings and plans, but design suggestions for accompanying furniture and landscape.

Craftsman Contradictions

Contradictory ideals were typical for Stickley, as for many early modern aesthetic theorists of the Arts and Crafts bent who tried to live in two ages at once, the handcrafted medieval period and the modern Machine Age. This led to essential conflicts within Stickley's encompassing vision. Stickley's search for artistic truthfulness, as found in rustic American hand-made craft, was a characteristic he shared with many early modern designers and architects. Although Stickley's concepts of the holistic life, including subsistence farming coupled with communal life and furniture making, was a short-lived experiment, it has had a long lasting aesthetic influence on American interior design. More modern architects and furniture designers, particularly Greene and Greene and Frank Lloyd Wright, shared his integrated Arts and Crafts visions. Although Stickley is recognized as the founder of the American Craftsman style, its finest aesthetic equivalents are to be found in the joinery of Greene and Greene and the furniture of Frank Lloyd Wright.

MODERN FURNITURE AND DECORATION

The Furniture of Frank Lloyd Wright

While Wright's Prairie style furniture made beautiful abstract sculpture, it was not furniture as we usually define it. Because Wrightian architecture and interior spaces were so low-ceilinged and strongly horizontal, the upright furniture articulated a critical interior vertical element. Furniture was visually a solid opposition to the cubic space of the room. Chairs, tables, and rugs defined and subdivided space. His furniture was certainly not an ergonometric extension of the human body, for as women in corsets in 1900 knew, design unsympathetic to the human body can feel aesthetically arrogant to the user. Wright or wrong or upright, Prairie furniture made a strong statement. Wright was so powerful an architect at this time as to demand a kind of fealty from his clients, which they gave him. He expected clients not only to employ him, but to continue to live a total Wrightian life long after his work was finished and not to move the furniture about willy-nilly. Wright as a designer has long inspired a cult-like adherence to his Wrightian look, and to some extent this pervasive feeling has obfuscated the actual beauty of his vision. It is interesting to note that late in life, Wright commented that the chair was a meaningless object, for he felt that the human was only meant to assume the upright or the reclining position. Sitting was not a human practice. Well, no, not in a Wright chair. One wonders in retrospect, however, whether Wright's complete plans of *organic* architecture meant "to grow naturally from the site" were drawn while he was standing upright or lying down.

Wright's spreading Prairie homes, for which the most important of his furniture was created, were built during the decade of 1889–1909. One notes how modern these homes were for the time, and would still be today, when seeing that women within his Prairie houses were still wearing ankle-length black dresses with bustles. Thus, Wright no doubt understood that his clean-lined vision would be threatened if clients were to install their former retrograde furnishings within his new architecture, and therefore he dictated not only the design of the cabinets, breakfronts, chairs, tables, benches, beds, lamps, and chandeliers, but carpets and all internal fixtures, as well as the permanent placement of the furniture and fixtures he had designed for the site.

Wright's chairs were, like mission furniture of the time, solid hardwood, and they were exceedingly upright, with closed or slatted back, some high backed, some low, some barrel shaped (Heinz 2000). His furniture was consciously arranged within his architectural spaces. From domestic architecture, to stained glass windows, to dining table and chairs, to forks, he had an all-encompassing vision of the home, and his furniture was as modern as his forward-looking Prairie houses. Thus, high-backed, upright dining chairs arranged symmetrically about a dining table defined the interior cube of the room as if they themselves were partial walls confining the table. Though Wright wrote about the importance of the family within the home, the image his furniture projects to

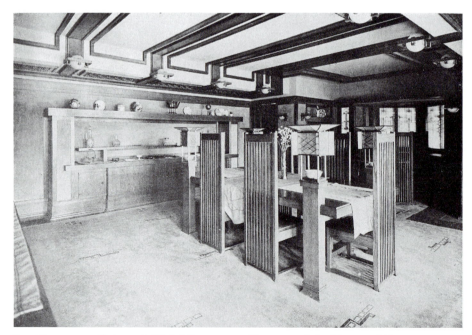

Furniture as sculpture. A Wrightian room. Courtesy of the Library of Congress.

us now seems not one of loving family and children relaxing together about an evening meal, but of strangers in a restaurant assuming rigidly correct posture and silence over a 10-course dinner. The simple geometry and hierarchy in Wright's furniture forms, however, may have seemed more modern and free in their day when compared to the overwrought and oppressive interiors of Victorian homes.

To appreciate Wright's furniture, one has to keep in mind both aesthetics and the milieu. These works were aesthetically revolutionary for their early modern day. Wright's emphasis and intention was not only to seat, but to define space aesthetically. It was not meant only for domestic relaxation, but to stimulate visual acumen through the environment of the early modern home. The chair was not meant to be appreciated as an object alone, though it would be a beautiful thing even alone, but as part of an overall design concept of the total home environment.

Furniture as Museum Object

Modern furniture has now become classical. One expects to see these works not as a place to sit, but as an object to contemplate, and thus, ironically, Wright's derision of the sitting position has come to fruition in the museum. The most important design collections, including the Museum of Modern Art and the American Wing of the Metropolitan Museum of Art in New York, display Frank Lloyd Wright furniture, as well as other American designers, including Louis Comfort Tiffany, and Greene and Greene, of the early modern architectural era. A series of modern rooms can be found among the traditional decor of the Huntington Library, Museum, and Botanical Gardens, where the interiors and furnishings of Greene and Greene have been recreated within a model of a California home, near Pasadena, where their Gamble House is located. Greene and Greene and Wright were truly original and involved in the new concept of total design, very early modernists internationally, designing complete environments for their clients' home lives.

Early modern American visions and styles were likely precedents and complements of German and Austrian concepts of total architecture. Forms and theories of the Werkbund, the Bauhaus, and the Wiener Werkstadt shared aesthetic ideals with these designers and anticipated modern design movements such as French Cubism and Dutch De Stijl. As object of art, the furniture of Frank Lloyd Wright was dramatic, revolutionary and influential, for here was the chair as abstract object in space, rectilinear, geometric, and beautiful. The reader may encounter these rare chairs not only in their native Prairie habitat, but also in captivity in museums.

Reference List

"The Harmonious Home." 1920. *Chicago Tribune,* weekly column.

Heinz, Thomas A. 2000. *Furniture of Frank Lloyd Wright.* Salt Lake City, UT: Peregrine Press (color illustrations).

Linoff, Victor, ed. 1991. *Illustrated Mission Furniture Catalog 1912–13, Come-Packt Furniture Company.* New York: Dover (catalog illustrations).

Stickley, Gustav. 1906. "The Craftsman House: A Practical Application of Our Theories of Home Building." Reprinted in *The Best of Craftsman Homes*. Santa Barbara, Peregrine Smith, Inc., 1979, 67–71.

Tiffany, Louis Comfort, and Laurelton Hall. 2007. *An Artist's Country Estate*. Metropolitan Museum of Art, New York. Exhibition, November 21, 2006–May 20, 2007.

Landscaping and Outbuildings

OUTBUILDINGS

Outbuildings for Necessity and Labor

As the early modern architectural era moved toward simplification, the parts of the home were integrated and drawn together. There were more simplified, more hygienic homes for more classes of people as the country's economy democratized after the introduction of income tax in 1913. Home simplification and streamlining implied a slow disappearance of the many outbuildings of the past, as the self-sufficient, multibuilding small bungalow or attached-barn farm home was replaced with the suburban dwelling, as a changing world meant a changing home and incorporation of its subsidiary buildings. Homes were advancing, though sporadically and interrupted by war and economics, slowly toward the concept of the more compact machine for living in as French architect Le Corbusier would later christen the modern home of the 1920s.

Indoor plumbing plants, heat, and electricity, as well as access to streetcar and the new automobile, changed the physical structures of modern life markedly from 1901–1920. The physical plant of the home had not been so modern since Roman engineering ran the world. For example, hygienic indoor plumbing eliminated the need for the most infamous of all outbuildings: the rural outhouse or the inner city slum privy, as well as the public urban bathhouse. Public water supply and sewers meant that well houses would disappear as the individually drilled home well would be capped off. Rain barrels, too, disappeared from the home with a regular supply of running water. Central heating added the coal bin to the basement, but eliminated the woodshed. Electric

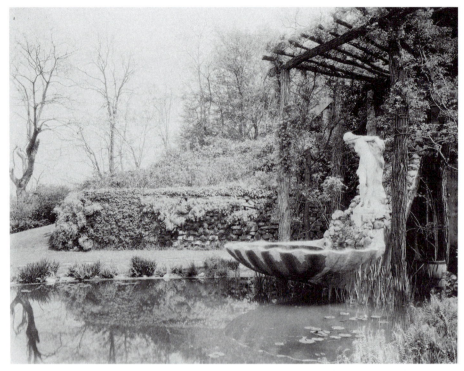

Modernism meets antiquity: A grotto landscape. Courtesy of the Library of Congress.

kitchen appliances, especially the refrigerator, replaced the icehouse, the chicken coop, the vegetable cellar, the dumb waiter, and the summer kitchen. As horsepower replaced the horse, the garage replaced the porte-cochere, the stable, and the livery.

As the country urbanized and suburbanized, fewer homes had need of a barn, and this once necessary outbuilding became a picturesque anachronism in America by the mid-twentieth century as its stone walled fields in Vermont and Connecticut went fallow. In cities, as urban symbols such as water towers atop tenements, outdoor latrines, back alleys, and gas lamps disappeared, utility poles with multiple lines of electric overhead wiring and electric lamps appeared, as well as elevated trolley tracks above avenues, changing the streetscape of early modern cities. Outbuildings decreased in number about the home from 1901–1920, but simultaneously, new technology begat new urban structures during the early modern architectural period.

Outbuildings for Leisure and Sport

Increasing income and suburbanization meant that the upper- and middle-class American home could begin to add some leisure and the structures built exclusively for leisure. Observing the decline in outbuildings for necessity and labor, versus the increase in structures for sport and leisure, one can note economic and social mobility in America of 1901–1920. Thus, with rising income for more Americans came the advent of new outbuildings: terraces, ornamental iron fences, arbors, gazebos, pergolas, boat houses, green houses, glass conservatories, garden sculpture and follies for the rich, and porches with screens for the middle class.

Swimming pools with cabanas and tennis courts were enjoyed as early as 1901 on country estates, but by the middle of the early modern architectural era, such luxuries were becoming rare but possible amenities for some suburban homeowners. The *Chicago Tribune* in 1910 bragged that swimming pools in glossy lawns were disarming summer's heat and that the fine crop of swimming pools burst forth on lawns and terraces and in courtyards. Swimming, tennis, golf, and boating were popular for the white flannel pants and white bucks-attired leisure of the upper class, and members-only golf courses and country clubs with 18-hole courses became popular leisure landscapes with extensive outbuildings for sport in the first decades of the twentieth century. The Country Club in Brookline, Massachusetts, where the Masters has been played, was established by this time, as well as dozens of private membership golf clubs. A number of 9-hole private golf courses on estates, such as the Rockefeller's private course in Pocantico Hills, Westchester, New York, were a private luxury. A golf course was actually an extravagant use of land in the early modern architectural era, a major display of land wealth, upon whose manicured grass a great deal of time and nutrients have been expended in America.

Horses upgraded their social class, from workers to leisure class, during the early modern architectural era. Horseback riding became a sport of the rich, and stables, picturesque outbuildings finished outside in shingles and inside in polished board and batten wood paneling, gave horses on East Coast estates better quarters than most Americans. It is said that Teddy Roosevelt housed both his horse and his manservant nearby when he arrived at Harvard. Irish immigrants were a great boon to the horse world, for they knew the animals. Jumping rings, white fences, and green paddocks defined a leisurely lifestyle. Bridle paths crossed blithely through private land, and red-coated fox hunters rode to hounds, unhounded about their private sport well into the 1950s. Bridle path trails connected the great estates of Long Island until the open tracts of land were subdivided into mid-century suburbs. Sadly, coincidental with the writing of this book, the last public livery stable in Manhattan, renting horses for riding the trails of Central Park, has closed, and as the horse trots further off the American landscape, we are diminished by the loss of its beauty and majesty.

Playhouses

Perhaps the most amazing outbuilding of this era was the hand-built playhouse for upper-crust children. The great estates included classy quarters for playing house that exceeded the full-sized homes that most people were living in. One wonders if pretend servants' quarters and sculleries were included in the playhouse plans. There were the beautiful precedents of historical playhouses in Newport, Rhode Island, on the Vanderbilt property of the Breakers, and in Tarrytown, New York, at Lyndhurst, as well as an expansive early modern era playhouse at the Rockefeller's Kykuit. The Coonley Playhouse (1908, River Forest, Illinois), however, a product of a modern-day fantasy, a sophisticated modern child's place adjoining the home's private swimming pool, was a Frank Lloyd Wright designed architectural indulgence if ever there was one. Wright also designed the somewhat more public River Forest Tennis Club (1906) in suburban Chicago, a contemporary of the Forest Hills Tennis Club in suburban New York. Members-only country clubs, perhaps a kind of pretend place for adults, were the social rage among homeowners in the developing upper middle-class suburbs, emulating the exclusivity and prejudices of the pre-income tax robber baron leisure class who had preceded them.

Front Yard, Back Yard: Display Versus Play

The individual, single family home was affected by the concept of landscape. The front yard became the place for a visual landscape display to the neighborhood, as well as a necessary buffer from the street, particularly as the automobile made inroads into the suburb. The rear yard, which had once been the place only for ash cans, hanging laundry, and a family vegetable garden, began to be seen as a private place for calm enjoyment. Adirondack chairs were placed under the back elm, and lemonade saturated with sugar was squeezed, bringing family, friends, and mosquitoes together in a great American tradition. With the American invention of the lot as outdoor room, the home was expanded, and the suburban landscape was transformed into a new kind of outbuilding to the American home. Thus, the present American suburban front yard and back yard dichotomy of display versus play began in the early modern architectural era.

The Importance of Public Playgrounds

Sadly, the street from 1901–1920 was becoming a place more for cars and less for friends, and hoops and stickball. Simultaneously though, children were just beginning to be acknowledged as real persons who would benefit from and enjoy the revolutionary concept of outdoor backyard play. The first convention of the National Playground Association met in 1907 in an attempt to advance a national playground movement. Urbanization, industrialization, and the rise of the automobile, then as now, had made land for childhood games forever inaccessible to disenfranchised classes of children whose homes were the tenements and slums of the early twentieth-century city. The most socially constructive and empathic use of landscape in the early modern architectural era was the emerging concept of the urban public playground for children. As a humane society, we must continue this work and now employ our land use and social policies to rectify this injustice by reintroducing the simple concept of outdoor play to the school day, school yard, and back yards of our homes, and by making creative, active, and safe public play space for all classes of children a priority in our landscape.

THE LANDSCAPE

The Meaning of Landscape in the Early Modern Era

Important integrated relationships between architecture and landscape, as well as between landscape and human welfare, were developing in the early modern architectural era. The great American homes of 1901–1920, and even the not so great homes, demanded great American landscapes. Land has traditionally, since feudal days, represented wealth, and land is no doubt called *real* estate because it is tangible wealth. As Beaux-Arts city mansions and country estates were enhanced with sculptured Italian gardens, formal French parterres and allées, and rolling English lawns, America acquired its most sophisticated private landscapes before 1913, when money was untaxed and immigrant gardeners, particularly Italian workers who were trained in formal landscaping, were unfairly low paid and readily available.

The permanent philanthropic contributions of these great estates came later in the century when these landscapes were opened to the public. Private gardens and arboretums, where native and rare plants and trees flourish, such as the Coe Estate, Planting Fields on Long Island, and Wave Hill in Riverdale, both in suburban New York, preserved massive tracts of land and dramatic vistas that are now open for public enjoyment. It would be virtually impossible to evolve the mature landscapes of Long Island, the Hudson River, and Connecticut now, had they not already been created in the early modern architectural era. There exists a difficult ambiguity in American gardens and landscape, for historically, the great estates represented a harshly class-divided society; however, today we can thank the legacies of the early modernists for creating and preserving many of our most dramatic landscapes and parks.

Heavily urbanized cities particularly felt the need for parks and playgrounds, not only for pleasure but for health and welfare, as well. Bridgeport, Connecticut's Beardsley Park, and City Park, Denver, Colorado (1917) are good examples of such parks as urban escape. Landscape amenities afforded cities better access to clean air and clean water; there was even a dairy in Central Park supplying fresh

American Landscape Painting and Photography

The sublime qualities of the American landscape, the wilderness of the West in particular, were brought to eastern Americans first and most vividly via the dramatic landscape paintings of masters such as Edwin Church (1826–1900), Thomas Moran (1837–1926), and Albert Bierstadt (1830–1902), long before tourism and photography made great parts of the country visible or accessible. Important American landscape painters, who still lived and exhibited widely during the early modern architectural era, displayed the heretofore unknown western scenery of the Rocky Mountains, Yosemite, Yellowstone, the Grand Canyon, and Monument Valley to enthralled audiences. The Hudson River, too, in the eastern wilderness had held a nostalgic place in art since the 1800s, providing the subject matter of some of the classical works in the America oeuvre, and many late nineteenth-century and early twentieth-century Americans were moved by the displays of Frederick Church's painted panoramas of Niagara Falls. Church first began painting in the eastern wilderness, eventually moving from Niagara on to the spaces of the West. Thomas Moran painted western landscapes in Yellowstone, and Bierstadt, with his European influence, was drawn to the dramatic sites of Yosemite and participated in early expeditions to the West. Bridal View Falls in Yosemite provided much inspiration to these painters, and Yellowstone even has a colorful canyon site appropriately named Artist Point. The great landscape paintings brought the dramatic meaning of wilderness to the American public in the early modern architectural era, thus encouraging the salvation and preservation of American landscape.

By the early modern architectural era, tourism and photography together entered the American landscape scene. In the Grand Canyon, architect Mary Colter designed an isolated but functional photography studio, with Native American decorative motifs, on the very edge of the south rim, to produce personal mementos of travel for visitors. Though it is difficult today to reach the National Parks, in 1901–1920 it was a major trek to such places, and travelers were eager to document their presence at the great American geologic sites. The wealthy Scripps family, for example, took a month off, traveling from San Diego by train and horse-drawn station wagon to arrive at the Grand Canyon, where they were suitably photographed on a mule

(continued)

train above the great expanse of the canyon. Americans as well as Europeans fortunate enough to experience it in 1901–1920 were awed by our landscape. One might attribute to the landscape painters and the early travel photographers the American public's first grasp of our own almost infinite spaces.

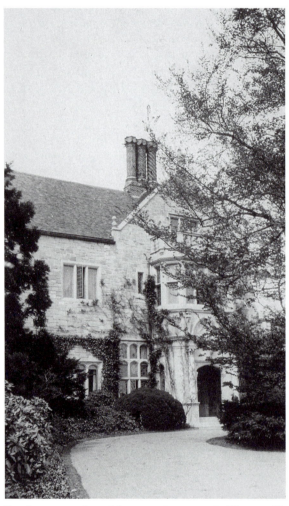

Landscape and architecture integrated: The traditional estate of the early modern era. Planting Fields, Oyster Bay, New York. Courtesy of the Francis Loeb Library, Harvard Graduate School of Design.

milk to the city's tenement-dwelling children at this time. Nature was synonymous with beauty, but also with public health. Landscape was a balm for urban wounds. Newly planned suburban developments ringing the city, in the Bronx and Queens, and in Westchester County, Nassau County, and western Connecticut, brought architecture into contact with landscape to create a modern, middle-class environment of health and comfort accessible by commuter rail. Planned suburban developments, such as Forest Hills and Sunnyside, Queens, included treed interior courtyards and walkways between apartment houses in New York. As the middle class began to advance above economic parity, they had the ability to enhance their homes with some plantings, making life at home more palatable.

Middle-class homeowners now understood that trees and shrubs enhanced their Traditional style houses and grounded a home in a tiny taste of nature. Previously, landscape had been relegated to gardening and flowers and left politely to the ladies of the upper class. A number of women, however, had always been committed to nature, had greatly advanced the appreciation of the humane qualities of the garden, and were not abashed to be moved by the beauty of trees and flowers (Griswold and Weller 2000). Such important early garden aficionados as writers Gertrude Jekyll (British) and Beatrix Farrar (American) (1872–1959) had drawn attention to the importance of the soothing space of landscape, not just to counteract the city, but to surround the suburban home in blooms. Designs and landscape journals became more significant and structured as the century and the suburban home progressed, and the Garden Clubs of America, founded by Helena Rutherford Ely (1858–1920), promoted an appreciation of gardening among women.

The growing American sense of the personal and public importance of open space and plantings coincided with the democratization of housing and the professionalizing of modern landscape architecture during 1901–1920, resulting in the founding of the American Society of Landscape Architects. Some landscape architects associated with the early modern architectural era include: Guy Lowell (1870–1927), who created Planting Fields; Arthur Shurcliff (1870–1957), designer of the Williamsburg, Virginia, restoration; Kate Sessions (1857–1940), who designed landscapes for the cubic modernism of Irving Gill in San Diego; and Fletcher Steele (1885–1971), who would take modern abstraction into landscape in Naumbkeag, Stockbridge, Massachusetts, later in the 1930s (Birnbaum, FASLA, and Larson 2000). There was consensus in the early modern architectural era, based on the theories and designs of early landscape architects Frederick Law Olmsted, Calvert Vaux, naturalist John Muir, and architect and president Thomas Jefferson, that nature enhanced health, welfare, and psychological peace though its beauty.

ESTATE LANDSCAPES IN EARLY TWENTIETH-CENTURY AMERICA

Country Estates as Formal Extensions of the Beaux-Arts

Just as the Beaux-Arts in architecture dictated a formal plan of axial arrangement of rooms in sequence, so, too, did Beaux-Arts landscape architecture dictate an axial arrangement of garden spaces. These spaces, or parterres, and rows of trees, or allées, culminated in sculpture or scenic vistas. This style exhibited not only manicured formality, but was composed of highly structured, geometric spaces, very flat, creating visual vistas toward a distant view, a garden folly, or a sculpture. Sculpture within this Classical style was, of course, Greco-Roman or a copy of such. Beaux-Arts landscape brought a feeling for antiquity and the Renaissance to the American "aristocracy." One could look, just as the Medici had, from one's drawing room outward into a fully designed landscape of terraces, balustrades, clipped grass, water features and fountains, sculpture, gravel paths, green linear plantings, and flowering roses.

Excellent examples of Beaux-Arts landscapes of 1901–1920 can be visited all about America today. Many of the first and finest can be seen in the estate areas of New York's Long Island and Hudson River Valley, in Connecticut, and Washington, D.C. The prime New York examples are Kykuit, the Rockefeller Estate in Pocantico Hills, Wave Hill in the Bronx, Planting Fields on Long Island, and the Otto Kahn Estate, which is based on the vision described in the poem "Kubla Kahn." Some of the finest gardens in Washington, D.C. are found at Dumbarton Oaks in Georgetown. Beaux-Arts landscape architecture was intended to induce awe. It was extremely labor intensive and could only exist as long as American immigrants were available who knew the tenets and upkeep of the clipped formal garden. As America became more even socially, less of a master–peasant economy, precision-created gardening declined, as did the country estates to which it had belonged.

Topiary Landscape

The Beaux-Arts landscape was nature contained, with geometry and the human hand directing flora. As such, it was clearly an imported style, in exact opposition to the basic American sense of land as wilderness. Of all landscape styles, topiary was at once the most constrained and the most whimsical. Topiary gardens represent the complete mastery of nature by the human hand, clipping trees and shrubs into visual forms not within their nature. The green forms of animals, or abstract sculptural forms, create a strangely beautiful, imaginary, structured landscape. Such gardens were rarities of the eastern estate gardens of America of the early modern architectural era. One can today be found in Bristol, Rhode Island, named Green Animals.

The first topiary garden in North America was the Hunnewell Topiary in Wellesley, Massachusetts, a treed suburb west of Boston (Hayward 2006). One can view this clipped landscape from across Lake Waban, near Wellesley College, which is itself a dramatic landscape including arboretum and greenhouses designed on land that once was owned by the Hunnewells. The Hunnewell Topiary, on the National Register of Historic Places, is composed of carefully trimmed spruce, pine, and hemlock with long shadows thrown from each plant. The strange landscape of the topiary takes on a stillness that is the perfect living tableau of a post-Impressionist Pointillist painting. Until recently, this magical landscape could be viewed while swimming or canoeing at the Lake Waban Swim Club, a quirky century-old upgraded swimming hole on the Wellesley College campus. Long before that, the Hunnewells had toured their guests about the lake to view their lakeside Italian gardens and topiary via their private gondola.

Campus Landscapes

Wellesley College and other contemporary nineteenth- and early twentieth-century picturesque college campuses together represent some of the most creatively designed landscapes in America. (Campuses are private, though often open to public enjoyment.) Many incorporate sculpture within the landscape setting. American picturesque college landscapes of note include, but are certainly not limited to: in the East, Princeton University, whose revivalist buildings, like Wellesley's are by architect Ralph Adams Cram; in the West, the University of Arizona, Tucson, and the University of Colorado, Boulder, by Olmsted, are striking.

Many beautiful campuses partake of more urbane antique eighteenth-century models based on enclosed yards and greens, such as Harvard University and Brown University, predating the emotive nineteenth-century picturesque. On the other hand, Columbia University by McKim, Mead, and White and the Massachusetts Institute of Technology by Welles Bosworth, exemplify the highly organized geometry of the urban nineteenth-century eastern Beaux-Arts campus. In the West, the California Institute of Technology in Pasadena epitomizes the Spanish influenced campus of covered arcaded walkways, courtyards, palms, and tropical shade trees.

Planting Fields, English Manor House on Long Island Landscape

One of the finest of the private estates homes of the early modern architectural era, melding architecture with landscape, is the Coe Estate, Planting Fields, Oyster Bay, New York. Exceptional both as architecture and as land-

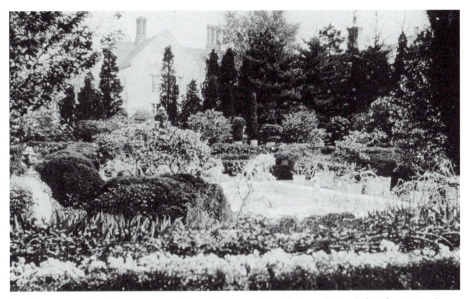

A picturesque landscape transplanted trans-Atlantic to a Long Island estate. Courtesy of the Francis Loeb Library, Harvard Graduate School of Design.

scape, the Traditional style limestone Tudor Revival mansion (1918) by architects Walker and Gillette sits like an English manor house within a picturesque British estate, magically transplanted trans-Atlantic to Long Island's North Shore, on grounds designed by landscape architect James Greenleaf and the Olmsted Brothers (1910). The Coe family invested money and care in their outstanding collection of trees, creating not only an architectural estate but an arboretum, appropriate to the name Planting Fields. Moving mature specimens at great expense across Long Island Sound via barge to the property, the landscape designers arranged the important trees artistically about the great lawn. Sweeping views of lawn punctuated by giant copper beech trees today continue to create the sense of green expansiveness fully expressive of the possibilities of eastern American land. A rich family's Arcadian dream has become in time a park for the public family (open to the public), for the landscape and mature beauty of Planting Fields are now fortunately preserved for posterity by New York as Planting Fields Arboretum State Park.

PARK LANDSCAPES IN EARLY TWENTIETH-CENTURY AMERICA

National Parks and Urban Parks

The early modern era, in which America now spread from Atlantic to Pacific, meant the end of the frontier and its open-ended sense of land. On one hand, the concept of endless land was mythic, but on the other, it meant that land was an exploitable resource for human enjoyment and consumption, with little intrinsic value, that could be left unprotected. From 1901–1920, major advances in understanding the necessity for protection of open land were made. True wilderness existed in the West, and thanks to

Kykuit, Landscape and Sculpture

Original, open-minded, antique, modern—a unique vision of the visual arts of architecture, landscape, and sculpture has evolved at Kykuit, The Rockefeller Estate. This is a place that recalls simultaneously Beaux-Arts classicism and mid-century modernism. The home, north of New York City, began with the construction of the mansion by architects Delano and Aldrich for oil magnate John D. Rockefeller in 1909; the extensive site overlooking the cliffs of the Hudson River was landscaped and engineered by architect Welles Bosworth. The mansion is both refined and informal, of granite blocks and Palladian windows. In a mixture of motifs, for example, the mansion features an Italianate portico and classical detailing, played against the rough-hewn regional granite and gneiss reminiscent of local historical Dutch farmhouses.

An unusual American expression of the mutual relationship of nature and visual art, Kykuit is homestead, art collection, and landscape creation. There is not on this estate the sense of the stricture of style that is so often the province of the socially or artistically unsure; aesthetic rules are folly here. This was a place where people collected passionately, a home of a free-thinking people who happened to be rich. The family philanthropy was extended both to art museums by Governor Nelson Rockefeller, including the Museum of Modern Art and the Metropolitan Museum of Art, and to American landscape through the protection of National Park land by Lawrence Rockefeller, including Acadia and Grand Teton National Parks. Kykuit is symbolic of these myriad philanthropic commitments.

The Kykuit landscape is at once proper and on the verge of eccentricity; the art romantic, primitive, and modern. Flame-like Art Nouveau Tiffany torches light the Renaissance Revival front portico, yet turn to the west and the view of the Hudson River includes the abstractly cool form of modernist sculptor Brancusi's "Bird in Flight" bronze (replica, original in the Museum of Modern Art). A massive modernist Henry Moore sculpture overlooks a sunny golf course, while faux stalactites and dripping ferns hang from dark, hidden grottoes footsteps away. Everywhere, from the rolling green hills, to the planted topiary terraces, to the Brancusi bird and the secret gardens, the significance of Kykuit is of landscape and sculpture and of nature as articulated by art.

such early modern environmentalists as Presidents Theodore Roosevelt and Woodrow Wilson, wilderness still exists today in protected national parks, the earliest being Yellowstone in Wyoming and Yosemite and Sequoia in California. Although the parks predated the official act, President Wilson signed the National Park Service Organic Act of 1916, landmark legislation in defining American attitudes toward land that had been begun under President Theodore Roosevelt. With the Olmsted Brothers, Daniel Ray Hull (1890–1964) helped to advance the visual style we associate with our park landscapes and their outbuildings. "The formation of the National Park Service in 1916 quickly produced a design ethic. Today, these parks contain a rich architectural legacy: The distinctive NPS Rustic-style building" (Kaiser 1997).

The Olmsted Home and Landscape, Fairsted

Even as the giant National Parks were being founded in the West, eastern cities were building parks in heavily industrialized and domestically developed regions. Cities with foresight had earlier set aside urban parks or sites for parks, the most famous of which were New York City's Central Park (1857) and its sibling in Brooklyn, Prospect Park, both by Frederick Law Olmsted (1822–1903) and Calvert Vaux (1824–1895). So great is Frederick Law Olmsted's influence on American landscape that when we look at our parks and landscapes, we often think we are seeing untouched nature, when in actuality, we are seeing an Olmsted visual invention. One might even call it a feat of trompe-l'oeil, or fool the eye, landscape.

The "wilderness" of Central Park in the middle of Manhattan Island is still one of the most amazing feats in urban history—that the most densely populated city in the country, on a skinny island, should have a miniature wilderness at its core, surrounded by skyscraper apartment homes—is unexpected, to say the least. One may be astounded to learn that those picturesque rock outcroppings, Manhattan schist and gneiss boulders, curving lakes, miniature forests, and grassy swards were not just there. They were carefully exposed or placed there by steam shovels and hand trowels to the specifications of Olmsted, creating one of the most naturalistic manmade environments in history (Olmsted 1928).

On a much smaller scale, Olmsted designed Fairsted, his own home in Brookline, Massachusetts, a microcosm landscape of the many types of terrain he created in parks. Fairsted, a simplified version of the sweeping landscapes of his parks, is located in one of the outstanding early suburban places in America, a streetcar suburb with mature landscape amid the built environment. (Fairsted is open to the public as the Frederick Law Olmsted National Historic Site). Today, one can fully appreciate Olmsted's American vision best perhaps via a rowboat in Central Park, from the Ramble or the open Sheep Meadow, looking toward 5th Avenue or Central Park West. This sight is one of the truly American landscape views, for it encompasses, in counterpoint, the two most significant indigenous, contrasting aesthetics of America: skyscraper and wilderness.

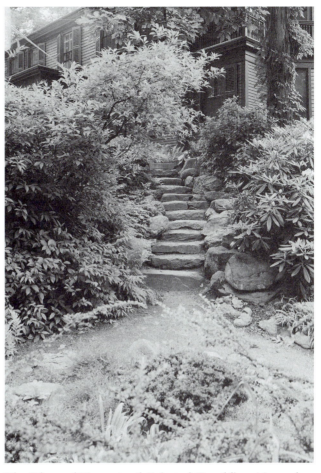

The Olmsted Homestead, Fairsted. Brookline, Massachusetts. Courtesy of the Library of Congress.

Back to Nature

As the urbanized concepts of the city park, the garden city, or the streetcar suburb were taking hold during 1901–1920, there was a counter movement of "back to the land" in such places as Craftsman Farms, Gustav Stickley's communal home in New Jersey. Stickley held fast to an anti-urban mythic, picturesque sense of the home as cottage or bungalow, as an extension of the land, specifically symbolized by his shingle, stone, and log cabin. The Craftsman vision was so complete that Stickley published his home plans in conjunction with correct Craftsman landscape, describing appropriate cottage gardens and tree and shrub selections. Just as Stickley felt that the home interior should reflect the exterior domestic architecture, so, too, did he believe the plantings should be part of the total environment of the home.

SUBURBAN LANDSCAPES IN EARLY TWENTIETH-CENTURY AMERICA

"Substantial Suburban Undertakings": Town Planning, Land Use and Landscape in the East

In announcing that "Town Plan Helps Future Land Value, Artistic Foresight Becomes a Permanent Protection for the Future," the *New York Times* (1924) proclaimed, "There has been a marked awakening to the utilitarian value of beauty and good taste. A comprehensive plan with regard to landscape and houses to interpret the spirit and need of the people in terms of recognized principles of art is now essential to the most substantial suburban undertakings." The new and pervasive sense of land protection influenced the home by linking the idea of domestic architecture to land in the early modern architectural era. Thus, the city expanded into the suburb, and the newspaper added a special section on real estate. Many excellent streetscapes were created in this time within suburban developments that can serve as models for current projects. Though it sometimes escapes our conscious perception, as we explore a neighborhood we find visually inviting, we are unconsciously enjoying particular components of the streetscape. A well-defined street is calming because it observes principles of proportion and regularity where it should. For example, setbacks of the houses are even; street trees are planted along the sidewalk. Perhaps a canopy of leaves touches, forming an arch above our heads as we walk down this street.

Nature, proportion, and a sense processional through the space of nature make landscape live about our homes. The American garden suburb was based on the English Garden City, the theory and designs of which had been laid out by Ebenezer Howard's *Garden Cities of Tomorrow* in the nineteenth century. In America, modern suburb and theory would be advanced by recently built environments discussed in books such as urban planner Clarence Stein's *Toward New Towns for America* (1978). The association of personal and public health and welfare with access to trees and open land, sunlight, and fresh air was a revolutionary concept and reflected the democratization of the eastern and midwestern suburban American home. Even the names of the first American planned suburbs, Forest Hills Gardens, Sunnyside, Chestnut Hill, Riverside, Oak Park, conveyed the importance of landscape and deciduous trees via their nomenclature. American place names, actually, have often reflected an appreciation and an association of nature, landscape, and water with well-being: such as, Brookville, Cold Spring, Locust Valley, Boulder, Lone Pine, Wellesley, and Providence.

"Perpetual Sun" and the Building Boom of the 1920s: Landscape Did Not Escape

"In the Land of Your Dreams, Southern California! Perpetual Sun . . . Summer Sea Breezes, Tropical and Semi-Tropical Verdure" bragged an advertisement in the real estate section of the *Los Angeles Times* in 1920. Orange groves and a different American dream were for sale in California and Florida in the 1920s. At first, it seemed so escapist to have a home away from home, to seek and find a place amid palms. In the words of Kevin Starr in his history of California, "Southern Californians were showing an intense relationship to the stunning shoreline . . . Middle-class families would spend an entire month on the beach . . . living in tents . . . The seaside villages and summer tent cities of the 1910s developed in the 1920s into a string of beach towns running from Laguna Beach . . . to Malibu . . . where a sea-and-shore-oriented lifestyle, as yet free of . . . suburban sprawl, flourished with a special charm" (Starr 2002).

Southern California, a modern place rich in twentieth-century architecture but poor in vegetation, sorely cried out for serious scientific planting and ecological planning. Eventually billboards selling fruit and nuts, as well as the very land that grew them, were to be the last crop produced by large tracts of California's arable land. Even the desert was not immune to over-development; the last of the great desert date palm groves could still be discovered among the polluting automobile development along Route 66 in Palm Springs. Until recently, this operating date farm, a wonderful piece of Americana, was continuously showing its faded color film in the visitors' center on the wonders of date fertilization. Even Death Valley in the 1920s had its crazy date palm farmer and hotel entrepreneur, struggling to make a go of it in 130 degrees Fahrenheit. At the end of the early modern architectural era, land was hot, hot, hot, especially in California and Florida in the 1920s, as the world went wild in stock market speculation and land development.

In Florida, Flagler ran his railroad on a bed of sand to Key West and lost it to a hurricane. Eventually whole sections of the Everglades, one of the rarest riparian environments in the world, was diverted and filled in for development. The current concept of wetlands was meaningless during the first half of the twentieth century, based no doubt in an old idea that swamps were evil, disease-causing things to be eradicated by infilling. Much of the colonial and nineteenth-century city of Boston, for example, had been built on landfill dumped into the harbor and Charles River tidal basin, and in the mid-twentieth century even marshy parts of Olmsted's Emerald Necklace were infilled and shamefully paved for a parking lot. The Los Angeles River basin became an environment scarred, paved with concrete and freeways. Suburban wood, swamp, and desert were despoiled in the land rush. Reversing seemingly irreversible harm done to American landscape from the 1920s through the mid-twentieth century is crucial and now becoming a significant planning issue in the early twenty-first century.

Lots of Trees Versus Lots without Trees

As the pace of home building accelerated during 1901–1920, so, too, did the breaking up of large open tracts of land into repetitive rectangular lots. Subdivisions of lots were drawn up on paper by speculative developers in office buildings, rather than by landscape architects such as Olmsted, and subsequently executed upon the land, often with little thought given to the topography of the site and even less to existing trees. This meant that a road, sidewalk, or house within a planned subdivision might run directly through a century old oak or beech. Because bulldozers run in one direction, forward, many an ancient tree has been cruelly destroyed in America, as landscape has come second to "progress." For nearly a century, Americans have been loving their landscape literally to pieces.

Fortunately, there has always been a more thoughtful ecological strain in American landscape, those who understood the longer range implications of trees and land. One of the greatest accomplishments of the early modern architectural era was the planting of trees all over America, particularly street trees, an underappreciated American environmental and aesthetic achievement. American trees planted in the Northeast included oak, sugar maple, fruit trees, and white pine. Elms, sadly, were blighted during this time. Southern trees planted were pine and cypress. The Midwest had prairie grasses with cottonwoods. The desert Southwest had the saguaro cactus. California was planting palms, citrus groves, eucalyptus, and date palms in the deserts. Arbor Day was celebrated annually in American schoolhouses linking children with nature, nationalism, early environmentalism, health and welfare, and a general sense of goodness with landscape.

Geometry and the Tree

America of the 1920s was taming the wild and making it safe for bungalows. A few proponents of landscape, however, were actively seeking to bring plantings to the desert in conjunction with the development of homes. Among them were philanthropist Ellen Brown Scripps and landscape designer Kate Sessions, both working with modern architect Irving Gill. Together they brought eucalyptus trees from the plants' native Australia to San Diego's desert by the sea environment (although imported species are no longer considered a good thing). By planting the groves in conjunction with modern architecture, Scripps and Gill introduced not only the simplified aesthetic of white facades to southern California, but emphasized the subtle relationships of built environment to nature, of home to yard, of architecture to landscape, and the aesthetic dichotomy of abstract solid geometry to the sensuous lines of a tree.

Protecting the American Landscape Legacy

We have inherited some beautiful landscaped homes and towns in America from the generation of 1901–1920, but likewise we have inherited the responsibility of the stewardship of our environments. Single-family homes and apartment houses moved into open landscape during the early modern architectural era, at best creating sites designed with order and processional, shaded pathways, picturesque arrangements of buildings and parks, public transit, good access to shops, and real neighborhoods. Homes, too, can be important factors in saving the environment for future generations, and those who believe that offer these suggestions to homeowners: Please do not offend nature by callously cutting down a tree, sheltering home to wildlife, in 15 minutes, that has taken 100 years to grow. As we would not countenance the burning down of our own homes, we should not with abandon despoil our living landscape legacy. Also, if we insist on growing the water-wasting American front lawn in the East or the Midwest that belongs in Britain, to improve it, mow it diagonally from the house and avoid putting poisons on the grass. In the dry West, think of low-water landscaping without grass at all. The desert is beautiful because it is dry, not in spite of it. Nature does not line up its trees and shrubs and cacti, and therefore neither should we. Nature's aesthetic is not neatness; it enjoys variation and irregularity, even decay, within its encompassing vision.

Trees, Tribulations, and Aspirations

"Twelve Arguments for Trees," published a century ago, reminds us today that trees are the natural expression of form and function.

> Trees are beautiful in form and color, inspiring . . . appreciation of nature.
> Trees enhance the beauty of architecture.
> Trees create . . . love of city and home.
> Trees . . . educate citizens, especially children.
> Trees encourage outdoor life.
> Trees purify air.
> Trees cool the air in summer.
> Trees improve climate, conserve soil and moisture.
> Trees . . . shelter birds.
> Trees increase the value of real estate.
> Trees protect pavement . . . from the sun.
> Trees counteract adverse conditions of city life. ("Plant a Tree" 1909)

This seems a good place to exit the remembered places of 1901–1920. For no greater summation, nor greater tribute, to the tribulations and aspirations of the homes and landscapes of the early modern architectural era can be made by the author of this book, than those simple words from 1909 above, to "enhance the beauty of architecture," to "create . . . love of city and home," and to "counteract adverse conditions of . . . life."

Reference List

Birnbaum, Charles A., FASLA, and Robin Larson. 2000. *National Park Historic Landscape Initiative, Pioneers of American Landscape Design*. New York: McGraw-Hill, 475–483.

Griswold, Mac, and Eleanor Weller. 2000. *The Golden Age of American Gardens, Proud Owners, Private Estates, 1890–1940*. New York: The Garden Club of America and Harry N. Abrams, 15–16.

Hayward, Allyson M. 2006. *Private Pleasures Derived from Tradition, The Hunnewell Estates Historic District, Arnoldia*, vol. 64, no. 4. Cambridge, MA: Arnold Arboretum, Harvard University, 33.

Kaiser, Harvey H. 1997. *Landmarks in the Landscape, Historic Architecture in the National Parks of the West*. San Francisco: Chronicle Books, 17.

Olmsted, Frederick Law. 1928. *The "Greensward" Plan for the Improvement of the Central Park, 1858, Forty Years of Landscape Architecture, Central Park and Frederick Law*

Olmsted, Sr. Ed. F. L. Olmsted, Jr. and reprinted by MIT Press, Cambridge, MA, 1973, 214–232.

Real Estate section. 1924. *New York Times.* (18 May): 1.

Starr, Kevin. 2002. *The Dream Endures, California Enters the 1940s.* New York: Oxford University Press, 10.

Stein, Clarence S. 1978. *Toward New Towns for America.* With an introduction by Lewis Mumford. Cambridge: M.I.T. Press, 1957.

"To Plant A Tree." 1909. *Chicago Tribune* (28 July): 13.

Appendix: Excerpts from Gustav Stickley's *The Craftsman*

THE CRAFTSMAN: CREATIVE AND COMMERCIAL CONCEPT

The Craftsman style was, in Gustav Stickley's encompassing early modern vision, appropriate to every home and every lifestyle in America, from farm to city. Stickley (1858–1942) was a very modern man, for he understood the synergy of the modern domestic environment with the modern economy and was early to integrate his own design ideals and creativity with the pragmatic necessities of the developing American consumer economy.

Craftsman style was thus a broad design and commercial concept, including product design, education, marketing, production, distribution, advertising, and public relations. The Craftsman magazine, which began publication in 1901, was the visual and theoretical foundation the operation, integrating all Stickley's ideas within an attractive graphic style, selling the total design concept to the public. Through the voice and visuals of The Craftsman, Stickley brought his wares, as well as his philosophy, to public attention throughout America from 1901–1920.

The variety and harmony of Stickley's vision is clear in this selected issue of his magazine. One notes the overall simplification of the graphics, beginning with the modern aesthetic of the cover design and integrated throughout. Clear typography, quite plain for the era, yet just sinuous enough to be graphically striking, sets a visual standard for the publication. The earth-toned brown cover and beige, rather than stark white, paper integrates the volume.

THE CRAFTSMAN: FEBRUARY 1911 ISSUE

Subtle sophistication by the editor is evident in this issue, through the inclusion of significant artists and architects of the day, persons outside the Arts and

VOL. XIX, No. 5   FEBRUARY, 1911   25 CENTS

THE CRAFTSMAN

"The lyf so short, the craft so long to lerne"

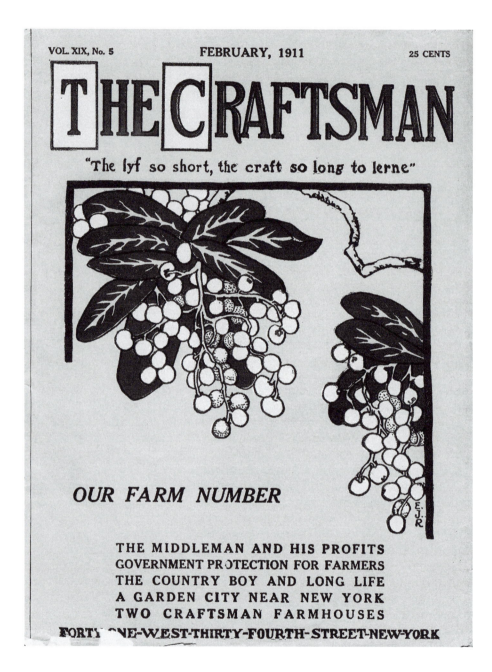

OUR FARM NUMBER

THE MIDDLEMAN AND HIS PROFITS
GOVERNMENT PROTECTION FOR FARMERS
THE COUNTRY BOY AND LONG LIFE
A GARDEN CITY NEAR NEW YORK
TWO CRAFTSMAN FARMHOUSES

FORTY-ONE-WEST-THIRTY-FOURTH-STREET-NEW-YORK

Crafts circle. Art photographs by Alvin Langdon Coburn were abstract and high style. British suburban home designs by the English architect C.F.A. Voysey were international style setters in the early twentieth century. The innovative urban planning and landscape design of Forest Hills Gardens, by architect Grosvenor Atterbury and landscape architect Frederick Law Olmsted, were internationally significant in the early modern architectural era. Stickley's early publication of this important project linked his vision of America with Britain via the new Garden City Movement. Through the recognition of highly regarded contemporary creative artists and architects, Stickley raised the aesthetic level of his publication, and by association, of his Craftsman style. This selected 1911 issue of *The Craftsman* attests to Stickley's wide vision of the Craftsman style.

The Craftsman Style: Farm, City, Suburb

Though Stickley called this "The Farm Issue," it is certainly not limited to rural pursuits. The issue speaks equally to the life of the city and the suburb, interspersing articles about rural farming and observations of rural life with the more urbane forms of the city. For Stickley, farm was as much a concept as a reality, hearkening back to an American Arcadian ideal of the land; this back-to-the-farm philosophy of 1901–1920 would prefigure many theorists of American regionalism of the 1930s. Craftsman Farms in Morris Plains, New Jersey, which is now a museum, remains the physical reality of Stickley's ideal integration of home, handcraft, and farm. (www.stickleymuseum.org.)

Suburbs and Skyscrapers: England and America

Dispersed amidst abstract skyscraper scenes and homey farm homilies, the most significant articles in this issue deal with the suburb, a developing housing configuration of the early modern architectural era, influencing both British and American homes. This issue of *The Craftsman* sought to link the American aesthetics of the Craftsman style to the more sophisticated British aesthetics of the Arts and Crafts movement.

Here in the February 1911 issue, Stickley published creative home designs by one of the most influential domestic architects of early twentieth-century Britain, C.F.A. Voysey. By showing Voysey's chic suburban designs in the same issue as Stickley's more humble house plans, Stickley gave an excellent introduction to the meaning of the modern middle-class home and upgraded his own design level by making an association with Voysey. Also published in this issue were works of the well-known traditionalist American architect Grosvenor Atterbury, as well as the most influential American landscape architect of the day, Frederick Law Olmsted. This article on Atterbury and Olmsted's plans for Forest Hills Gardens, with its pen and ink illustrations of Tudor homes and town, can be considered a classic piece in the history of *The Craftsman*.

"At Once Practical and Picturesque": Forest Hills Gardens

Stickley advanced the new concept of the suburb, with homes, commuter train, shops, and town center, through one of the most significant articles ever published in *The Craftsman*, "A Garden City for the Man of Moderate Means," by architectural critic Edward Hale Brush. This article suggests that the foundation of American urban theory was to be found in the landmark antecedent of the British Garden City Movement and that these homes and towns were "practical and picturesque." Here, among the pen and ink illustrations of a revivalist yet modern Tudor town, architectural critic Brush complements the work of architect Grosvenor Atterbury and landscape architect Frederick Law Olmsted for establishing a "standard of beauty in town planning" and for planning their community "with a noble architectural standard, based on a foundation of honesty and simplicity."

A GARDEN CITY FOR THE MAN OF MOD-ERATE MEANS: BY EDWARD HALE BRUSH

ITH the building of a garden city in America we are brought to a consideration of the value of such a movement in combatting our nation-wide cry for in-dividuality of expression. Probably our inane atti-tude toward individuality, our absurd national egotism has been made more manifest in architecture than in any of the other arts, and yet, as a matter of fact, since we have given up imitating good architecture we have very largely devoted ourselves to designing bad buildings. We have seemed to regard startling eccentricity as genius and whimsicality as originality, at the very least, and so going about our undisciplined individual ways we have dotted our pleasant country landscapes with houses showing so little thought in construction or adaptation or appropriateness that the result is embarrassing to contemplate.

We seem to have overlooked the fact that the *purpose* of expres-sion is to have *something* to express. A train of cars is not run pri-marily to prove its capacity for motion, but really to carry some-thing. And the actual value of affording opportunity for the indi-vidual is that unhindered he may express wise purpose and sincere understanding, not that he may unhampered prove to a suffering world his lack of thought and failure to appreciate that the right to express, is absolutely involved with the power to express beauty.

There is a vast difference between the individualist and the egotist, and by their works shall ye know them—apart. Of the individual conception of real beauty we cannot have too much in architecture. On the other hand, we must welcome most heartily an attempt like the Garden City at Forest Hills, Long Island, to prove the impor-tance of establishing a standard of beauty in town building, and of guaranteeing that standard to the public by placing the building in the hands of artists of imagination and training. This most significant, if not the first, garden city in America was born of the desire of Mrs. Russell Sage to devote a part of the large fortune left her

FOREST HILLS:
THE RAILROAD
STATION FROM
THE HOFFMAN
BOULEVARD.

445

A GARDEN CITY FOR PEOPLE OF MODERATE MEANS

by her husband to create something of permanent value to the country; a practical investment, perhaps, but also a means of education to all those of moderate means seeking the peace and comfort of a model village, where would be an opportunity of living without great expense and in charming homes; of having a bit of a garden and congenial neighbors; and all this, of course, within easy commuting distance of New York and in surroundings that are at once picturesque and yet along main traveled roads. Naturally, Mrs. Sage is not attempting to supervise or in any way be responsible for the

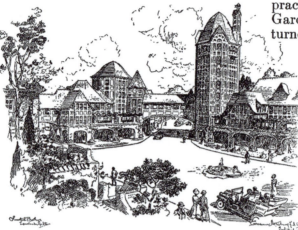

practical details of this Garden City. She has turned over the management to the Sage Foundation Homes Company.

Both the projectors and directors of Forest Hills Gardens were convinced from the start that buildings of tasteful design, well constructed of brick, cement or other permanent

STATION SQUARE AT FOREST HILLS: STORES AND HOUSEKEEPING APARTMENTS.

material, were really most economical in the long run, even if involving a greater expense at the start. They were also more durable, safer, with greater picturesque possibilities. And so the houses of this City, which is being erected, as in a way a memorial to Mr. Sage, will be, if the plans are carefully carried out, at once practical and picturesque, comfortable and durable. Now that the new Pennsylvania tunnel is finished, Forest Hills Gardens is within a quarter of an hour's ride of Herald Square, so that the resident of this unique village will be much nearer the central business portion of New York than if living north or south on the actual island.

Already in England the garden city movement has been productive of most interesting and practical results. Beautiful suburbs have been established about London, near enough to render business in the metropolis perfectly practicable; far enough away to permit interesting architectural design and a chance for home gardens. There are also many societies in England as well as all over Europe for the building of garden cities for laboring people, where every

446

A GARDEN CITY FOR PEOPLE OF MODERATE MEANS

man has his garden and every woman her opportunity to live somewhat out of doors, and to have real neighbors near at hand. The idea of all this kind of community architectural work is to make life more economical, more nomical, more beautiful, more interesting for women, more 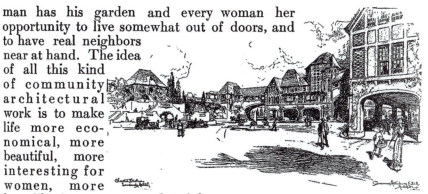 homelike for men, more cheerful and sane for children. The value of the work is so tremendous that it is somewhat of a surprise that it has not been undertaken on a large scale before in this country.

FOREST HILLS RAILROAD STATION, STATION SQUARE.

It is a matter of most widereaching good fortune that the first building of a beautiful suburban city should have been placed in the hands of an architect who is already famous as a designer of original, significant and beautiful American domestic architecture. We know of no man in this country more capable of handling the architectural difficulties in such an undertaking and evolving therefrom the right kind of beauty than Mr. Grosvenor Atterbury. He is an artist of wide experience, most adequate professional training and genuine architectural ideals. That he is to work out the architectural salvation of this garden city with Mr. Frederick Law Olmsted would indicate that a higher ideal of beauty will be achieved than we have ever hoped for in our suburban existence. One has only to glance at the illustrations of this article to realize that these two

SINGLE FAMILY DWELLINGS AT FOREST HILLS.

men have planned a noble architectural standard for the town, and have based it on a foundation of honesty and simplicity. The houses are beautiful in design; where ornament is used it seems inevitable, and the relation of one house to another shows a harmony only conceivable where there is a fundamental architectural principle underlying a diversity of effort in building.

447

A GARDEN CITY FOR PEOPLE OF MODERATE MEANS

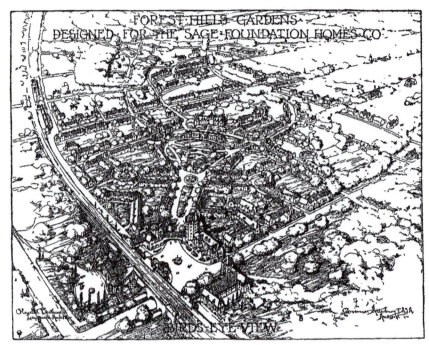

DETAIL PLAN OF THE CONSTRUCTION OF FOREST HILLS: THE FIRST GARDEN CITY IN AMERICA.

The question will naturally arise as to what opportunity the individual will have in this "model town" for the expression of his own particular ideas in home building. According to the prospectus, the individual will have his opportunity, within limits. The company will not build the whole town. It will leave a large part of the tract to be built up by the individual purchasers of plots, exercising a sufficient guidance over their choice of plans and development of their land to ensure a general harmony with the admirable architectural scheme devised as a standard for the entire community. On this point Mr. Atterbury himself says:

"While a very large proportion of the land area to be developed will undoubtedly be sold without building improvements, the Homes Company, in order to set a standard and control more surely the architectural character of the future town, has planned to erect and hold, certainly for a time, a large number of dwellings. To this end designs have been prepared for an initial operation contemplating different groups of buildings, involving an expenditure in land improvement and building construction of a million and a quarter

448

A GARDEN CITY FOR PEOPLE OF MODERATE MEANS

dollars. The majority of the buildings to be erected in this first operation, which will be largely confined to the more expensive and central property, are in the form of contiguous houses; the detached and semi-detached types of dwellings of various grades and sizes being necessarily possible only on less central and lower-priced portions of the property. The different types of buildings included in these groups cover as wide a range as is permitted by the economic conditions, which necessarily determine also their distribution and location on the property. Adjoining the railroad station and forming the Station Square are three- and four-story buildings containing stores, offices and restaurants, and in the upper stories small non-housekeeping apartments, for both men and women. From this center out toward Forest Park, which bounds the property on the southeast, the houses are planned to correspond to the varying values of the lots, as determined by their size, location and prospect, the larger single-family dwellings containing ten or twelve rooms, the smaller four or five. While they will vary greatly in size, arrangement, cost and architectural treatment, an attempt will be made to make them alike in their domestic and livable character. From an architectural point of view our greatest opportunity will lie in that general harmony of design which is possible only where the entire scheme of development is laid out and executed under a system of coöperation by the various experts engaged in it."

Not only will Forest Hills Gardens be educational along architectural lines but it will establish a precedent and inaugurate methods along certain practical channels of real-estate operation. It is proposed in this experiment to formulate regulations for the distribution of real estate which may be accepted by operators handling property of similar character throughout the country, with consequent elimination of waste in energy and money. A matter which has not in the past received much consideration.

As to the details of the architectural scheme perhaps one can obtain the best idea through the classification of the buildings into groups as follows:

Group One. Station Square, including the railroad station and a group of buildings adjoining containing shops, offices, a restaurant and accommodations for some three hundred or four hundred people, consisting mainly of small non-housekeeping apartments for men and women, in connection with which there is provided a squash court as well as a certain number of small studios.

Group Two. A block of small single-family houses, with thirteen feet frontage, two or three stories in height, containing four rooms and bath.

Group Three. A block of single-family houses of seventeen feet frontage, two stories in height with attic, seven to nine rooms and bath.

Group Four. A block of ten single-family houses, with seventeen feet frontage, two stories in height and containing five rooms and bath.

449

A GARDEN CITY FOR PEOPLE OF MODERATE MEANS

Group Five. A block of single-family houses with twenty feet frontage, two stories and attic in height and containing six to eight rooms and bath.

Group Six. Three blocks of single-family houses, with twenty feet frontage, two stories in height with attic and containing eight to ten rooms and two baths.

Group Seven. Three blocks of single-family houses with twenty-six feet frontage, three stories in height, containing ten to twelve rooms and baths and toilets.

Group Eight. A block of workshops and flats, twenty feet frontage, two and three stories in height, the former containing workshops or stores with three rooms and bath above, the latter workshops and stores on street level and six rooms and bath in upper stories.

Group Nine. A row of semi-detached two-family houses on shallow lots of fifty feet frontage, containing two stories, each unit consisting of six rooms and bath all on one floor.

Group Ten. A row of semi-detached two-family houses on lots of twenty-seven feet frontage, two stories in height, each unit containing five or six rooms and bath all on one floor.

The drawings reproduced here speak for themselves as to the attractiveness and architectural impressiveness of Mr. Atterbury's plans for the buildings of the above groups. As may be seen, the arrangements afford considerable latitude for differences in income, taste, number in family and habits of life among the prospective residents and yet preserve the harmony of the scheme from both architectural and operative points of view. It is not going to be a town where a low-paid mechanic or day laborer can afford to live, and in view of the ill-advised and unauthorized announcement that it was to be a workingmen's colony there may be some regret or disappointment at this. But the members of the Sage Foundation hint that in future the funds in its possession may also be used to provide better housing for wage-earners of this class. The homes at Forest Hills will, however, be within the means of well-paid mechanics, workers on small salaries, etc.

The type of dwelling architecture in the garden city needs for its effectiveness the shrubbery and flowers, the frequent open spaces and the curved street lines which will be noticeable features of the village. The center of the town will have that air of dignity and solidity observed or felt in many old-world cities but usually lacking in America. The shops and business resorts of various kinds will take their places as appropriate parts of the picture, not marring the landscape but contributing to the general attractiveness of the town as well as being of value from the point of utility.

The graceful lines of the winding streets will not only help to preserve the rural aspect of the village and be more pleasing from the æsthetic standpoint, but they will also add to public convenience by affording a more direct means of circulation. The reduction of minor streets to a width appropriate to their character results in economy in road construction and saving of land. This saving will enable the company to provide more public open spaces and more

450

A GARDEN CITY FOR PEOPLE OF MODERATE MEANS

space between the houses or groups of dwellings. The latter, instead of continuing in solid blocks from one street to another will be broken up into smaller units. The spaces between the blocks, together with a setback from the street, will give a general feeling of openness to the entire village. Thus, though on account of the nearness to Manhattan a certain degree of density of population will be economically necessary, the general aspect of things will be more like the real country than is customary in places where prices of land are correspondingly high.

The idea of the Homes Company management is to rent a certain proportion of homes, but to afford every encouragement to the homeseeker to acquire ownership of the property. Terms of sale will be as low as may be consistent with a safe business proposition, where the funds invested are expected to earn only what they would in a savings bank. The buyer may exercise his discretion as to employing his own builder or having the company do the construction. All grading, paving, planting, parking and sewerage construction will be done by the company.

If the expectations entertained at Forest Hills Gardens can be realized the Sage Foundation will succeed in providing healthful and attractive homes to many people, will demonstrate that tasteful and natural surroundings pay in suburban development, will encourage more economical methods of marketing land and will suggest imitation of its methods in many particulars. The latter point is perhaps the most important of all. Who can say how far-reaching the effect may be?

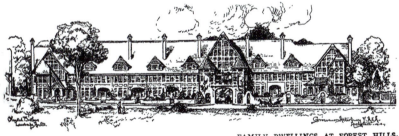

FAMILY DWELLINGS AT FOREST HILLS.

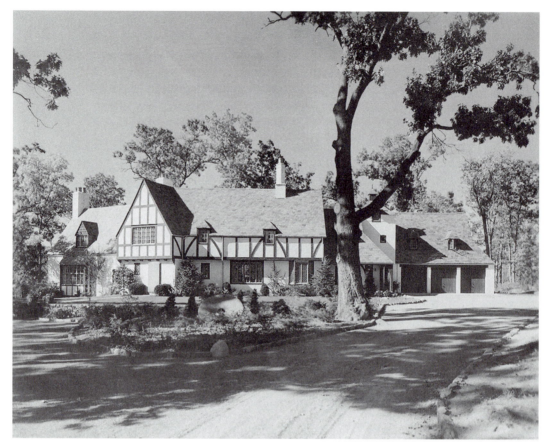

American Historical Revival Home. Courtesy of Royal Barry Wills Associates.

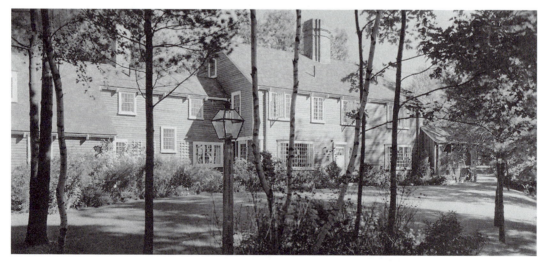

American Historical Revival Home. Courtesy of Royal Barry Wills Associates.

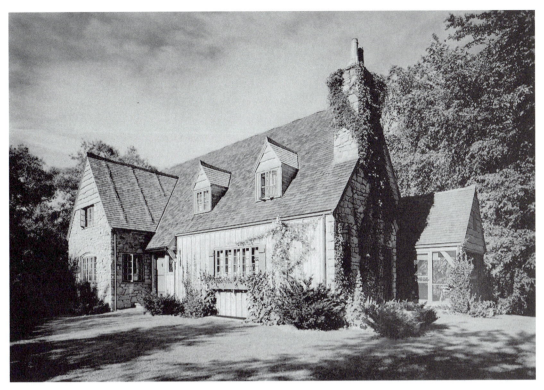

American Historical Revival Home. Courtesy of Royal Barry Wills Associates.

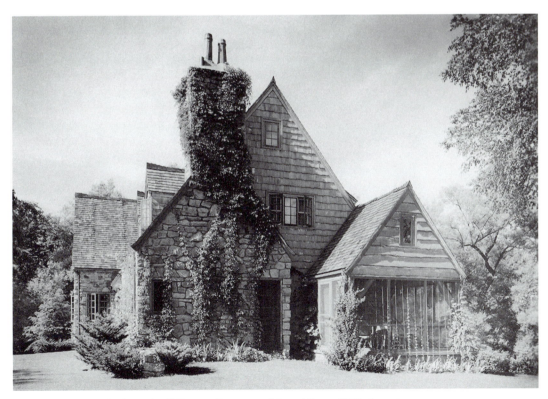

American Historical Revival Home. Courtesy of Royal Barry Wills Associates.

Glossary

Aesthetics: The theory and philosophy of the beautiful.

Alberti: A Renaissance theorist of the visual arts.

Allée: (French) A linear processional of trimmed trees or hedges in a garden.

Armory Show: 1913 New York art exhibition of American Ash Can School painters and invited French modern artists.

Ash Can School: Social Realist painters of the early twentieth century in New York's Greenwich Village known for painting urban life as observed.

Atrium: Open central courtyard within a Mediterranean influenced home.

Axial: Referring to a composition arranged along lines.

Balloon frame: American invention in the 1830s of lightweight wooden construction, which allowed more construction because it did not require master carpenters nor heavy timbers.

Bauhaus: *Building house.* Modern German design school, known for simplified functional objects and modernist theory of its founder, architect Walter Gropius. The school operated between 1919 and 1933.

Beaux-Arts: French architectural style based on formal design principles and Classical motifs; influential in turn of the century architectural education and American style.

Bungalow: An informal type of small American house with heavy roofline and deep, overhanging porch.

Cantilever: Architectural extension into space, unsupported on one end.

Clapboard: Long, narrow wood board used in siding.

Classical: Styles based on the Greek and Roman Orders; also refers to Classical Revival Styles.

Classical Revival: Nineteenth- and twentieth-century architectural references to the Classical past.

Classicism: Art, architecture, or knowledge based in the Greek or Roman past.

Clinker brick: Malformed, burned brick, once discarded, sometimes used by modern architects.

Colonial Revival: American style of the nineteenth and twentieth centuries bringing back the motifs of seventeenth- and eighteenth-century America.

Colter, Mary: (sometimes spelled Coulter) Architect of many buildings in the Grand Canyon National Park, as well as other designs.

Concrete: Mixture of cement, crushed stone, and water.

Constructivism: Modern art movement based on the interpenetration of planes.

Craftsman Style: Early Modern style of Gustav Stickley and followers in American architecture, decorative arts, and handcrafts.

Cubism: Modern style of painting based on reduction of forms into geometric masses.

Curate: (verb) to bring together art of a certain style in an exhibition or museum.

Density: (housing) housing units per acre.

Domestic architecture: Architecture of the home, or domicile.

Early modern era: The period of 1901–1920.

École des Beaux-Arts: Parisian architectural style and school that trained students in the classical style of architecture (literally, School of the Beautiful Arts).

Émigré: One who migrates to America, either by choice, or as a refugee.

Flemish bond: Decorative style of brickwork.

Focal point: Place to which sight is drawn.

Functional: In architecture, building in which the style reflects the use.

Geometric architecture: Buildings with aesthetics reflecting the basic forms of the square, the triangle, and the circle.

Gill, Irving: American early modern architect of the simplified concrete, geometric style of Southern California.

Gropius, Walter: Modern architect, founder of the German Bauhaus, and émigré to America.

Header: Brick turned short end out.

Herringbone: Diagonal brick pattern.

High modernism: Mid-twentieth-century modern style.

Highrise: Modern building with elevator, also skyscraper.

In situ: Meaning *on site;* or constructed on site.

International Style: The Modern architectural style of the 1920s–1950s in Europe and America consisting of simplified form.

Joinery: The contact between parts of architecture.

Le Corbusier, or Corbusian architecture: The most important French modern architect and architectural theorist of the twentieth century.

Linoleum: Early modern kitchen floor covering of felt and linseed oil layers.

"Machine for living in": The Corbusian ideal of the home as an aesthetic and functional object.

Mies van der Rohe, Ludwig: German Modern architect and émigré to the United States.

Mission Style: Simple American Craftsman Style, usually found in California and the West, having a "mission," or based on Spanish missions of the west.

Modernism: Twentieth-century artistic movement emphasizing simplicity of form and abstraction.

Mortar: Mixture containing cement between bricks.

Mortice and tenon: Heavy wooden building constructed of slotted, joined beams.

Motif: A repeated visual pattern or literary reference within a work of art, often having cultural or historical meaning.

National Historic Landmarks Sites: American places of significant design or events in history.

National Parks: American landscapes preserved by the U.S. Federal Government.

One point perspective: Technique of Renaissance art used to create the illusion of space on a flat surface.

The Orders of Architecture: Doric, Ionic, Corinthian.

Organic Act: The Congressional law that established the National Parks in 1916.

Organic Architecture: Frank Lloyd Wright's expression of materials and nature in architecture.

Parterre: A formally designed garden.

Perspective: The illusion of the creation of space.

Philanthropic housing: Experimental, social movement in improved housing conditions for the poor and middle class, supported by donations of the wealthy, of the early modern era.

Picturesque: Having the qualities of informality, irregularity, and naturalistic design.

Porte-cochere: Covered carriage entrance in front of a house.

Post-and-lintel: Fundamental form of architecture, in which point supports hold roof aloft; found in ancient Greek architecture as well as in modern wood and steel beam buildings.

Post War: Generally refers to the period just after World War II in America and Europe, the 1940s–1960s.

Prairie style: The style of the important American modern architect Frank Lloyd Wright. His horizontal aesthetic of the home was based on the flat lines of the plains of the Midwestern United States.

Prototype: The original model for the normative, replicable building type or design form. The prototype is a theoretically and aesthetically significant concept intrinsic to modernism, related to the concept of the Typeform in architecture.

Public transit or transportation: Urban or suburban rail, streetcar, or bus, operated for everyone; as opposed to the private automobile.

Refugee: Émigré forced to migrate; many early twentieth-century immigrants were refugees.

Renaissance: Fifteenth- and sixteenth-century Italian flowering of painting, architecture, and sculpture.

Retarditaire: Out of date even in its own day.

Richardsonian Romanesque: Emerging modern style based in the work of architect H.H. Richardson, with heavy masonry and arches.

Shingle Style: Early modern movement in architecture, producing softly shingled wooden picturesque houses.

Social Realism: Early modern art movement, showing truthfully the conditions of the urban poor.

Speculative housing: Homes built by a developer with the intent to make a profit.

Stretcher: Brick turned long end out.

Suburb: Organized housing configuration contiguous to a city, often connected by public transit.

Taylorism: Early efficiency theory based on time and motion studies.

Tenement: Minimal urban apartment house dwelling, usually for the poor, having shared toilet and no elevator, approximately 4 to 8 stories in height.

Tilt-up construction: Patented modern concrete method used by architect Irving Gill in California.

Triple-decker: A three-story apartment building with one apartment per floor.

Typeform: Normative, repeatable, or standardized form.

Urban and regional planning: Organized thinking and designing for the city and environs; including public transit, housing, foot paths, schools, parks, and playgrounds.

Vernacular: Referring to the common building style of a particular period or place, such as buildings, usually houses, designed by nonarchitects. May also include urban or rural background buildings.

Vigas: Natural logs used as protruding ceiling cross beams in homes of Spanish and Native American architecture in the Southwest of the United States.

Wrightian: A design by Frank Lloyd Wright or stylistically similar to that of Wright.

Resource Guide

HISTORICAL ARCHIVES

Most historical archives of original documents are available only to qualified scholars, with prior approval and appointment. Students are therefore advised to use the reference libraries of their educational institutions.

Carnegie Observatories' Photograph Collection, Archives and Special Collections, The Huntington Library, Museum, and Botanical Gardens, San Marino, California, holds the photographs and scientific papers of the California Institute of Technology concerning the building of the Mount Wilson and Mount Palomar Telescopes and housing for scientists.

The Huntington Library
1151 Oxford Road
San Marino, CA 91108
http://www.huntington.org.LibraryDiv./LibraryHome

The Gropius Archive, Harvard University, contains writings and correspondence of architect and Bauhaus founder Walter Gropius, on the design of his own home in Lincoln, Massachusetts, and to his Arizona stays in a dude ranch and significant information on his emigration.

Note: This is the resource guide for Part I of the volume (1901–1945). For the resource guide to Part II (1921–1945), see page 323.

The Gropius Archive
Houghton Library, Harvard University
Cambridge, MA 02138
http://hcl.harvard.edu/libraries/#houghton

Rotch Library, Architecture and Planning, Rare Books Room, Massachusetts Institute of Technology, Cambridge, Massachusetts, contains many important early modern books, including early twentieth-century plans for San Francisco.

Rotch Library, Architecture and Planning
Massachusetts Institute of Technology
77 Massachusetts Avenue
Cambridge, MA 02139
http://libraries.mit.edu/rotch/

Scripps Institution of Oceanography, University of California San Diego, Archives and Special Collections, La Jolla, California. Original letters, papers and photographs of architect Irving Gill, concerning his early modern architecture are found here, in particular, pictures of the site plans for this institution and designs and photographs of the 1908 director's house by architect Irving Gill.

Scripps Archives
Library, Scripps Institution of Oceanography
University of California San Diego, La Jolla, CA
www.scrippsarchives,ucsd.edu

BOOKS, JOURNALS, AND ARTICLES

Allen, Frederick Lewis. 1931. *Only Yesterday.* New York: Harper & Row.

Allen, Frederick Lewis. 1954. *The Big Change, America Transforms Itself 1900–1950.* New York: Harper & Row.

Anderson Stanford, Leslie Cormier, Jacqueline Gargus, Felipe J. Prestamo, Charles Rusch, and Lydia Soo. 1986. "Architectural Design as Research Programs: The Schools at Cranbrook by Eliel Saarinen." *Places* 3 (2): 59–69.

Baca, Elmo. 1996. *Romance of the Mission, Decorating in the Mission Style.* Salt Lake City: Gibbs Smith Publisher (illustrated).

Birnbaum, Charles A., FASLA, and Robin Larson. 2000. *National Park Historic Landscape Initiative, Pioneers of American Landscape Design.* New York: McGraw-Hill.

Brooks, H. Allen. 1972. *The Prairie School: Frank Lloyd Wright and His Midwest Contemporaries.* Toronto: University of Toronto Press.

Brush, Edward Hale. February, 1911. "A Garden City for the Man of Moderate Means," *The Craftsman* xix (5): 445–451 (pen and ink illustrations of Forest Hills).

"California Architects: Greene & Greene, Polk, Gill." 1913. *Architectural Record* xxiv (December).

Cormier, Leslie Humm. 2004. "Walter Gropius." *Encyclopedia of 20th-Century Architecture,* vol. 2. New York: Routledge (Fitzroy Dearborn), 563.

Cormier, Leslie Humm. 2004. "The International Style." *Encyclopedia of 20th-Century Architecture,* vol. 2. New York: Routledge (Fitzroy Dearborn), 681–685.

Cormier, Leslie Humm. 1993. "Gropius House, Lincoln, Massachusetts." *International Dictionary of Architects and Architecture,* vol. 2. Detroit: St. James Press (originally published 1984, 1986, Brown University), 1993, 947–949.

Cormier, Leslie Humm. 2004. "Urban Planning." *Encyclopedia of 20th-Century Architecture,* vol. 3. New York: Routledge (Fitzroy Dearborn), 1379–1382.

Cormier, Leslie Humm. 1984. *The Woods End Colony: An Architects' Refuge in America.* Master's thesis, Brown University, Department of History of Art and Architecture.

Craftsman Farms Foundation. 1999. *Gustav Stickley's Craftsman Farms A Pictorial History,* ed. David Cathers. Parsippany, NJ: Turn of the Century Editions.

Flagg, Ernest. 1907. "American Architecture as Opposed to Architecture in America." *Architectural Record* × (October): 178–190.

"The General Contractor." 1903. Monthly column, including Modern Plumbing, Elevators, Fireproofing. *Architectural Record* xiii (January): 120.

Giedion, Sigfried. 1978. *Space, Time and Architecture, The Growth of a New Tradition.* Cambridge: Harvard University Press, 1941.

Glenn, John. 1907–1946. *Forest Hills Gardens,* vol. 1. New York: The Russell Sage Foundation.

Goff, Lee. 2002. *Tudor Style, Tudor Revival Houses in America, 1890 to the Present.* New York: Universe Publishing.

Gottfried, Herbert, and Jan Jennings. 1988. *American Vernacular Design 1870–1940.* Ames: Iowa State University Press.

Gowans, Alan. 1986. *The Comfortable House: North American Suburban Architecture 1890–1930.* Cambridge, MA: M.I.T. Press.

Gray, Stephen. 1990. *Gustav Stickley after 1909.* New York: Turn of the Century Editions (reproduction of 1909 catalogue).

Gray, Steven, ed. 1987. *The Early Work of Gustav Stickley.* New York: Turn of the Century Editions (reprint of catalogs 1901–1905).

Griswold, Mac, and Eleanor Weller. 2000. *The Golden Age of American Gardens, Proud Owners, Private Estates, 1890–1940.* New York: The Garden Club of America and Harry N. Abrams (color illustrations of gardens).

"The Harmonious Home." 1920. *Chicago Tribune,* weekly column.

Hayden, Dolores. 1981. *The Grand Domestic Revolution: A History of Feminist Designs for American Homes, Neighborhoods, and Cities.* Cambridge, MA: M.I.T, Press.

Hayward, Allyson M. 1997. *Private Pleasures Derived from Tradition, The Hunnewell Estates Historic District, Arnoldia.* Cambridge, MA: Arnold Arboretum, Harvard University.

Heinz, Thomas A. 1982. *Frank Lloyd Wright.* New York: St. Martin's Press.

Heinz, Thomas A. 1993. *Frank Lloyd Wright: Portfolio Furniture.* Salt Lake City, UT: Peregrine Press (color illustrations).

Hines, Thomas S. 2000. *Irving Gill and the Architecture of Reform, A Study in Modernist Architectural Culture.* New York: The Monacelli Press.

Hitchcock, Henry-Russell. 1982. *Architecture: Nineteenth and Twentieth Centuries.* New York: Penguin Books.

Hitchcock, Henry-Russell. 1942. *In the Nature of Materials, The Buildings of Frank Lloyd Wright 1817–1941.* New York: Hawthorn Books, Inc. (reprinted New York: Da Capo Press, 1982).

"How to Build Tenements." 1900. *New York Times* (12 October): 11.

Jekyll, Gertrude. 1982. *Home and Garden.* London: Longmans Green & Co. (reprinted by the Antique Collectors' Club, England, 1982).

Jordy, William H. 1972. *American Buildings and Their Architects, Progressive and Academic Ideals at the Turn of the Twentieth Century,* vol. 3. New York: Doubleday and Company.

Kaiser, Harvey H. 1997. *Landmarks in the Landscape, Historic Architecture in the National Parks of the West.* San Francisco: Chronicle Books.

Lancaster, Clay. 1984. *American Bungalow 1880–1920.* New York: Abbeville Press.

Linoff, Victor, ed. 1991. *Illustrated Mission Furniture Catalog 1912–13, Come-Packt Furniture Company.* New York: Dover.

Longstreth, Richard. 1983. *On the Edge of the World, Four Architects in San Francisco at the Turn of the Century.* Cambridge, MA: The Architectural History Foundation and M.I.T. Press.

Louis Comfort Tiffany and Laurelton Hall. 2007. *An Artist's Country Estate.* Metropolitan Museum of Art, New York. Exhibition, November 21, 2006–May 20, 2007.

Lupton, Ellen, and J. Abbott Miller. 1992. *The Bathroom, the Kitchen and the Aesthetics of Waste, A Process of Elimination.* M.I.T. List Visual Arts Center and Princeton, NJ, Architectural Press. Exhibition, Cambridge, MA, May 9–June 28.

Maddex, Diane, and A. Verntikoff. 2003. *Bungalow Nation.* New York: Harry N. Abrams (illustrated).

Mather, Christine, and Sharon Woods. 1986. *Santa Fe Style.* New York: Rizzoli (exceptional photography by Paul Hardy).

McCoy, Esther. 1960. *Five California Architects.* New York: Reinhold Publishing Corporation.

Newcomb, Rexford. 1927. *The Spanish House for America.* Philadelphia: J.B. Lippincott Company.

Olmsted, Frederick Law. 1928. *The "Greensward" Plan for the Improvement of the Central Park, 1858, Forty Years of Landscape Architecture, Central Park and Frederick Law Olmsted, Sr.* Ed. F. L. Olmsted, Jr. and reprinted by MIT Press, 1973.

Poppeliers, John C., S. Allen Chambers, Jr., and Nancy B. Schwartz. 2003. *Historic American Buildings Survey, What Style Is It? A Guide to American Architecture.* Hoboken, NJ: John Wiley & Sons.

"To Plant A Tree." 1909. *Chicago Tribune.* (28 July): 13.

Pulos, Arthur J. 1983. *American Design Ethic A History of Industrial Design to 1940.* Cambridge, MA: The MIT Press.

Real Estate section. 1908. *New York Times.*

Real Estate section. 1919. *Chicago Tribune.* (11 May).

Real Estate section. 1919. *Los Angeles Times* (11 May).

Rifkind, Carole. 1980. *A Field Guide to American Architecture.* New York: Plume.

Roth, Leland M., ed. 1983. *America Builds, Source Documents in American Architecture and Planning.* New York: Harper & Row Publishers.

Roth, Leland M. 1983. *McKim, Mead & White, Architects.* New York: Harper & Row.

Roosevelt, Theodore. 1918. "Housing After the War." *Architectural Record* (July): 151.

Scully, Vincent J., Jr. 1979. *The Shingle Style and the Stick Style.* New Haven, CT: Yale University Press.

"17 House Designs of the Twenties, Gordon-Van Tine Co., (1923)." 1992. New York: Dover Publications.

"A Short Bibliography and Analysis of Housing." 1921. *Architectural Record* (February): 181–185.

Starr, Kevin. 2002. *The Dream Endures, California Enters the 1940s.* New York: Oxford University Press.

Stein, Clarence S. 1978. *Toward New Towns for America*. Introduction by Lewis Mumford. Cambridge: M.I.T. Press, 1957.

Steiner, Frances H. 1985. *Frank Lloyd Wright in Oak Park & River Forest*. Chicago: Sigma Press.

Stern, Robert A. M. 1983. *Gregory Gilmartin and John Montague Massengale, New York 1900, Metropolitan Architecture and Urbanism 1890–1915*. New York: Rizzoli International Publications, Inc.

Stickley, Gustav. 1906. "The Craftsman House: A Practical Application of Our Theories of Home Building." Reprinted in *The Best of Craftsman Homes*. Santa Barbara, Peregrine Smith, Inc., 1979, 67–71.

Stickley, Gustav. 1906. "Furniture Making in This Country." Reprinted in *The Best of Craftsman Homes*. Santa Barbara, Peregrine Smith, Inc., 1979, 187–195.

Stickley, Gustav. 1906. "The Natural Garden." Reprinted in *The Best of Craftsman Homes*. Santa Barbara, Peregrine Smith, Inc., 1979, 152–155.

Stickley, Gustav. 1906. "Our Native Woods and the Craftsman Method of Finishing Them." Reprinted in *The Best of Craftsman Homes*. Santa Barbara, Peregrine Smith, Inc., 1979, 221–229.

Stickley, Gustav. 1912. *The Best of Craftsman Homes*. Santa Barbara: Peregrine Smith, 1979.

Stickley, Gustav. 1903–1916. *The Craftsman*. (Monthly magazine published by Craftsman Farms, Parsippany, NJ, 1903–1916, illustrated with photographs, drawings, and house plans.)

Sturgis, Russell. 1900. "The Art Gallery of the Streets." *Architectural Record* (July): 92–112.

Sturgis, Russell. 1901. "Architects and Architecture" column. *New York Times* (21 September).

"The Work of McKim, Mead & White." 1906. *Architectural Record* (September).

"The Work of Carrere & Hastings." 1910. *Architectural Record* (June).

"Town Plan Helps Future Land Value." 1924. *New York Times* (18 May): RE2.

"Twentieth Century's Triumphant Entry." 1901. *New York Times* (1 January): 1.

"Uncle Sam, Landlord." 1919. *New York Times* (29 June): 82.

United States Geological Survey. 2006. "The Great 1906 San Francisco Earthquake, Earthquake Hazards Program." Available at: usgs.gov.

"A Universal Cry for Smaller Houses." 1921. *Chicago Tribune* (21 July): 62.

Veiller, Lawrence. 1920. *A Model Housing Law*. New York: The Russell Sage Foundation.

White, Charles E., Jr. 1927. *The Bungalow Book*. New York: MacMillan Company.

Wills, Royal Barry, Associates. 1993. *Houses for Good Living*. Stanford, CT: Architectural Book Publishing Co.

Wilson, Henry L. 1993. *California Bungalows of the Twenties*. Reprint, original date unknown, 1920s. New York: Dover Publications.

Wilson, Richard Guy. 2004. *The Colonial Revival House*. New York: Harry N. Abrams.

Winter, Robert, and Alexander Vertikoff. 2004. *Craftsman Style*. New York: Harry N. Abrams Publishers (color illustrations).

Wright, Frank Lloyd. 1954. *The Natural House*. New York: Horizon Press.

HISTORICAL NEWSPAPERS AND JOURNALS

These historical newspaper and journal sources, in particular, offer valuable and varied insights into the early modern architectural era. One can observe the illustrations and the writing styles of the sources, in addition to the content, to find the flavor of the time.

The New York Times The newspaper of record for national and international affairs, as well as for art and architectural criticism of the era. The more florid style of the earlier part of the century gave way to serious journalism and economic news by the teens.

The Chicago Tribune The voice of the Midwest, with similarities to both a big city and a small town paper. Many pages devoted to the life of the socialite, and therefore openly illustrating societal inequities of the day. Regular home columns, and much concerned with contemporary architectural developments.

The Los Angeles Times Like the city it represented, this paper was filled with bungalows, real estate developments, and exclamation points!

Architectural Record An excellent source documenting the stylistic and social concerns of the architectural profession in America. Illustrated, with critical comments by well-known architects, as well as entire issues devoted to outstanding architectural firms, such as McKim, Mead, and White.

The Craftsman Published by Gustav Stickley from 1903–1916, with articles on the Craftsman home life, illustrated by photographs, drawings, and plans of Craftsman style house and furniture designs.

WEB SITES

Arnold Arboretum, Harvard University, Cambridge, MA. www.Arnoldia.arboretum. harvard.edu. Includes a periodical on the history of landscape design.

Asilomar, Monterey, California. www.visitasilomar.com. Provides illustrations and history of the bungalow camp designed for the YWCA by early modern architect Julia Morgan.

Edison & Ford Winter Estate, Florida. www.efwefla.org. Gives information on winter homes and workshops of two important American inventors, open to the public.

Fallingwater, Pennsylvania, Frank Lloyd Wright, architect. www.paconserve.org. One of the most important modern homes in America, open to the public for tours.

Frank Lloyd Wright Preservation Trust, Oak Park, Illinois. www.wrightplus.org. The Web site of the Frank Lloyd Wright Home and Studio, open to the public, and nearby early modern homes by Wright, for walking tours.

Frick Collection and Frick Art Reference Library, East 71st Street, New York., www. frick.org. An important art collection and home of an American industrialist, open to the public.

Glass House, New Canaan, Connecticut, Philip Johnson, architect. www.philip johnsonglasshouse.org. Important mid-twentieth-century modern home in the International style, open for tours by appointment.

Gropius House, Lincoln, Massachusetts. www.historicnewengland/visit/homes/ gropius.org. The American modern home, showing a synthesis of American and European aesthetics, of the émigré architect and founder of the German Bauhaus, Walter Gropius, open to the public.

Historic New England. www.historicnewengland.org. Formerly known as Society for the Preservation of New England Antiquities, this organization preserves and opens historical American homes from the seventeenth to the twentieth centuries to the public.

Historical Newspapers. www.ProQuest.com., A site containing editions of *The New York Times, The Los Angeles Times, The Chicago Tribune,* and others of the early twentieth century, by subscription or in libraries.

Huntington Library, Art Collections, and Botanical Gardens, San Marino, California, www.huntington.org. A Web site showing collections include paintings, books, and botanical specimens on a landscaped estate, including rooms of Greene and Greene furniture, open to the public.

Isabella Stewart Gardner Museum, Boston, MA. www.gardnermuseum.org. Museum and mansion home of an American art collector, open to the public.

Kykuit, The Rockefeller Estate, New York. www.hudsonvalley.org. A Web site about the architecture, Hudson River landscape architecture, and modern art collection of an American philanthropic family, the Rockefellers, open to the public for tours.

Lower East Side Tenement Museum. www.tenement.org. An authentic, re-created American tenement of the early modern architectural era, showing the lives of the immigrant poor.

Metropolitan Museum of Art, New York, www.Metmuseum.org. The Web site for the world renowned encyclopedic art museum, including examples of furniture and architecture of Frank Lloyd Wright and decorative arts of Tiffany, open to the public.

Museum of the City of New York, New York. www.mcny.org. Archival photographs, documents, and decorative arts of the city.

Museum of Fine Arts, Boston, MA. www.mfa.org. A major museum of art, including works of Paul Revere and other important collections of American decorative arts.

National Archives of the United States of America, Washington, D.C. www.archives. gov. A resource for researching documents on American history.

National Park Service. www.NPS.org. The site of the National Parks of the U.S., which provides preservation of landscape and dramatic open spaces, established during the early modern era, protecting such sites as Yosemite, Yellowstone, Acadia, and Grand Canyon National Parks.

National Trust for Historic Preservation. www.nationaltrust.org. Advocacy organization dedicated to saving historic American architecture and cities.

Old House Journal. www.oldhousejournal.com. Magazine source for useful hands-on historic home preservation and illustrations.

Planting Fields Arboretum, Brookville, New York. www.plantingfields.org. An early modern Long Island private estate and landscape, now a public state park.

Sagamore Hill National Historic Site, Oyster Bay, New York. www.nps.gov/sahi. The home of early modern era President Theodore Roosevelt, open to the public.

Scripps Institution of Oceanography, University of California San Diego, La Jolla, California. www.sio.ucsd.edu. Illustrations of the site of Irving Gill's early modern Scripps Director's House.

Smithsonian Museum. www.smithsonian.org. Valuable illustrations and site for historic American decorative arts, including the collections of the many museums on the National Mall in Washington, D.C., as well as the Cooper-Hewitt mansion, the National Design Museum, New York.

Stickley's Craftsman Farms, New Jersey. www.stickleymuseum.org. Illustrations of the exterior and interior of the home of Gustav Stickley, and information on the American Arts and Crafts Movement, open to the public.

United States Geological Survey. www.USGS.gov. Contains scientific information for the public, and illustrations of historical earthquake damage, particularly of the Great San Francisco Earthquake of 1906.

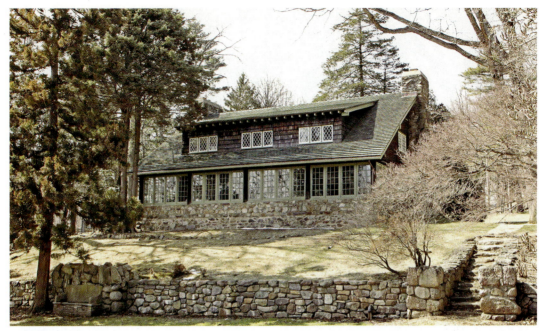

Crafting the Craftsman style. Gustav Stickley's bungalow at Craftsman Farms. Photograph by Ray Stubblebine, used by permission of The Craftsman Farms Foundation, Inc., Parsippany, New Jersey.

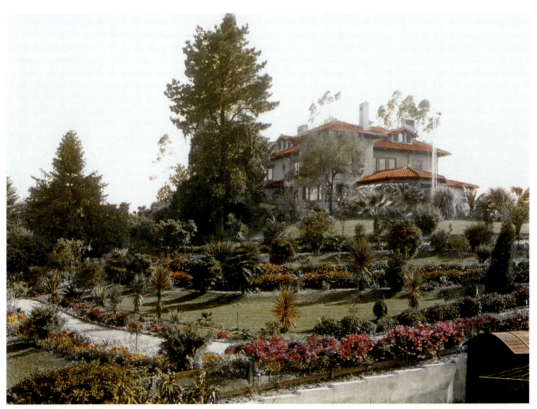

A place amid palms. California Spanish Revival. Courtesy of the Francis Loeb Library, Harvard Graduate School of Design.

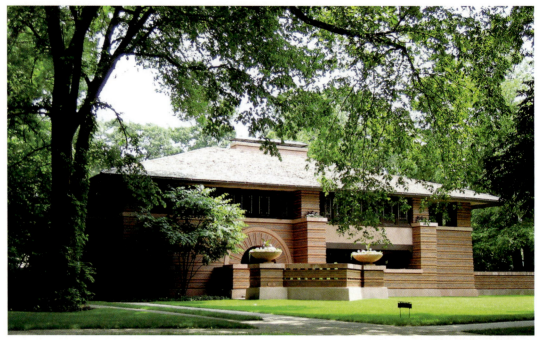

Organic architecture and the Prairie style: The Heurtley House, Frank Lloyd Wright, Oak Park, Illinois. Courtesy of Craig Stewart.

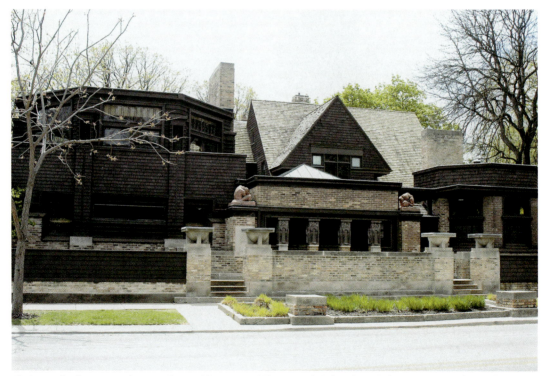

Geometric forms and organic architecture: The Frank Lloyd Wright Home and Studio, Oak Park, Illinois. Courtesy of Addison Godel.

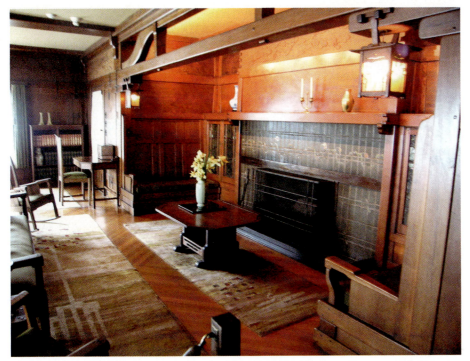

The hand-crafted home as art form. The Gamble House, Greene and Greene, Pasadena, California. © Greene and Greene Archives, Huntington Library, USC.

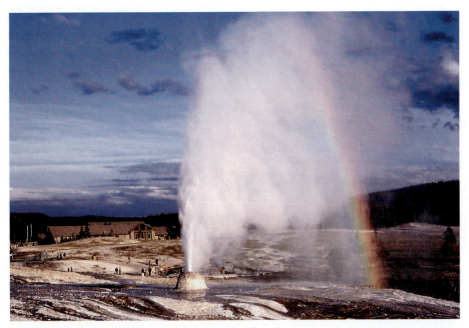

Beehive Geyser is located on Geyser Hill in the upper Geyser Basin of Yellowstone. During an eruption, the narrow cone acts like a nozzle, projecting the water column to heights of 130–190 ft. Courtesy of the National Park Service.

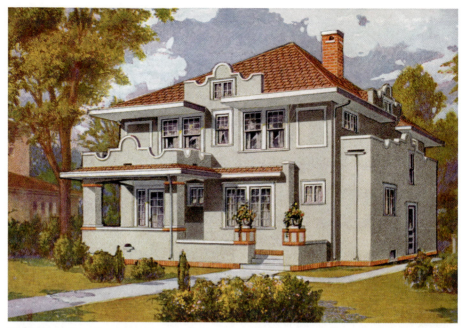

The Alhambra. Sears, Roebuck, and Co., Honor Bilt Modern Homes, Chicago and Philadelphia, 1923.

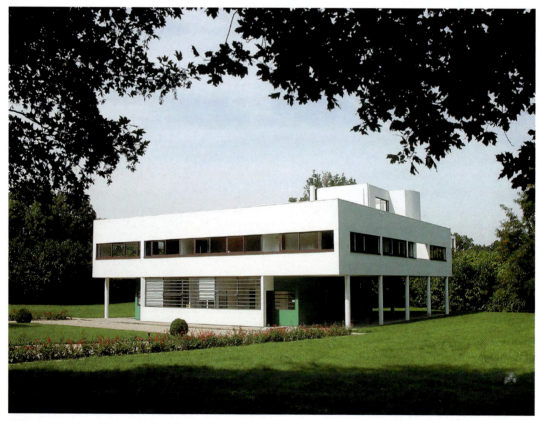

Villa Savior, Le Corbusier. Courtesy of Parandeep.

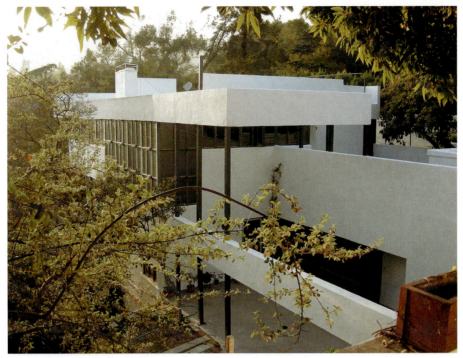

Lovell Health House, Richard Nuetra. This was the first steel-framed house constructed in the United States. Courtesy of Steven Keylon.

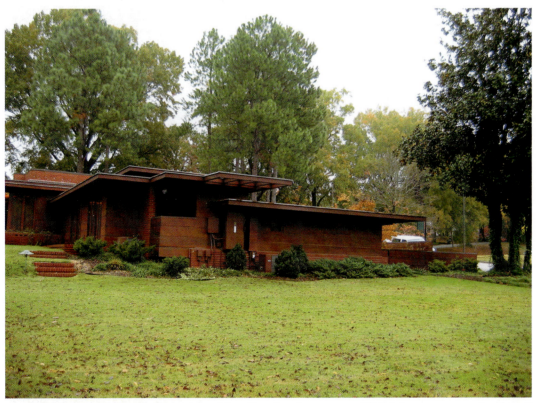

Usonian house, Frank Lloyd Wright. The Usonian house was Wright's answer to the "small house problem." Courtesy of Janet Powell.

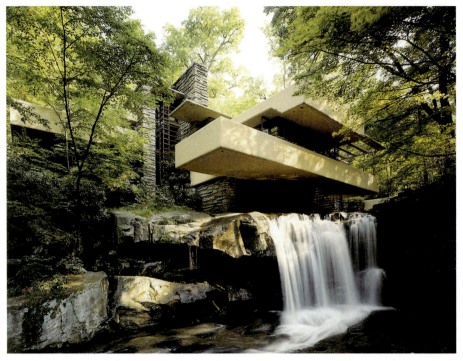

Falling Water, Frank Lloyd Wright. This is Wright's masterpiece and one of the best known houses of all time. Courtesy of the Library of Congress.

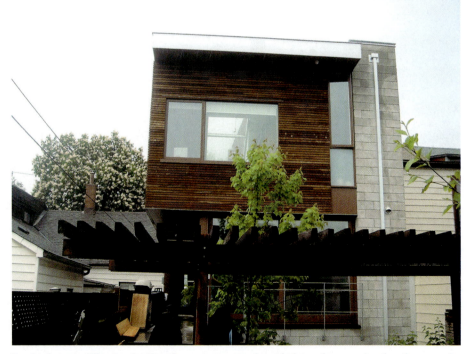

Levitt house. The Levitt Brothers mass produced these houses in the thousands. The house has come to symbolize suburban sprawl. Courtesy of Pema Hagen.

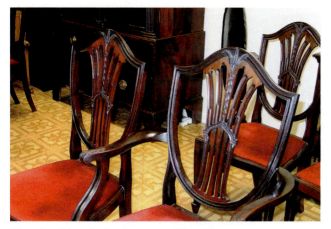

Hepplewhite chair. Courtesy of Ben Harper.

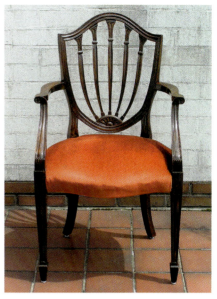

Sheraton chair. © Aperture8 | Dreams
time.com.

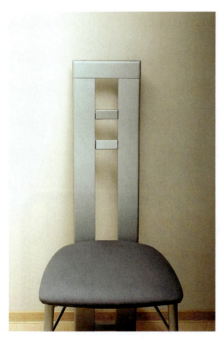

Art Deco chair. © Igor Terekhov | Dreams
time.com.

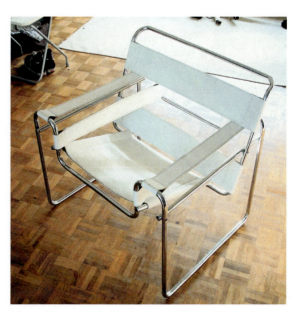

Marcel Breuer chair. Courtesy of Easy Skywalker.

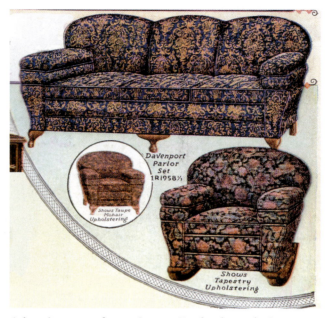

Advertisement from Sears, Roebuck and Company, 1926. The primary piece of furniture in the living room was a sofa. Sears, Roebuck, and Co., Chicago and Philadelphia, 1926.

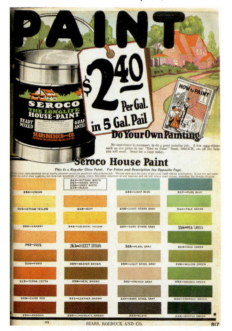

Paint advertisement, Sears, Roebuck and Company, 1926. Color schemes were changing the late 1920s and 1930s from neutral colors and patterns to the bolder look. Sears, Roebuck, and Co., Chicago and Philadelphia, 1926.

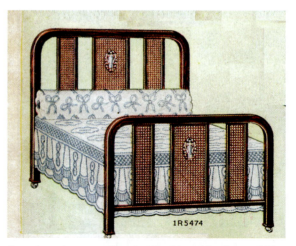

An advertisement for a typical steel bed as sold by Sears. Sears, Roebuck, and Co., Chicago and Philadelphia, 1926.

PART TWO

Homes in the Depression and World War II Era, 1921–1945

Neal V. Hitch

Introductory Note

During the early decades of the twentieth century, the societal concept of housing moved from the Victorian values of domesticity to a concept of the *modern* home. The modern home defined the discussions of housing between 1921 and 1945. Modernism, as a design movement, embodied basically three ideas; formal innovation, a desire to create something new, and a tendency toward abstraction. Modernist houses included plain walls, flat-roofs, ribbon windows, and open floor plans.

Modern, however, also applied to the new technological systems placed in the house during the early twentieth century. The comfort and convenience of new bathrooms, new kitchens, electricity, and new heating systems were new *modern* concepts. From the outside, however, the typical new modern house of the period usually looked like a traditional house.

What was less obvious was the way in which the single-family house became the catalyst that moved most families into a larger community of consumers. This occurred through the acceptance, desire, purchase, and use of the small, everyday appliances that increasingly represented the modern ideas of comfort and convenience. Electricity, plumbing, and communication systems such as the telephone and radio began to be integrated into the very core of the house.

During the 1920s, Americans in a new middle class began both to desire and purchase new houses filled with these technological systems. To fulfill the burgeoning dream of home ownership, builders and real estate professionals began to construct and market smaller houses. These new houses, constructed all across the country during a housing boom between 1922 and 1929, were what came to be known as "modern homes."

The transformation of the American home from the Victorian manse to the small modern house is the story told in this book. The development and spread of the small house paralleled the rise of technological systems that defined the small house. Simultaneously, both governmental and nongovernmental agencies pushed the development and marketing of new homes during the period. By the 1940s, the ownership of a small home had become a defining value of the middle and working classes. This was no accident.

CONTENT

"The Transformation of Life in America, 1921–1945" provides an account of the historical context of housing during the 1920s, 1930s, and 1940s. During this period, monumental changes took place in society and the economy. The period began with the substantial economic growth of the booming 1920s. Mass acquisition of automobiles changed the relationship of the house to the community and changed the relationship of the family to the house. The boom years were quickly followed by the dramatic decline in the economy during the depression of the 1930s. Many people retrenched within their homes; many people lost their homes. From 1941 to 1945, a wartime economy and the military service of nearly 18 million people brought an end to the depression and a rise in national income.

"Styles of Domestic Architecture, 1921–1945" discusses the styles of houses that dominated the period. Historians would describe most of the houses built during the 1920s and 1930s as *vernacular,* that is, common houses built without an architect or designer. Architectural historians characterize the period in terms of the dominant new style of modernism. Across neighborhoods and developments, however, houses deceivingly appeared to be traditional.

Most new house building was not under the control of architects. Builders, realtors, and developers controlled the majority of new construction. Here, the planning of new developments and neighborhoods was as important as the styles of houses built. This included development on the periphery of cities, developments serving minority homeowners, and even housing developments for the military.

During the first decades of the twentieth century, technological changes in both the construction industry and in the house itself altered the nature, plan, and concept of the house, as is discussed in "Building Materials and Manufacturing, 1921–1945." Changes involved mostly the perfection of technologies introduced in the late nineteenth century. The house, and the construction systems and technological systems in the house, systematically became standardized between the 1920s and the 1940s. At the same time, images of the new twentieth-century home in various media negotiated household and cultural change. Technologies such as the radio and the telephone had dramatic affects on both the interior and on the social culture of the house. A modern, media-driven culture replaced Victorian domesticity.

The house plan and layout symbolized much of this transformation, as explained in "Home Layout and Design, 1921–1945." Changing family relationships and changing gender relationships affected areas of the house such as the kitchen.

Specific private and government-sponsored organizations and programs promoted and marketed the transformation of the house. A network of organizations and individuals sought to use modern housing to stabilize capitalism after 1917 and after 1929 sought to use modern housing to revitalize the economy. Housing policy and federal programs became institutionalized after 1934, and with the backing of the government, whether intentional or unintentional, the designs of houses became standardized by the mid-1940s.

"Furniture and Decoration, 1921–1945" discusses the individual rooms in the small house of the 1920s and 1930s and the furniture placed in these rooms. The transformation from the Victorian home to the modern home occurred in changes to individual rooms. Technology tended to remove the specialized functions of individual nineteenth-century rooms, and the multifunctional living room came to dominate the house.

Traditional styles of furniture and decoration, such as Colonial Revival and Arts and Crafts, dominated the living room, as well as other rooms between 1921 and 1945. By the mid to late 1930s, the aesthetics of modernism began to be commercially successful.

Community builders and utopian developments all had the community and the automobile at the heart of new housing. First the automobile transformed the neighborhood into the near-urban neighborhood. Then the car culture led to full-fledged suburbs. Yards and lawns, however, started with the development of the individual lot, as is discussed in "Landscaping and Outbuildings, 1921–1945." Homeowners often received a blank canvas on which to create outdoor spaces. Many books and magazines informed them on how to best create their lawns and yards. The yard was also tied into services, particularly through the basement. The basement often served as a technological service area, typically for laundry, heating, and food storage. Once a builder completed a house and the homeowner moved in, landscape and the outbuildings served as indispensable to living in the house.

The themes that run through this part of volume 3 of *The Greenwood Encyclopedia of Homes through American History* reinforce the importance of technology to the modern home. The period, however, also saw the transformation of the house into the typical forms we live with today. Revival styles and bungalows typified most new houses throughout the 1920s and 1930s. But by the 1940s, architects and builders began to blend the traditional styles of housing with modernist planning principles. The open floor plan, the open kitchen, and the elimination of the tight cluster of rooms typical of the small house of the 1920s became standard planning principles of postwar housing in the late 1940s. The years between 1920 and 1945, therefore, constitute one of the significant transformative periods in the history of housing in the United States.

Timeline

1920	November: Election of President Warren G. Harding.
	First commercial radio broadcast KDKA in Pittsburgh.
	Eighteenth Amendment prohibits the sale and manufacture of alcohol.
1921	February: Herbert Hoover accepts Warren G. Harding's offer to head the Commerce Department.
	Frank Lloyd Wright builds concrete block houses in California, such as the Millard House of 1921 and the Storer House of 1922, with a geometric grid, determined by the module of the block.
1922	Founding of Better Homes in America Movement by Marie Meloney, publisher of the *Delineator,* a women's magazine.
	Housing boom begins, moving from 247,000 new houses constructed in 1920 to 716,000 houses constructed in 1922.
	J. C. Nichols begins development of his famous County Club District in Kansas City, eventually building over 6,000 homes.
	Fiske Kimball publishes *Domestic Architecture of the American Colonies and of the Early Republic.*
1923	June 4: President Warren G. Harding dedicates the "Home Sweet Home" house on the Washington Mall.
	August: President Harding dies in office. Calvin Coolidge becomes President.

Le Corbusier published one of the most successful books on the Modernist aesthetic, *Vers Une Architecture,* or *Towards a New Architecture.*

Richard Neutra immigrates to the United States.

1924   Better Homes movement reorganized into a not-for-profit corporation housed within the Department of Commerce.

RCA engineers design a reasonably-priced six-tube receiver and begin marketing and selling the first modern family radio.

1926   September 18: Category 4 hurricane known as the Great Miami Hurricane devastates Florida, ending the land boom and beginning an economic down turn in land speculation prior to the depression.

Warner Brothers introduces talking movies.

Walter Gropius completes the building of the Bauhaus in Dessau, Germany.

1927   Production of Model T Ford ends. Ford plants retooled to produce Model A Ford.

October: *The Jazz Singer* is first successful talking movie.

November: John D. Rockefeller, Jr. commissions Dr. W.A.R. Goodwin, the rector of Bruton Parish, to purchase buildings and complete a restoration plan for Williamsburg, Virginia.

1928   Construction starts of new housing begin to decline.

Home Modernization Bureau founded by private business in order to emphasize remodeling and to push commercial sales of building materials.

Sears, Roebuck Company introduces the Craftsman line of tools.

November: Herbert Hoover elected President.

Richard Neutra designs the Lovell Health House, which becomes an icon of modernism in America.

1929   October 24–29: Stock Market Crash leads to the Great Depression. The Dow Jones Industrial Average sinks from 400 to 145. The New York Stock Exchange loses $5 billion of share values.

1930   Construction begins on the Empire State Building in New York City.

Le Corbusier completes the Villa Savoye near Paris.

1931   Conference on Home Ownership and Home Building is initiated by President Hoover through the Better Homes organization.

1932   Opening of the International style exhibit of modernist architecture at the Museum of Modern Art in New York categorizes the modern architecture aesthetic.

Frank Lloyd Wright publishes *An Autobiography* and *The Disappearing City* and opens the Taliesin Fellowship.

November: Franklin D. Roosevelt elected as President.

Statistically worst year of the depression.

1933   First 100 days of the New Deal.

1934   Housing Act of 1934 creates Federal Housing Administration (FHA) and Minimum Standards for housing in the United States.

1936   Frank Lloyd Wright builds Jacobs House, built in Madison, Wisconsin, which is the best example of a Usonian house.

1937   Frank Lloyd Wright's masterpiece residential project Fallingwater is constructed.

FHA receives new director and begins to excel as a government institution.

1939   September 1: German forces march into Poland, and war breaks out in Europe.

1941   December 7: Japanese attack on Pearl Harbor. United States enters World War Two.

1945   September 2: VJ Day. Signing of formal surrender ending World War II.

The Transformation of Life in America

On June 4, 1923, President Warren G. Harding dedicated the "Home Sweet Home" house, on the Washington Mall. The building was a small model home designed to look like a typical house from the time when America was still a group of colonies. The "Home Sweet Home" house served as the national demonstration house of the Better Homes in America movement, an organization devoted to promoting the ownership and improvement of housing across the United States. Sponsored by the General Federation of Women's Clubs, the house was the centerpiece of a national Better Homes Week with a "mission of raising the standard of homes and home life in America."

The house was Colonial Revival in style, and furnishings followed the colonial period. The house, however, was "built according to the best standards and its equipment follow[ed] the most modern ideas." Amazingly, building contractors constructed the house in just three weeks. It opened specifically to coincide with the national Shriners convention in Washington, where the building served "the double purpose of model or demonstration house for the better homes campaign and bureau of information for the Shriners" ("President to Open" 1923).

With over 500,000 visitors coming to Washington during the week, the "Home Sweet Home" house made a "specially favorable opportunity for a better homes campaign." The Shriners had come from every city and town in the country. Seeing modern appliances and a model kitchen and bath all put together in a small house designed to reflect the values of the early colonists allowed them to embark on a "new study of their home problems" ("J. H. Payne House" 1923).

The demonstration house was designed by the architect Donn Barber along the lines of the 1720 house in which John Howard Payne lived in East Hampton,

New York. In 1822, Payne wrote the song "Home Sweet Home," which by the early twentieth century had become a symbol of the American dream of home ownership. During the 1920s, the reference could be found in many advertisements and building campaigns. Dr. Jason Noble Pierce even preached a sermon about the song at the First Congregational Church in Washington in May of 1923. The entire Sunday service was devoted to "interest of better American homes" ("J. H. Payne House" 1923).

The "Home Sweet Home" house illustrated the combined efforts of the government, manufacturers, and voluntary associations to promote a prototype of the new suburban American home, the Colonial Revival. It was not by accident that the demonstration house was built in Washington. Secretary of Commerce Herbert Hoover was the chairman of the advisory council of Better Homes in America. In an article in the *Washington Post,* on April 22, 1923, John Gries, the chief of the division of building and housing at the Department of Commerce, clearly articulated the federal government's position on housing as well as the reason for model homes like the "Home Sweet Home" house. He stated, "The American people will advance as individuals and as a nation largely as they are determined to improve their living standards. There is nothing so stimulating to character and usefulness as the desire for a better home. The more intelligently the American people develop their homes, the happier and more prosperous the country will be" ("J. H. Payne House" 1923; "President to 'Open Home Sweet Home' " 1923).

By the 1920s, housing in America had become the cultural icon representing the achievement of an increased standard of living. Throughout the 1920s and 1930s, and into the 1940s, housing served as the sign that the owner had attained the status of middle class. But housing also introduced new technology to most Americans and became a significant driver of the economy. Housing, in short, became the most important artifact of culture associated with the lives of the typical American family.

It is the characteristics of this new cutting edge housing that will be discussed in this section of volume 3. The same dynamics at work in the society and the economy fundamentally altered the nature of housing during the early decades of the twentieth century. Many of the changes in housing were directed by a large domestic housing reform movement, the Better Homes in America movement was one example. These domestic reforms were not new ideas, but it was not until the 1920s and 1930s that a critical mass of housing had been built in order for the changes to be transforming in nature.

THE YEARS OF FRAGMENTATION, BOOM, AND BUST

The years between 1921 and 1945 can be characterized by a sudden fragmentation in many aspects of the social and economic fabric of the United States. The forces associated with the organizational society and progressivism ushered in the new America of the 1920s. Significant sectors of society substantially unraveled, but progressivism continued, especially in the modernization of housing. The organizational society intensified, and in the 1920s and 1930s specialization increased in most areas of business, culture, and life.

At the turn of the century, the United States was at the threshold of a new modern society, a new modern economy, and new modern housing. At least

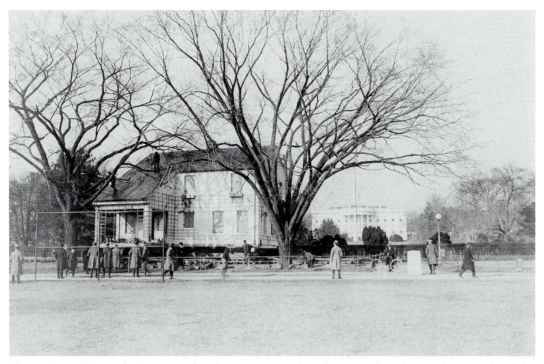

Home Sweet Home being moved to its permanent location, passing the south grounds of the White House, 1924. Courtesy of the Library of Congress.

four characteristics distinguished this new society. The first was the development of an industrial complex. The second was the dependence on technological change for economic growth. The third was diversity in the social structure. The fourth was vast changes in the foundation of cultural life (Nash 1971).

The organizational society served to specialize and professionalize. Engineering became a major component of business. Engineers fine-tuned production techniques and brought efficiency into the factory. Workers specialized in specific areas of the workplace.

Professional organizations developed into effective institutions controlling entire trade groups. Significantly, the National Board of Realtors was founded in 1908. But during the 1920s, these institutions grew from infancy into professional organizations that participated in advocacy and policy during the massive growth in business output through the Second World War.

The new economy was spearheaded by the emergence of big business—businesses that had systematically organized in order to achieve greater control over production, supply, and profits. Food processing, textiles, steel, and lumbering all grew through vertical and horizontal integration. Many corporations began to control every process in the production chain, from raw materials to retail sales, in order to limit the loss of profit to middlemen. Canned meats, fruits, and vegetables found transportation along new roads and highways and large new markets in cities and towns. Steel, which had been a developing industry in 1870 with $128 million in procession output, had grown to a billion-dollar industry by 1900. These four industries—food production, textiles, steel, and lumbering—accounted for over half of the manufacturing income in the United States and employed over half of all workers engaged in manufacturing.

At the same time that business and society were organizing, a general atmosphere of reform permeated most of American society. Known as progressivism, reform affected almost all American institutions during the first two decades of the twentieth century. The reforms, however, initiated in the collective actions of individuals. Progressives, as individuals, were largely upper middle class. During the late nineteenth century, middle-class sons and daughters began to put into action the cultural lessons they had learned in their family parlors.

The rise of the middle class is described at length by Stuart Blumin in *The Emergence of the Middle Class.* Largely a result of the new managerial revolution in business, the new middle class applied scientific principals and efficiency to all political, economic, and social institutions. The use of the expert to solve problems became the focus of change.

Reform came from the top down and worked through the process of volunteerism. Reform was not government sponsored, it resulted from the efforts of the upper middle class in voluntary groups. Reformers attempted to uplift society through changing both the social and the physical environments where people lived and worked. This "environmental" approach is suggestive of the fact that progressives believed that if they could change the institutions affecting the individual, then the individual would change. Examples included raising women's wages in an effort to end prostitution, or tenement housing reform to improve health conditions.

By the 1920s, with the end of World War I, the progressive movement began to give way to other cultural forces. Many progressives became disillusioned with a society that could create the destruction experienced during the war. The idea that society progresses toward a better end had taken a step backward, and many intellectuals retreated into "art for arts sake."

Domestic reforms in housing, likewise, continued unabated and in fact were facilitated by the new societal and social dynamics of the 1920s. This, in part, was because reforms focused on cleanliness and health in modern bathrooms and kitchens, which were conveniences that most homeowners learned to want.

Modern conveniences came slowly to the average American home. Only after 1934 did over 80 percent of homes have electricity. Not until the late 1940s did over 80 percent of homes have running water and sewer systems. These figures, however, are misleading in that they are based on the modification of existing homes. What these figures show is a material culture lag that occurs in the remodeling of older homes.

The 1921 Recession and Cultural Fragmentation

Economic growth in the United States was steadily increasing during the decade before the First World War. This growth continued throughout the war owing to mobilization and war materials manufacturing. At the same, Americans complained about a disturbing inflation and a high cost of living. After the war ended, however, a decline in the global economy occurred rapidly. A mild retreat ensued between 1918 and 1920, but in 1921 the global economy fell

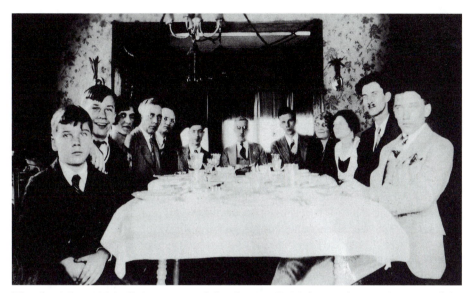

Thanksgiving 1931, dining room of the George K. Mahanna home. Courtesy of the
Ohio Historical Society.

sharply, plunging the United States into a disruptive recession. The end of war
materials production and returning veterans placed a tremendous strain on the
job market. Unemployment climbed to 11 percent. The surplus labor market
caused wages to fall. The gross national product fell nearly 24 percent between
1920 and 1922. This was twice the decline that the country would experience
during the later depression.

Meanwhile, reformers within the progressive movement separated themselves into two camps; one group concerned with social justice and one with
uplift. The forces behind social justice worked to improve race relations, the
lives of the working poor, and the health and safety of labor. The forces behind
uplift fought for prohibition and decency, what today we would call family values. The uplift movement was primarily influenced by the white Anglo-Saxon
Protestant population. The efforts to promote decency within society were
aided by an alliance with other religious groups such as Catholics. Both social
justice and uplift programs were focused toward the new immigrant classes.
But general reform never again had the power wielded a decade before. Progressive reforms did continue to impact American institutions into the Depression and New Deal years. Many New Deal programs were extensions of
progressive reforms. And at the state level, progressive reforms continued well
into the mid-twentieth century.

A mass of immigrants resisted integration into systems of American life.
Hispanics in the Southwest and eastern Europeans in the urban areas of the
East came into the country to find work in the new industrial economy. Industrialization created an urban revolution where the population migrated toward
cities and towns, changing the landscape from one dominated by agrarian lifestyles to one dominated by urban lifestyles. Immigration fueled this change.
Millions of immigrants came to work in the new industries, creating a population with significantly more diverse cultural backgrounds.

Not everyone saw immigration as a positive attribute of the new industrial society. Nativists wanted to put limits on the growth of foreign communities, which had speech, habits, and values alien to old stock groups.

In 1921, Congress passed an immigration act that established quotas based on how many people of any particular nationality were already in the country. The intention was to keep the current balance that existed. Immigration was cut from 800,000 to 300,000 people annually. In 1924, the National Origins Act banned all immigration from East Asia.

Nativism also resulted in radicalized activities, including a resurgence of the Ku Klux Klan. The Klan originated during Reconstruction and had disbanded in the 1870s. By the 1920s, however, white southerners had resurrected the organization as a vehicle to intimidate African Americans, Catholics, Jews, and foreigners. The Klan devoted itself to purging America of impure alien influences. By 1923, the Klan consisted of over 3 million members; by 1924, it had grown to 4 million. The organization did not just persecute minority members of society; it also advocated compulsory Bible reading in schools, enforced prohibition, and worked to make divorce unacceptable. In short, the objective of the Klan was to radically defend what they saw as traditional values.

Minorities were oppressed, and a large part of the population did not participate in mainstream society. A growing African American middle class, however, shared values and aspirations of other upwardly mobile Americans. For many of those living outside of the mainstream, housing was still a major issue.

The New America and the 1920s

The First World War was a fundamental turning point, separating the old society from the new modern world. After the war, observations on the changes taking place in perception, attitude, and direction pervaded the American population. The population of the United States grew throughout this period, both through birth and immigration. After seeing a decrease in growth during the war, 1923 witnessed a peak growth of 2,119,000 people. This was slightly larger than the largest prewar year. After 1923, the increase in population declined steadily. The 1930 census recorded 122,775,046 persons living in the United States.

The most spectacular change came in a great recovery and growth of the economy between 1923 and 1929. Although not evenly distributed, substantial material growth was obvious to everyone. Much of it was based on technologies that were not new but that had massive qualitative impact, which will be discussed more later.

During the 1920s, the dynamics of economic and cultural change along with this increase in population brought about a shift in housing in the United States. Housing had long been in short supply, resulting in overcrowding, especially in urban areas. The housing market boomed between 1919 and 1927. In 1924, 1925, and 1926, new home starts reached nearly 1 million each year, numbers that would not be seen again until the late 1940s. Most of this new housing, however, came in the form of small houses marketed to an expanding middle class. And as shrewd commentators noted at the time, as many people moved into new housing, the housing they left became available to those further down in the economic hierarchy. In this way, the population shifted into newer residences, and housing filtered down through the various income groups living in both rural and urban areas.

A CULTURE OF CONSUMPTION

During the 1920s and 1930s, the culture of America changed noticeably. The change consisted of a shift from a producer-ethic to a consumer-ethic and to a therapeutic ideal. People began to define themselves not by what they produced, but by what they bought or thought about buying. The result was a driving force to consume, to buy, to desire to own more stuff. Many aspects of changing business practices became fundamental to the new consumer culture. The branding of specific products moved many products from a local to a national market. The 1920s ushered in a new consumer-oriented culture.

Abundance became the unifying character in the culture. The idea of success was universal. Anyone could attain success and mobility. Displays in windows and in advertisements allowed people to envision what they could buy in the future. They could consume by proxy. This democratized shopping. New stores often offered more than merchandize; they offered social destinations as well.

During the 1920s, countless self-help books instructed the individual how to develop a personality. The development of personality helped the individual live in a mass society. Personality differentiated the individual from the crowd. The performance of personality attracted others. Throughout the 1920s and 1930s, magazines, advertising, housing, and new institutions linked consumption to the personality.

Supermarkets and mail-order catalogs offered consumers the opportunity to get new national brands and offered manufactures outlets to attract new consumers. By the 1930s, national chain stores such as A & P and Walgreen's offered standardized product lines. By buying name brands, consumers could count on product consistency and price. Mail-order catalogs brought national brands to rural households; every homeowner had access to the same merchandise. By 1927, over 75 million Sears, Roebuck catalogs had been distributed. The products and styles seen in advertisements could be purchased by almost anyone.

The abundance and availability of consumer goods affected the relationship of the individual to the local community. Mass communication particularly aided in creating communities of consumption. Advertisers used print as a medium to convey messages about products. These advertisements presented images that told readers to emulate the middle class and professionals. To be middle class was to buy certain things imbued with middle-class values.

The radio offered a medium that reached into over 30 percent of the homes of America by the mid-1930s. Radio used methods including the interweaving plot, eavesdropping, and the crooner to advertise products, shying away from direct advertisement. Many of these advertisements used uplift to market a product. By 1931, most restrictions were lifted from radio advertising and commercials pushed new forms of coercion.

In 1924, one-third of all buyers were women. Moving away from the Victorian ideals of domestication, the typical daily routine for women changed from church-related activities to shopping. The new shopper worked for a salary rather than wages. Families also held middle-class values as important.

Mobility was a key to success. Continuing to improve one's station also meant continually moving into better neighborhoods and better houses.

Though consumer culture began to drive the new economy of the 1920s, the incomes produced were not evenly distributed. The business classes did very well. A new emergent managerial class working in steady jobs with salaried positions offered a new market for cars, radios, and houses. The working classes did not benefit in the same proportion. Workers did not get boosts in income from new products being manufactured.

Farmers fared worse, losing income. In 1920, farm income comprised 15 percent of the national total. By 1929, farm income only accounted for 11 percent. The average farm income dropped to one-fourth of the average nonfarm income.

In part, the loss of individual income resulted from gains in production stimulated by new technology. The number of tractors in use on American farms increased by 400 percent and 35 million new acres went into cultivation. The result, however, was overproduction. During the 1920s, the bottom dropped out of several commodity markets, including corn and grains. By the end of the 1920s, the farmer could not sell many agricultural products for what it cost to produce them. Over 3 million people left farms during the decade and moved to larger cities.

The Automobile as the Symbol of Consumption

The symbol of consumer culture was the automobile. During the 1920s, a new economy based on mass production and distribution created great affluence for many middle-class groups in America. Total wealth in the United States increased from $74 billion in 1919 to $104 billion in 1929. New industries developed in the 1920s based on technological innovations instead of the processing of raw materials. The manufacture of electrical appliances became a booming industry. American factories produced millions of refrigerators, washing machines, irons, fans, and toasters. In 1919, the Radio Corporation of America (RCA) began manufacturing radio receivers. Radios sold in the millions each year during the 1920s and 1930s. Automobiles, another new industry, became the poster child for success in the new economy. The sale of new cars exceeded 5 million a year between 1921 and 1929. The resulting value of the industry totaled 12 percent of all manufacturing. The auxiliary industries, such as road construction, petroleum production, and large-scale rubber and glass industries, had as much impact in job creation and wealth. There are few better examples of the technological achievements of the new businesses than the Ford Motor Company.

Both the assembly line and mass-produced consumer goods existed prior to Henry Ford. The success of the Ford Motor Company, however, changed the way American corporations understood mass production. Ford solved the mass-production requirements by introducing a single model, the Model T, put together on an assembly line. On the assembly line, workers stayed in one place, and the car came to them. In this system, a worker would complete a single step in the production process, such as dry mounting a single part or setting a bolt. They would complete the step, however, all day long as quickly as physically possible. Model T Fords started coming off the assembly line in mass in 1914.

The key to Ford's success lay in the company's ability constantly to drive the price of their product down. In 1908, when the Model T touring car was first introduced to the market, the car sold for $950. After the introduction of the assembly line, the price dropped to $550. By 1924, the price had come down to $290 (Volti 2004).

The Ford Model T did not have many innovations, but it was reliable, sturdy, and easy to drive. The height of the chassis allowed the car to drive on the poor roads of the time. The top speed was only 40 miles an hour, but owing to the condition of most roads, this was adequate. The simple construction allowed owners to do maintenance and minor repairs. The car also could be fitted with accessories in order to plow a field, saw wood, or power a washing machine.

By 1927, when the Model T went out of production, 15,007,033 cars had been built and sold. By 1923, over half of the automobiles on the road in the United States were Ford Model Ts. In rural areas, the automobile broke the isolation of rural life. Farmers became some of Ford's best customers. Urban dwellers learned the attractions of "the open road" that had earlier brought wealthy people to utilize autos. Day trips and the resulting development of rural attractions became commonplace.

By the late 1920s, several automobile manufacturers offered new cars in varying styles and colors. In 1920, Alfred P. Sloan, Jr. became president of General Motors. The company had acquired several other smaller independent manufacturers, and under Sloan's leadership GM branded a series of semiautonomous divisions that catered to different customers and different economic groups. Chevrolet, Oldsmobile, Buick, and Cadillac all served to meet the needs of different segments of the population.

Sloan also introduced a new marketing strategy: the annual model year. Starting in 1923, the General Motors chassis and power train remained the same, but changes to body styles and interiors occurred every year. In 1927, the company introduced the first automotive design department of any manufacturer. The marketing of the new styles was very effective, and millions of customers replaced serviceable cars that appeared stylistically out-of-date. This "deliberate obsolescence" came to be applied to other consumer goods—including housing.

Again with a first, in 1919, the General Motors Acceptance Corporation was established to promote credit sales. Buying cars on credit became a trend in the market. A customer could put one-third down and finance the balance over the next 12 months. Ford, who had always sold cars cash only, refused to go along with the new scheme. By 1926, almost 70 percent of all automobiles were sold through monthly financing arrangements. Ford's market share slipped, and General Motors dominated with 47 percent of the U.S. market by the end of 1928. Ford then introduced the Model A and began to compete on General Motor's terms. Though the car never had the market dominance of the Model T, Ford remained competitive throughout the 1930s and 1940s (Volti 2004).

Car Culture

The automobile affected daily life for most people. Even if you did not own one, the car increasingly changed how families understood time and distance. This can be illustrated by looking at the story of one typical family.

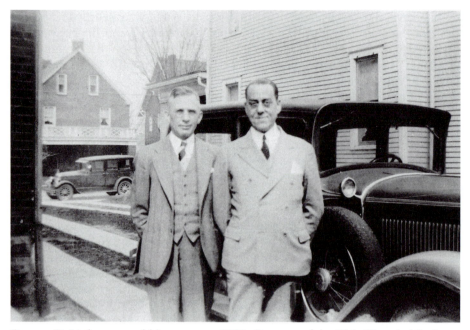

George K. Mahanna and his new car, 1930. Courtesy of the Ohio Historical Society.

George K. Mahanna and Frances Marian Gineva, of Columbus, Ohio, married on January 2, 1909. They had met the summer before at Rader's Neil Avenue Dancing Academy in the heart of a very Victorian neighborhood. They moved to a new house rented at 445 South Eighteenth Street. On January 21, 1910, they took a "horse cab" to the Protestant Hospital on North Park Avenue to have their first child.

By the fall of the next year, the family had moved several streets over to 216 East Ninth Street. George and Frances participated in very typical Victorian cultural activities. November 5, 1911, was no exception. The day was warm and sunny, and in their home they held calling hours with "no fires and the doors open." Almost everyone in the family called, and one Aunt stayed for supper. After supper, at about 10:00 P.M., the family walked Aunt Lucy to the High Street streetcar, "stopping into High-Eleventh Drug Store for refreshments." These activities were all part of the community function of the walking street. Upon returning home, they hired another "horse cab" to take them to the hospital to have their second child.

On May 1, 1912, the family moved again, to another house rented at 154 East Eleventh Avenue. Their third child came a couple years later, on October 14, 1914. This time, however, something had dramatically changed. George called the doctor, Dr. Inglis, who "brought his car by and took the family to the hospital." Just before the delivery of their next child, born in December 1916, the family attended a music recital at the residence of some friends. They came home at 10:00 P.M. and called a "taxi motor" to transport them to the hospital.

Between 1910 and 1916, the Mahannas had lived in three different houses in the same neighborhood and had four children with the same doctor in the same hospital. The condition of their lives had not changed that much, but their use and interaction with the street had changed.

By December 1918, they had moved into a new house, renting a double on Euclid Avenue. By this time they had five children. George worked as a salesman selling candy for the Walter M. Lowney Company. In 1920, they purchased the double, moved into the other side, and rented out the half they had lived in previously.

In 1924, at the age of 39, and after renting various older homes and working for the same company for 15 years, George bought a Studebaker touring car, and the family moved into a brand new small modern house at 249 Kelso Road. After buying the car, the entertainment activities for the family changed. They took several road trips, including three trips out of state within four years. The Mahannas represent the families that strove to attain better housing, new consumer goods, and the experiences of travel beyond their neighborhood. They left their stories in a photo album. When the family purchased a car, the world became a little smaller. Most of the pictures they kept were of the three trips they took. Their memories of travel they evidently shared with each other in the home as well (Mahanna family scrapbook).

DAILY LIFE CHANGES

An automobile parked outside of a house allowed movement away from Victorian parlor culture into modern culture. The transportation and communication revolutions altered the activities of most middle-class Americans. The automobile and the commercial activities now available to the family contributed to transforming the function of home. In 1930, the author of a book on the history of American housing claimed that, "entertainment, as a result of ease of transportation and communication, has almost gone from the homes of a large per cent of American families. They give dinners at clubs and restaurants and entertain at amusement places . . . The automobile has replaced the parlor." The automobile changed the parlor-culture custom of visitation and opened up a wider spectrum of leisure opportunities for family members. These leisure activities, however, no longer required intimate communication with other people in the community. The automobile transported the consumer to places such as parks, movies, or restaurants, large public places the commercial success of which depended on patrons who arrived by private transportation (Allen 1930, 145).

The rise of the automobile played the largest role because private transportation opened up so many new opportunities for businesses that relied on leisure dollars. In 1913, there were just 1,258,000 automobiles registered in the United States. This amounted to one car for every 75 people. In 1921, the number of registered vehicles had reached 9,346,195—one car for every 11.6 people. By the end of 1930, there was one car for every 5.3 people with total registrations in excess of 23 million.

The movie industry is a good example of the new leisure activities. By 1931, there were 22,731 motion picture theaters throughout the country. Silent movies had been the mainstay of the industry; a film would be shown accompanied by live music. In 1926, Warner Brothers introduced a new system where music, sound effects, and dialog recorded on a wax disc was synchronized with the film projector. Many theaters did not invest in the new sound equipment until the success of the movie *The Jazz Singer* in October of 1927.

Movie attendance doubled after 1926, and by the end of 1931, 14,805 theaters had been wired for sound. Walt Disney introduced one of the first animated talking pictures in 1928, *Steamboat Willie,* which also introduced Mickey Mouse. The Academy of Motion Picture Arts and Sciences began the Academy Awards in 1929. By 1930, attendance at movie theaters exceeded 100 million a week. This was during a period when the population just exceeded 122 million. When people said that everyone went to the movies, they may have been right. In 1933, the report of the President's Research Committee on Social Trends concluded of the motion picture industry that, "the important role it plays in the leisure time of the masses can hardly be exaggerated" (President's Research Committee on Social Trends 1934, 941).

W. F. Ogburn, a social scientist working out of the University of Chicago, charted the increases and decreases in recreational spending. Between 1929 and 1941, attendance and popularity of the vaudeville theater, social clubs, radio, golf, and fraternal organizations all decreased. Activities that required less personal interaction or more travel, such as gambling, sporting events, sightseeing, amusement parks, and motion pictures, all increased dramatically. Gambling increased over 1,000 percent (Ogburn and Nimkoff 1955, 133).

All of these forces introduced around the car deeply affected patterns of housing in the United States and, more particularly, the shift to suburban housing. Car culture could affect the lives of individuals and families, in part, because of the development of roads and highways. Mark Rose, in *Interstate Express,* argues that suburbanization did not enter into the highway decision process, but rather private interests such as car manufacturers and oil companies pressured Congress to fund highways. Suburbs followed as an afterthought to highway construction. In *From Streetcar to Superhighway,* Mark Foster argues that early developers financed the construction of roads into new developments, but the federal government invested deeply in highway construction between towns and cities. The federal government favored the use of cars over all other forms of transportation. The automobile served as the chief mode of transportation for the suburbanite, but highways were also the chief mode of transportation for the military (Rose 1990; Foster 1981).

TECHNOLOGY

As will become clear in the chapters that follow, a number of changes in technology were fundamental to changes in housing in the interwar period. Most important were the technological systems that became connected into each modern house.

Historian Mark Rose shows how the rise of gas and electric companies and the distribution of these services changed everyday life and also how the technology itself became an agent of cultural change. He argues that the employees of gas companies acted as agents of social change when they stepped out to sell gas and create markets. In a similar argument, Ronald Kline shows how women became agents for marketing new technologies, and thus agents of cultural change. Kline pushes his argument of cultural change further by arguing that end users of new technology became agents of change themselves in some cases. Similar studies have been completed about the development of city sewer systems and household plumbing (Rose 1995; Kline 2000).

Technology shaped culture, but of course technology cannot be viewed separately from the culture that created it. New studies in the theory of technology even suggest that artifacts themselves have agency. Under this model, technological artifacts became the interface of emergent cultural change with which most of the population came into contact. Few artifacts exhibit this tendency better than the house. Under this proposition, changes in housing during the early twentieth century embodied cultural change as an artifact of that culture. The artifact, however, still cannot be disassociated from the cultural changes that created it.

ART OUTSIDE OF THE MAINSTREAM

In addition to the social force of technology, changes in architectural ideas affected the ways in which Americans viewed many buildings—not least because the new ideas involved technology fundamentally.

As the 1920s began, despite the beginnings of modernization in housing, a Beaux-Arts classical education dominated art and architecture discussions in both Europe and the United States. Nevertheless, the art deco movement was rapidly replacing the style in major new works of architecture. The Beaux-Arts style embodied an approach embracing the grand traditions, including symmetry, a hierarchy of spaces, and grand monumentalization. Art deco, on the other hand, celebrated what was new and modern. The style could be found in architecture, industrial design, and visual arts and could be considered an amalgam of many different styles that had been influential at the turn of the century, including constructivism, cubism, neo-Egyptian, and Art Nouveau.

Using materials such as chromium plate, stained glass, and colored tiles, art deco buildings relied on applied ornament to convey the design style. A good example would be The Chrysler Building, built between 1928 and 1930 in New York City. The 77-story skyscraper reflected Egyptian and Mayan influence as well as contemporary art deco considerations. Another good example is the Empire State Building, which was built between 1930 and 1931.

In both product design and automobile design a new style emerged based on advances in the aviation industry. This new style was sometimes referred to as Streamline Moderne. The aerodynamic shapes resulting from scientifically applied principles on airplanes were adapted to cars and even everyday objects, such as refrigerators or toasters. The Chrysler Airflow, designed in 1933, had rounded corners and a streamlined appearance, very different than the typically boxy Model A, for instance.

These commercial and industrial design styles originated with design philosophies from artists working at the leading edge of current art. These artists were collectively known as the avant-garde, those in the front. Members of the avant-garde became extremely disillusioned after the First World War and turned to pure art as a way of making a better world.

The shift to art within avant-garde circles was a response to a lack of faith in politics. During the 1920s, cubism, surrealism, and Dadaism had come into fruition as styles of art that reflected a rejection of existing culture. In Germany, the Bauhaus, a school of art and architecture, operated from 1919 to 1933. The

Bauhaus style, characterized by simplified forms, rational functionality, and the idea that the individual artist's hand could be aided by mass production, had a profound influence on modernist and avant-garde design in every area of design in the twentieth century.

During the 1930s, the art circles in America absorbed the best of the European avant-garde. Many came to avoid Nazi persecution during the political rise of Adolph Hitler. Walter Gropius and Ludwig Meis van der Rohe, both past directors of the Bauhaus, came to New York and would come to define the new modernist architectural style in the United States. Paul Klee, who taught at the Bauhaus and was a leading figure in the Dada movement also came to New York. The leading figure in the surrealist movement, Salvador Dali, emigrated to New York as well.

During the 1940s, the avant-garde in America practiced the aesthetics of life as art. They rejected both communism and modernism and envisioned a future in which art would be synonymous with life. Through the canonization of modern forms, the members of the avant-garde saw themselves not as reactionary to the existing styles that they were rejecting, but as transforming current culture into something new. The perfect example of this is the Seagrams Building designed by Mies Van Der Rohe in the mid-1950s. The glass and steel structure, which became the symbol of the modern business age, was designed as a commentary on new technology and a symbolic rejection of stylistic elements, exactly what European modernism was rejecting in the 1930s.

In rejecting the current culture and envisioning a new culture, the members of the avant-garde were rejecting mass culture. New cultural identities placed the individual within the confines of a mass culture where they followed a sterile existence. These identities stemmed from the new consumer culture that came to dominate the United States in the 1920s.

THE MAJOR PATTERNS IN AMERICAN HOUSING

Technology, art, business, and social developments in general made the movement toward suburbanization a characteristic of American society and housing by the 1930s and 1940s.

In the older "walking cities," wealthy people lived on linear streets radiating from the central business districts of town. People of lesser means lived behind the large homes off the alleys or above storefronts. These inclusive neighborhoods offered opportunity and security to the underprivileged. The children of the working class had daily contact with the upper classes and had opportunity to work for them or see them as role models. This pattern of neighborhood development was consistent throughout the late nineteenth century. Big cities had multiple business districts owing to the craft system, and there were countless small towns throughout the country. Many of these neighborhood systems are still evidenced by the many large Victorian homes radiating from every small town in the Midwest.

People in rural communities lived a very different existence. The one consistent pattern was that in rural America there seems to have been very little change. As individuals and families moved further west, frontier patterns of development were very consistent. Housing in rural areas needed to be self sufficient, as there were typically very little or no municipal services. By 1934, only 30 percent of rural farms had electricity. Eventually, the new consumer culture leveled many of the cultural differences between rural localities and metropolitan areas.

Developers experimented with the first suburbs by developing the border-lands around large cities. For example, Lewellin Park, outside of Philadelphia, had been developed during the late 1870s. Early suburbs, however, were exclusively for the rich and often served as retreats from the city, where the primary residence was located. With the invention of the electric trolley, whole new areas of the city were opened for development. These new "streetcar suburbs" were almost exclusively middle class, but as stated before with the horse cars, they were extensions of the walking city where all community and social services were available in the neighborhood. The opportunities of home ownership and mobility attracted the new middle class. Many authors site health and gentility as the reasons for the flight from the city. More recently authors have been citing the reason as escape from the new immigrants, who were often Catholic and thought not to embody middle-class values.

The automobile, new styles of single family housing, and prosperity all coalesced during the first two decades of the twentieth century around the development of near-urban neighborhoods. Progressive era beliefs in efficiency led to the development of smaller houses that could be built more inexpensively with less emphasis on style. At the same time, new kitchen appliances became available, and housewives learned to use these "labor saving" devices. Ronald Tobey, in *Technology as Freedom,* describes this change in housing during the 1920s (Tobey 1996).

In the near urban neighborhoods, new developments combined both the traditional elements of the walking city and the flexibility of automobile transportation. For a brief time, during the development of the interstitial areas around cities, between streetcar lines, the pedestrian and the automobile coexisted. The new houses in these neighborhoods did not contain the fancy trim or the parlors of the older Victorian homes. They contained elements such as large front porches, sidewalks, and living rooms, things promoting community and family, both of which had been advocated by Progressive reformers.

Between 1929 and 1945 there was a hold on most private construction, but major changes to the processes of housing development occurred. By 1932, people in the real estate industry began to advocate for a change in housing construction, arguing that if a house could be designed to be built for under $6,000, then the majority of the working class could afford a home through a mortgage. Owing to this, members of both the savings and loan industry and the real estate industry invested much time and energy to develop efficiency in home construction. Many local savings and loans actually had a model in their offices showing the type of home for which they would lend money.

After 1945 there was a need for housing. There had been a shortage before the war, but as men began to return home the shortage increased to drastic proportions. The need for housing fell to large building corporations who could mass manufacture standard housing using the minimal requirements to receive mortgage guarantees in the form of FHA and VA loans. Developers such as the Levitt Brothers built 6,000 homes a year. This was dramatic given that a large builder during the 1920s could build 20 houses a year.

FHA minimum requirements were not meant to be the only way to build housing, but like other unintended consequences, in order to compete in the market, builders had to build only what was minimally required. Jackson in *Crabgrass Frontier* (Jackson 1985) and Mark Hise in *Magnetic Los Angeles* (Hise 1997) both have documented the importance of FHA guarantees even when FHA financing was not going to be used. The idea that the government could guarantee mortgages was enough to get construction financing. Advertisement campaigns for the new government program were so successful that FHA designation became the stamp of trusted quality instead of the minimum requirements that they actually represented.

After the Second World War, all of the countries that had been involved suffered from a housing shortage. The suburb was a priority of the United States. In searching for housing typologies after the war to meet the great demand for housing, European countries chose a different model. Scholars have developed several reasons for the American exception. Work comparing postwar suburbia to housing developments in Sweden and France show that European housing trends differed in the role of a strong central government, transportation, and cultural systems. In both countries, the middle classes rejected suburbanization as a solution to their housing need. In part, the rejection occurred owing to well-developed public transportation and centralization of jobs within urban areas. Both examples serve to show how large developers, interest group politics, and a wide acceptance of the automobile as the primary mode of transportation created the suburbanization movement in the United States.

The United States was set apart from the rest of the world by a predisposition to a suburban desire and the institutionalization of federal programs that favored corporate developers. As housing came to the forefront of the economic debate in the mid-1930s, economic leaders determined that construction starts could be used as an economic indicator. At that point, housing became a central aspect of governmental policy. Indeed, as housing began to be a political issue, authors vigorously expanded the historiography of housing and suburbanization in the late twentieth century.

Many scholars have focused on cheap available land and the acceptance of the automobile as the chief reason for suburban development. New highway systems allowed access to the hinterlands where rural property could be developed at low cost. The automobile mobilized the population, but it did not create availability or housing demand. A new conceptual understanding of the American home had created the demand for postwar housing.

During the early 1920s, the conceptual understanding of the American single-family home was transformed from an implied sign of social standing to a consumer-based commodity. The ownership of a home became the primary goal of significant numbers of middle-class Americans, over the quality, style, and visibility of the house. Within this transformation, most people understood and accepted the social implications of home ownership, which had a leveling effect on the segment of the population willing to invest in a new home. Indeed, the detached, single-family residential house became the essential understanding of the American Dream.

THE GREAT DEPRESSION, THE FEDERAL GOVERNMENT, AND HOUSING

Beginning in 1929, the United States entered into the Great Depression, a period of profound disruption and change. In 1921, the nation had experienced its worst recession and its largest drop in gross national product. But this had passed. Many economists, as well as the general public, thought that the stock correction and recession in 1929 would soon pass as well. President Hoover, therefore, focused voluntary cooperation between business and government as a policy toward the economic downturn. This had worked very effectively during the 1920s.

By the end of 1930, however, the economy appeared no better. The annual total of bank closures doubled to 1,352, and businesses continued to fail. The gross national product fell 12.6 percent from its 1929 level. Private businesses decreased construction expenditures, and employees began to be laid off work. By the end of 1931, another 2,294 banks had failed. By early 1932, over 10 million people were unemployed, and nearly one-third of all workers were employed only part time.

The basic economic and social institutions failed during the beginning of the 1930s in most local areas. These local institutions included banks, businesses, and families. The total breakdown of both economic and social institutions created a societal crisis. At this point, both businesses and wealthy individuals began to call for the federal government to do something. In their attempts to save society, federal officials attempted to save or revive basic social institutions—one of which was now understood to be private home ownership.

In January 1932, Hoover persuaded Congress to create the most radical and innovative program to date, the Reconstruction Finance Corporation (RFC). This was a government program making tax dollars directly available to private financial institutions. The intent of the RFC was to save banks, railroad companies, and the private ownership of housing. Many charitable institutions had their money invested in railroad stock. Insuring the stability of banks and railroads insured the stability of many other institutions.

The effects of the declining economy can be clearly seen in the figures of annual housing starts. Throughout the housing boom of the 1920s, builders erected nearly 1 million houses a year. In 1928, housing starts stood at 810,000. In 1929, the early effects of a recession could be noticed when only 753,000 houses were constructed. This number continued to drop; 1930—509,000 houses; 1931—330,000 houses; 1932—134,000 houses; and 1933—93,000 houses.

In 1933, Franklin D. Roosevelt became president. Unlike Hoover with his volunteerism, but exactly like the direct federal intervention of Hoover's later programs, Roosevelt sought to use the resources of the government to stimulate the economy.

The Roosevelt administration quickly created, among other measures, the Home Owners' Loan Corporation (HOLC), modeled loosely after Hoover's Reconstruction Finance Corporation, to stabilize the home mortgage industry. In 1932, over 250,000 families had lost their homes. During the first half of 1933, more than 1,000 home foreclosures occurred each day. Over half of all home mortgages were technically in default. The HOLC allowed mortgage holders to turn in defaulted loans for guaranteed government bonds. The program served as a homesaver for thousands of American families. By the end of the depression, one out of five home mortgages had been refinanced by the HOLC.

HOUSING UNDER THE NEW DEAL

During the second half of the 1930s, New Deal legislation created more permanent programs aimed at the societal reforms. In the development of housing, New Deal legislation also played a large part. Many New Deal liberals called for massive public housing programs, on European models, to solve the nation's housing problems. Roosevelt, however, felt more strongly about the encouragement of private industry than about public housing. Housing projects, though, were advantageous as almost one-third of the unemployed worked in the building trades. Government money would be spent on public housing, but reform in housing did not occur, and by the end of the New Deal the single family home became the de facto federal policy.

The Public Works Administration (PWA) and Works Progress Administration (WPA) developed into very successful programs that continued to put money into economy. The PWA improved on its predecessors and used the construction of public buildings as a means to stimulate local economies. Between 1933 and 1939, the PWA helped construct over 70 percent of the new schools built in the United States, over 65 percent of the new public buildings, such as courthouses, and over 35 percent of new hospitals.

The PWA also served as the first government program aimed at creating housing. Under the direction of Harold Ickes, the PWA initiated slum clearance and low-cost housing projects. Ickes stumbled with courts ruling that the federal government could not claim eminent domain to acquire land for housing. The PWA started just 49 projects with a total construction of under 25,000 residential units.

Senator Robert Wagner, who had sponsored the labor relations act, was also interested in passing major housing legislation. In 1937, the Wagner-Steagall Housing Act passed congress and was signed into law. The act created the United States Housing Authority (USHA) as a public corporation within the Department of the Interior. The USHA made 500 million in loans available for low-cost housing. By the end of 1940, over 350 housing projects had been completed.

The bill, originally seen as a liberal victory, had multiple amendments placed on it at the last minute that restricted its potential. A critical mass of federal housing projects could not be developed in order to change the hold of private housing development. One of the key amendments mandated that for any new low-cost housing built, an equal number of slum housing would be torn down. This "equivalent elimination" clause forever linked public housing with slum clearance. The conservatives in congress saw the passage of the Wagner housing act as their own victory (Radford 1996, 190).

The Federal Housing Administration (FHA) had been established in 1934. The inept directors, however, kept the agency from excelling; but after 1938, the housing act had been liberalized and a new director appointed. The potential of the FHA as a home building agency became realized just as public housing programs faltered.

Conservatives sought to expand the role of the government in the private sector, while at the same time limit the roll in public housing. Very telling was the comment made by James Moffett, the director of the FHA, about Ickes' WPA housing projects. Moffett quipped that if continued, the program would "wreck a 21-billion-dollar mortgage market and undermine the nation's real estate values" (Leuchtenburg 1963, 135). During the passage of the Wagner housing act, many organizations mobilized to voice their opposition, including the U.S. Chamber of Commerce, the National Association of Real Estate Boards, the U.S. League of Building and Loans, and the National Retail Lumber Dealers Association. These organizations were all tied directly to the residential housing market. The lumber dealers are a good example of why organizations saw public housing as a threat. They understood that modern public housing, by and large, would be built from new modern materials such as steel, concrete, and glass. The lumber industry explicitly saw itself tied to single-family residential development (Radford 1996, 188).

WORLD WAR II AND THE END OF THE GREAT DEPRESSION

The Depression in America was a small part of a global economic crisis. During the 1930s, America dealt with the crisis through the liberalization of government relief programs and through the development of interest group politics. In Europe, the crises resulted in the rise of fascism. In Asia, the similar economic conditions were partly responsible for the territorial aggression of Japan. In the late 1930s, another world war loomed on the horizon.

In September 1939, Hitler's armies invaded Poland. The defense budget stood at $1.9 million. The unemployment rate in America was still above 17 percent. In 1940, Roosevelt asked Congress for $4 billion in defense spending, 50,000 airplanes a year, and a two-ocean navy. Only $2.2 billion was approved. In the spring, The Netherlands and Belgium surrender to Germany after invasion, and in June, France fell.

By 1940, the United States was in the eleventh year of the Depression. The transformation of public opinion and government policy from depression to a wartime economy was occurring. In August of 1940, the Hoover-created Reconstruction Finance Corporation funded a new entity, the Defense Plant Corporation. In September, the Selective Service and Training Act became law, establishing a peacetime draft and a 1,200,000 man army with 800,000 reserves.

In many respects, the United States had entered the war by the late 1930s. The Depression ended, however, with the passage of the Lend-Lease Act in March 1941. The legislation authorized the President to supply military and other goods to any country deemed vital to the defense of America. In the first year, Congress approved $112 billion in Lend-Lease aid. Additionally, defense spending in America grew from $2.2 billion to $13.7 billion. In December, after the bombing of Pearl Harbor by the Japanese, the United States officially entered the war. By 1942, the army had grown to 3,859,000 men, and defense spending had soared to $49.4 billion (Vatter 1985).

The new war economy affected housing in some parts of the country. During the war years there was little population growth, but the population migrated toward work in wartime industries. Over six million people left farms and farm communities between 1940 and 1945. The Pacific Coast received the largest increase due to this migration. Between 1940 and 1943, one and a half million people moved to California.

In areas where large war factories were constructed, large developers also constructed housing for war workers. This was especially true for the factories constructed to meet Roosevelt's demand for 50,000 airplanes a year. In order to secure funding, builders constructed most of these homes to meet FHA requirements.

The war caused lasting affects in society as well as in the housing industry. The war and the successful wartime economy caused a redistribution of wealth in the United States. The Servicemen's Readjustment Act of June 1944, the GI Bill, made it possible for returning veterans to attend college and to purchase homes, among other things. Veterans could secure a VA loan through the FHA. The bulk of the population did not own homes, but returning veterans and their young families found that a new VA home mortgage was cheaper than paying rent. This had a tremendous potential effect on housing as over 11 million people served in the military during the war.

By 1945, housing starts began increasing and large-scale residential development became the norm. With the end of World War II, the United States truly became a suburban nation with the wave of homes built to supply the needs of returning veterans. Through this critical mass of housing, programs such as the Better Homes in America movement and the Own Your Own Home campaign were finally fulfilled.

Reference List

Allen, Edith. 1930. *American Housing: As Affected by Social and Economic Conditions.* Peoria, IL: The Manual Arts Press.

Blumin, Stuart M. 1989. *The Emergence of the Middle Class: Social Experience in the American City,* 1760–1900. New York: Cambridge University Press.

Foster, Mark. 1981. *From Streetcar to Superhighway: American City Planners and Urban Transportation, 1900–1940.* Philadelphia: Temple University Press.

Hise, Greg. 1997. *Magnetic Los Angeles: Planning the Twentieth-Century Metropolis.* Baltimore: John Hopkins University Press.

Jackson, Kenneth. 1985. *Crabgrass Frontier: The Suburbanization of the United States.* New York: Oxford University Press.

"J. H. Payne House to be Reproduced," *Washington Post,* April 22, 1923, 43.

Kline, Ronald. 2000. *Consumers in the Country: Technology and Social Change in Rural America.* Baltimore: John Hopkins University Press.

Leuchtenburg, William E. 1963. *Franklin D. Roosevelt and the New Deal, 1932–1940.* New York: Harper & Row.

Mahanna family Scrapbook. AV11, Ohio Historical Society.

Nash, Gerald. 1971. *The Great Transition: A Short History of Twentieth Century America.* Boston: Allyn and Bacon, Inc.

Ogburn, W. F., and M. F. Nimkoff. 1955. *Technology and the Changing Family.* Boston: Houghton Mifflin.

"President to Open 'Home Sweet Home'," *Washington Post,* June 3, 1923, 44.

President's Research Committee on Social Trends. 1934. *Recent Social Trends in the United States.* New York: Whittlesey House.

Radford, Gail. 1996. *Modern Housing for America: Policy Struggles in the New Deal Era.* Chicago: University of Chicago Press.

Rose, Mark. 1990. *Interstate Express: Highway Politics, 1939–1989.* Knoxville: The University of Tennessee Press.

Rose, Mark. 1995. *Cities of Light and Heat: Domesticating Gas and Electricity in Urban America.* University Park: Pennsylvania State University Press.

Tobey, Ronald. 1996. *Technology as Freedom: The New Deal and the Electrical Modernization of the American Home.* Berkeley: University of California Press.

Vatter, Harold. 1985. *The U.S. Economy in World War II.* New York: Columbia University Press.

Volti, Rudi. 2006. *Cars & Culture: The Life Story of a Technology.* Baltimore: Johns Hopkins University Press.

Styles of Domestic Architecture

Today, most historians would not think of housing between 1921 and 1945 in terms of style. They would consider development practices that began to change the nature and idea of the neighborhood. They would consider model developments and model homes. They would think in terms of suburbanization. They would think in terms of consumer-driven, mass-manufactured housing.

Architectural historians would discuss the houses of this period in terms of style. There was a Colonial Revival style. There was also the style of modernism, or the New International Style. Most of the houses constructed in the period, however, they would contend, were vernacular.

Vernacular forms of housing are the houses built outside of the formalism of design as a cultural process. In the twentieth century, architects typically performed the design process. But most new house building was not under the control of architects. Instead, builders, realtors, and even individual homeowners all built homes during the first half of the twentieth century.

Many of these houses had stylistic elements that made them look as if they were conforming to a style. But even so, the majority of houses built during this period had the character of square or rectangular wood framed boxes with gabled roofs, filled with new technological systems such as electricity, plumbing, and heating.

A new high style of architecture called *modernism* emerged during the 1920s and 1930s as well. This style embraced the simplification of form, use of technology, and elimination of applied ornament from the structure. If the Colonial Revival houses that lined the streets of the new developments in most cities and towns could be characterized as vernacular boxes, then the modernist homes looked like highly designed boxes. The flat roofs, plain stucco exteriors, and banded windows could not have been more different than the typical Colonial Revival house.

Modernist housing received much attention in the press and in architectural publications. The International Style, as it came to be known, created forms and appearance that were clearly outside of the mainstream. Many of the architects working within the stylistic principles understood the forms to be culturally transformational. They thought modernist houses would make life better. The ideas, however, were not universally accepted.

The small houses constructed during the first decades of the twentieth century were also considered, and called, *modern*. Modern in this sense really meant that the houses incorporated the latest technologies. These technologies, and technological systems, were confined in well-defined boxes. These houses depended on the integrated systems that ran the new technologies, and therefore existed in developments planned and laid out with lots for multiple houses to be constructed in a single defined area. These areas were called additions or subdivisions.

New styles of small houses, including the Colonial Revival, the Craftsman bungalow, and the American foursquare were all basically the same type of house. New houses saw the removal of the parlor replaced by a multiuse living room. The living room came very close to replicating the conception of the Colonial Hall House type, where the majority of activities occurred in one room.

Both technological and social changes served to effect housing. The automobile had a tremendous effect on the house because in many ways it replaced the parlor. Changes in the culture eliminated the social rituals surrounding Victorian culture. People now drove to places of social interaction that were outside of the home. Additionally, by the 1920s, Progressivism had resulted in efficiency of kitchen design and the standardization of kitchen and bathroom layouts.

The Hall House type went through one more change during the twentieth century that proved a dramatic twist to the type and is illustrative of the period after 1934. During the postwar housing boom, the Levitt Brothers revived the typology of the Colonial house type in their new mass produced developments. Efficiently designed to embody the minimal space required for a family to live, the Levitt house provided a nice conclusion to the type. The reasons that made the type so prevalent during the colonial period, ease of construction, flexibility, and cost, were the same reasons that it became the ideal mass-constructed and mass-marketed house type. Of course, this was made possible in large part by the minimal home requirements established by the FHA.

The Levitt house type, a rectangular, gabled, one-story building, was based on the salt box. The idea evoked by the type was still marketable in the 1940s, and the house was built in the thousands. This house type's continued relevance within the housing culture is both an indication of change and an indication of the consistencies within American culture.

PLANNING OVER STYLE

Realtors, builders, and developers did not over concern themselves with style. Nevertheless, residential structures that lined the streets of many neighborhoods built from the 1920s to the 1940s looked very similar. Contemporary builders and suppliers labeled the seemingly endless stream of new houses as revival styles. In many cases the massing, plan layout, and room nomenclature remained the same from house to house.

Houses differed from each other by their exterior appearance. Professionals within the building and real estate industries did not adhere to a particular list of styles, but houses with different features could be labeled as New England Colonial, Dutch Colonial, Half Timber, Modern English, Italian, and Spanish Mission. And what happened was simply that as plans were developed by numerous builders, lumber companies, plan companies, and architects, these professionals designed houses with different exterior features applied to the shell of the house to provide character. The character of the structure, however, was superficial. One professional wrote, in fact, that the "styles in a frame house are many— almost as numerous as the architects"(*Classic Houses of the Twenties* 1992, 6–7).

The various names associated with the Colonial Revival styles, therefore, varied by who was writing advertisements and who was selling the houses, but they generally referred to a set of very similar types. As early as 1910, builders could list the various styles as Colonials, Queen Ann and Dutch Roofs of various brands; Swiss Chalets, Bungalows, Romanesque, Picturesque, Grotesque, Frontier, and many other kinds. People within regional housing networks marketed the idea that if a house was to be "beautiful, symmetrical, of enduring charm and general appeal," then it had to "observe certain fundamental principals and traditions." The fundamental traditions had been the "results of centuries of thought and experiment" by "architects and builders." What was occurring here was the transfer of a cultural shift; a romantic view of the past, placed onto modern housing (Arthur 1910, 271–272).

Development was the term given to the acquisition and subdivision of large tracts of land in order to provide multiple individual lots for the construction of houses. This included platting streets and assigning parcel numbers to lots, the process of mapping and registering the lots with the county recorders office. Typically, in this early stage of development, municipal services such as water, sewer, and gas would also be run to the individual building lots. The companies, or in some cases even the men who performed this work, were called developers. These near universal terms will be used to describe the process that brought individual houses to market. The process can also be called the housing delivery system.

Development occurred in a variety of patterns, but it often began the same way. Marc Weiss has accurately called the companies that performed this work "community builders" (Weiss 1987, 1). These developers bought farm acreage outside of city limits, subdivided the land into individual parcels, and then sold the lots to builders and speculators. Individual lots were sold to owners or builders who then constructed the houses.

In an alternate scenario, some developers bought land and controlled the development from subdivision through construction. Here, the developer had much more control in shaping the look of the development. Often, under this development scenario, restrictive covenants within the property deed were utilized to control development. Restrictions embodied the attitudes and values of people at that time. Outside of Kansas City, a local developer named J. C. Nichols purchased a garbage dump, a racing track, and an old brick kiln. Beginning in 1922, Nichols constructed over 6,000 homes and nine golf courses in what became known as the Country Club District. In his development, people bought "permanently protected homes, surrounded with ample space for air and sunshine" (Jackson 1985, 177).

To protect houses, Nichols used consistent setback regulations, determining the distance from the lot lines that homes had to be constructed. Additionally, the new development became racially segregated through self-perpetuating deed restrictions. In the Country Club District developments, Nichols became one of the first developers to utilize deed restrictions to control his developments for 25 years after the homes had been built.

NEAR-URBAN NEIGHBORHOODS

Near-urban neighborhoods constituted the critical stage by which American housing in general shifted in the 1920s. Near-urban neighborhoods, which one can still see standing today, are typified by residential streets lined with boxy, medium-sized houses on lots with an average size of 40' by 140'. These neighborhoods were developed on land purchased outside of the city limits and platted to extend the linear street grid of the existing urban fabric.

The pattern, with many varieties of advertisement and promotion nationally, did not depend on population or even geographic area. Near-urban neighborhoods existed in developments such as West Haven in Indianapolis, Indiana; Over-the Pike outside of Wheeling, West Virginia; and in Vernon Heights in Marion, Ohio. Similar neighborhoods and houses have existed in Helena, Montana; Syracuse, New York; and Decatur, Illinois.

Developed during the 1920s, but many platted prior to that time, near-urban neighborhoods combined sidewalks and porches with alleys and rear one-car garages. A distinguishing characteristic of these neighborhoods was that they were both automobile- and pedestrian-friendly. Streets in the neighborhood typically dead-ended into commercial corridors, and people living on the street worked at, or were patrons of, the services available and accessible at the end of the street. Early in the 1920s, often the commercial corridor also served a streetcar line. The street, in this case, connected the community with a larger work environment, while the neighborhood still offered basic services within walking distance. In fact, a major selling point of these neighborhoods was this proximity to both services and public transport.

Many near-urban neighborhoods fall into the category considered today as inner-ring suburbs. In current city planning, a new model of metropolitan spatial structure differentiates an inner-ring and an outer-ring of suburban development. Inner-ring areas were often developed before post–World War II suburban development. These areas today are experiencing decline. Not all inner-ring suburbs, however, would be considered near-urban neighborhoods. In Martin's Ferry, Ohio, for example, postwar suburban development never encircled the town, and so the near-urban streets effectively operated as suburbs. In the near-urban subdivision, developers extended the existing street grid.

The marked difference between near-urban neighborhoods and the typical postwar subdivision is that near-urban neighborhoods were typically inclusive of both the automobile and the pedestrian. Near-urban neighborhoods often combined single-family detached houses with duplexes and multifamily structures. At the end of the housing boom in the late 1920s, housing developments tended to eliminate the pedestrian in favor of the car.

Historian Clay McShane has noted that one of the chief differences of the new automobile-based suburbs—which constituted the next stage and succeeded the near urban stage—was that the suburbs were exclusively upper middle class. Developers focused the new suburban neighborhoods toward those individuals buying cars. This new trend toward neighborhoods accessible only by automobile became the standard during the 1930s and on into the 1940s (McShane 1994).

PLANNED DEVELOPMENTS

During the 1920s, planned developments began to share a larger role in housing production. Many of these developments increasingly relied on the development skills of realtors rather than builders. Carolyn Loeb has described the residential pattern that realtors negotiated within the existing network of housing professionals as "entrepreneurial vernacular" subdivisions. She found that social and economic changes in the building industry "placed realtors, rather than architects or building-craftsmen, in a position to determine the shape and direction of subdivision development." Shifts in the nature of building, specifically the new small square houses, and the rise of professionals "enabled realtors to champion a type of housing they were ideally suited to create"(Loeb 2001, 4).

Large-scale development is often associated with post–World War II housing construction, but all of the prerequisites were in place by the 1920s. Additionally, as shown by near-urban development, the agents, systems, and design solutions already existed by the time realtors and community developers began to construct planned developments after 1945.

One example of Loeb's entrepreneurial vernacular development was the construction of housing in Dearborn, Michigan, by the Ford Motor Company. To stimulate housing development near an existing Ford plant, Ford created the Dearborn Realty and Construction Company. Working with a Detroit architect, Albert Wood, the company produced 250 housing units between 1918 and 1921.

Wood had self-published a booklet titled "Community Homes" in which he argued for the creation of neighborhoods and services in extendable modular forms and rejected the wasteful system of speculative subdividing and building. He laid out plans for blocks of 10 to 13 houses with a common landscaped courtyard. Wood had suggested that the "few farsighted real estate operators who are making it their business to plan and develop property in its entirety, from the subdivision of the acreage to the completion of all the improvements, including the houses, should be encouraged" (Loeb 2001, 25).

This is exactly the activity in which Wood was able to participate while working with the Dearborn Realty and Construction Company. The first buildings to be erected were a planing mill, a lumber warehouse, and a plumbing and tin shop. Bricks, lumber, piping for heating systems, windows, doors, casing, and molding were all bought in bulk and shipped to the site. Dearborn Realty standardized all of the parts, which were then precut and assembled and then taken to individual house building sites. These techniques introduced the Ford assembly line philosophy into housing construction. The bulk purchase and standardization reduced the cost to produce homes. Savings included at least 10 percent per home on the heating system alone (Loeb 2001, 40).

The workforce used to construct homes came from existing Ford employees. These employees had limited connections to the building trades. They were borrowed from their regular jobs in Ford factories and assigned to specialized tasks at the construction site. Anywhere from 250 to 500 men could be found working at the site at any one time.

AFRICAN AMERICAN NEIGHBORHOODS

Andrew Wiese, in his book *Places of Their Own,* discusses the fact that historians of suburbanization have left out the place of African Americans in the history of housing development between 1920 and 1940. Wiese points out that after the Civil War, many African American families moved to the edge of southern cities. This followed established patterns prior to emancipation where free blacks set up residences at the edge of towns where they could commute to town but avoid interference in their daily lives. Most African Americans in the south were farmers who lived in rural areas, but the region was also home to suburban enclaves of African American communities.

Many African American suburban developments lacked the basic infrastructure of paved streets, sewer, gas, electricity, or city water. The housing condition was very poor. But, as African Americans swelled urban areas after emancipation, developers subdivided land in these peripheral areas and marketed land to African Americans in areas where they had already established a foothold.

At the start of the 1920s, the suburban landscape around most cities was a suburbia of "smokestacks, cemeteries, scrub trees, and rutted streets; a suburbia of steel mills, workers cottages, trailer camps, gap-toothed subdivision, makeshift housing, vegetable gardens all coexisting with the prim residential blocks of the middles class." It was areas such as these where African Americans built houses and neighborhoods. These areas were largely blue-collar communities where residents both worked and lived (Wiese 2004, 12).

By 1940, 1.5 million families lived in areas described by the U.S. census as suburban. During the Great Migration of the 1920s, waves of African Americans moved to northern and western cities following the development of large industrial manufacturing businesses. By 1940, nearly 500,000 African American families lived in suburban areas outside of the South.

Many of the small suburban enclaves developed into large communities. In Durham, North Carolina, and Atlanta, Georgia, African Americans lived in more than half a dozen settlements just outside of the city. Five such communities existed just outside of Charlotte. In 1940, sociologist Charles S. Johnson reported that in many cities and towns most all of the African American settlements were "located at the edge of town," with "no white areas beyond them." Many cities absorbed these communities as they grew. Jesse Owens lived in one such community in Columbus, Ohio, when he won four gold medals at the 1936 Olympics in Berlin. Hank Aaron lived in a similar community in the 1940s in Toulminville, Alabama, during his childhood (Wiese 2004, 18).

WORKERS' HOUSING

Workers' housing remained relatively unchanged from the late nineteenth century through the early twentieth century. As builders and developers constructed more housing during the 1920s, older declining housing stock without modern facilities was filled by immigrants and the working classes. Robert and Helen Lynd, in their study of Muncie, Indiana, during the 1920s noted that:

> The poorer working man, coming home after his nine and a half hours on the job, walks up the frequently unpaved street, turns in at the bare yard littered with a rusty velocipede or worn-out tires, opens a sagging door and enters the living room of his home. From this room the whole house is visible-the kitchen with table and floor swarming with flies and often strewn with bread crusts, orange skins, torn papers, and lumps of coal and wood; the bedrooms with soiled, heavy quilts falling off the beds. (Lynd and Lynd 1929, 99)

The Lynds also noted that the "working man with more money leeway" often lived in a two-story house, a bungalow, or a cottage with a "tidy front yard." As industrialization increased the need for workers, however, developers occasionally filled the need for working-class housing as well (Lynd and Lynd 1929, 101).

In Detroit, over 11,000 houses were constructed in 1923 alone. Many of these houses were the small near-urban houses built for the new middle class, but many were designed specifically as single-family detached houses for the working class as well. Carolyn Loeb has investigated this type of working class development in detail (Loeb 2001).

One such development, discussed in *Entrepreneurial Vernacular,* was the area of Brightmoor, set up by a realtor named B. E. Taylor. Between 1921 and 1925, Taylor purchased 28 separate parcels of land, subdivided them into 15,511 lots, and began to sell lots and build houses himself. By 1925, almost 4,000 houses had been constructed, supporting a population of 11,319.

The Brightmoor homes were designed for working-class people and had been built without any of the modern services associated with the new modern housing. That is, the houses had been constructed without furnaces, bathrooms, or basements. At completion, the development had no paved streets, no streetlights, and no running water. Until 1924, when water and electricity services came in from Detroit, water was provided by a water wagon. Even as late as 1938, only 75 percent of the homes in Brightmoor had flush toilets.

In 1924, the typical house in Brightmoor cost $2,000. Advertisements for the development explicitly tied the houses to local industry, stating that the main street of the neighborhood ran right to the front door of the Ford Highland Park plant. Taylor kept the prices of his houses low by building on the periphery of the city without any modern services. He waited for the city to incorporate the neighborhoods, then the city paid for the service infrastructure.

In Brightmoor, Taylor filled an expanding market for home ownership within working-class housing. This market had previously existed with owner–builder housing that will be discussed in a later chapter. Areas outside of regulated developments, where the working class constructed their own homes, often differentiated themselves from the traditional subdivided landscape in which the developer constructed paved roads and services. Here, however, Taylor used professional resources to produce the basic level of housing that characterized working-class areas that had grown ad-hoc. In this way, he extended the speculative real estate market into a new market, which had either been independent or underserved (Loeb 2001, 83).

HOUSE STYLES AND TYPES

The Colonial Revival and the Small House

Between 1921 and 1945, the revival styles dominated the new housing market. The Colonial Revival house revived the English Hall house as a modern typology. The design precedents were both historical, like the "Home Sweet Home" house in Washington, and interpreted from a variety of available sources.

There were many books on Colonial house types written in the early twentieth century. *American Colonial Architecture, Its Origins and Development,* by Joseph Jackson, first published in 1924, was typical of these. In the book, Jackson gave a cursory look at the early architecture of the colonies, placing emphasis on similarities and style developments. Other studies within the discourse of architectural history included Fiske Kimball's *Domestic Architecture of the American Colonies and of the Early Republic,* published in 1922. Kimball was a noted architectural historian from the University of Virginia, and his book was based on a series of lectures that he had given at the Metropolitan Museum of Art in 1920.

The idea of a colonial revival in the United States is somewhat of an oxymoron. The period when many of the cultural elite began to look backward came at the same time that culture took a massive leap forward. Nowhere is the revival more clear than in the movement to preserve and restore Williamsburg, Virginia.

Colonial Williamsburg and the Restoration Movement

Williamsburg, Virginia, was the seat of government and the economic and social center of the Virginia colony from 1699 to 1779. The town of Williamsburg contained approximately 300 houses in an area of about a square mile. The resident population had been nearly 3,000 in the sixteenth century. In 1779, the seat of government moved further inland to Richmond, and Williamsburg became a quiet college town.

In the 1920s, the population of the town was 3,778. During the years, several of the historic buildings had been destroyed, particularly during the Revolutionary and Civil Wars. Other buildings had been torn down so that the wood could be reused. The core of the historic town, however, still contained the essential elements of the colonial plan and a critical mass of historic buildings.

In 1925, John D. Rockefeller, Jr., heir to the Standard Oil fortune, attended a lecture given by Dr. W.A.R. Goodwin, the rector of Bruton Parish church in Williamsburg. Dr. Goodwin had directed the restoration of the church in 1905 and advocated the restoration of the entire city to its colonial appearance. In November of 1927, Rockefeller commissioned Dr. Goodwin to proceed with the restoration plan and purchase necessary buildings.

Almost the entire area of the colonial city was purchased. By 1935, the restoration plan had been completed, and Colonial Williamsburg had opened as a historic site. Within the town, 66 buildings had been restored, 88 buildings had been reconstructed, and 442 twentieth-century buildings had been torn down.

The restoration work was overseen by the Board of Advisory Architects of the Restoration. Restoration architects, carpenters, or specialists did not exist.

The Williamsburg Decalogue

1. That all buildings or parts of buildings in which the Colonial tradition persists should be retained irrespective of their actual date.
2. That where the Classical tradition persists in buildings or parts of buildings great discretion should be exercised before destroying them.
3. That within the "Restoration Area" all work which no longer represents Colonial or Classical tradition should be demolished or removed.
4. That old buildings in Williamsburg outside the "Restoration Area" wherever possible should be left and if possible preserved on their original sites and restored there rather than moved within the "Area."
5. That no surviving old work should be rebuilt for structural reasons if any reasonable additional trouble and expense would suffice to preserve it.
6. That there should be held in the mind of the architects and in the marking of buildings the distinction between *preservation* where the object is scrupulous retention of the surviving work by ordinary repair, and *restoration* where the object is the recovery of the old form by new work; and that the largest practicable number buildings should be preserved rather than restored.
7. That such preservation and restoration work requires a slower pace than ordinary modern construction work and that in our opinion a superior result should be preferred to more rapid progress.
8. That in restoration the use of old materials and details of the period and character, properly marked, is commendable when they can be secured.
9. That in the securing of old materials there should be no demolition or removal of buildings where there seems a reasonable prospect that they will persist intact on their original sites.
10. That where new materials must be used, they should be of a character approximating the old as closely as possible, but that no attempt should be made to "antique" them by theatrical means.

Williamsburg became a training ground for the development of a new professional specialization. In 1928, the advisory board published restoration guidelines, a document comprised of 10 fundamental points known as the Williamsburg decalogue. These guidelines, authored primarily by Fiske Kimball, provided direction for research, investigation, and restoration decisions. Architects and historians researched buildings, completed architectural investigations, documented every building, and completed restoration plans.

In the end, the restoration and the interpretation of Colonial Williamsburg set a professional standard that is still practiced today. The restoration of historic homes followed from the same principals that made revival styles popular for new homes. William Graves Perry, an architect who worked on the Williamsburg project summed up nicely the meaning placed on the colonial style of architecture. He stated, "the architecture in its simplicity and breadth possesses strength that is robust and articulate, scale that is imposing and generous, and dignity that is calm and eloquent. As such it speaks to us plainly as the expression of the life of a people" (Perry 1935, 363).

The Bungalow

The single story and the story-and-a-half bungalow was a dominant style in many neighborhoods during the 1920s, though it had become very popular in the decades before. The house was characterized by wide eaves and roofs that swept down low to cover large porches. Precedents for the bungalow originated in the West Indies as an architectural type that was suited to the extreme heat of the tropics.

The bungalow rose to prominence in southern California at the turn of the twentieth century and remained popular almost everywhere in the country

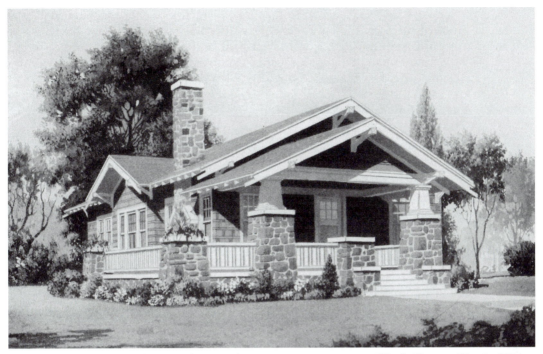

Bungalow style house, the Dresden. Wardway Homes, Montgomery Ward, Chicago, Illinois, 1924.

throughout succeeding decades. In 1923, one builder advertised a whole street of new bungalows in the Takoma Park area of Washington, D.C. In *The Seattle Bungalow* (2007), Janet Ore describes, in detail, the bungalow style houses and the people that lived in them in Seattle, Washington.

A very typical bungalow would be one story with low-sloping gables and a large porch. Windows usually consisted of double hung units with a multi-pane sash over a large single pane sash. Unenclosed eave overhangs and exposed rafter ends were also very common.

The houses had several exterior features that were defining attributes of the style. These included the use of large brackets to support the eaves and horizontal spans supported by columns at each end of the porch roof. Horizontal banding often emphasized the connection of the house to the landscape, as did the use of natural materials including wood shake, wood clapboard, and stone. The house could also have details such as window boxes and balconies.

Semi-Bungalow

The semi-bungalow is a style that upon first look could be considered strictly vernacular. And, in fact, rightly so. Houses that fit the style, however, can still be found in abundance throughout the country. Typically, the style had a side-gable with a shed dormer and roof eaves sloping into a shed roof over the porch. In many examples, the house had a large central gabled dormer rising out of a roof that sloped down to cover the porch. Because the roof continued down over the porch, in some designs the windows of the second-story dormer opened onto flat roofed cutouts with rails.

The semi-bungalow took the basic elements of the bungalow style and placed them on the facade of a two-story modern home. Eave brackets and exposed roof rafter ends were typical, as well as the use of natural materials. The use of band boards to separate the first story from the second story was common, as was the use of wood shingles on the second story.

Dutch Colonial Revival

The Dutch Colonial Revival represents one of the most typical house plans of the 1920s and is a hallmark of twentieth-century Colonial Revival designs. The precedents for the style were Dutch colonists who settled in New Amsterdam, which became the colony of New York after 1665. The style was characterized mainly by the incorporation of a gambrel roof, a shape often associated with a barn roof. This roof covered much of the second story, with a large dormer on each elevation incorporating windows. The urban legend told about the original Dutch houses is that in the eighteenth century the gambrel roof covering the second story allowed the house to be taxed as a one-story house instead of a two-story house.

The Dutch Colonial Revival styles all had the gambrel roof. Through traditionally the second floor was enclosed with the roof framing, builders conventionally framed the two story house and created the look of the gambrel roof through the application of eaves. In many examples, the eaves on the front of the house slope into a small porch roof.

Typically, the house was designed with side facing gables and a symmetrical front facade. In this design, the house often contained gable end chimneys. Round or elliptical windows in the gable end or used as dormers were common. Clapboards or wood shingles typically clad the exterior. A side entry was also occasionally used.

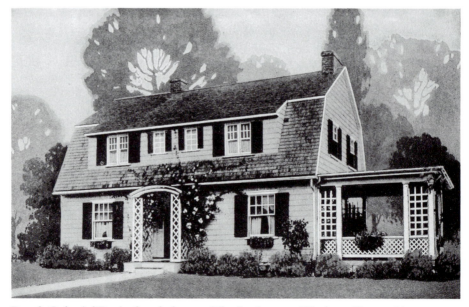

Dutch Colonial Revival style house, The Lexington. Wardway Homes, Montgomery Ward, Chicago, Illinois, 1924.

Spanish Mission

Mission Revival architecture had its origins in the early Spanish missions in California. Quickly constructed missions shared many characteristics owing to the limited materials and building skills available during the Spanish colonization of California. The buildings had large adobe walls covered with plaster, few windows, and red clay tile roofs. Many of these structures still stand and even today are iconic of the history of southern California.

As a style, the height of Mission Revival architecture occurred in California during the first decade of the twentieth century. During the 1920s and 1930s, modern adaptations of Mission architecture resulted in applied exterior decoration, known as Mission Revival, Spanish Revival, or Spanish Mission Revival.

The style was characterized by low-pitched clay tile roofs, arches set on piers, curved gables, and exterior walls finished with stucco. The iconic dormers or roof parapets often owed their designs to the roof lines of actual Spanish missions. The house relied on exterior decoration to express the stylistic elements, and the interiors often did not reflect the same style.

The Mission Revival style was prominent in the Southwest. In areas in southern California, the style could be ubiquitous in entire neighborhoods. Certainly, the forms worked best aesthetically in areas with a desert climate. Because of the marketing in catalogs, however, occasional Mission Style homes can be found throughout the country.

English Half-Timber

English Revival styles had their precedents in seventeenth-century English, vernacular timber-framed houses. In the English houses, the structural timbers that supported the house were left exposed on the exterior, and builders filled the spaces in between with waddle and daub, brick, or lime plaster.

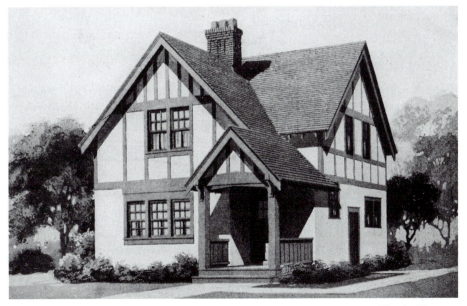

English Half-Timber, The Parkway. Wardway Homes, Montgomery Ward, Chicago, Illinois, 1924.

The revival styles popular in the 1920s incorporated the look of the English half timber, but largely as an applied ornament. A conventionally wood framed house could be transformed with wood siding and a stucco finish. Band boards at each story and the large false timbers over the front porch were defining features of the style. Often, builders would place heavy trim around the windows as well.

Very typical of the style was "The Parkway" featured by Montgomery Ward and Company in 1924. This house had an exterior finish of "stucco with sufficient half timbering to break up side walls and prevent any suggestion of plainness." With a "quaint porch" with "sturdy roof brackets and paneled gable end," the ad copy proposed the style suggested "quiet and rest" (*Wardway Homes* 1924, 14).

New England Salt Box/Cape Cod

The Cape Cod had precedents from styles modeled after the half-timber cottages of England brought to America in the seventeenth century by New Englanders. The president of Yale University, the Reverend Timothy Dwight, described the modest one-story or story-and-a-half houses that dotted the New England landscape as a style and coined the term "Cape Cod" in *Travels in New England and New York,* published in 1821.

The small size and functional room layout made the style ideal for the mass-consumption of housing in the mid-twentieth century. Steeply pitched roofs, side-gable orientation, and symmetrically placed windows and doors characterized the houses. Many Cape Cods also had dormers placed on the front of the house, allowing additional room for small upstairs bedrooms. Shutters, which had been an indispensable part of storm protection on the early colonial houses, had become largely decorative by the twentieth century, inoperable and fixed to the sides of the windows.

The revival type houses represent stylistic treatments of the six- or seven-room modern house more than styles. They can all be categorized as subsets of the Colonial Revival styles. What is noticeably apparent, however, is how similar the houses were in interior plan and layout. This will be discussed in a later chapter.

Military Housing

At the close of the First World War, the U.S. military embarked upon a campaign to reduce standing forces. As a result, appropriations for maintaining existing military facilities in the United States were curtailed to a minimum. During the late 1920s, the need for expansion came to the forefront of a heated debate in both Congress and the press. The Army met the challenge of expansion and modernization with the planning branch of the Quartermaster General known as the Construction Service.

Within this service, the Army employed architects, engineers, and construction managers to design and build new facilities for the military. Many of the Army's new designers and planners came from the private sector. The absorption of professionals into the department sped up design and construction time and eliminated many contracting obstacles. These professionals also brought current thought and ideas about the small house into the military.

In 1926, funding to increase the number of military personnel and improve military bases began to be approved by Congress. In 1927, the media became

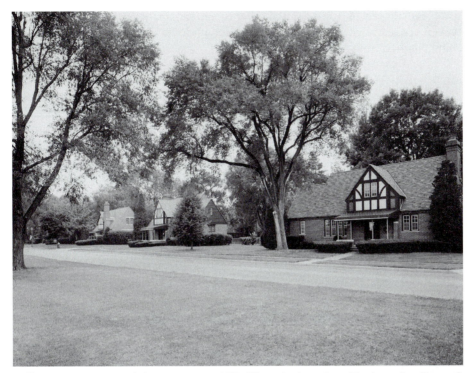

Officers Quarters, Wright-Patterson AFB, Historic American Engineering Record. These streets on the air base looked just like suburban housing developments. Courtesy of the Library of Congress.

aware of the current condition of military housing. In January, the *Philadelphia Record* reported the Secretary of War as saying, "our officers and enlisted men, their wives and children, are in many posts housed in war-time shacks, hastily constructed for temporary use, many of them utterly unfit for human habitation." In the fall, the Army Chief of Staff, General Charles P. Summerall, denounced the housing on Army posts as disgraceful while on a tour of several bases. Summerall stated, among other comments, that soldiers had better housing in German POW camps. A congressional investigation into the condition of housing at military bases across the United States ensued ("Army Housing a 'National Disgrace'" 1927).

The housing problem existed throughout every branch of the military, but especially in the air corps. New airfields had been built through emergency construction during World War I. The majority of air service quarters consisted of temporary structures that were thrown together with a life expectancy of one to two years. The poor condition of the housing affected the quality of officers staying in the air corps. Officers understood that "the right type of enlisted men will not be attracted to stay by the air service unless they are comfortably housed" (Savage 1927).

Owing to the concerns, between 1927 and 1933, Congress appropriated nearly $80 million for the military housing program. In 1933, the Quartermaster Corps received $61 million from the Federal Emergency Administrator of Public Works. These funds provided for 660 projects at 65 bases and resulted in the construction of 1,636 buildings or structures nationwide. Military architects prepared plans and specifications for 647 detached officers houses and 66 semidetached houses.

A good example of a typical housing project is the new officer's quarters at Patterson Field in Ohio. By October 1933, the Quartermaster Corps had completed plans and specifications for the Officer's Quarters project. One of Dayton's leading architects, Louis Lott, reviewed the plans for the base. He found the plans favorable, but commented that the houses were of "medium good design in vogue ten to fifteen years ago and cannot be said to be abreast of the times." He recommended a "smaller, more compact kitchen" and a larger living room with a dining alcove. Lott also suggested that the number and size of rooms exceeded the needs of most officers. He advised that the houses should be made smaller (Lavoie and Herrin 1994, 26).

Lott had considerable experience with revival styles. He received a local AIA award for the design of the C. C. Blackmore Home, one of the region's best examples of half-timbered Tudor Revival architecture. The army hired Lott to revise the housing plans in order to cut construction costs and to update the styles.

The quartermaster awarded the contract for constructing the housing project in March 1934. Work commenced on the million-dollar WPA project in a "mass production" system, where each construction phase was completed on all structures concurrently. Crews erected each house with a concrete foundation, brick walls with wooden framing and millwork, and shingle tile roofs. Construction went according to schedule with only minor change orders, such as the addition of a coat closet and coal room. On July 1, 1935, the army accepted the project as complete, and officers and their families began to move into the new homes (Lavoie and Herrin 1994).

The officers quarters resembled a typical suburban development. The 91 detached and duplex quarters sat along tree-lined streets. A boulevard cut through the center of the planned community with a green space and central axial reflecting pool. Designed in the Tudor Revival style, the brick houses were one-and-a-half and two-and-a-half-story with stucco and half-timber detailing on a front gable. Design details included quoining at the corners, pointed-arch stone lintels, steeply pitched gables, and chimney pots. Many of the houses were small, containing less than 1,800 square feet. The larger houses contain 2,400 square feet.

Every two houses shared a two-car garage located in between the structures. A common drive between the houses allowed access from the main road. The garages had less detailing than the houses, but they were constructed with brick walls and tile roofs. Landscaping and other features were provided for the officer's quarters. The most notable feature was the central ornamental pool, referred to as the Turtle Pond. Built with Civilian Conservation Corps funds, the base constructed the pool as a recreational facility for use as a wading pool in the summer and an ice skating rink in the winter.

High-End Housing

During the 1920s, 1930s, and 1940s, there was dramatic difference between the typical developments where most people lived, the larger homes of the wealthy, and houses designed by cutting edge architects for specific clients. The revival styles and bungalows dominated suburbs and near-urban neighborhoods. Larger homes, both in urban areas and on the fringe of suburban development, were still being constructed.

Many of the large homes of the wealthy shared the same construction techniques and design styles of the revival style small houses; they were just bigger. At a time when the average house sold for around $5,000, houses could be purchased outside of Washington, D.C. for $22,500. These brick homes with Colonial detailing contained eight rooms and two baths. The realtor selling the home noted that "every possible means has been provided to make you comfortable and to protect you against the heat." They were also clear to inform that "whoever gets it will have not only an ideal home, but a good investment" ("You've Been Looking for These Very Homes" 1923).

Clients who truly wanted something different, something that set their houses apart, turned to architects working with new forms and styles that were revolutionary to the housing market. New forms came directly out of the cultural and societal dynamics that characterized the early decades of the twentieth century. Architects working with new theories were known as modernists.

MODERNISM

The high style houses of modernism were not ubiquitous throughout the United States. In fact, the handful of the best examples could be all placed into a single book. Colin Davies, in his book *Key Houses of the Twentieth Century* (2006), provides a succinct, chronological catalogue of the best modernist houses in both the United States and Europe. Between 1921 and 1945, Davies includes seven houses in the United States, four by Frank Lloyd Wright and two by Richard Neutra.

As Davies suggests, in architectural history, the modernist architects and the houses they designed dominated the last century. With the ordinary house buying public, however, they failed to win approval. Modernism, Davies states, "is both the architectural profession's greatest success and its greatest failure" (Davies 2006, 16).

Internationally, the 1920s saw the development and completion of some of modernism's most important masterworks. Walter Gropius completed the building of the Bauhaus in 1926, in Dessau, Germany. In 1927, Eric Mendelsohn completed the Schocken department store, also in Germany. Alvar Alto completed his famed tuberculosis sanitarium in Paimio, Finland, in 1929. That same year Mies van der Rohe unveiled the pavilion for the German Werkbund at the Barcelona Exposition. In 1930, Le Corbusier completed the Villa Savoye near Paris. Today, these are all defining buildings in the history of architecture.

Le Corbusier and the Modernist Vision

Le Corbusier, born Charles Edoard Jeanneret, was a French architect and theorist. During the 1920s and 1930s, he pursued a vision that architecture could be used to uplift society and that quality housing for the working poor would lift them from the cultural of poverty. Efficient modern housing was a way to provide a modern ethos to the lives of the working class.

Le Corbusier was one of the most influential architects of the modernist movement. Through his writing and his architecture, he became the dominant figure in modernist theory. His ideas on urban living became the cornerstone of many post–World War Two reconstruction developments, and his imitators continued to build and develop a modernist utopian vision of housing in western cities into the 1960s and 1970s.

By the early 1920s, Corbusier had developed architectural theories on how housing should meet the demands of the Machine Age. The architect should aim to simplify design and remove all applied ornamentation. Refined architectural design could equal the efficiency of a factory assembly line. To fulfill these theories, Le Corbusier developed standardized housing types that he envisioned mass-produced like the automobile in order to solve the housing shortages of industrialized countries.

In 1923, Corbusier published his radical ideas in a book called *Vers Une Architecture,* or *Towards a New Architecture.* The book became one of the best selling architectural books of the twentieth century. In this manifesto, Le Corbusier described the house as "a machine for living in" and created forms that would bring the discipline of the factory into the home. To accomplish this, he proposed a new structural system using steel columns and masonry slabs, which he referred to as the Domino concept. The load-bearing interior columns of the rectangular structure allowed the exterior walls to be wrapped with glass causing sunlight to fill the open, free-flowing plan of the house.

The machine aesthetic used by Le Corbusier was tempered by a desire to introduce nature into the house. Corbusier saw cities as dark and chaotic and urban housing as destructive to humanity. The standardized housing types he developed would offer a humane, healthy housing alternative.

One of Le Corbusier's most famous houses using his machine aesthetic principals was the Villa Savoye outside of Paris. The house is one of the best examples of Le Corbusier's goal to create a machine for living in. The result of many years of design, the Villa Savoye was finally constructed between 1929–1931. Reflecting Corbusier's design theory, the house was based on a modular system with human proportions; a structural system of "pilotis" raised the house off of the ground. The house had an abstract sculptural design with no applied ornament, and the open floor plan allowed space to flow between functions of the house. Ribbon windows opened the interior of the house to the outdoors, and a roof garden tied the house back to the natural setting that it displaced. The garage was integrated into the house, where the automobile came in underneath the raised portion.

The design ideas of Le Corbusier were unique, but many other architects worked within the modernist theories as well. This included the work of Richard Neutra and Frank Lloyd Wright. All of these architects worked within a similar set of design beliefs. These beliefs included that cultural changes in society should result in new forms of housing; the open plan and introduction of light into the home offered better living conditions, and the house should be integrated with nature. Though the shape and massing of the houses could be very different in the work of Le Corbusier and Frank Lloyd Wright, at its core the design of the architecture resulted from a similar reading of modern industrial society.

Richard Neutra

Richard Neutra was a key figure in the modernist movement in the United States and can serve as an example of how many architects were thinking in new ways and designing a new style of house for the twentieth century. A native of Vienna, Austria, Neutra was influenced by Otto Wagner and Adolf Loos, both architects working within a new "Machine-Age" metaphor. Loos is credited with leading a personal crusade to eliminate applied ornament from architecture. His 1910 Steiner House, a house with sleek, stark stucco exteriors and bands of casement windows, is considered one of the earliest predecessors of architectural modernism. Neutra spent time with Loos touring buildings and meeting with architects and artists at local Viennese cafes. In the 1920s, Neutra moved to Berlin to work with the young avant-garde architect, Eric Mendelson.

Neutra idealized the work of Frank Lloyd Wright, who he knew from the 1910 German publication of Wright's work by Wasmuth. Wright's organic forms, sophisticated circulation, and ability to be monumental without symmetry left Neutra with the desire to "go to the places where he walked and worked." The work of Henry Ford also inspired Neutra to look toward the United States as an outlet for a new housing aesthetic. In fact, one of his later students suggested that "Neutra came to America because America was the home of Henry Ford . . . Europeans were prepared to worship the machine" (Hines 2005, 36, 57).

In 1923, Neutra immigrated to the United States. He worked on a variety of projects, and in 1924 he was hired to work in the office of Frank Lloyd Wright for a year. In 1925, Neutra moved to Los Angeles, which had been his destination upon moving to America. He worked for a variety of architects and collaborated with a good friend, Rudolph Schindler, who had immigrated a few years before. Schindler had also worked for Wright and had moved to California to oversee Wright's buildings there. In 1928, Neutra received one of his most important commissions, one that would also come to define modernism in the United States, the Lovell Health House.

Health was a major reform movement in the late nineteenth and early twentieth centuries. In housing this translated into better kitchens and baths, sanitary floors and wallpapers, sleeping porches, and a lot of white paint. One of the leading advocates of the health reform movement was Philip Lovell. A physician from New York, Lovell moved to California and became very successful advocating exercising, vegetarianism, and nude sunbathing. In 1928, Lovell hired Neutra to design a home that would incorporate his healthy living ideas and that would rival the new International movement. The Lovell Health House became an icon of modernism in America.

The Lovell Health House was a three-story box of steel and concrete built into the side of a hill; it was the first all-steel framed house built in the United States. The exterior had plain white geometric facades, punctuated by steel window bands. Additional bands of white concrete broke out of the box to become landscape elements and garden walls. On a conceptual level, the Lovell Health House was a series of geometric planes that overlapped, cantilevered, and ran through one another. Glass filled the voids where the planes punched through one another or where intersections broke the planes.

The plain white, smooth faced interior walls mimic the exterior, creating open spaces where a living room, dining room, and library all shared a large rectangular space inside the plain white box. The rooms, all opened to one anther, but the spaces were defined by breaks in the planer elements of the ceiling and floor.

Frank Lloyd Wright

How does one write about a brief period of an architect who had a significant career that spanned from 1886 to 1959? Between 1929 and 1934 Wright saw the completion of only two homes. It was during this period, however, that most Americans became aware of his work. Then, in 1937, Americans learned about the construction of his most well-known and significant house, Fallingwater. Because of Wright's innovation in plan, his concern about the environment of the house, and his focus on new materials and methods, his work reflects the era in which we are talking.

During the 1910s, Frank Lloyd Wright designed high-end homes for wealthy clients. Working with forms and materials evoking nature and a blurring of inside and outside, Wright designed houses based on a theoretical approach to architecture. His design theories included the strong use of a grid as an organizing element. This was especially true in the reinforced concrete block houses, such as the Millard House of 1921 and the Storer House of 1922, built in California. Here, the geometric grid, determined by the module of the block length, organized the house as well as the landscape. Wright allowed the demands of the site to penetrate into the grid system, and then he further used the grid to unite inside space with outside space.

Another Wright design strategy was the investigation of the complex relationship of form and material. Throughout his career, Wright searched for a comprehensive order that integrated both composition and construction. Wright found, in his studies of nature, a fusion of structure, form, and space, and he sought to incorporate this into his houses.

In 1929, Wright had several projects about to begin. These included a large resort hotel in Arizona and an apartment tower in New York City. Both of these projects, as well as future work, were put on indefinite hold after the stock market crash in October. With no work, Wright turned to lecturing and writing to support his family.

In 1932, Wright's *An Autobiography* and *The Disappearing City* were published, and he opened the Taliesin Fellowship, an architectural school at his home in Wisconsin. In the midst of the Great Depression, Wright had begun to think about new approaches to a home of modest means. His focus became creating a post-Depression solution to what he called "the small house problem." Taliesin would become an incubator for what Wright referred to as his "Usonian" house (McCarter 2005, 196).

Wright's Prairie style houses offered a design type that allowed unlimited variations in site, materials, and plan. The Usonian followed this design strategy as well, except the houses all incorporated the same building system. This system included brick walls that rose directly from the ground and lapped board parapets, small extensions above the roofline.

Another design innovation that characterized the Usonian house was a kitchen that opened into the living and dining spaces. Wright labeled this "the workspace." This design innovation would have dramatic affects on the open floor plan of housing in the 1960s.

Wright proposed cost savings by eliminating features of the typical American home: visible roofs were replaced with flat roofs; the garage was replaced with a carport; the large basement was replaced with a cellar used for fuel, heater, and laundry.

Many of the innovations incorporated into the Usonian house were based on new technologies. Wright placed heating in the floor. In a system he called "gravity heating," hot water pipes laid on a bed of crushed rock and encased in concrete heated the house from the floor up. Utilizing gravity, heat rose from the floor causing cold air to flow down to be heated at the floor again. The system provided consistent heat without drafts or cold spots. In fact, because heat came from the floor, the house felt warmer even when kept at lower temperatures.

The carport, as well, was a Wright invention. The modern car, he reasoned, only needed to be protected from the elements. It did not need a separate building modeled after the carriage house where horses were often stabled.

The Usonian houses incorporated all of the hallmarks of Wright's designs, an open floor plan, an integration of the house with the natural surroundings of the site, a human scale and honest use of materials, and a focus on spatial quality.

The House as Design Philosophy

One of Wright's career-defining achievements was the residence known as Fallingwater in Pennsylvania. Built in 1937, this house embodied Wright's domestic architecture principles. Fallingwater achieved perfection in its relationship to the site, and it is the epitome of Wright's design philosophy of integration between site and house and use of natural materials that relate to the site. The plan of Fallingwater mimics the elevations, with the large stone massing of the walls creating planer elements. The terraces create abstract planes in elevation; the walls create abstract planes in plan. The house is situated on a stream with a series of cantilevering terraces stretching over the water mimicking the natural stones and flowing water of the falls below the house. The most common image of the house shows this view, the large vertical native stone masses juxtaposed with the buff stucco terraces and the natural rocks and foliage of the creek bed. In fact, the controlled natural views are meant to be seen from inside the house with the main floor having natural views in three directions. Two of the views open onto terraces where concepts of inside and outside bleed into one another—one terrace opening up to the upstream side of the house and one terrace opening up to the down stream side of the house. Each bedroom on the second floor opens onto a terrace, as well as the gallery bedroom on the third floor.

The living room and dining rooms are one large area. A natural stone floor connects spaces throughout. Built-in features provide seats and, to some extent, differentiate spaces. A large stone, a site feature, was left in place, built around, and incorporated into the fireplace. This one design element illustrates the perfection of Wright's design ideas. The natural formations of the site intrude into the interior space. They become the hearth, the center of the family house.

CONCLUSION

The revival styles and bungalows typified most neighborhoods throughout the 1920s and 1930s. Modernist planning concepts, however, began to be integrated into the small house by the 1940s. Changes to the floor plan of the house opened the living room and kitchen, eliminating the tight cluster of rooms typical of the small house of the 1920s in favor of the open floor plan introduced by the modernists. This is clearly illustrated by the house developed by the Levitt brothers and constructed in the thousands in Levittown, a residential development that would come to define postwar housing development.

The Levitt House, mass manufactured after World War Two and the house that would come to symbolize the rise of suburban sprawl, was in fact a hybrid of the revival style house imbued with modernist planning principals. The carport attached to the side of the house allowed the car direct access to the rear kitchen entry. The primacy of the automobile was a direct reflection of both Le Corbusier and Frank Lloyd Wright. The car port was actually a Wright invention.

The kitchen, dining room, and living room of the Levitt House occupied one space within the open floor plan. A large central fireplace separated and defined the spaces. The use of the hearth to define space has its precedent in Wright's Usonian houses. The rear picture window, an iconic image of the Levitt House, is very similar in intent to the ribbon windows designed for working class apartments in Le Corbusier's Weissenhol Stuttgart. The design concept of Levitt House then, could be read as a modernist working-class apartment with a steep gabled roof and a front yard.

The postwar Levitt House, built with the exact same plan across open potato farms outside of New York, completed the utopian vision laid out by the modernists. During the 1940s, the Levitt brothers were able to capitalize on the house as a factory built commodity, exactly like the early Ford automobile. They established a production method that produced one new house every four days. This provided an economically viable housing alternative for young couples and returning veterans. The commodification of the house became possible due to the development of new technologies and building methods, the same methods that had shaped the new small house at the beginning of the 1920s.

Reference List

"Army Housing a 'National Disgrace.'" 1927. *Literary Digest.* (5 November).

Arthur, William. 1910. "Suggestions for Building a Modern Dwelling." *The Building Age* 32: 147–148, 217–218; 34: 227–228.

Classic Houses of the Twenties: Loizeaux. 1992. New York: Athenaeum of Philadelphia and Dover Publications, 1927.

Davies, Colin. 2006. *Key Houses of the Twentieth Century: Plans, Sections, and Elevations.* New York: W.W. Norton.

Dwight, Timothy. 1821. *Travels in New-England and New-York.* New Haven, Conn.: T. Dwight.

Hines, Thomas S. 2005. *Richard Neutra: and the Search for Modern Architecture.* New York: Rizzoli.

Jackson, Joseph. 1924. *American Colonial Architecture, Its Origins and Development.* Philadelphia: David McKay Co.

Jackson, Kenneth. 1985. *Crabgrass Frontier: The Suburbanization of the United States.* New York: Oxford University Press.

Kimball, Fiske. 1922. *Domestic Architecture of the American Colonies and of the Early Republic.* New York: C. Scribner's Sons.

Lavoie, Catherine C., and Dean A. Herrin. 1994. "Wright-Patterson Air Force Base, Brick Officers' Quarters, Area A, Dayton vicinity, Greene County, OH." HAER Report OH-103.

Le Corbusier. 1931. *Towards a New Architecture,* translated from the French by Frederick Etchells. London: J. Rodker.

Loeb, Carolyn S. 2001. *Entrepreneurial Vernacular: Developers' Subdivisions in the 1920s.* Baltimore: The John Hopkins University Press.

Loizeaux. 1992 [1927]. *Classic Houses of the Twenties (Loizeaux's Plan Book No. 7).* Athenaeum of Philadelphia and Dover Publications: New York.

Lynd, Robert, and Helen Merrell Lynd. 1929. *Middletown: A Study in Modern American Culture.* New York: Harcourt, Brace and World, Inc.

McCarter, Robert, ed. 2005. *On and By Frank Lloyd Wright: A Primer on Architectural Principles.* New York: Phaidon Press.

McShane, Clay. 1994. *Down the Asphalt Path: The Automobile and the American City.* New York: Columbia University Press.

Montgomery Ward and Company. 1924. *Wardway Homes.* Chicago: Montgomery Ward.

Ore, Janet. 2007. *The Seattle Bungalow: People and Houses, 1900–1940.* Seattle: University of Washington Press.

Perry, William Graves. 1935. "Notes on the Architecture." *The Architectural Record* (December).

Savage, W. E. 1927. "Why and How an Airplane is Static Tested." *Aviation* (14 November): 1164–1166.

Weiss, Marc. 1987. *The Rise of the Community Builders: the American Real Estate Industry and Urban Land Planning.* New York: Columbia University Press.

Wiese, Andrew. 2004. *Places of Their Own, African American Suburbanization in the Twentieth Century.* Chicago: University of Chicago Press.

"You've Been Looking for These Very Homes." 1923. *Washington Post* (17 June).

Building Materials and Manufacturing

During the first decades of the twentieth century, technological changes in the house and in the construction industry fundamentally altered the nature of house and housing. Much of the change involved the perfection of technologies introduced in the late nineteenth century. Technological systems snaked throughout the house behind walls and in floors. Component parts of both the house and the systems in the house became standardized at the same time that changes in advertising and consumption patterns brought images of the new twentieth-century home to almost everyone.

Engineers integrated technological systems, such as electricity, gas, water, and sewerage, into the house as well as down streets and into neighborhoods. Utilities companies integrated the house into the system of the city. Controlled by forces far away from the home and hidden from view, or in the case of wires on poles, taken for granted, technology directly affected the house. This occurred mostly in urban areas up to 1934, and then the systems increasingly affected rural areas as well. The systems, however, tied the house itself directly into a larger network of communication and services that were, before 1934, unmistakably urban in nature.

The changes brought by new technology and materials were mass marketed through a variety of outlets, but especially through magazines and catalogs. Images of new smaller homes permeated daily activity. Whether one picked up a Sunday newspaper, a *Ladies' Home Journal,* or a Sears, Roebuck catalog, pictures of new houses, new appliances, and new lifestyles were everywhere. With house construction peaking in the mid-1920s, one could often not get away from the new houses themselves.

In the last several years, historians have studied technological systems and have provided in-depth analysis of how these systems negotiated the terrain between municipal development and private enterprise. Thomas P. Hughes (1983) became a pioneer in looking at technological systems outside of time and place, to investigate the pattern and sociological process of networks.

The installation of modern technological systems into homes required the prior introduction of utility systems into neighborhoods. Given the substantial investment, such installations made more sense economically in newly developing areas. By 1921, almost all new housing came ready-made with technology installed and hidden. Homebuyers never saw the systems. They saw the results of the systems through appliances and attachments, such as an iron or a telephone. Such evidence of the technology was used every day.

COMFORT AND CONVENIENCE IN THE HOUSE OF THE 1920s

The house was the catalyst that moved the family into a larger community of consumers. What made this occur was the small, everyday appliances that increasingly began to represent the modern ideas of comfort and convenience. Electricity in the home is a good example. Housing experts initially understood electricity to be strictly a safe, efficient replacement for gas lighting. During the late nineteenth and early twentieth century, contractors wired new homes for lights but did not include outlets for appliances. This is understandable as very few businesses manufactured electrical appliances at that time. As late as 1920, 80 percent of home electricity in the United States was used for lighting and 15 percent for ironing (Cowan 1983, 93).

After the turn of the century, electrical companies aggressively marketed electrical devices, often sending representatives door to door. In some cases, these salesmen allowed housewives to trade older, nonelectric devices for new appliances. In southern California, energy company salesmen accounted for 80 percent of total appliance sales by 1915. In Denver, Colorado, a salesman for the Denver Gas and Electric Company, Roy Munroe, sold the first electric iron in Denver in 1905 and won a contest for the most irons sold in 1915. A long-time employee before entering sales, Munroe "merged his knowledge of gas and electric appliances and consumer tastes" to become a leading salesman and eventually manager of the sales department (Horowitz and Mohun 1998, 95–114; Rose 1995, 99).

The use of technology in the home served to solve the "servant problem." Housing advocates understood the servant problem to be the difficulty of finding good, cheap, trustworthy domestic help. For generations, young unmarried women, often immigrants, served as domestic servants in homes. One expert on domestic technology, Ruth Schwartz Cowan, states that in all of her primary research, she has never come across a household between 1660 and 1860 that did not at some point have hired or boarded help. By the early twentieth century, however, social and economic changes made domestic service undesirable for most young women. A servant's hours were long. A live-in domestic servant began to work before the family woke and finished after the family had gone to bed (Cowan 1983, 28–29).

The importance of domestic servants working in the house at the turn of the century has been recorded by Ethel Spencer. In her memoir (1983), Spencer told how her mother "engaged newly arrived immigrants, trained them, taught them to speak English and make bread, and then sadly lost them to husbands eager to take over such jewels" (Spencer 1983, 30). The Spencer family hired servants to help run their Pittsburgh household at a cost of $1.50 a week during the late nineteenth century. In contrast, by the early 1920s the cost of a domestic servant in Muncie, Indiana, had become $10 to $15 a week. Tellingly, women who were interviewed in Muncie from the "business class" were half as likely to have a full-time servant as their mothers had been. Why was this? Because of the "increased opportunities for woman to get a living in other kinds of work" (Lynd and Lynd 1929, 169–170).

At the turn of the twentieth century, technology redefined business and manufacturing. Many people who worked in domestic service found new work in manufacturing. Factory jobs provided opportunity for economic improvement and the possibility of escape from a defined servant class. In 1870, women working as servants accounted for 60.7 percent of all women employed. In 1920, only 18.2 percent of employed women worked as servants. Young women chose to work in new factories rather than as domestic servants.

Cheap labor became scarce in the marketplace of the twentieth century. Additionally, the new middle class did not have the wealth to purchase a new home and hire multiple servants to do the traditional tasks associated with homeownership. Technology became the servant within the new modern house.

MATERIAL CULTURE AND TECHNOLOGY

Objects affected the way people worked and entertained within the home. Builders, housing experts, and homeowners all saw electricity as a great modernization. But the devices and appliances plugged into electrical systems actually changed life. "Anything that simplifies house work is a boon in homes without servants," stated one advocate of electricity in the home. In a two-story model home, called the "Electrical Home," in San Francisco, sales representatives exhibited 31 electrical appliances said to be "every device invented to date in which electricity plays a part." According to published reports, visitors understood the use of electricity to be the future of the home. To the "woman whose electrical possessions included only the familiar toaster, coffee percolator and indispensable flat-iron, the Electric Home was a revelation" (Hollis 1920, 70, 72).

The house became the environment in which the middle class interacted with technology and negotiated the cultural change that technology brought into the home. The house functioned as part of a larger consumer culture. Goods associated with the home were increasingly marketed to institutional customers, such as hotels, railroads, hospitals, restaurants, and schools. In this way companies placed their products in public settings where customers would take notice and become familiar with certain devices or even brands. As people embraced this new culture, through increased social activities, technology caused the house to evolve in form. By the 1920s, cultural activities were taking place outside of the home. Once the social rituals that had made the house a center of social display had been removed, the house was redesigned to serve the functional needs of technology.

HEATING SYSTEMS

Though not often thought about, contemporaries understood that improvements in heating technology had a lot to do with the modern, smaller house of the 1920s and 1930s. One housing expert suggested that "not only must a modern house look well and be of good construction, but the mechanical equipment: heating, plumbing, and electric wiring, must be practical and so worked out as to contribute to the comfort of the family." Heating was an elemental part of this comfort. During the first decades of the century, experts argued that "heating is by many considered to be of first importance; to be cold is even worse than being hungry" (Randall 1919, 140).

Heating technology progressed for several decades moving into the 1920s. Victorian homes had heating, but the furnaces were not always reliable and did not always provide an adequate level of comfort. The Spencer family of Pittsburgh lived in a Queen Ann Victorian house built in 1885. They originally installed a coal-fired furnace intended to heat only the first floor "and the coldest room on the second floor." All of the second floor rooms had fireplaces. The family bought coke, a fuel made from processed coal, by the train-car load, splitting the load with a family member who lived across the street. A hired laborer used a wheelbarrow to move the coke from the pile on the street to an iron coal chute emptying into the basement (Spencer 1983, 25).

Inefficiency of early furnaces could also result in costly expenses. In some cases furnaces consumed so much fuel, without really warming the house, that homeowners could not afford to use them. Resorting to older iron stoves, however, one in each room, just increased the labor and extra trouble to keep multiple stoves clean.

As early as 1914, another housing expert credited new heating technology as the cause of changes to the house plan. He observed that homeowners heated most "moderate priced houses" by a furnace or hot water by the first decade of the twentieth century. The new technology in furnaces eliminated the concern of heating individual rooms and created an environment where houses could be designed and built with large openings "made between the hall and front room, and that and the dining room" (Arthur 1914, 18).

By the 1920s, heating units had become more efficient. In newly constructed houses, the placement of the furnace became an important aspect of the construction. Technological systems were no longer afterthoughts or retrofits. They were integrated into every aspect from design to construction. Specialists had to install the heating units, meeting technical specifications to insure that the apparatuses would work correctly. Building officials adapted construction regulations as well. Heat-pipes passing up through the walls had to be covered with asbestos paper. This lessened the danger of fire, but also kept pipes from inefficiently radiating heat.

In 1919, a house planner argued that "the modern furnace is a very different article compared with that of twenty years ago." The planning of the house determined the success of the new furnace. "It is obvious that a compactly planned house can be more easily heated by a furnace than a house which is spread over a considerable area . . . If a furnace is to be used, it should be considered in the construction of the house, and ample opportunity given to run the pipes without cramping" (Randall 1919, 140).

The new heating installations in the new houses still required the storage of coal and the daily or hourly feeding of the furnace. The storage of coal was a significant part of the requirements of the cellar during the 1920s. Yearly maintenance required homeowners to take care of the heating systems during the summer. Someone had to clean all the old coal and ashes out of the furnace or boiler, clean the boiler flues with a brush, and then brush off the inside doors and the firepot. Smoke vents also had to be taken down, cleaned, and put back up.

During the winter, the heating system required constant attention in order to run smoothly and provide comfort in the home. Most heating plants would heat a home effectively when stoked, with a little coal thrown into the fire once in the morning and once at night. The coals inside needed a light shaking each day and a thorough shaking down once a week. The ashes, once collected, had to be taken out of the house and placed in as ash pit in the rear yard.

Most of the work and processes involved with new furnace systems in the new home involved gender spheres. As one contemporary noted, the husband "doesn't care what kind of house she builds as long as he can pick the furnace." But as one author noted, "Every heating system must be run with care and intelligence. Many perfectly good systems are unsatisfactory because of ignorance, neglect or both. Take a lesson or two from the man who installs your work. Learn how to keep a clear and bright fire, how to bank the fire at night, and bring it up quickly in the morning. You ought to know these things, even if you do not run your own heater" (Whitton 1927, 49; Randall 1919, 198).

During the 1920s, improvements to heating technology kept pace with other technologies in the home. The Spencer family, as mentioned previously, replaced their original coal furnace in January of 1928. The new furnace used more coal than the old furnace, so soon they converted the unit to gas. Though the new furnace still did not heat the second floor of the house, the family "ceased to be slaves of the furnace" (Spencer 1983, 25).

Another family installed a new system, stating that "in the place of the stoves which were our reliance for warmth in the cold weather, but which left the hall and several rooms cold, we have a furnace in the basement which provides a genial temperature all over the house." Indeed, as heating systems improved, they became an important aspect of new homes. Builders understood that, as a system, heating was as important to homebuyers as were other technologies. By 1930, advertisements in the *Building Age,* a journal marketed to contractors, could assert, "Modern Heating helps sell houses" (Jones 1919, 204; American Radiator Company 1930, 5).

MODERN HOUSEHOLD PLUMBING

Indoor plumbing became an integral part of houses during the late nineteenth century. Much like heating, technological innovations of the twentieth century did not serve to supplant the design of the early systems as much as improve them.

In 1912, an article in the *Building Age* described a house in Wichita, Kansas, with water supplied to the bath, the laundry tray, a basin, and a sink, all from a 200-barrel cistern in the basement. The water was pressurized into the water lines by an electric pump made by the Dayton Manufacturing Company. The basins, bath, laundry tray, and sinks had soft, hot and cold water. The basin in the bathroom also had city water supplied by a separate faucet. An article about a house in Boston described a $2' \times 2' \times 3'$ copper lined water tank in an attic that served a very similar system. Very commonly, rainwater filled tanks like this directly from the gutters on the roof ("A House in Wichita, Kansas" 1912; "A Shingled Dwelling in a Boston Suburb" 1910).

These types of systems were common to late nineteenth- and early twentieth-century urban houses. Many homeowners had similar plumbing systems retrofit into their homes. Plumbers installed these early plumbing systems through the open plumbing method. Drainage piping was exposed outside of the walls so that the homeowner could be certain that "sewer gasses" were not leaking out into the house. These gases were viewed as harmful and a cause of disease.

As mechanical contractors perfected the design and installation of systems, many professionalized or branched out into supply businesses. Some moved into the design and supply of technological innovations. Many water pumps, water heaters, and other devises developed because early installers understood the need for such devices.

Other contractors became recognized as leaders in incorporating new technological features. Homebuyers, therefore, saw their work as more desirable in achieving a modern home. Modern is perhaps somewhat of a misnomer. Many systems at the turn of the century may have been modern when installed, but quickly went out of date. At Paul Laurence Dunbar's house, a house in Dayton, Ohio, a bathroom fixtures consisting of a zinc-lined wooden tub, a hot water boiler manufactured by the Dayton Manufacturing Company, a marble lavatory, and a flush toilet with a high tank were installed in 1894. This bathroom was still being used in 1934 and still exists today.

In contrast to this, in July 1920, the Probst Brothers installed a new bathroom in Warren G. Harding's home in Marion, Ohio, in preparation for the summer's "Front Porch Campaign." The bathroom included the latest plumbing fixtures available. The company installed an $18'' \times 24''$ cast iron, enameled sink with a back and apron costing $27.25. The sink contained three water faucets, one for hot water and one for cold water, both served by an external cistern pressurized by an electric pump in the basement. The third faucet was a tap for city water. The bathroom contained a toilet with a vitreous bowl, a Mahogany seat, and a cast iron tank. The toilet cost $43.50. The company also installed a 60" bathtub with a base and a "standing waste with china knob," at a cost of $76.50. The plumbing company installed the bathroom with all manner of nickel-plated accouterments, such as a combination soap and tumbler holder, a toilet paper holder, a soap holder with opal tray, and opal towel bars with nickel plated posts. This was a very expensive bathroom for 1920, but remarkably typical of the *Building Age* descriptions, the fixtures were sleek, white, and modern. So modern looking, in fact, that in 1963 curators removed them from the house assuming that there was no way they could have been from the 1920s.

During the mid-1920s, modern bathroom fixtures, such as the ones installed in the Harding home, became widely available. Companies such as Sears, Roebuck and Company and Montgomery Ward & Co. offered complete sets in their catalogs. American Standard and Kohler both standardized their fixtures and sold to wide markets. Porcelain soon replaced both iron and marble fixtures as desirable, and contractors placed standard fixture packages directly into new homes constructed with plumbing systems hidden away in the walls. The idea of the modern bathroom had arrived.

ELECTRICITY AND THE MODERN HOME

Of all the technology systems in the home during the first decades of the twentieth century, electricity brought the most significant change to the modern household. Most of the appliances that worked to solve the servant problem functioned only when attached to an electrical system. As such, most of the electrical devices available to the homeowner were thought of as labor-saving devices. For anything to work, the home obviously had to be equipped, or wired, with an electrical service, which had to be connected to a larger network of local electrical production.

Before the early 1920s, housing experts considered electricity not as a necessity, but as a luxury. In older homes, as noted previously, electrical systems had been installed for lighting and not for the general use of household electrical appliances. However, as the twentieth century wore on, housing advocates argued that builders and homeowners should prepare for the expansion of electricity in the home by providing systems that included future uses. In an article in *House Beautiful,* in 1916, an author asked, "Why use electricity only to light your home? Why not transform housework with some of the many electrical household appliances now on the market?" The article then showed many of the new devices available (Derby 1916, 146).

By the early 1920s, electricity had grown to become the primary utility in the home. New homes in urban areas came specifically equipped with installed electrical systems. In 1923, in an article in *House and Garden,* one author contended that the buyer of a new home "will say little about the style of his house or the period of his furniture, but he will want to know everything you can tell him about electricity [and] the new methods of heating." Electricity and the devices it ran had become the "most modern" way of "making the home safe and sane" (Peyser 1923, 37).

To be utilized conveniently, with future use in mind, electrification in the home had to be planned. The planning and installation of electrical systems had to foreshadow the actual purchase of many electrical devices by the homeowner. Much like today, few homeowners came into their new home with every conceivable electrical appliance. In fact, during the 1920s, many standard appliances had not even been invented.

Owing to the general lack of electrical outlets in homes, many early electrical appliances came with electrical plugs that fit into light sockets. Some very early systems had a few light-socket style wall receptacles. Houses in which systems had not been planned with future uses in mind resulted in a "percolator and toaster connected to the chandelier above the dining-room table." Additionally, in order to use a vacuum, some homeowners were "obliged to unscrew a lamp from the lighting fixture and replace it when through using the cleaner" (Zillessen 1920, 163).

Homeowners conceived of the electrical system as it directly related to the use of household electrical devices. They understood the technology only as it related to the specific use, or the future use, of electrical devices. The placement of outlets in every room explicitly implied buying other devices and appliances. Having electricity made the homeowner a future consumer of appliances.

WHAT APPLIANCES DID CONSUMERS BUY?

In a 1918 article titled "Electricity in the Home: Which One Shall We Buy First?" one expert related a story of a friend who wanted to "start in and get some of these electrical appliances." She informed the author that she wanted "to pick them up gradually, from time to time, until we are equipped as we should be." She thus explicitly established a pattern of consumption based on a prioritized list of electrical devices to be used in the home. At the top of the list was the suggestion to get an "electric flatiron first." If summer was coming, the author suggested a fan second, stating that it would "freshen up the sleeping rooms and the nursery before bedtime and bring more rest." Next, came an electric heating pad, "just the thing for warming the bed on the sleeping porch before you climb in on cold nights." After this came a succession of appliances: a tableside grill, a toaster, a waffle iron, coffee pots, and secondary items such as a "tea kettle, hot cup, immersion heater, curling iron, vibrator." The vibrator was understood at the time to be used for massaging muscles for health purposes (Whitehorne 1918, 372).

During the first decade of the twentieth century, advertisements for electrical devices had to convince consumers of the need to purchase. The first electrical devices typically replaced existing nonelectrified devices in the home. Admen sought to promote the modern use and convenience of the appliances by identifying electrical devices with social status and respectability. These campaigns worked very well, and by 1937, the author of a government publication could state:

> Household electrical appliances are not considered as luxuries but rather as necessities in efficient housekeeping. With the present low cost of the appliances themselves and the low cost of the electricity to operate them, it is really more economical to use many of them than to try and get along with old-fashioned methods and equipment on hand. (National Resources Committee 1937, 325)

Equipping the Home

Housing experts in the first decades of the century offered suggestions about how to install the new modern electrical systems. Outlets needed to be placed where appliances were going to actually be used. Often this involved placing outlets in the floor for lamps that would sit on desks; placing outlets halfway up the wall where it would be convenient to plug in an iron; or, very common, in the center of the dining room floor for electric cooking appliances used at the table. The homeowner would have to know what appliances would be used and where furniture would be placed in order to install wiring like this.

In 1927, the New York Edison Company, an electric company, commissioned a book called *The New Servant: Electricity in the Home.* This book included a chapter suggesting how a home should be wired. One expert suggested that "any woman who wishes to plan her wiring for economy as well as convenience would do well to locate, in theory, the chief articles of furniture in her room before she begins to assign locations for receptacles." The author acknowledged the modern trend in living rooms to "provide the owner one large room which in turn serves as a parlour, music room, and library." Since this was the "type of living room found in the great majority of modern houses," the author discussed the "electrical equipment to cover general living-room needs" (Whitton 1927, 32, 28). Lighting trends in the living room moved toward eliminating one large central chandelier in favor of brackets at suitable points along the walls, as well as floor and table lamps. A minimum of three "convenience outlets" provided electrical connections for a floor lamp or a table lamp and a point where a vacuum cleaner or an electric heater could be plugged in. With just three outlets per room, care had to be given in placing them so that they did not wind up behind a piano or bookcase.

Likewise, planning electrical outlets in the dining room posed additional considerations. The author suggested that there was "hardly a room in the house where electrical facilities will be more frequently employed." One outlet needed to be centrally placed to be used for a "vacuum cleaner, an electric radiator, or an electric fan." A moderate demand existed for "one outlet to go under the dining room table, to serve as a source of supply for electrical table cooking devices" (Whitton 1927, 34).

The most common early electrical appliances would today be considered very common, indeed. A study completed in Philadelphia in 1921 found the electric iron as the number one device, in use in 87 percent of "Modern homes" and in 90 percent of "Better class" homes. Homeowners evidently thought a vacuum cleaner was very important as well. Listed as second, 83 percent of modern and 84 percent of better homes had vacuums. The washing machine placed third, showing up in 28 percent and 32 percent, respectively. Next came the electric fan. Less than 10 percent of houses had an electric coffee percolator. For all classes of homes, the refrigerator and radio were not listed as even 1 percent in 1921 (Nye 1997, 268).

New homebuyers did not conceive of technology as independent from the house. The unity of the house and technology can be seen in the way in which electrical appliances were marketed and sold. During the introduction of new appliances and systems, electrical companies found that educating consumers was an important first step in developing customers. Often these companies hired salesmen who went door to door demonstrating appliances in order to mediate the transition from Victorian culture to modern culture. These individuals and institutions served as "agents of cultural mediation" and transformed the dynamic between producers and consumers of electricity.

Refrigerators

Refrigeration in the house became one of the hallmarks of home modernization. By 1910, the traditional icebox had taken its place as a modern convenience in the modern kitchen. Many house plans even adopted configurations to make the management of the icebox more convenient. The icebox was typically placed at the rear of the home, in the kitchen near an exterior door, or in an enclosed back porch area. The icebox required ice deliveries and thus was connected to the yard, street, and community.

According to housing experts, the "modern scheme of living" made artificial refrigeration in the kitchen a necessity. The traditional icebox, seen as the answer to these modern needs in 1910, had, by 1925, become labeled "the old-fashioned ice box." Homemakers, however, continued to purchase millions of iceboxes until 1930 (St. John 1925, 404).

The technology of refrigeration changed the way in which foods could be cooled in the home. In the early nineteenth century, the icehouse was a common outbuilding in most large residences. Traditionally, ice would be harvested and stored in a protected, often underground, vault packed with sawdust as an insulator. In this way, many wealthy people had ice throughout a large part of the year. Additionally, outbuildings built on streams or springs could keep foods, such as milk and cream, cool throughout the year. In the same way, ice harvested from frozen rivers and lakes could be sold in urban areas and used to cool foods in specially created insulated iceboxes. When commercial electrification in the late 1880s allowed large industrial refrigeration, new large commercial icehouses began to produce ice throughout the year in urban areas.

The word refrigerator came into use sometime around 1803 with the invention, by a Maryland farmer, of a device for the transportation of butter to market. As late as 1926, however, only 34.6 percent of the population was using refrigeration to protect foods. In many homes, people used cellars and, in the winter, even living rooms to store food. When temperatures rose above 60 degrees, however, these spaces became entirely inadequate (King 1926, 13).

In most homes, the basement contained storage rooms specifically for food. It was a common practice throughout the nineteenth century and into the twentieth century to have a vegetable cellar in the basement. This was typically the furthest room away from the heater. The vegetable cellar usually had a plank door and was filled with wooden shelves. Because of the small size of the basements, often the room was located next to the coal cellar. Larger homes could also have a specific room set aside for the storage of wines.

The principle of artificial refrigeration is to provide an environment in which perishable food can be stored in temperatures between 32 and 50 degrees Fahrenheit. Below this, foods will freeze, and above this, bacteria begin to multiply rapidly, and food spoils.

The commercially manufactured icebox contained two compartments, one for a large block of ice and one for the storage of food. Air circulated around the block of ice and then passed though the other compartments to keep food cool. Models that placed the ice on the top of the compartment worked well because the heavier cold air dropped to the bottom of the box.

During most of the 1920s, when new homeowners purchased a "refrigerator," they were purchasing an icebox. From 1923 through 1927, families purchased more than a million iceboxes a year. Electric refrigeration, however, began to grow as advances in technology made the systems more reliable. Advertisers were quick to promote electrical refrigeration. The limited number of units sold during the 1920s, however, is a clear indicator that this technology was slow to affect the average modern kitchen. Even a 1922 author describing the merits of the electrical refrigerator noted that "for good, legitimate reasons, the majority of us must continue to use a refrigerator which requires icing" ("Electricity or Ice" 1922, 77).

Ruth Swartz Cowan, in her seminal work, *More Work for Mother,* discusses the early development of the electric compression machine and the competition between gas and electricity as a power source. The first household electrical refrigerators were produced in 1918 by Kelvinator. General Electric entered the market in the mid-1920s. Though studies found natural gas systems to be more efficient, General Electric decided to pursue an air-cooled electrical unit. The fundamental key to GE's development of the electrical refrigerator unit was the fact that an electrical refrigerator ran 24 hours a day and thus served to increase demand and profitability of home electrical service. GE's "Monitor Top" refrigerator went into production in 1927. Virtually unlimited advertising funds pushed the Monitor Top to the top of the market and guaranteed the success of the electrical units.

The icebox had one major drawback in the efficiency conscious world of the 1920s. The units required a routine of constant maintenance and attention. It is not surprising, therefore, that sales of electric refrigerators increased every year. It was late in the decade, however, before the electric refrigerator displaced the icebox in the new home. In 1920, manufacturers sold 737,000 iceboxes compared to just 10,000 electric refrigerators. Between 1926 and 1935, however, manufacturers had sold 8,255,000 electric units. Owing to these numbers, even as late as 1936, only 34.2 percent of homes that had been wired for electricity had an electric refrigerator (National Resources Committee 1937, 316, 317).

The advance in household electrical refrigeration can be best illustrated by one manufacturer. In 1931, Sears, Roebuck and Company developed an inexpensive electric refrigerator in order to expand what they saw as an untapped market. The company bought the patents of an existing unit and hired refrigeration engineers to design an appliance that could be easily repaired.

The innovations included a removable freezing unit and a removable electrical unit that the customer could remove and return for repair. Other innovations included the use of aluminum shelving that was guaranteed not to rust and was much cheaper to produce than the stainless steel that other companies had been using. The result was a serviceable appliance that could be manufactured for an affordable price.

The Sears, Roebuck merchandising department had noted that 60 percent of all refrigerators sold in the United States had been four cubic feet in size, but most families wanted to buy a six-cubic-foot unit. Sears produced a new line of refrigerators named the "Coldspot" and sold a six-foot unit for $149.50, the price of the standard four-foot unit.

Within 10 years, the Coldspot became one of the best selling consumer appliances. The promotion of this refrigerator and the relaxation of credit terms resulted in high sales. In Cleveland, one housing survey showed that the Sears Coldspot accounted for only 7.3 percent of electrical refrigerators purchased by consumers in 1934 but accounted for 32.4 percent of all refrigerators purchased in 1939 (Emmet and Jeuck 1950, 390–392).

Shelley Nickels, a historian of technology, argues that the refrigerator was designed for the high-end market during the 1920s, but after 1930, the "streamlined curve, vegetable drawer, and door handle" were designed for the mass market as part of the servantless house. For instance, refrigerator doors needed to be designed so that they could be opened by a homemaker with both hands full (Nickels 2002, 694).

Table 1

**Sales by Year of Refrigerators and Houses, National Resources Committee
1937, 317; U.S. Bureau of the Census. 1975, 646**

Year	Electric Refrigerators Sold	Iceboxes Sold	Residential Unit Constructed
1920	10,000	737,000	247,000
1921	5,000	571,000	449,000
1922	12,000	760,000	716,000
1923	18,000	1,139,000	871,000
1924	30,000	1,282,000	893,000
1925	75,000	1,231,000	937,000
1926	210,000	1,290,000	849,000
1927	390,000	1,116,000	810,000
1928	560,000	980,000	753,000
1929	840,000	1,053,000	509,000
1930	850,000	419,000	330,000
1931	965,000	282,000	254,000
1932	840,000	213,000	134,000
1933	1,080,000	244,000	93,000
1934	1,390,000	276,000	126,000

BUILDING THE HOME

The building delivery service traditionally had been based on a local organization of individuals in the community. From the local lumberyard to the local builder, the delivery of housing had a tradition of servicing individual clients. The cost of new housing restricted the residential construction of single detached houses to those who could afford to absorb the cost.

By the turn of the century large construction contractors dominated commercial building. Contractors specializing in railways, commercial structures, multiresidential complexes, or public works generally had large facilities, equipment, and permanent staff (Doucet and Weaver 1991, 565). The local market, however, dominated the residential house building market.

The community was involved in all aspects of the building of housing. The typical house builder lived in the community and was active in community organizations. William Orbaugh had a typical family construction business in Ohio. Between 1922 and 1927, over 50 percent of the homes he built were in walking distance of his business office. His son John, who worked in the family business, and two of his daughters also lived within walking distance. William was a very active member of the local Presbyterian church and was a member of the Knights of Pythias and the Odd Fellows.

The local builder was in need of increasing his productivity and reducing the cost of construction. The cost of construction increased five fold between 1905 and 1920. But, with the increased population of the United States and technological innovation, the residential building boom of the 1920s created a demand that the local builder was able to tap (Doucet and Weaver 1991, 563).

By 1920, the single-family detached house took 30 to 50 specialists to complete. The local builder served as a coordinator of tasks. The builder, typically a carpenter, often completed the framing as well as the finish work and hired a series of subcontractors. Excavators, masons, tinsmiths, plasterers, glaziers, and painters all had been primary subcontractors; by the 1920s, electricians and plumbers were added to the list.

By 1906, common electrical symbols had been established by architects, electricians, and contractors. By 1922, there was the common standard of at least one electrical outlet per room. General Electric, in 1930, was advertising electrical systems with the questions, "are there enough outlets for comfort and for an elastic decorative scheme? Is there a switch accessible to every door?" In the advertisement General Electric offers contractors to write for a free book, "Housewiring Data for Builders" Standardization resulted in increased efficiency in many areas of the construction process. (Doucet and Weaver 1991, 567; *American Builder,* 1930; General Electric 1930).

The emergence of electrical construction tools had a dramatic effect on the efficiency of the contractor as well. The large circular saw had been invented in 1804 for use in lumber mills by the British Admiralty Board. By the turn of the century, the use of the tool was the "most important breakthrough in a highly competitive industry's search for labor-saving practices." Between 1859 and 1896 the production cost of material provided by lumber mills had decreased by 2,000 percent (Doucet and Weaver 1991, 571). The introduction of portable electric hand tools during the 1920s and 1930s had an equally astounding impact.

New Efficiencies and Home-Building Products

Introduction of Power Tools

During the 1920s and into the 1930s, electrical hand tools began to appear in the construction industry. During the first decades of the twentieth century, large electrical tools changed shop production, but electric motors were still too big and heavy to be made into hand-held portable tools. The technological advancements in portable tools often came from small companies already in the tool business.

In 1910, S. Duncan Black and Alonzo G. Decker started a small machine shop in Baltimore, Maryland. The Black & Decker Manufacturing Company specialized in producing machines designed by outside clients. In 1916, the company began designing their own electrically powered tools. Black & Decker designed the first universal motor for use in a hand-held electrical tool, and the first application was a 1/2-inch portable drill with a pistol grip and trigger switch. The tool weighed 21 1/2 pounds and cost $230. This was at a time when the average construction worker earned $5 a day. In 1917, the company received a patent for the drill and built a large manufacturing plant outside of Baltimore. The firm began one of the first mass-media campaigns for an electrical tool in 1921 by advertising in the *Saturday Evening Post.* In 1946, the company introduced the first inexpensive home utility line of tools specifically marketed to homeowners. The first tool introduced was a small 1/4-inch drill. By 1950, over 1 million of the drills had been sold.

In 1922, Raymond DeWalt, while working for a lumber milling shop, perfected the first radial arm saw. DeWalt's design used a movable motor and saw mounted on an arm that could rotate to any angle and be tilted, raised, and lowered. The production output of this one piece of equipment equaled four men. In 1924, the DeWalt Products Company formed to commercially market the DeWalt "Wonder Worker." Demands for increased productivity in the construction industry at the start of the Second World War resulted in a dramatic increase in product sales for the DeWalt company. The company grew rapidly beginning in 1941.

Porter-Cable began business in 1906 as a machine and tool shop. In 1914, the company entered the power-tool market with a line of lathes for machining small parts. Increased demand caused by the First World War allowed the company to expand by buying other smaller tool companies. One of these, the Syracuse Sander Manufacturing Company, included a line of disc sanders.

During the early 1920s, a young engineer named Art Emmons came on staff to lead product development at Porter-Cable. Emmons literally revolutionized the home-building industry. In 1926, Porter-Cable unveiled the first portable belt sander, the "Take-About Sander." The portable sander mechanized one of the hardest tasks on a jobsite, finish sanding. In 1929, Emmons invented the helical drive circular saw and the first electrical floor sander. Emmons' design for the circular saw, lightweight and compact, became the most common design for the circular saw in the country.

In 1932, a builder, William Brown from Highland Park, IL, was asked how important power equipment was to his work. His reply showed the extent to which labor-saving electric tools had become integral to the local builder.

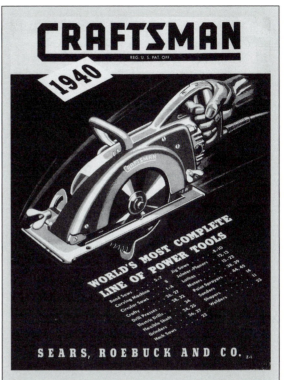

Cover, 1940 Sears Craftsman catalog. Note the variety of tools offered by 1940. Courtesy of the Library of Congress.

The Craftsman line of tools began in 1927 when Sears, Roebuck and Company decided to create a brand of superior tools. Only tools that met exacting standards would be marked with the Craftsman brand. The brand first appeared on a line of saws. The 1929 fall catalog featured Craftsman power tools for the first time.

By 1940, the Craftsman power tool catalog carried 17 types of electrical tools. The 9-inch tilting-blade "floor-type" table saw sold for $89.50. Smaller bench saws with tilting blades sold for as little as $8.95. The catalog had a range of band saws and jig saws. Shapers, joiners, laths, and drill presses also came in a variety of sizes and price ranges.

Small portable power tools included only drills and a "new electric hand saw." The catalog contained five styles and sizes of hand drills. The small 1/4-inch "Companion" Utility Drill for "general work around the shop, garage and home" sold for $9.45. The Craftsman Heavy Duty drill was built for the heaviest production work in garages and factories and sold for $48.95. At

(continued)

$14.95, the Craftsman 1/4-inch Pistol Drill was "tremendously popular," in a "new small size which [was] rapidly taking the place of large, unwieldy drills." The drill weighed 2 3/4 pounds.

The electric hand saw was of heavy duty construction and was built for production use. The saw had a 7-inch blade and weighed 18 pounds. Sears marketed the saw as the "ideal tool for contractors." The saw was designed for "day after day of continuous service" and would "pay for itself many times over in actual saving of time and labor." Using the electric saw was the "modern way to build," eliminated "tedious hand sawing," and "cuts down on labor cost." The saw cost $87.50. This would be the equivalent of buying a $1,300 saw today.

"Important? We couldn't get along without it," he said. "That power saw does the work of five men." The increased use of electrical tools was also necessary to compete with other builders. "No up to date contractor today can afford to get along without electric power equipment," said Mr. Brown. "We use electric saws and floor surfacers to great advantage, and just as soon as business picks up, we will add many more pieces of modern electrical equipment, such as mortisers, drills, planers, and others that we know will make our workmen more efficient" ("Power Saw, Planning, Speed up $15,000 Modernizing Job" 1932, 33).

Beaver Board, Gypsum Wallboard, Sheetrock, Drywall

Wallboard, as a building product, is a material of the twentieth century. Marketed as a cost saving expedient, various materials were sold. The wallboards, however, were seen as temporary or less than desirable until the Second World War, when their advantages in labor savings created a shift in the construction industry.

An early wallboard product, marketed as Beaver Board, was invented in 1903 in Beaver, New York. In 1906, the Beaver Manufacturing Company began producing the ground wood and paper product for commercial and residential use. Beaver Board came in a thickness of 3/16-inch and in widths of 32 and 48 inches. The finished side featured a decorative pebbled surface that could be painted or stained.

The boards could be placed directly over framing or they could be fastened to existing plaster finishes. In 1921, the Westside Lumber Company advertised the material saying, "fix old rooms, cover cracked and falling plaster, build new rooms in the attic or other waste space." Beaver Board continued to be sold throughout the 1920s. The company could not weather the decline of construction in the late 1920s, however, and was purchased in 1928 by the Certain-teed Product Corporation who continued to produce and market the material throughout the 1940s and 1950s (Westside Lumber Company 1921).

The United States Gypsum Company (USGC) manufactured a similar material during the same time, though with a very different outcome. A trust formed from 30 smaller independent gypsum rock and plaster manufacturing companies, USGC consolidated plaster resources across the continent at the beginning of the twentieth century. The new company combined the operations of 37 mining and calcimining plants, which produced plaster for both agricultural and construction purposes. In 1909, the USGC purchased the Sackett Plaster Board Company. This company produced an innovative product, a thin layer of crushed gypsum sandwiched between two layers of paper. This nonwarping, nonflammable wall board began production in 1916 and was soon known by the trade name Sheetrock.

The temporary building material did not have a large market. Builders and homeowners preferred the traditional plaster and lath systems, which were known to be durable and permanent. The World's Fair hosted in Chicago in 1933 featured buildings finished mostly with Sheetrock panels. The first major marketing campaign for the new material resulted directly from this boon, but did not result in a substantial increase in sales.

The Second World War, however, resulted in the wide acceptance of the gypsum board panel. The necessity to increase the speed of construction caused builders and developers of government projects to look for innovative ways to cut construction time and costs. The USGC Sheetrock product could be nailed directly to framing studs eliminating the time-consuming steps of installing lath and then waiting for the multiple coats of plaster to be finished and cured. A Sheetrock produced wall went up dry and could be painted almost immediately. Hence, contractors referred to the product as "drywall."

After the war, gypsum wallboard became the perfect material for use in the mass-produced residential housing market. Builders familiar with the product, used as a wartime necessity, continued to incorporate the material because of its economic advantages. The time savings resulting from the use of the Sheetrock more than compensated for loss of the advantages of a traditional plaster finish. By the late 1940s, gypsum wallboard became the standard finish material for house interiors.

Efficiency in Quantity

By the end of the 1930s, the local contractor was having to combat the emergence of corporate construction. The standardization that made mass production available to the local builder was also used very effectively by large corporations. The local builder found that by reproducing the same floor plan in one location, he could speed productivity and make more money. In this way, builders could also compete with larger corporations that provided housing through the use of mail order. Economics dictated that the builder construct houses with simple plans that they had become very familiar with. Efficiencies of scale dictated that "a hundred houses can be constructed at one time more economically than single dwellings" (Allen 1930, 162).

The standardization of materials, used to create efficiency in the local building process, also allowed the development of mass production in housing. The Sears, Roebuck Company was probably the most effective in marketing mass-produced precut housing packages. Sold through catalogs, the Modern Homes program enabled homebuyers to chose from a variety of styles. Simply by filling out the order form, one could purchase a precut house that would be delivered to a lot. Contemporary housing critics noted that, "one may take a catalogue and pick out a house, write an order and have most of it shipped to the point designated, ready to assemble." Catalog sales trended "toward uniformity in houses" (Allen 1930, 159). All Sears' homes were delivered by rail and came in order of building sequence. Explicit instructions enabled anyone to build the home, and a guarantee insured that the home would meet expectations after construction.

Each piece of the home was numbered for ease of construction. It was possible for the homeowner to construct the house himself, but it was typical for the homeowner to hire a contractor to do the construction.

Sears tried to make buying a home as easy as ordering an automobile or radio. Starting in 1919, they offered their homes from regional sales offices. People were able to choose, modify, and order a house from a representative in a setting that was similar to every other purchase that they made. By 1930, Sears had 350 salespeople in 48 sales offices.

LUMBERYARDS AND HOUSING

The growth of house construction in many communities required the need for a local lumber supplier. The local lumberyard became a major employer and educator of new housing in the community. Railroads serviced the local lumberyard, which were always located on a rail line. Shipments came from regional suppliers to be stocked and delivered within a small local area by truck or wagon. The local lumberyard viewed the education of the consumer as one of the primary function of advertising.

The Westside Lumber Company serviced the building needs of the west side of Columbus, Ohio. The business was one of four lumberyards operated by the Doddington Yards. Elija Doddington opened the original Doddington Lumber company in a central downtown location. During the early twentieth century, the Doddington Yards expanded into developing communities on the west side, the east side, and the north just outside of the downtown. The new lumberyards were located on major street arterys, at rail crossings, on the periphery of the city. A general manager operated each of the yards independently, while the availability of a central mill work allowed custom orders to be done in-house.

The lumberyard became very progressive in their advertising. In 1924, the advertising campaign changed from selling lumber and building materials to selling the idea of home ownership. The early ads in 1922 stressed the economic advantage of home owning. In bold letters, advertisements told the consumer to "pay rent no longer," and to put money into "a home of your own, and not into a landlord's pocket." According to many housing advocates, the payment of rent did not further the future security of individual property ownership. In one advertisement, the inclusion of a quote by a well known religious figure gave buying a home a moral twist; "Billy Sunday says: 'The man who sings Home Sweet Home in a rented house is kidding himself and serving the landlord' " (Westside Lumber Company 1920).

MARKETING HOUSE PLANS AND MATERIALS

Housing styles, plans, and technological systems were promoted in a wide variety of outlets. These included savings and loan offices, lumberyards and materials dealers, newspapers, plan catalogs, and magazines. Of the available outlets, much of the existing evidence for the widespread dissemination of housing plans and styles is contained in retail catalogs and ladies' magazines. The various outlets permeated the average homeowner's, or perspective homeowner's, daily environment and helped established the market for the materials and technologies that went into houses. For instance, between 1909 and 1928, Sears, Roebuck and Company sold 41,200 homes. During this same time, Aladdin Homes, a rival, sold approximately 32,000 houses. These companies had an enormous impact on the housing market in terms of marketing and advertising.

That is, the impact of advertisements for prefabricated housing far outweighed the number of houses actually bought and constructed. Considering the 73,200 houses constructed by these two companies, during the housing boom from 1922 to 1929 nearly 6 million homes were constructed in the United States. The percentage of the marketplace that prefabricated housing commanded was slight, though the impact of the marketing of such houses cannot be overstated. In 1906, the Gordon-Van Tine Company allocated $50,000 and hired the Chicago advertising firm of Lord & Thomas to promote their new catalog homes. Within eight months, their print advertisements had reached 40,000,000 households, just under half of the population of the country. The media blitz that accompanied the new modern house type established the small, middle-class house as the house type of the future.

Few of the catalog companies have kept records of when and where their homes were built. Sears is working toward creating a database of existing catalog homes, but this is a time-consuming task. The catalogs themselves catered to the rural market by also offering barns and outbuildings. It is also unknown how many of the catalog homes sold in the United States were erected in rural areas or urban areas.

Catalogs and Magazines

Housing styles, plans, and technological systems were especially promoted in housing catalogs and women's magazines. What the catalogs and magazines show, when one looks at the evidence, is a standard housing plan marketed to middle-class couples, often in outlets available primarily to women.

The distribution of home plans also became a marketing scheme used by wholesale publishers as a way to expand additional products through established methods of distribution. The Curtis Publishing Company, the publisher of the *Ladies' Home Journal,* initiated a specific home plan service, creating its own demand through ads in the magazine. The company would hire architects to design homes and then would mass-produce these designs for publication and sale. Well-known architects designed special house plans that could be purchased for just one dollar. Plans were published with interior views of individual furnished rooms, and from the pictures, prospective buyers could visualize how the house would look and should be used after completion. These advertisements were specifically marketed to women, and in this way, they promoted the consumption of certain types of houses to the average home seeker.

For the dollar, a would-be buyer received an envelope with the home plans, specifications, and four white sheets of paper on which a model of the house was printed. The model could be punched out of the paper and glued together, allowing the purchaser to see what the house would look like when built. This distribution medium was extremely effective and reached a vast market. Indeed, the Curtis Publishing Company printed over 16,000,000 magazines every month.

The distribution of home plans in different media was remarkably extensive. This flood of images allowed new homebuyers to accept the small modern house as not just a legitimate consumer purchase, but the only housing option. The magazine campaigns were so effective that the desire for the ownership of a single-family detached house became the cultural norm in the United States. Many studies have shown that for families with children it became the only consideration. Stanford White, a member of the prominent architectural firm McKim, Meade, and White, gave the editor of the *Ladies' Home Journal* credit for this change when he stated, "I firmly believe that Edward Bok has more completely influenced American domestic architecture for the better than any man in his generation" (Gowans 1986, 46).

If the average housing consumer was inundated with images of new modern house plans in magazines, they were doubly aware of the houses offered by mail-order companies. The marketing campaigns that the manufacturers of prefabricated housing launched reached new heights. One only has to think of the still lingering fascination with houses sold by Sears to understand this.

The housing campaigns of catalog businesses were distributed to people far and wide. The importance of the precut housing industry to the actual production of housing has been grossly overestimated by historians and the general public alike. But the effect of the catalogs at building desire, especially in rural areas, was remarkable. Historic preservation professionals have focused on Sears, Roebuck and Company, often pointing out how many of the houses are left. But many companies supplied prefabricated houses, and many companies supplied premade house plans.

Sears, Roebuck and Company

Sears, Roebuck and Company entered the housing market in 1908 with a catalog of housing plans called "Modern Homes." Sears offered to supply all the lumber and materials needed for the house as well. Starting in 1916, Sears, Roebuck offered precut houses for which all the lumber came cut to size. Their advertisements told the homebuilder to "hang his saw upon a nail."

Sears "Modern Homes" began between 1895 and 1900 with the creation of a department to handle building materials, though technically the term "Modern Homes" would not be used until 1911. High expenses had kept the original building materials department from being profitable. As late as 1906, the department sold almost $1.2 million in material but posted a net loss of $35,000. The department was to be liquidated by F. W. Kushel, but he instead proposed to reorganize, and starting in 1908 with the first issue of the homes catalog, the department began to turn a profit.

From 1908 to 1925, the Modern Homes Department was consistently profitable. After the issue of the first homes catalog, the department began to grow quickly. In 1909, Sears, Roebuck purchased a lumber mill in Mansfield, Ohio, in order to improve service. In 1911, a lumberyard was constructed in Cairo, Illinois, to simplify distribution. In 1912, a millwork plant was purchased in Norwood, Ohio. In this way, Sears, Roebuck and Company began to control all the aspects of material production for the entire house. The department wrote the first bill of sale for a complete home in 1909 and made the first house mortgage loan two years later. By the end of 1912, over $2.5 million in sales had been reached, and $649,000 in mortgage loans had been written.

Most sales still consisted of assorted mail-order building materials. Owning the production capability to produce entire homes, however, allowed the company to begin producing precut houses sold through the "Modern Homes" catalog. Precut housing saved money in three ways. First, the company bought lumber in the most economical lengths instead of longer lengths. Second, second-grade lumber could be purchased and converted to first-grade lumber by cutting out knots where smaller lengths needed to be precut. Third, with all the waste lumber removed, freight charges were considerably reduced. By 1920, the combined annual sales of the building department had reached $6 million.

Between 1921 and 1926, the sales of building materials became second to the sale of precut "Modern Homes." The operation changed from being a standard mail-order department to an administrative unit with manufacturing operations and a sales force. The company established regional sales offices in Pittsburgh, Cleveland, Cincinnati, and Dayton, in 1921. The following year, offices opened in Chicago, Philadelphia, and Washington, D.C. In 1924, a sales office opened in Columbus, Ohio, and in 1925 an office opened in Detroit, Michigan. With continued expansion, however, expenses increased to 20 percent of sales, and profits decreased from 15 to 10 percent of sales.

The company produced and sold prefabricated houses from 1913 to 1940. Throughout the 1920s, Sears was the largest manufacturer of precut houses, offering over 370 different styles and shipping houses from coast to coast. In a few cases, Sears, Roebuck supplied houses for entire company towns.

Gordon Van Tine

The Gordon Van Tine Company started business in 1906 in Davenport, Iowa. Originally a local supplier of specialty lumber, the company expanded into the direct sales of millwork after the business passed to the sons of the original owner. Their first retail catalog listed more than 7,500 pieces of millwork, and within a year they were the largest specialized mail-order company in the country.

In 1910, the firm entered into the precut housing market with a national advertising campaign. Gordon Van Tine experienced growth in sales and operations during the 1910s and 1920s and became very profitable. By 1915, the company had purchased a fourth lumber mill, operating mills to cut lumber in St. Louis, Washington, D.C., and Mississippi. Sales slowed drastically during the 1930s. Unable to recover from the Depression and a new wartime economy, the firm ceased business during the Second World War.

Montgomery Ward and Co.

Montgomery Ward and Co. entered the housing market in 1910 with a catalog of house plans. By 1912, their "Building Plans for Modern Homes" catalog contained 80 pages and offered 66 different house designs. By 1918, they had changed the name of the catalogs to Wardway Homes and offered both "Ready-Cut" and "Not-Ready Cut." The Ready-Cut system was explained as the "scientific cutting" of all the lumber "exactly according to the architect's drawing." This eliminated "all chance for mistakes." Copy in the Wardway Homes catalog stated that the carpenter "simply takes the piece the plan calls for, slips it into place and nails it up" (Montgomery Ward 1924, 8).

If ordered Not-Ready Cut, the lumber came in standard mill-run lengths and had to be cut to fit by the carpenter. In 1924, the savings between the two systems ranged between $74 and $110 on houses costing $1,298 to $1,995. According to the company, the Not-Ready Cut system, though costing more owing to the labor costs associated with cutting the lumber at the site, provided the advantages of easily altering Wardway house designs.

The Wardway Homes catalogs offered many different styles of houses. These included the Square Home, the Southern Colonial, the Colonial Bungalow, and the English Style. Most of these distinctions had to do with the exterior trim details and were not totally indicative of a high style. In the 1924 catalog, house designs were closely split between square house and bungalow concepts; 26 designs showed two-story houses with square plans, and 30 designs showed a one-story or one-and-a-half story bungalow design. Ten other house designs showed small one-story homes often labeled cottages or small homes.

Within the Wardway Homes catalog, the company suggested that their success owed to the thought and effort that went into their designs. A "staff of experts," chosen because they were "specialist[s] in some phase of home building," designed each home. According to the catalog, each house was studied after being built in several different climates and revised until every detail was just right. A comparison of Wardway Homes and Gordon Van Tine homes offered in catalogs during the 1920s showed several identical models. Evidently both companies bought designs from the same source. Wardway Homes continued in business until 1931, when the last mention of the Montgomery Ward precut housing venture appeared in a regular catalog (Montgomery Ward 1924, 5).

Aladdin Homes

Three precut housing companies had offices in Bay City, Michigan, founded principally as offshoots of the most successful and longest operating precut housing business. Aladdin served as the pioneer of the precut housing market and provided precut homes from 1906 to 1982. Two brothers, Otto E. and William J. Sovereign, founded the company in 1906 after seeing first hand the success of a local mail-order boat business in Bay City.

Otto Sovereign had a background in advertising and newspaper reporting. During the first year they offered "knocked-down Boat Houses and Summer Cottages," a market readily available from the mail-order boat companies already operating in Bay City. During the second year, the brothers scraped enough money together to place a one-time advertisement in the *Saturday Evening Post*. By 1910, the company had begun to prosper with sales over $87,000. By 1913, sales had reached $565,000, with a total of 2,400 houses shipped and sold. During the 1920s, sales averaged 2,000 houses shipped each year, with a peak of 3,650 in 1926. During the 77 years of business, the company sold more than 50,000 homes.

Lewis/Liberty Homes and Sterling Homes

Two other precut housing companies followed in the success of the Aladdin Company. It is unknown how close the ties were between the companies.

Perhaps the early success of Aladdin Homes sparked the interest of others in Bay City, or perhaps the Sovereign brothers had a falling out with working partners who then started their own companies based on what they had seen at Aladdin Homes. Both the owners of the Lewis Manufacturing Co. and Sterling Homes had ties to the organizational network utilized by Aladdin to produce precut lumber for their business, and both started very similar businesses within the first six years of Aladdin's success.

Lewis/Liberty Homes began in Bay City, Michigan, as a planing mill owned by Miss Adna G. Lewis. Her family had founded a local lumber business in 1896. By 1907, the Lewis Manufacturing Co. supplied cut lumber for the Sovereign brothers of Aladdin Homes. Adna Lewis had business ventures with Aladdin, at one point being listed as a vice-president within the company. In 1914, the Lewis Manufacturing Company began to produce its own line of "Easy-Built" homes, introducing a Lewis-Built Homes catalog with 105 different designs. Lewis provided houses very similar to houses in other catalogs, houses typical of those being built in near-urban neighborhoods. One of their designs was even labeled the "Semi-Bungalow." During the late 1920s, the company changed its marketing strategy and began publishing a catalog of less expensive houses under the name Liberty Homes.

Sterling Homes began to produce catalogs of prefabricated houses around 1915. The owner of the company, W. D. Young, also owned three lumber mills and was known as the world's largest producer of maple flooring. Though the company went bankrupt in the late 1920s, another family lumber concern bought Sterling Homes and issued catalogs of prefabricated houses until 1971.

SELLING AND FINANCING HOUSES

Sears, Roebuck and Company changed the marketing of prefabricated houses in a way that no other company could hope to. Starting in 1911, Sears, Roebuck offered financing for homes they sold through their catalog. Credit would be advanced for both material and construction labor. Typically, monthly installments lasted for five years at 6 percent interest. Sears financing increased even after the stock market crash in 1929. Sales of their precut houses peaked that year, with half of the $12,050,000 representing sales on credit (Stevenson and Jandl 1986).

Montgomery Ward maintained a strictly cash business. In catalogs, the company stated, "We buy and sell Wardway Homes Only for Cash!" They also stated, however, that if a customer did not have "the ready cash in hand," they could "arrange with a local bank to furnish all or any part of the amount" (Montgomery Ward Co. 1924, 1).

Both the local savings and loan and the local lumberyard, therefore, had to compete with self-financed, mail-order sales. Lumberyards worked especially hard to keep business in the local community. In Collingsville, Illinois, the Savings and Loan League and local lumber suppliers worked together to combat Sears, Roebuck and Company home sales. They took a full-page advertisement in the local newspaper that featured Sears, Roebuck house names and numbers. The ad read, "We will build the houses that Sears, Roebuck talks about for 10 per cent less than their prices. We will give you grade marked yellow pine and turnkey jobs on fifteen years or on any other time that Sears Roebuck offers." The advertisement was very successful and allowed the building delivery process to stay within the community of Collingsville. The cooperation of the savings and loan and the lumber industry halted the Sears marketing plan in their region (Lieber 1931, 446).

Lumberyards, suppliers, and builders often offered their own plan books to compete with the national companies. Of course, national companies in fact produced the plans used by local businesses. The West Side Lumber Company, in Columbus, had several plan books available for people interested in building a "modest home." By 1930, the *Building Age,* a journal marketed to contractors, featured an article on "how to conduct your advertising campaign to attract a greater number of prospects," declaring that "big profits result from newspaper advertising." The article provided as examples ads showing plans and house elevations of small modern houses (Casey 1930, 56).

All of the catalogs served to codify what the house should be and how it should be used. Pictures of interiors and cutaway views of the house showed how rooms could be furnished. These diagrams exposed homeowners to ideas about what consumer items should be purchased for the inside of the house. One author even suggests that Sears began selling houses in order to create expanded markets for the existing furniture in their catalogs (Thornton 2002).

CONCLUSION

The marketing techniques that became standard in the 1920s were unproven and cutting edge during the first decade of the twentieth century. Many of the early builders and businessmen making, installing, selling, or advertising new technologies and new houses did so through small businesses. Not until these first few businesses began to change public perception and desire for new houses did larger businesses and corporations become involved and thus create institutional changes after the Depression and World War Two. Even so, the marketing of the new house plans and styles proceeded through myriad small- and medium-sized business who published books, flyers, catalogs, and advertisements, all aimed at getting a piece of the new twentieth century housing market. To the market, this advertising had the effect of a concerted campaign for change in housing and was a precursor to even more dramatic institutional change that would occur in the 1930s.

Even though plan books and advertisements pushed the idea of the revival styles, as early as 1910 one builder noted that "the latest favorite, the 'square house,' is probably the most sensible of any [style] for the average family." Contemporaries viewed the changing house of the twentieth century as a real benefit. Housing experts argued that the sensible family wanted this style of house, a dwelling that provided the most modern and up-to-date functional plan without the exterior accouterments of a typical style. Modernist architects provided cutting-edge designs that were also filled with new technological systems, while local builders provided a market-driven alternative in the neighborhoods that provided the perfect escape from older crowded urban areas that did not have the amenities of the new modern lifestyle (Arthur 1914, 33).

Contemporaries simply referred to the new houses as modern homes. The term *modern* had direct implications for what the plan of the house would be and what physical services would be provided. Where form and social rituals dictated late Victorian housing in the 1870s, 1880s, and 1890s, the modern "conveniences" of electricity and plumbing dictated the typical dwelling in the 1920s, 1930s, and 1940s. Much was changing culturally in the lives of the typical family, but the incorporation of modern kitchens, bathrooms, electrical wiring, telephones, and radio truly ushered in the modern age for the typical middle-class family. A standard interior configuration for the twentieth-century house would be the outcome. Furnishing these new homes would also become a priority.

Reference List

Allen, Edith Louise. 1930. *American Housing: As Affected by Social and Economic Conditions.* Peoria, IL: Arts Manual Press.

American Radiator Company. 1930. Advertisement. *Building Age* (April): 5.

Arthur, William. 1914. *The Home Builders' Guide: A Treatise for Those About to Build, Covering the Selection of the Site, the Planning of the Rooms, and Proper Materials to Use in Construction.* New York: David Williams Company.

Casey, Harry A. 1930. "Wuxtra! Wuxtra! Big Profits Result from Newspaper Advertising," *Building Age.* April, 56–58.

Cowan, Ruth Schwartz. 1983. *More Work for Mother: The Ironies of Household Technology from the Open Hearth to the Microwave.* New York: Basic Books.

Derby, Richard. 1916. "Electricity Domesticated." *House Beautiful* 39: 146–147.

Doucet, Michael, and John Weaver. 1991. *Housing the North American City.* Montreal: McGill-Queen's University Press.

"Electricity or Ice." 1922. *Good Housekeeping* (May): 77.

Emmet, Boris, and John E. Jeuck. 1950. *Catalogues and Counters: A History of Sears, Roebuck and Company.* Chicago: The University of Chicago Press.

General Electric. 1930. Advertisement. *American Builder,* 50.

Gowans, Alan. 1986. *The Comfortable House: North American Suburban Architecture, 1890–1930.* Cambridge, MA: MIT Press.

Hollis, Elaine. 1920. "Electrifying the Home." *Sunset* (October).

Horowitz, Roger, and Arwen Mohun, eds. 1998. *His and Hers: Gender, Consumption, and Technology.* Charlottesville: University Press of Virginia.

"A House in Wichita, Kansas: A Frame Dwelling with Stucco Exterior and Brick Trimmings—Some Details of Construction." 1912. *Building Age* 34: 507–510.

Hughes, Thomas P. 1983. *Networks of Power: Electrification in Western Society, 1880–1930.* Baltimore: John Hopkins University Press.

Jones, Louis C. 1919. "The New House Versus the Old." *House Beautiful* 46: 204.

King, E. Clark, Jr. 1926. "The Advantages of Electrical Refrigeration." *Better Homes and Gardens* (July): 13.

Lieber, Philip. 1931. "What Sears-Roebuck Financing Means to Us," *Building and Loan Annals,* 446, 447.

Lynd, Robert, and Helen Merrell Lynd. 1929. *Middletown: A Study in Modern American Culture.* New York: Harcourt, Brace and World, Inc.

Montgomery Ward Co. 1924. *Wardway Homes.* Chicago: Author.

National Resources Committee. 1937. *Technological Trends and National Policy: Including the Social Implications of New Inventions.* Washington, DC: National Resources Committee.

Nickels, Shelley. 2002. " 'Preserving Women': Refrigerator Design as a Social Process in the 1930s." *Technology and Culture* 42: 693–727.

Nye, David E. 1997. *Electrifying America: Social Meanings of a New Technology, 1880–1940.* Cambridge, MA: MIT Press.

Peyser, Ethel R. 1923. "The Electrically Equipped Home." *House and Garden* (January): 37–39.

"Power Saw, Planning, Speed up $15,000 Modernizing Job." 1932. *American Builder* 54: 33.

Randall, Daniel. 1919. "Heating Your House." *House Beautiful* 46: 140, 198.

Rose, Mark. 1995. *Cities of Light and Heat: Domesticating Gas and Electricity in Urban America.* University Park: Pennsylvania State University Press.

St. John, F. J. 1925. "Artificial Refrigeration: Ice without the Iceman," *House Beautiful* 57. 404, 433.

"A Shingled Dwelling in a Boston Suburb." 1910. *Building Age* 32: 369–371.

Spencer, Ethel. 1983. *The Spencers of Amberson Avenue: A Turn of the Century Memoir.* Pittsburgh: University of Pittsburgh Press.

Stevenson, Katherine Cole, and H. Ward Jandl. 1986. *Houses by Mail: A Guide to Houses from Sears, Roebuck and Company.* Washington, D.C.: Preservation Press.

Thornton, Rosemary. 2002. *The Houses That Sears Built: Everything You Ever Wanted to Know About Sears Catalog Homes.* Alton, IL: Gentle Beam Publications.

U.S. Bureau of the Census. 1975. *Historical Statistics of the United States from Colonial Times to 1970, Bicentennial Edition, Part 2.* Washington DC: Government Printing Office.

Westside Lumber Company. 1920. "Homes are not Built From Rent Receipts." *Hilltop Record* (2 March).

Westside Lumber Company. 1921. Advertisement. *Hilltop Record* (12 May).

Whitehorne, Earl E. 1918. "Electricity in the Home: Which One Shall We Buy First?" *House Beautiful* 43: 372.

Whitton, Mary Ormsbee. 1927. *The New Servant: Electricity in the Home.* New York: Doubleday.

Zillessen, Clara H. 1920. "The Electric House." *Ladies' Home Journal* 37: 163.

Home Layout and Design

The concept of the modern home defined housing in the 1920s through the 1940s. The term *modern,* however, had two very different meanings. Modernism as a design movement embodied basically these three ideas; formal innovation, a desire to create something new, and a tendency toward abstraction. These design manifestations appeared in art, product design, furniture, and architecture (Wilk 2006). The modern house, however, was modern because of the new technological systems run throughout its walls. The idea of comfort and convenience in the house was a new *modern* concept.

By the early 1920s, the house began to be marketed to a new middle-class home-buying segment of the population. The house was filled with technological systems, and the house also became smaller. The typical house constructed by a builder, realtor, or developer during the 1920s, 1930s, and 1940s consisted of a nearly square or rectangular plan approximately 25 feet in at least one dimension, containing between 1,000 and 1,200 square feet of living space. The house usually had three basic rooms on the first floor, including a living room, a dining room, and a kitchen. Two or three bedrooms could be located on the second floor, or on the first floor in the case of a single-story house. Many small houses were designed by architects, and architects designed and built very large traditional houses during the period. But, the "modern" small house type was a new form.

Signature architects designed and built housing as well, many in the modernist, or International, style. These homes were most often for wealthy clients looking for one-of-a-kind, high-designed homes. These houses incorporated new technological systems, and had spatial relationships resulting from the cultural changes that were affecting most new housing in the early twentieth century. Modernist houses, however, looked very different than the typical small

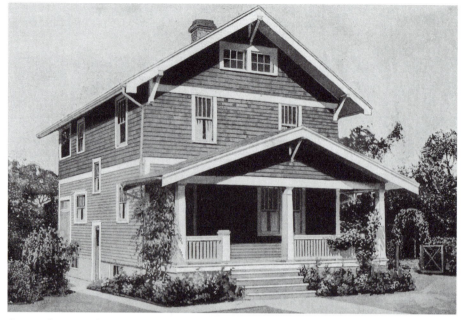

Square house, The Hampden, "a square home of splendid proportion," Wardway Homes, 1924. Dover Pictoral Archives.

middle-class house designed from traditional forms. The modernist house type was a also a new form.

Historians have noted the rise of the small middle-class house. One has concluded that the "ideal house" had a "simplified design and standardized layout." Others have noted the predominance of "modern, simpler houses." Local builders had accepted the square plan by the turn of the century, and national experts, such as Frederick Thomas Hodgson, had written several articles on the new house type in trade journals such as the *National Builder* and *The Carpenter*. The small house proliferated, however, during the housing boom of the 1920s (Clark 1986, 163; Wright 1980, 191, 244). Discussions of the modern home will refer to the smaller, compact houses of the early twentieth century that were designed for the middle class in America.

The small, square house plan revealed a changing culture in the United States. This was seen in the emerging consumer culture. It was also seen in the change within family relationships. Housing for the working class retained a meagerness that upheld social position. But cultural changes were reflected here as well. Victorian domesticity gave way to the influences of a modern media driven culture. The house symbolized much of this change.

Though somewhat of a generality, the transformation from the Victorian home to the modern home can be illustrated in the changes to individual rooms. The rooms and the plan of the modern house served technological systems explored in the last chapter. Technology tended to remove the specialized functions of individual nineteenth-century rooms, as will be shown in detail in the next chapter. Technology also influenced the entire layout of the individual house, creating the small house. This will be discussed below.

The central feature of the house from the 1920s throughout the 1940s was the living room. This was true whether in a traditional neocolonial house, a bungalow, or a signature architect-designed premiere example of modernism. Usually the first room in the house to be entered, the living room filled the front of the house and provided access to the rest of the home. The living room became the center of family activities, and the living room linked the family to the rest of the house.

In many of the homes designed in the new International Style, an open floor plan was central to the house. Here, the kitchen, dining

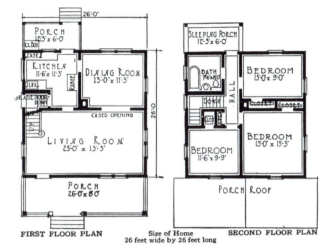

Square House Plan. The Hampden, Wardway Homes, 1924. Dover Pictorial Archives.

room, and living room flowed through one another without intermediate walls. And the life of the house became focused on what could be considered the ultimate expanded "living" room. The concepts used in creating new modernist house plans became standard house planning principals in the 1960s and 1970s, but in the 1920s and 1930s they were radical concepts.

By the second decade of the twentieth century, people understood the changes in the house to be reflective of the cultural changes around them. Many people did not see the *modern* house, whether they meant the inclusion of modern conveniences or whether they meant the new modernist styles, as entirely good for society. In 1921, a nationally syndicated editorialist wrote, "It is a pity that the real pleasures of the good old fashioned American home are being usurped by the fleeting mirage of excitement in the modern day method of living, for just as sure as the home loses its attraction to the individual the nation loses its impetus of progress and prosperity" (Greig 1921, 5).

The architectural plan dominated the discussion of housing during the 1920s; it was very important because it was the primary convention to illustrate a house in two dimensions. In 1928, Frank Lloyd Wright published an article in *Architectural Journal* titled "The Logic of the Plan." Here, Wright stated, "To judge the architect one need only look at the plan. He is master then and there, or never" (McCarter 2005, 344).

The architectural plan, though, is really nothing more than the individual rooms of the house placed in some sort of order. These individual rooms became a key feature of the development of the small house. They were components that formed into a whole. Understanding each component is an easy way of understanding the house.

House plans were available through many sources and were widely circulated through magazines, housing catalogs, newspapers, pamphlets, and advertisements. They were so widely circulated that the average person in the United States had the opportunity to see a plan image several times a day. All of these available house plans served to establish the concepts of space and lifestyle that we still live with today.

HOUSE PLANS AND TYPES

Houses, house plans, and house types were varied through the decades between 1921 and 1945. To get a sense of what was typical, what was unique, and what would become ubiquitous, four house plans will be discussed in this section. These house plans represent a cross section of single-family, residential structures. There are literally hundreds of house plans that could be discussed, but, by looking at a few houses in detail, an idea of what was available and what was built can easily be understood.

Bungalow

The bungalow house, discussed here, is laid out as a rectangle, 28 feet wide and 44 feet long. A large porch and terrace transitioned the house from outside areas of the house to the interior. Entry is made off of a large porch in the center of the front facade.

The predominate room in the bungalow and semi-bungalow house styles was the elongated living room that one entered into from the porch through the front door. In the Dresden, from Wardway Homes, this room was 18'-6" by 13'-6." A large hearth, the focus of the room, stood centered in the left exterior wall. The dining room, a den, and bedrooms were accessed of the living room. Thus, the living room was the central connector of the private family bedrooms and the service areas of the house.

One entered the dining room directly off the living room through a wide cased opening. A large triple window allowed the room to be flooded with light. The room also connected with the kitchen and hall, with a linen closet.

The kitchen was in the back of house, accessed through a swinging door from the dining room. The kitchen included modern amenities for the period, including a range, sink, built in broom closet, and built in china case. Off of the kitchen was a separate vestibule with a space designated for an icebox. Stairs off of this vestibule allowed access to a ground floor exterior rear door and stairs to the basement.

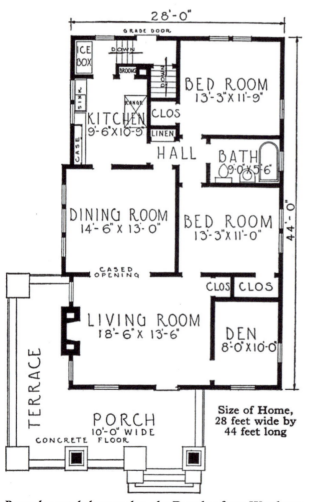

Bungalow style house plan, the Dresden from Wardway Homes, 1924. Dover Pictorial Archives.

The bungalow reflected a plan that at once embraced modernity while also looking back to traditional icons in the home. The open floor plan between the living room and dining room was a clear break from the individual rooms of the nineteenth century, which were closed to keep heat in. With the advent of modern heating systems, rooms began to open up during the first decade of the twentieth century. By 1920, the open floor plan of the modern home was standard. Here, the central fireplace, once the focus of heat and life, became a symbolic focal point of the traditional family gathered around the hearth.

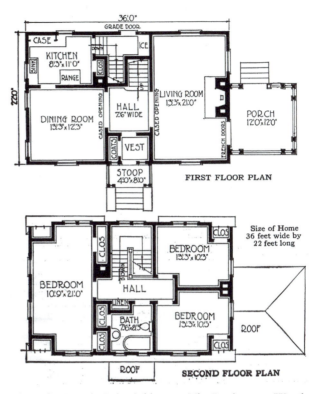

Dutch Colonial

The Dutch Colonial plan, discussed here, is 22 feet long and 36 feet wide. Entry is made through the center of the front facade.

Characteristically, the Dutch Colonial was a two-story house with the main rooms on the first floor divided by a central stair hall. This

Plan of a Dutch Colonial house, The Lexington, Wardway Homes, 1924. Dover Pictorial Archives.

"hall house" plan is the traditional plan of earlier seventeenth-century homes throughout colonial America. In the Lexington plan, offered by the Montgomery Ward Company, entry through the front door places one into a small vestibule. From here, a central hall is entered allowing access to the rest of the house. To one side of the hall the living room is entered through a cased opening. To the other side, entry is made into the dining room through a similar opening. A stair in the hall goes upstairs to the bedrooms.

The living room in this Dutch Colonial is very similar to the living room in the Bungalow. The elongated room, approximately 13' × 21', has a centrally located fireplace on the exterior wall. A set of double French doors allows access to a sun parlor that extends to the side of the house.

The separation of the living room and dining room offers a more formal living arrangement than the open floor plan of the bungalow. But, like the bungalow, the kitchen is accessed from the dining room through a swinging door.

The second floor contains three bedrooms and a bathroom, all located off of a central hall. By looking at the plan, it is clear where the family lives in the house. The living room, dining room, and sun parlor form the core of the accessible public space. The kitchen became the female sphere of the house, and the bedrooms became an individual's retreat from the family life of the first floor. Though it should be noted, between 1920 and 1945, many people lived in homes like this with extended family members and often boarders. The individual room is somewhat of a misnomer because, in reality, there could be an individual family in each of the upstairs bedrooms.

Architectural historian Richard Harris has referred to persistence of lodging as the "flexible house" (Harris 1994). Large-scale migration, shifting patterns of investment, and economic downturn all created tensions within housing markets. Families doubling up or taking in lodgers provided flexibility in the housing market that helped cope with different cycles. The housing boom during the 1920s, followed by the Depression in 1929, then the Second World War in 1941, created cycles that resulted in increased levels of lodging within private family homes. The proportion of single lodgers in urban areas fell from 11.4 percent in 1930 to 9 percent in 1940. Apartment vacancy rates during the first few years of the 1930s, however, increased dramatically, because both single householders and whole families who could not afford to pay rent moved into the homes of family members and "doubled up." Lodging declined as the economy picked up again at the end of the 1930s. But with the migration of workers to new war materials factories after 1940, areas typically where housing was in demand, lodging increased throughout the war years (Harris 1994).

THE KITCHEN

Modernization within the house changed the kitchen more than any other room. As Gwendolyn Wright clearly illustrates, by the turn of the century, "Every article or book on the home reiterated the point that the kitchen was the most important room in the modern house" (Wright 1980, 239).

Though plumbing had been introduced into the home in the late nineteenth century, during the 1920s, domestic engineering and technological advances dramatically altered the impact that the kitchen had on daily life. Until the 1920s, when people wrote about modern conveniences, they were writing primarily about the kitchen or the bathroom. After the 1920s, the radio and telephone became the objects of conversation, and people took the modern kitchen and bath for granted.

The kitchen, as well as the bathroom, added additional construction costs to the average house. Some homebuilders constructed small houses without these modern facilities. These houses, however, were often built in rural areas or economically depressed neighborhoods. For the middle class, the purchase of a small house depended on modern conveniences, such as the kitchen and bath.

By the mid-1920s, the kitchen had achieved a standardized arrangement with elements that could be found in all modern homes. The layout, once perfected by domestic engineering principles, remained very consistent. In 1910, one housing expert suggested that the chief elements of the kitchen were the "sink, gas stove, cabinet, table and pantry" (Arthur 1910, 148). In 1923, Another expert wrote that the common elements included the "range, sink, work table, china cupboard, refrigerator, and service to the dining room" (Robinson 1923, 73).

Domestic engineering principles fundamentally altered the nature of the household kitchen. From the early nineteenth century through the early twentieth century, domestic engineers and housing experts argued for an improved kitchen. The goal of this new kitchen was a room designed with the fewest number of steps needed to prepare meals.

The small compact space efficient kitchen used progressive engineering principles and new technologies to equip the house with a place for a single housewife to prepare modern meals on a modern time schedule. The kitchen had been one of the largest rooms in the house in older Victorian homes. By the 1920s it had become one of the smallest. Housing reformers, architects, and home-owners all thought that the space could be used to better advantage in other rooms of the house.

THE PANTRY

In laying out the home of the early twentieth century, the transitions be-tween rooms mattered almost as much as the primary rooms themselves. Most rooms in the house were empty rectangles and achieved purpose of use through the placement of furniture. Others required design and layout to be functional, ac-cording to a plan. Off of the kitchen, the pantry was one such room. Intended to be more than just a storage area, the pantry was a connection between the food services of the kitchen and the food consumption of the dining room.

For large suburban houses, a butler's pantry, also called a pass pantry, served as an area for a cupboard set aside for the dining room dishes. In this way, the finer dishes used for eating did not have to be mixed with the cookware and kitchen utensils. In larger or more expensive homes, the pantry could also have a sink for washing the dining room dishes. This

In 1923, Eugene Robinson wrote an architectural text book. He specified that in a large suburban house the kitchen should be 13 feet square, stat-ing:

The kitchen occupied by the housewife for a comparatively short time each day while she per-forms the light kitchen duties required in a little house may be very small indeed, and usually the smaller the better. In this type of kitchen the economic principles of kitchen design should be applied stringently, so that the range, sink, work table, china cupboard, refrigerator, and service to the dining room should have the proper eco-nomic relation. The saving of steps is especially important when the work of the house is done by the housewife herself.

Usually a service pantry is not desirable in a small house, a service cupboard opening from both the dining room and the kitchen being a great labor-savings device. The sink should be adjoining to the service cupboard counter, so that the dishes having been passed through from the dining room may be washed and replaced in the cupboard ready for the next meal with the mini-mum amount of handling. The drain should be at the left of the sink, with the china cupboard above and facing it, if possible. All of the kitchen equipment should be compactly arranged, with perhaps a small storage pantry in the rear of the rear. (Robinson 1923, 73–74)

arrangement was a vestige of the nineteenth-century, or even earlier. Often, large kitchens included formal relationships dictated by the hierarchy of house servant work.

Small house design eliminated many of the functions of servant spaces and smaller subservient rooms. And as the twentieth century progressed, bringing with it innovations in commercial canning, the rise of brand items, and the chain grocery store, the storage need of the kitchen began to change. One ex-pert argued that "a small kitchen usually means a small pantry, but unless there is a storeroom in the basement a large pantry is desirable, for there seems to be no end of material that should find a place in this room." Unlike the pass pan-try between the kitchen and dining room, such a storage pantry was usually at the rear of the kitchen. Here, a smaller pantry could be conveniently accessed from a rear door entering the back of the house from the garage, or the side of the house from a driveway. With the removal of the pass pantry, a swinging door between the kitchen and dining room allowed ease of moving food, but still kept out food odors (Arthur 1914, 23).

FROM HALL TO PARLOR TO LIVING ROOM

In the earliest forms of housing, one room served as the central public room, *the hall*. Situated around the hearth, or fireplace, the hall became a multifunctional room providing the basic needs of shelter, warmth, and food. By the seventeenth century, specialized rooms had begun to replace the dominance of the hall. The parlor and chamber added spaces dedicated to entertainment and sleeping, and the hall began to serve the separate function of reception. Throughout the eighteenth century, the hall became the transitional area between a series of more intimate public rooms and, often, second floor bedrooms. Eventually, the hall became an area dedicated to receiving guests who quite often were escorted into the parlor, which had become the central public room of the house.

The parlor, therefore, became the most important room for social entertaining in the nineteenth-century house. The parlor served as the social and family hub of a refined life. A parlor and a few good pieces of furniture were prerequisites even in the lower-income search for gentility. Richard Bushman describes the use of the parlor not only for entertainment, but also for training young adults in the finer aspects of genteel behavior. The parlor was the outgrowth of a larger cultural change. He writes, "We assume that house lots will have yards with lawns and shrubbery, that houses will make space for formal entertainment, that everyone will own books, take baths, carry handkerchiefs, eat with a knife and fork, forgetting that all this once had to be learned" (Bushman 1992, 447).

The parlor became antiquated by the early twentieth century. The genteel parlor culture of the nineteenth century radically transformed into a culture that depended on material gain and personal expression. The fast pace of twentieth-century urban life needed a fast-paced physical environment. Parlor culture was steeped with gender and class biases and did not relate to new consumer driven mass culture. The need for formal visitation in the parlor was replaced by casual entertainment outside of the home.

As leisure increased, the role of the home changed. Parlor reformers sought to change the parlor from a place of social entertainment to a room for living during the homeowner's leisure moments. The new living room that developed became a multifunctional family space serving the needs of changing family functions.

During the late nineteenth century, many families in houses with a specific, set-aside formal parlor used another room for daily activities. A sitting room or back parlor would be filled with older furniture where daily family activities could take place without disturbing the parlor. Thomas Schlereth discusses this type of catchall room for everyday family activities in Victorian houses. He suggests various names associated with the room, such as "second parlor, the drawing room, music room, sitting room, or living room" (Schlereth 1991, 122–123). The transformation of the parlor and sitting room into the idea of the living room took time in each individual household, but occurred roughly between 1890 and 1913. In remembering her Victorian home in Pittsburgh, one author recalled that her parent's parlor "went through many transformations and toward the end of our occupancy of the house, it became a living room" (Spencer 1983, 107).

The Telephone in the Modern Home

The layout of the home in the twentieth century was affected by the artifacts of the new technologies that were brought into the home, for example, the telephone. The telephone altered formal relationships of the parlor, connected the kitchen to the outside world, and made an in-home business office more valuable. The telephone also connected the family to larger social networks outside of the established neighborhood or local community. Writing about the history of the parlor, Katherine Grier (1988) notes the connection between the Victorian social custom of "calling" and the new use of the telephone. Victorian domesticity required the housewife to stay home and keep parlor hours in order to stay connected to local social networks. The telephone allowed the modern, middle-class housewife to stay connected without the social ritual of the parlor. Fischer, in his book *Calling America,* quotes a women in California who chose to communicate by telephone rather than "go the five miles just for a short visit" (Fischer 1992, 237). Robert and Helen Lynd documented that during the 1920s in Muncie, Indiana, many families used the telephone as a substitute for visiting (Lynd and Lynd 1929, 273–275).

In the modern home, the homeowner typically leased a telephone from the phone company. Because of this business model, local companies offered few choices of types or styles. Early telephones came in two basic types, the wall-mounted phone or the candlestick phone. The wall-mounted phone could be placed conveniently on the wall at the height of the caller's mouth. The candlestick telephone could be placed on a desk or table. On a desk, just the mouthpiece and handset were visible, and the internal workings, the magneto bell and generator, had to be placed out of the way under the table, on an adjacent wall, or attached to the table itself.

The telephone was typically installed in a den or office, or in the kitchen or back hall, and as the twentieth century wore on, in the dining room. The den and office were male-dominated spaces of the home. In the office, the phone became an extension of the male-dominated business world. The phone here connected the home to the virtual networks of the work environment.

To at least one expert, placing a telephone in a hall where conversations could be overheard was an "abomination." Here, visitors could overhear "the price of their roast," or the family could overhear someone "tell a white lie for society's sake." The writer suggested that the phone be kept in a closet or upstairs where "the family alone" were the "listeners in" (Wright 1917, 140).

Installing the phone in the kitchen created a new area from

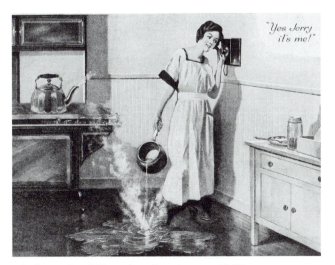

Kitchen. *Good Housekeeping,* August 1922.

which to manage the household. Domestic reformers promoted the idea of the housewife as an efficient home manager. Part of this efficiency became balancing informal conversation and household communication with housework. Advertisements reinforced the idea as well. A woman taking time from preparing a meal to talk to "Jerry," which could be either her husband or a female friend appeared in one such advertisement (*House Beautiful* 1920, 161).

The telephone niche placed in the wall between the kitchen and dining room became a common design feature during the 1930s. The phone niche established a central place for the phone book, notepads, and pens, the social communication node that attached the modern family to the community. The telephone, placed in the kitchen or hall, then, removed social connection in the home from the parlor, and hence the front of the house, to the rear of the house, the new female sphere.

Telephone companies originally conceived of the telephone as a technological system to be used as a tool for business, placing the telephone in the den or office. It is clear that users of the technology did not adhere to the proponents of the new communication system, but they adapted the technology to their own needs, most particularly social conversation. In this case, consumers and not engineers ultimately determined the outcome of the cultural impact of the technology.

The phone in the home was seen by telephone companies as the equivalent of the business phone. Telephone salesmen often promoted units to be used for the efficient ordering of goods and services by the housewife, who was seen as a household administrator. This vision worked well with ideas emerging from both advertising and home economics.

In the home, however, telephone users mediated the technology with the needs of the home and their own uses. Women, increasingly comfortable with phone use, began to use the technology for their own purposes. Selected studies in 1930 found that 25 to 40 percent of calls made or received by housewives were commercial, and 30 to 50 percent were social. In the home, women, and not men, pursued what they wanted from the new technology, that is, conversation. Fischer, in fact, argues that because of this the telephone was an icon of modernity at the turn of the century (Fischer 1992, 232–235).

The Radio in the Modern Home

Both the piano and the phonograph were technologies by means of which music entered the house during the first two decades of the twentieth century. By 1914, annual manufacturing totals exceeded 500,000 phonographs and 323,000 pianos. Both permeated late nineteenth-century culture. Craig Roell, in *The Piano in America,* repeats an old vaudeville joke; "Do you play the piano? No, but I play the phonograph" (Roell 1989, 48). Ubiquitous in the home at the turn of the century, by 1923 both the piano and the phonograph were being eclipsed by the radio, an object that had more effect on the interior layout of the house in the twentieth century than any other technological artifact.

The piano was the center of musical entertainment in the Victorian parlor. Activities often revolved around music. Again, the Lynds recorded that in Muncie many families had a piano in the living room, and "spontaneous singing" was a "part of the fun of any and all gatherings" (Lynd and Lynd 1929,

245). The height of the piano's popularity occurred between 1870 and 1890. Peak sales, however, came in 1909. After 1921, the decline of the piano was directly proportional to the increased sales of the radio.

The invention of the phonograph, and then the radio, brought variety of music into the home. Both affected the layout of the house by creating a living room of passive musical activity instead of active musical activity. The activity associated with the new radio fad, however, initially occurred in the attic and garage. Building a radio kit in the garage or listening through earphones up in the attic began to connect individual listeners to the transmissions of a larger nation. As fun as this was, the tinkerer became more isolated from the rest of the family.

As an invention, the radio has been important for redefining masculinity in the home. In part, the radio served to make the pleasure of music acceptable for men. Being active in exploring nature was the traditional Victorian pastime of manly activity. When men began to "tinker" with first the automobile and then the radio, a male-dominated sphere returned to the house. But just in certain areas. One of these areas, though, was the new modern living room.

Home-Built Radio Sets

During the beginning of the radio phenomenon, young men often built their own radio sets from scratch. Before commercial radio production, there were not radios at stores that could be brought home and plugged in. Early sets, both crystal and then even the early tube sets, were purchased as kits and put together. The crystal set consisted of an aerial, an induction coil, a crystal detector, and a pair of headphones. Also necessary, was a piece of galena crystal with a "cat's whisker." Costing $10 to $35 apiece, crystal sets were extremely popular. In fact, Westinghouse was producing 25,000 sets a month by 1922 and could not keep up with demand (Douglas 1999, 52).

The aerial had to be positioned high enough to collect waves from the air and had to be grounded, often by attaching one end of the wire to a water pipe. In some cases, the aerial could be as much as 85 feet of wire attached 30 feet in the air from the house. Aerials cluttered the skylines of many neighborhoods, and some people shopping for new homes even looked for locations with good reception.

Why did young men build radios? For them, the act of building the sets de-mystified science and engineering. The hobby also began to give many young men a solid grasp of electricity and electronics. Crystal sets were fairly simple, requiring no power source. A wire wound around an oatmeal box with the two ends connected to wooden posts could be used for a coil. A brass track and slider placed on top of the coil acted as a tuner. One end of the wire would be attached to the aerial and the other end attached to the headphones. Douglas, in her book *Listening In,* suggests that though reception was very poor, "thousands of tinkerers" fashioned their own sets during the first decades of the century (Douglas 1999, 52).

One of these young amateurs, Edwin H. Armstrong, had begun experimenting with wireless gadgets in his attic workroom in 1905 at the age of 15. In the Signal Corps during the First World War, Armstrong began to work on the development of transmitters using vacuum tubes. While with the army

The First Commercial Radio Broadcast

The first regularly scheduled broadcast of voice and music over the radio is credited to Frank Conrad. A Westinghouse employee in the radio division, Conrad held multiple patents for radio advances he made during the First World War. When his work slowed at Westinghouse after the war, he began experimenting with the broadcast of sound in a makeshift station he set up in his garage at his home in a suburb of Pittsburgh. People with home-built radios began tuning in to hear Conrad's experimental broadcasts.

The Joseph Horne Department Store put an ad in the *Pittsburgh Sun* announcing that the store had radio sets for sale that could pick up the Conrad radio program. Harry P. Davis, Conrad's supervisor, saw the ad and had a vision of the future. The next day, Davis held a conference with Conrad and other officials to see if the company could build a more powerful transmitter at the Westinghouse plant in Pittsburgh that could offer regularly scheduled programming. If this could be done, Westinghouse could enter the market manufacturing radios so that people could listen to their broadcasts.

The new station received a license and the call letters KDKA from the Department of Commerce on October 27. The first radio station with the intent to appeal to a mass audience, KDKA began broadcasting at 8:00 P.M., November 2, 1920. With much publicity, the new station began broadcasting by announcing up to the minute returns during the presidential election between Warren G. Harding and James M. Cox.

The station continued to broadcast regularly. The first broadcasts emanated from Pittsburgh nightly between 8:00 P.M. and 9:30 P.M. This was soon expanded to include daytime hours. Though typically the transmissions had an effective range of less than 200 miles, on a clear night the station could be heard in Illinois. The success of KDKA was not readily apparent. For one reason, Westinghouse did not begin producing radio units in large numbers until more than a year later. The station had, however, set the stage for things to come.

In 1921, just a year later, radio mania swept the country. Large companies, newspapers, churches, stores, and private individuals paid for a license and entered into the experimental radio market. New licenses included WIP in Gimbel Brothers Department Store in Philadelphia, WEAF in New York owned by American Telephone & Telegraph Company, and the

in 1918, he designed an eight-tube receiver of unusually high quality. This receiver, the Radiola Superheterodyne, revolutionized the radio industry because it offered reliable, clear reception that, with the attached loudspeaker, itself an invention of the early 1920s, could be heard by multiple listeners (Douglas 1987, 40).

Armstrong had invented the first commercially marketable radio. His device ran on batteries, could be easily tuned, and did not require an antenna. In 1922, Armstrong sold a perfected receiver to the Radio Corporation of America (RCA). By 1924, RCA engineers had reduced the unit to a reasonably-priced six-tube receiver and had begun marketing and selling what could be thought of as the first modern family radio.

The culmination of the technology occurred in the mid-1920s when the A-C tube was invented, allowing the radio to run on electricity. A cheap and practical A-C tube began to be produced by RCA in 1927, and the radio became a home appliance plugged into an outlet in the living room. Companies such as RCA, Magnavox, Zenith, and Philco immediately began to market console sets resembling fine furniture. Companies designed and marketed radios specifically to be placed in the living room.

The radio quickly became a fixture in American living rooms. By 1928, the radio had revolutionized home entertainment and American culture. In the 25 years previous to 1928, 19,000,000 automobiles had been produced. In the 30 years previous, 13,000,000 phonographs had been sold. In the previous half a century 18,000,000 phones had been installed. But in six years, between 1922 and 1928, 7,500,000 homes were equipped with radio sets, with a listening audience of one-third of the population. This increase in radio came during the same time that the housing boom produced more single-family homes than ever before in history (Douglas 1987, 77).

During the month of June 1939, the Cleveland Council of Parent-Teachers Associations distributed and collected household report forms, labeled the "Seventh Cleveland Home Inventory." The reports were intended to show family buying habits, and they were distributed across the entire economic population of Cleveland. The report established a good baseline for understanding what products and consumer goods were purchased and used in individual households. Every one of the 5,873 families inventoried had a radio. Thirty percent of the radios had been purchased before 1931. Slightly more, 32 percent, had been purchased within the last three years, between 1936 and 1939 (*Cleveland Home Inventory* 1939).

(continued)

Yahrling-Rayner Piano Company's station, WAAY, in Youngstown, Ohio. By the end of 1922, 690 different radio stations operated throughout the country (Douglas 1987).

TYPES OF ROOMS IN HOMES OF 1921–1945

The common way to both design a house and market a house was through the house plan. Plans were published in the countless books, magazines, and catalogs mentioned before. By looking at roughly 600 of these house plans, some conclusions can be reached about the layout of the typical house.

The most common room among all the plans was the living room. In fact, every one of the 600 houses contained a living room. Not one of the house plans contained a parlor. The next most common attribute of the early twentieth-century house was the connection of the living room and dining room. In 78 percent of the house plans, the dining room was located directly off of the living room. In 444 of the plans, a door or set of doors separated the two rooms. In the rest of the plans, the connection was an open doorway creating an open plan within the first floor of the house. The average house plan published in catalogs or magazines, therefore, had a 12-foot by 18-foot living room with a direct connection to a dining room and a kitchen on the first floor.

In about one-third of the homes, a hall provided a transition from the outside to the interior family rooms. In most cases, the hall contained a coat closet. Fifteen percent of the homes included a vestibule as the transition between entry and living room. Rather than receive visitors or a place to take off a coat and hat, the vestibule kept out the dust and the cold from the outside. A few houses had a vestibule that entered into a hall.

The main rooms of the house were very standard. Some of the plans, however, also contained what could be called a feature room, an added room based on specific function. The additional room was one of the key features in separating one house layout from another. Out of the 600 house plans, 21 contained a den, 9 a sewing room, 7 a library, and 2 a music room. Eighteen of the plans contained a sleeping porch on the second floor.

Just over 8 percent, or 51 of the plans, contained a sun porch or a sun room. Though not significant in total numbers, sun rooms were often a featured bonus room in magazines. These rooms, presumably placed on the south elevation, were used as casual living areas, often furnished with wicker suites similar to those popular for living rooms.

Table 2
Distribution of Rooms from 600 Plans Published 1917–1927

Distribution of First Floor Rooms

	Percent of Total	*Total Number*
Living Room	100%	600
Living Room — 11' 12' or 13'	62%	373
Kitchen	100%	596
Dining Room off of Living Room	78%	468
Hall with entry	28%	170
Vestibule	15%	89

Distribution of Bonus Rooms

Pantry off of Kitchen	14%	84
Sun Room	8.7%	52
Breakfast Room	6.7%	40
Den	3.5%	21
Sleeping Porch	3%	18
Sewing Room		9
Library		7
Washroom Room		6
Music Room		2
Alcove off of Living Room		1

Kitchens possibly showed the most difference between plans. Fourteen percent of the plans contained a pantry in the kitchen. Seven percent of the kitchens contained a breakfast nook, an area set aside with a built-in table for eating quick meals.

MODERNISM AND HOUSE LAYOUT

The stylistic composition, lack of gabled roofs, and plain facades with ribbon windows marked modernist structures as very different from traditional styles of housing. The floor plans and layout of the houses, however, had many similarities. The Lovell Health House, for instance, had a living room with a fireplace, a dining room, a kitchen entering into the dining room through a swinging door, and a sun room off the dining room. A smaller library was placed off of the living room, opposite the dining room. On the top floor of the house, three bedrooms surrounded two bathrooms. A small sleeping porch was accessible from each bedroom. A study, the same size as the bedrooms, also existed off the hall at the top of the second floor stairs. The first floor also contained a pair of guest bedrooms.

This house had all of the components of the traditional six- and seven-room moderns. The wealthy clients who commissioned signature architects to design modernist houses could afford a larger house with guest bedrooms and multiple feature rooms. The architects designing these homes had to satisfy the basic requirements necessary in any house. They had the ability to experiment with layout, however, once freed from the traditional forms.

The largest difference in layout of the typical modernist house was a very open floor plan. Most modernist houses could be characterized by a very open main floor, where the living room, dining room, and other main living areas flowed through one another. These spaces also included innovative responses to circulation, access, and the use of materials.

Frank Lloyd Wright and House Layout

Frank Lloyd Wright had more influence on American domestic architecture than anyone else in the twentieth century. His early work,

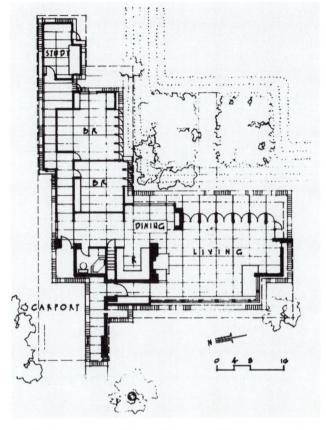

Jacobs house plan, Wright, Usonian 1936. Courtesy of the Library of Congress.

however, did not share the kind of influence that his later work would have. Though Wright's Prairie style architecture was uniquely visionary, not one of the 600 plans discussed above show any relation to his work.

Wright's designs for his Usonian houses would be another matter. Wright designed 26 houses in the Usonian style. The layout of these homes followed his existing ideas of developing interior and exterior space and using natural materials. But they also embraced Wright's fundamental understanding of the automobile and its effects on what would become suburbanization. Usonian, after all, stood for the utopian vision of a detached house and an automobile for every family. The design intent was Wright's answer to the small house.

The Jacobs House, built in Madison, Wisconsin, in 1936, is the best example of a Usonian home and can be used to illustrate the design and layout of the style. Much like the twentieth century model home, the core of the Usonian house was the living room.

Wright designed the house in an ell, with the bedrooms along one leg and the main living areas along the other. The living room is a large rectangle with a fireplace on the interior end wall and is the dominant and largest room of the house.

What makes the living room unique is its relationship to the kitchen. The kitchen sits in the middle of the house, at the intersection of the two legs of the house. No longer tucked in the back of the house out of the way, or a room where servants could work unseen and unheard, here the kitchen becomes the heart of the house. In the Jacobs House, the kitchen is open to the living room, what will become a standard late twentieth-century and early twenty-first-century design feature. The dining room becomes a built in nook between the kitchen and living room.

The automobile plays an important role in the design scheme of the house. Opposite the kitchen where the two legs of the ell-shaped house meet, Wright placed what he called a carport. Much like a port, the carport served as a dock, so to speak, for the car outside of the home, but directly connected to the home. Upon arrival, the carport placed the driver and passengers at doors entering into the living room, or entering into the kitchen area. The doors compete, public space vs. service space. Yet, space flows freely around the kitchen so the two doors create an open service block at the center of the house.

HOUSING PROGRAMS

A Home Ownership Network

Specific private and government-sponsored programs served to influence the design and layout of housing during the 1920s and on into the 1930s. During the first decades of the twentieth century, programs, organizations, and housing advocates coalesced to create a network that disseminated information on new housing. Carolyn Loeb has called this the "home-ownership network." This network formed to specifically change housing policy in the United States. In 1917, the aim was to use housing to stabilize capitalism; after 1929 the aim was to stabilize the economy. During the 1920s, federal involvement took the form of government-sponsored voluntary programs. After 1934, a national housing policy and federal programs became institutionalized, focusing mainly on the financial structure of housing (Loeb 2001, 149).

The federal government was actively participating in the home ownership network in order to promote home ownership as the foundation of American citizenship. Specific government agencies endorsed the suburban ideal as both attainable and desirable for the middle class. Government and nongovernment organizations disseminated information on housing through the cooperation of local individuals and businesses.

The home ownership network worked at the local level to produce a standardized housing layout. This occurred through the efforts of the local lumberyard, local bank, and local builder. The efforts to disseminate housing information down to the local level, however, took place on a national scale through federally sponsored programs. Herbert Hoover's Department of Commerce opened information channels between various interest groups, many which operated at the local level. Through federal efforts, lenders talked to builders, and builders talked to suppliers. Federal officials believed this type of cooperation could achieve housing policy goals. The modernization of existing housing helped stabilize families, raised living conditions, and employed construction workers and material suppliers.

As an example of how this worked, banks played an ever-increasing role in financing federal government programs. Banks provided funds, but they also promoted what type of work homeowners should finance. In one case, a bank janitor in Elizabeth, New Jersey, built a model of a house for a program the bank was advertising. One side of the house showed a dilapidated structure and the other showed what the house would look like once repaired and painted. The house was a "before and after" model with one-half of the house made of unpainted material, while the other half was neatly finished with modernization repairs and white paint. A booth set up near the model allowed bank officials to answer questions about the loan program. This case is an example of how many local institutions made great efforts voluntarily to support and promote large national programs ("Janitor Constructs Tiny Housing Show" 1935).

The savings and loan and banking industries had a large stake in the housing industry, even before 1934. In securing these loans, the local savings and loan promoted modern housing. In 1928, the Farm and Home Savings and Loan in St. Louis published a booklet called *The Modern Home*. In it, the company suggested, "When you have selected a location and have the plan of a home that you propose to build, call our office and let us explain our Loan Plan that will assist you to build your home" (Farm and Home Savings and Loan Association 1928).

The Architects' Small House Service Bureau

In 1919, a group of Minneapolis architects established a mail-order service to offer professionally designed house plans. The group believed that architect-designed small homes would be better for the public than the multitude of

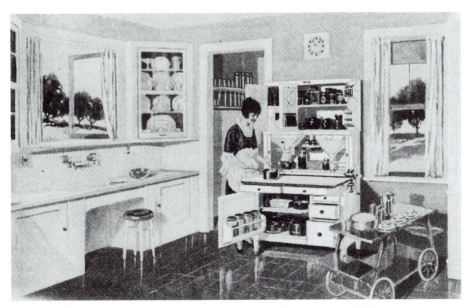

Modern Kitchen as presented in *Good Housekeeping*, August 1922.

free plans offered by various builders and materials suppliers. Their alternative was a set of blueprints and specifications for a small house, which they offered for six dollars per room. Success came quickly; by 1921 the organization had grown into a national service with 13 regional offices. The Architects Small House Service Bureau had been born.

Organized as a nonprofit corporation, the bureau received operating funds from practicing architects. Member architects prepared house plans as part of their private practices and gave these to the bureau to sell. An individual architect could be paid an hourly rate for the work it took to develop their house plans, but no one received royalties on the plans, which were sold to multiple buyers.

The Bureau offered approximately 400 different plans between 1922 and 1942. Successful house plans could be purchased and built multiple times. This seems to be the case as more than 5,000 houses across the states were built from plans sold by the bureau. In 1922, the Architect's Small House Service Bureau produced and distributed a pamphlet titled *How to Plan, Finance, and Build Your Home.* The book advertised how the architects within the bureau prepared plans that could be built economically. The bureau plans were designed specifically to "eliminate waste" and "to supply every home comfort and convenience within reason" (Reiff 2000, 208–209).

The American Institute of Architects and the Department of Commerce both endorsed the organization and its efforts to improve the quality of the small house. Like the precut housing catalogs, the program served as an educational tool for style and plan layout as much as it was a successful business. It also served to promote the role of the architect in a housing industry that began to favor the speculative builder and developer. This in fact may explain the bureau's inception as a nonprofit organization. Bureau-designed plans were advertised in newspapers every week, and nearly every women's magazine published an article about the service. The Bureau also distributed a yearly catalog.

Better Homes in America promoted the service and the plans developed by its architects. Literature often suggested the use of Bureau plans, and several communities built demonstration houses using Bureau plans. Don Barber, the architect of the Better Homes "Home Sweet Home" house on the Washington Mall, was an active member of the Architects' Small House Service Bureau.

It was not just the Commerce Department that took advantage of the planning activities of the Bureau. Both public and private organizations often requested plans to publish and promote through combined programs. Often, local newspapers ran the Bureau plans as advertisements for housing. *The Lima News,* in Lima, Ohio, for instance, ran a Bureau plan every Sunday for 10 weeks beginning in March 1922. The plans were run under the heading, "You Can Have an Architect Design Your Home." The *Decatur Daily Review,* in Decatur, Illinois, published house plans that could be purchased from the Community Service Department of the newspaper "in co-operation with the Architects' Small House Service Bureau" ("A Favorite Plan of Established Values" 1928). The Bureau, therefore, created many of the plans that people saw every day. In this sense, architects actually had a strong role in the development of the small house layout that dominated residential development during the mid-twentieth century.

The Home Modernization Bureau

In 1928, several business and industrial representatives, all of whom had previous organizational experience working with the Architects' Small House Service Bureau or sponsoring "Own Your Own Home" campaigns, formed the Home Modernization Bureau in order to emphasize remodeling and to push commercial sales of building materials. By 1928, new housing starts had begun to decline as the market for new housing became saturated. In contrast, more than 12 million homes, three out of every five, needed some form of modernization. The Home Modernization Bureau provided information to this market. Where most of the housing network programs pursued new construction, the Home Modernization Bureau advocated the remodeling of existing homes.

The Home Modernization Bureau opened offices in cities across the country. Using architects to design additions and improvements, the offices would produce drawings for contractors and homeowners who wanted to add to or remodel existing houses. The goal of the program was to modernize older nineteenth-century housing stock according to the standards of beauty, comfort, and convenience of the late 1920s. To accomplish this, the organization promoted model homes.

The president of the Home Modernization Bureau, Walter Kohler, epitomized the government/business alliance that fueled the for-profit motives of the organization. Kohler was president of the Kohler Company, a leading manufacturer of modern bathroom fixtures. He was also the governor of Wisconsin.

Kohler's leadership showcased how businesses within the housing industry worked together to provide and promote the suburban ideal of housing. As the developer of Kohler Village, a garden city for company employees, Kohler annually exhibited a model home fully equipped with Kohler appliances and fixtures. This model home consistently won an annual Better Homes award between 1925 and 1942. Kohler was thus able to use the Better Homes movement to market and promote Kohler Village and used the Kohler Village and the Home Modernization Bureau to market Kohler bathroom fixtures (Hutchison 1997).

Government-Sponsored Voluntary Programs

At the top of the housing information network was Herbert Hoover. In February 1921, Hoover accepted Warren G. Harding's offer to head the Commerce Department. Hoover's goal for the department was to centralize ideas and then decentralize the execution of those ideas. The Commerce Department created a national housing policy by advocating the single-family suburban home as the preferred residential model. The department did so by engaging the public through active cooperation and volunteerism.

Hoover's policies through the Commerce Department centered on the voluntary action of individuals and organizations. Under this model, the government used policy to direct the actions of individuals. The former Secretary of the Interior, Ray Lyman Wilbur, wrote in 1937 that Hoover proposed to solve problems within a "framework of strong local as well as Federal Government and the development of understanding and voluntary co-operative action among free men." Wilbur noted the several goals involved: one, to create a better public understanding of what constituted good housing; two, to create an interest in home ownership; three, to make available plans and specification of practical and attractive homes (Wilbur and Hyde 1937, 80).

The "Own Your Own Home" Campaign

During the First World War, the Department of Labor developed the "Own Your Own Home" campaign as a response to housing problems caused by mobilization. The chairman of F. W. Dodge, Franklin Miller, administered the program. Paul Murphy, a successful residential housing developer, assisted Miller. The program consisted of a public relations and advertising campaign aimed at promoting home ownership.

The idea of the "Own Your Own Home" campaign had come from local efforts to promote home ownership in cities such as Rochester, New York, Chicago, and Portland, Oregon. Murphy had successfully led the local campaign in Portland. The program he developed there featured a model bungalow, constructed and equipped with donated materials. The event ended with a marriage ceremony in the living room of the model home. The pastor preached on the merits of home ownership, and then the couple received $1,000 in furniture and other goods (Dunn-Haley 1995, 104).

Miller and Murphy moved to Washington to help facilitate wartime government programs as dollar-a-year-men, successful businessmen who came to work in Washington without government salaries. Miller immediately established a national advisory panel with members drawn from the United States League of Building and Loan Associations, the National Association of Real Estate Boards, and the National Federation of Construction Industries. With key national leaders in the housing industry disseminating information on the benefits of home ownership, the "Own Your Own Home" campaign capitalized on the for-profit motives of local community and business leaders.

The Department of Labor served as a clearinghouse for information on selling and buying houses. The U.S. Bureau of the Census reported that home ownership had dropped from 64.4 percent of all housing to 58 percent between 1900 and 1920. A 1918 publication from the Institute of American Architects indicated that between 1900 and 1910 home ownership dropped from 46.1 percent of the population to 45.8 percent. When nonfarm properties only were considered, home ownership was even lower.

Members of Congress and the Department of Labor understood the program as a way to combat the spread of bolshevism, which was seen as a major threat after the communist revolution in Russia in 1917. People who owned their own homes, it was believed, would have no interest in communism. The campaign used demonstration houses, newspaper and magazine promotions, radio broadcasting, and film to spread the patriotic message of home ownership.

After 1921, the Division of Building and Housing, within Hoover's Department of Commerce, continued the "Own Your Own Home" campaign. Two department employees, John Gries and James Spear Taylor, wrote a 28-page pamphlet titled "How to Own Your Own Home." The pamphlet advised prospective owners on all the major topics of homeownership including financing, house plans, maintenance, and location. Among other things, the booklet promoted the idea of credit, suggesting that borrowing to buy a home was "no disgrace." The booklet was sold throughout the 1920s through the Government Printing Office. The pamphlet was a success for the program, with 200,000 distributed the first year alone (Dunn-Haley 1995, 121–124).

The Better Homes in America Movement

Much like the "Own Your Own Home" campaign, the Better Homes in America movement was a successful small-scale nongovernment program that was co-opted and institutionalized by Herbert Hoover and the Department of Commerce. At the heart of the Better Homes movement was the promotion of local Better Homes exhibitions and programs. Each local committee sponsored a Better Homes week where builders, bankers, and material suppliers worked to promote the improvement of local housing. The aim of the program was to promote single-family residential houses. New homes and model homes were showcased in local and national events.

Established in 1922, the movement was the brainchild of the successful magazine editor Marie Meloney. Her women's magazine, the *Delineator,* sponsored a national housing competition in which local chapters exhibited model homes during a nationally designated Better Homes week. Meloney petitioned the government to promote her program. Hoover obliged, and in 1923 the Department of Commerce began to promote the Better Homes movement.

The roll out program for the Department of Commerce was the construction of a National Better Home on the Washington Mall. The "Home Sweet Home" house illustrated the combined efforts of the government, manufacturers, and voluntary associations to promote the recognized prototype of the suburban American residence, the Colonial Revival home. Meloney oversaw the construction and furnishing of the model house. Events such as the groundbreaking by Hoover and the dedication by President Warren G. Harding provided what Meloney had sought—widely covered national attention.

In 1924, Hoover oversaw the reorganization of the Better Homes movement into a not-for-profit corporation housed within the Department of Commerce. The Laura Spelman Rockefeller Memorial provided the initial funding, and top officials at the Division of Building and Housing became the directing officers of the nonprofit. Wilbur and Hyde, in their 1937 book, *The Hoover Policies,* state that over the next 10 years Hoover raised over $200,000 a year to support the program, which consisted of over 9,000 chapters with 30,000 members (Wilbur and Hyde 1937, 81).

Among other information, the national headquarters in New York distributed guide books on how to conduct a successful demonstration week. The guide books provided examples of demonstration homes that had been completed in other communities, including the 1922 national prize-wining demonstration house in New Haven, Connecticut. Pages devoted to committees that could be formed, as well their responsibilities, gave clear guidance to the local Better Homes delegates. One of the "chief objectives" of a demonstration home was to "exhibit a home well-balanced in all its features." The guide book provided suggestions of colors and furnishings for each room, down to the kitchen wall clock: "simple with clear figures" (Better Homes In America Advisory Council 1923).

Local initiatives made up the bulk of Better Homes activities. In May 1924, for instance, the city of Oakland, California, hosted a Modern Houses Exposition as part of the observance of National Better Homes Week. Held at the Municipal Auditorium, the exposition included special musical performances every afternoon and evening. One day featured an appearance by Wesley Barry, "the most famous boy in the movies." The exposition presented "the latest styles in home-furnishings, home equipment in furniture, draperies, gas ranges," and "household appliances of various kinds." Advertisements proclaimed that "under one roof the visitors will find everything from the architect's first drawings to the completely furnished and equipped home" ("Exposition to be Opened Saturday" 1924).

In October 1924, *The Columbus Dispatch* newspaper and the Columbus Retail Furniture Dealers Association hosted a Home Beautiful Exposition for the Better Homes in America week in Columbus, Ohio. The exposition included 13 homes and 1 apartment located throughout the city. The homes were open to the public "for everyone to see the latest modes in home furnishings" and "the newest labor-saving appliances for home comfort." During the first four days of the exhibition, 106,000 people had walked through the homes, greeted by hostesses from the City Federation of Women's Clubs ("These Built in Six Weeks for Home Beautiful Exhibit" 1924).

The Better Homes program continued to operate until the beginning of the Second World War. After the onset of the Depression in 1929, however, the focus of the program became home improvement. Information continued to be transferred to local committees in hopes of stimulating sales of home furnishings and building supplies as a means to local economic recovery.

President Hoover initiated a Conference on Home Ownership and Home Building in 1931 through the Better Homes organization. This became one of the most significant achievements of all of the organization's activities. In 1938, more than 16,000 Better Homes local committees still existed. Activity was still strong, and that year local initiatives resulted in the exhibition of more than 5,000 model homes. The Better Homes movement illustrates how private local programs can become institutionalized and spread nationally; the movement also provides an excellent example of how individuals and advocates within the housing industry viewed the modernization of housing as a significant government function (Dunn-Haley 1995, 131).

THE NEW DEAL AND MODERN HOUSING

In the aftermath of the Depression, the housing industry became one of the key industries targeted by the government as a means to stimulate the economy. Construction had always been one of the largest employers, but stimulating the construction industry also stimulated the lumber industry, quarrying, copper and iron pipe manufacturing, textile and appliance manufacturing, and many other industries. This one industry reached every part of the United States into almost every community. Programs with origins in working-class uplift, domestic reform, or fighting communism were reinvigorated as government programs to stimulate the economy. Providing ways to build or improve more houses became a foundation block of economic recovery in the 1930s.

Herbert Hoover laid the ground work for many of the programs that institutionalized the modern housing movement in the United States. The greatest influence within local and independent housing programs, however, came with the election of Franklin D. Roosevelt in 1933. Under Roosevelt's New Deal, housing became a major focus of the federal government intervention. Several of Hoover's housing programs continued throughout the Roosevelt administration. Key to both administrations was intervention in home financing.

The passage of the 1934 Housing Act institutionalized many local building practices and put into place the standard 30-year home mortgage industry that we still live with today. In general, the act guaranteed housing loans with insurance backed by the federal government. The intention of the act was to relax the requirements of private financial institutions in order to free up more money for lending. Once free from the risk of defaulting homeowners (under a federal insured loan the government paid the local bank for its loss), banks could lend money and free market forces would restimulate the housing industry, which had come to a halt after the onslaught of the Depression.

HOUSING ACT OF 1934

The Housing Act of 1934 changed the relationship of both financiers and builders to the housing industry. Though the federal program was loan insurance, to qualify lenders had to meet specific criteria established by the housing act. The act had three parts: Titles I, II, and III. Each addressed different areas of construction in an attempt to stimulate the building industry. The act also created the Federal Housing Administration. Policies and institutions resulting from this legislation had a tremendous impact on housing in America. According to urban historian Kenneth Jackson, "No agency of the United States government has had a more pervasive and powerful impact on the American people over the past half-century than the Federal Housing Administration" (Jackson 1985, 203).

Title I of the act addressed the modernization of homes. The act established a lending program by which a homeowner could receive a loan of up to $2,000.00 without any special collateral. The modernization of existing housing stock had already been a key factor in many nongovernmental and governmental agencies. Under the housing act, these programs received funding guarantees much like new housing initiatives.

Title II of the act addressed the lending of funds for the purchase of a new house. Banks had traditionally avoided risky housing loans by lending only 50 percent of the value of a home and often only over a period of three to five years. Many homeowners took second and even third mortgages to purchase a new home. The Housing Act required banks and savings and loans to lend 80 percent of the value of a home and established a payback period of 20 years at 5 percent interest. The federal government backed these loans so that the banks did not have anything to lose by making what was perceived as a risky loan.

In 1934, the Better Housing Program, established through Title I of the Housing Act, continued the goals of the Home Modernization Bureau. The program encouraged modernization by providing federally backed loans for home improvements. The Better Housing Program worked through local chapters to complete and promote model houses that had been renovated. Model homes, many of them renovated Victorian houses, were completed all across the country. In March 1935, Better Housing Program administrators issued a list of marketing ideas for local committee chairs. This list included:

1. Enlist the aid of your Water Department to stamp all of its water bills with a Better Housing insignia.
2. Milk bottle caps stamped with the emblem will get into every home.
3. Billboards in an artistic setting should carry the message.
4. Department stores might allot a display with a model house and erect a booth where literature can be distributed.
5. Lumber dealer, and other building-material dealer, trucks should carry a red, white, and blue "Better Housing" insignia.
6. Every store window should display a "We Are Cooperating" sign.
7. Full page and special sections can be run in the newspapers.
8. If you have a radio broadcasting station, enlist its aid.
9. Moving-picture houses will be supplied with films, devoid of advertising, which they can run.
10. House-to-house canvasses should be pushed to uncover any new jobs.
11. Ask your clergymen to point out the value of a Better Housing Program to develop improved social quarters and put men to work.
12. Aid of Boy Scouts might be enlisted to distribute a "Home Owner's Booklet" and a "14 Questions and Answers" pamphlet in every home.
13. A parade and building exposition will arouse the populace.
14. Let a model home be the focusing point around which these other features revolve.

Source: "Ideas for Committee Chairman," *Better Housing,* March 5, 1935.

STANDARDIZATION OF HOUSING

With the new focus on financing, federal programs shifted away from direct support of advertising and advocacy. The creation of the Federal Housing Administration, a new federal agency to administer the programs legislated by the 1934 housing act, had the largest impact on the housing industry in the twentieth century. The agency led the efforts to develop a strategy to guarantee mortgage loans. The intention of the housing program was to stimulate the building industry without direct federal expenditures. By guaranteeing loans, banks would have the incentive to free up the needed funding. By providing long-term amortization with small down payments, average families would be able to afford the loans.

In guaranteeing loans, the federal government also wanted a guarantee of what would be built. The FHA publications "General Acceptable Requirements" and "Minimum Requirements" established the parameters of the American home. The government specified a minimum house as a living unit for one family with sleeping, cooking, and dining accommodations with at least a separate bedroom, living room, kitchen, and bathroom. The house had to include the technological systems of the new modern house including plumbing, heating, and electrical power.

According to the new minimum standards of building practice, houses were to be placed on suburban lots and in developments with winding, tree-lined streets. In general, the FHA institutionalized the layout and design of most houses built after 1934. This design included the technology in the home, the neighborhoods the home sat in, and the culture associated with the new modern way of living in the home.

Imposing Standards, but also Conformity and Racial Segregation

Because the lending program was national in scope, FHA officials sought to limit agency liability by imposing design standards that guaranteed consistent construction practices and product. These standards included both the house and the types of neighborhoods and developments deemed to be desirable features with resale value. To get a loan guarantee, the house and neighborhood had to meet the standards. Kenneth Jackson discusses these aspects of the FHA in detail in his book *Crabgrass Frontier: The Suburbanization of the United States* (1985, 203–207). He points out that part of the consequence of these standards was the restriction of racially mixed neighborhoods, which were excluded from FHA financing by the practice of "redlining." This became a very important consequence causing, in part, the decline of many urban neighborhoods. Thomas Sugrue, an urban historian, has detailed how this redlining and decline worked in Detroit in his book *The Origins of the Urban Crisis: Race and Inequality in Postwar Detroit* (1996, 62–63).

Within neighborhoods, the FHA set up standard requirements for lot size, street setbacks, and separation between houses. The agency produced multiple pamphlets, booklets, and technical bulletins explaining the standards. Documents such as *Property Standards, Planning Neighborhoods for Small Houses,* and *Successful Subdivisions* all provided notes, diagrams, and directions for builders, developers, and lenders. For the house itself, the FHA established guidelines that promoted a detached, single-family suburban residence, which often became the various Colonial Revivals in style.

By making these standards a requirement of financing, the FHA institutionalized the type of house and floor plan advocated by the Better Homes movement, the Architects' Small House Service Bureau, the precut catalog companies, and many local builders. Not every house built after 1934 followed the guidelines, of course. Gwendolyn Wright points out that Frank Lloyd Wright houses did not receive FHA approval because of their low rating for "Adjustment for Conformity" (Wright 1981, 248–251).

The FHA also developed minimum standards for the construction of houses. Intended to ensure that houses would be free of gross structural or mechanical deficiencies, construction standards guaranteed that the house would be substantial enough for a 20-year mortgage. The housing industry accepted the standards as a positive step toward eliminating poor construction practices. In a 1938 *Cleveland Plain Dealer* article, one journalist reported the effectiveness of the construction standards enacted by the FHA. In Cleveland, at least, the standards resulted in "decent architecture, livable floor plan and soundness of work and materials." The new standards ensured "against terrific losses due to poor design of plan and bad construction over the years" (Monnett 1938).

The minimum standards delineated by the FHA were based on generally accepted construction techniques that most qualified contractors already practiced. Though the standards had to be enforced only for houses seeking an FHA guaranteed loan, the standards became the benchmark that most builders began to follow. By putting the standards into a codified, written form, the minimum requirements became universally accepted as standard residential building practice. There was little incentive for contractors to build above the minimum, and, in fact, in the tough construction market of the 1930s, building to the minimum requirement placed builders on a level playing field.

Builders submitted plans to FHA reviewers and received a "conditional commitment" of FHA approval. Though any building plan could be submitted, by designing homes using the minimum requirements as design guidelines, contractors were virtually guaranteed approval. In this way, the FHA publications resulted in the mass replication of similarly designed houses all over the country.

FHA and the Mobilization for World War Two

As the United States prepared for the coming of World War Two, the construction of new factories and new housing for factory workers became an early priority. The mobilization of war industries began in 1939. New factories needed to produce weapons and war materials were often built on the periphery of cities, decentralized in case of attack from enemy airplanes. The new factories required housing for workers, and this was often accomplished by the construction of complete company towns around the new plants.

Henry J. Kaiser, an industrialist famous for the construction of Victory ships, developed the entire town of Vanport, Oregon, in 1942 for employees of the shipyards. Vanport's population of 40,000 included many women, who made up nearly a third of the workers. The 24-hour production of the shipyards required Kaiser to maintain 24-hour child-care centers.

More than 15 million Americans migrated to war production centers looking for work. More than 500,000 people moved to Los Angeles alone to work in new aircraft plants. Westside Village, Toluca Wood, and Westchester all grew around airplane factories outside of Los Angeles. These cities did not develop as bedroom communities. Though they shared the curvilinear streets fronting rows of single-family houses with suburban development, these new towns housed a diverse population of semiskilled workers, skilled workers, laborers, managers, and professionals all supporting war production (Hise 1997).

During the war, developers and private builders followed FHA guidelines in order to secure federal construction financing. The FHA minimum standards established a baseline of a 624-square-foot, four-room house with a bathroom. Between 1930 and 1940, the FHA insured just 3 percent of new homes across the country. In Los Angeles, however, over 20 percent of new houses carried FHA mortgage insurance, and over 1 million new homes had been constructed.

In 1940, 16 percent of the FHA insured houses in Los Angeles had four rooms, and 48 percent had five rooms. Prior to 1939, the majority of new houses had six or seven rooms. FHA insured mortgages set a minimum standard that filled the requirements needed to house workers and their families in locations all over the country. After 1939, the majority of new houses contained the minimum four rooms (Hise 1997, 70).

The largest private builder of housing communities in the eastern United States became Levitt and Sons. The construction of defense housing near Norfolk, Virginia, provided the experience in mass production that would be applied to the postwar Levittowns in New York and Pennsylvania. These postwar developments followed the lead of wartime housing and conformed to the baselines established by the FHA.

Reference List

Architects' Small House Service Bureau. 1920. *How to Plan Finance and Build Your Home.* New Orleans, Louisiana: Southern Pine Association.

Arthur, William. 1910. "Suggestions for Building a Modern Dwelling." *The Building Age* 32: 147–148, 217–218.

Arthur, William. 1914. *The Home Builders' Guide: A Treatise for Those About to Build, Covering the Selection of the Site, the Planning of the Rooms, and Proper Materials to Use in Construction.* New York: David Williams Company.

Better Homes in America Advisory Council. 1923. *Better Homes In America: Plan Book for Demonstration Week June 4–10, 1923.* New York: Author.

Bushman, Richard. 1992. *The Refinement of America: Persons, Houses, Cities.* New York: Knopf.

Clark, Clifford Edward, Jr. 1986. *The American Family Home: 1800–1960.* Chapel Hill: University of North Carolina Press.

Cleveland Home Inventory: Seventh. 1939. Cleveland, OH: Cleveland Press.

Douglas, Susan. 1987. *Inventing American Broadcasting.* Baltimore: John Hopkins University Press.

Douglas, Susan. 1999. *Listening in: Radio and the American Imagination, From Amos 'n' Andy and Edward R. Murrow to Wolfman Jack and Howard Stern.* New York: Times Books.

Dunn-Haley, Karen. 1995. "The House that Uncle Sam Built: The Political Culture of Federal Housing Policy, 1919–1932." Ph.D. dissertation, Stanford University.

"Exposition to be Opened Saturday." 1924. *Oakland Tribune.* May 11.

Farm and Home Savings and Loan Association. 1928. *The Modern Home.* St. Louis: Author.

"A Favorite Plan of Established Values." 1928. *The Decatur Review.* February 10.

Fischer, Claude S. 1992. *America Calling: A Social History of the Telephone to 1940.* Berkeley: University of California Press.

Greig, James Ashton. 1921. "Make Yourself a Home!" *The Bucyrus Evening Telegraph* (2 August).

Grier, Katherine C. 1988. *Culture and Comfort: Parlor Making and Middle-Class Identity, 1850–1930.* Washington DC: Smithsonian Institution Press.

Harris, Richard. 1994. "The Flexible House: The Housing Backlog and the Persistence of Lodging, 1891–1951." *Social Science History* 18: 31–53.

Hise, Greg. 1997. *Magnetic Los Angeles: Planning the Twentieth-Century Metropolis.* Baltimore: Johns Hopkins University Press.

Hutchison, Janet. 1997. "Building for Babbitt: The State and the Suburban Home Ideal." *Journal of Policy History* 9: 184–210.

"Ideas for Committee Chairman." 1935. *Better Housing* (5 March).

Jackson, Kenneth. 1985. *Crabgrass Frontier: The Suburbanization of the United States.* New York: Oxford University Press.

"Janitor Constructs Tiny Housing Show." 1935. *Better Housing* (6 February).

Loeb, Carolyn S. 2001. *Entrepreneurial Vernacular: Developers' Subdivisions in the 1920s.* Baltimore: The John Hopkins University Press.

Lynd, Robert, and Helen Merrell Lynd. 1929. *Middletown: A Study in Modern American Culture.* New York: Harcourt, Brace and World, Inc.

McCarter, Robert, ed. 2005. *On and By Frank Lloyd Wright: A Primer on Architectural Principles.* New York: Phaidon Press.

Monnett, James G. 1938. "FHA Standards Bringing Results." *Cleveland Plain Dealer* (26 June).

Reiff, Daniel D. 2000. *Houses from Books: Treatises, Pattern Books, and Catalogs in American Architecture, 1738–1950: A History and Guide.* University Park: Pennsylvania State University Press.

Robinson, Eugene. 1923. *Domestic Architecture.* New York: Macmillan Company.

Roell, Craig H. 1989. *The Piano in America, 1890–1940.* Chapel Hill: University of North Carolina Press.

Schlereth, Thomas J. 1991. *Victorian America: Transformations in Everyday Life, 1876–1915.* New York: Harper Collins.

Spencer, Ethel. 1983. *The Spencers of Amberson Avenue: A Turn of the Century Memoir.* Pittsburgh: University of Pittsburgh Press.

Sugrue, Thomas. 1996. *The Origins of the Urban Crisis: Race and Inequality in Postwar Detroit.* Princeton: Princeton University Press.

"These Built in Six Weeks for Home Beautiful Exhibit." 1924. *The Columbus Dispatch* (9 October).

Wilbur, Ray Lyman, and Arthur Mastic Hyde. 1937. *The Hoover Policies.* New York: Charles Scribner's Sons.

Wilk, Christopher, ed. 2006. *Modernism: Designing a New World, 1914–1939.* London: V&A Publications.

Wright, Agnes Foster. 1917. *Interior Decorations for Modern Needs.* New York: Frederick A. Stokes Company.

Wright, Gwendolyn. 1980. *Moralism and the Model Home: Domestic Architecture and Cultural Conflict in Chicago.* Chicago: University of Chicago Press.

Wright, Gwendolyn. 1981. *Building the Dream: A Social History of Housing in America.* Cambridge, MA: MIT Press.

"You Can Have an Architect Design Your Home." 1922. *The Lima News* (3 March).

Furniture and Decoration

In 1921, a nationally syndicated editorialist wrote, "It is a pity that the real pleasures of the good old fashioned American home are being usurped by the fleeting mirage of excitement in the modern day method of living, for just as sure as the home loses its attraction to the individual the nation loses its impetus of progress and prosperity." On one hand, the effects of "modern day living" could be seen everywhere, especially in the home. One the other hand, a surprising amount of furnishings and decoration in the home revived styles that recalled the past. There were architects and designers that embraced the modernist vision of the future and designed both interiors and furniture that were new and exciting. For the majority of houses, however, living may have been modern, but furnishing was not (Greig 1921, 5).

It was the individual rooms in the small house of the 1920s and 1930s that took on modern functions. In fact, the individual rooms and their uses became a key feature in the development of new housing. The architectural plan came to dominate the discussion of housing during this period. This can be seen in how new houses were advertised and marketed. The components of the plan were the rooms in the house.

THE DESIGN OF INTERIORS

The design of interiors, whether in houses or apartments and whether by an architect, a builder, or a realtor, took into consideration standard furniture styles and placement. House design and interior design were intertwined when it came to the act of living in the home. The homeowner could not separate the two facets. People who rented and lived in apartments faced the same situations, only on a smaller scale with fewer rooms. In fact, housing advocates recognized and articulated that "in decorating we have always to bear that main fact in mind—that a room is a background against which we live." The purchase of the house or the decision to rent a specific apartment was conditioned by how a family intended to use and furnish the structure, and these decisions impacted the size and types of rooms the family thought necessary (Wright 1917, 3).

Interior design, therefore, involved how the homeowner or apartment dweller envisioned living in a room and then subsequently placed and exhibited furniture and decoration in each room. Interior design, as practiced by the upper half of the middle class in the United States, was disseminated particularly through monthly women's magazines and design advice books. To what extent the average reader listened to and followed this advice is not exactly known. Even at the time, design advocates understood that magazines were a little high-brow. In a November 1921 *Good Housekeeping* article, Margaret U. Barton stated, "It is well-nigh impossible for the average of us to adopt these books and articles to our modest homes and incomes, and interior decorators we can't afford" (Barton 1921, 34).

The furnishing of an apartment did not significantly differ from a house, except in scale. Apartments with a few rooms would typically be furnished only for those rooms. The pieces of furniture would not differ significantly from a house, and the discussion of furniture in this chapter will focus on furnishing the single-family home.

FURNITURE: TRADITIONAL STYLES TO MODERNISM

Traditional styles of furniture and decoration dominated the market during the 1920s through the 1940s. As one advocated commented, the "one clear-cut decorative tradition we have in America" is "our visible traditional background; the old houses and furniture of the early Colonial period." Indeed, this one expert suggested that it was "natural, for most of us, to turn first to this source in making plans for a home of our own" (Lockwood 1935, 159).

In 1923, the guidelines for demonstration houses for the Better Homes in America program suggested the use of traditional styles in outfitting the homes that millions of Americans walked through and understood as the ideal. The round or square dining room table was to be a "reproduction of Hepplewhite, Sheraton, or Georgian period" with Mahogany chairs with "damask seats" and "Hepplewhite backs." The sideboard was also to be "low, broad, after Hepplewhite or Sheraton" (Better Homes 1923, 39).

In the living room, furniture in the demonstration home was also traditional, but newer overstuffed furniture was to match. The library table was to be a "drop-leaf, Refectory type or modern Chippendale—in mahogany, weathered oak, or walnut, or Sheraton type of table." The sofa was to be "upholstered in either sage green or brown," the armchair was to be an "overstuffed chair in indefinite striped upholsterer's velvet in sage green," with a "satin cushion in corn color." The living room also contained a desk, a "reproduction in Sheraton, Hepplewhite, or Early English Oak" (Better Homes 1923, 37).

If the demonstration house was going to be a small cottage with a combination living room and dining room, then the furnishings were to be in the Craftsman style. The walls were to be "papered or painted with plain colors in grays, fauns or a light color such as greens, yellows, ect." A table, "oblong or square Crafts-man type in oak or pine," sat in the middle of the room. "Four simple wooden chairs" sat around the table. Two "wooden Craftsman oak or stained pine" chairs and a "Windsor type" chair in oak rounded out the furniture in the small house (Better Homes 1923, 38).

The 1927 Sears, Roebuck catalog carried a Queen Anne dining room table and a full Queen Anne period set of bedroom furniture. A dining room set marketed as "Spanish Renaissance" was characterized by "rich carvings, and massiveness of design." The pieces all had very fancy turned legs. Another complete set of living room furniture consisted of seven pieces in the mission or Craftsman style. This set included a library table, an arm rocker, a large arm chair, a taboret, a sewing rocker, and book blocks. This golden oak set retailed for $27.85, about a week's pay for the typical employee.

The majority of the furniture styles sold through Sears, Roebuck were ma-hogany, butt walnut, and walnut veneers. They were not attributed to a spe-cific style, but marketed as "right up to the minute in style." The pieces had matching inlay with "fancy scroll decorations," all finished in a rich brown mahogany. Heavy cast metal hardware in the "Early English" finish completed the traditional detailing of the furniture. A dining room set, in this traditional yet mass-produced style, included "fancy rosettes decorations on the corner posts" and "fancy turned legs touched with green enamel in harmonizing con-trast" (Mirken 1970, 860).

Furniture during this period began to be mass-produced using the indus-trial processes that characterized other products. Furniture, however, was one of the last industries to mechanize. The tradition of cabinetmaking drew on the guild system where an apprentice became a journeyman and then a master craftsman. Quality furniture placed emphasis on the craftsmanship inherent in each individual piece.

Beginning in the 1920s, the furniture industry took a cue from automo-bile manufacturing and began to mass manufacture furniture on the assembly line. Manufacturers referred to this as "straight-line manufacturing methods." Machines would mould, plane, sand, and groove boards in one operation. Turntables located along the assembly line enabled workmen to turn the case in any convenient position necessary for the work. Electric drills and other electric tools helped speed up production without lowering the quality of the product.

Furniture manufacturers had traditionally produced individual suites of furniture in multiple styles; mass-manufacturing resulted in companies producing more furniture in fewer styles. When the L. C. Phenix Company in Los Angeles adopted assembly line production they went from 200 individual styles of upholstered furniture to five. Seven men worked the davenport line. They stayed in position all day with stock being brought to them by stock boys. In the past, each of the craftsmen would have become an expert upholster. As one Phenix manager noted, under mass production, "all it takes to make an upholsterer for a line-assembly system is that he know how to drive tacks" (Pursell 1995, 135).

The Phenix Company assembly line could produce a two-piece living room suite in three hours. This same work under the old system of individual craftsmen took two to three days. Consequently, the company stopped working against orders on hand and worked against a production schedule. The company produced more furniture at a lesser price, but increased production also increased profits.

Factory built furniture provided custom-looking, well-built sets of furniture to many new houses. "Fine Overstuffed Davenport Suites" sold for $198 in Washington. An upholstered davenport from Sears, Roebuck, however, cost $49. "Craftsman" furniture, which at the turn of the century had been marketed as quality, individually produced pieces, was especially suited to mass manufacture. Though pieces differed in quality, a "3-piece quartered oak library suite" sold for $121 in 1921, and the seven piece from Sears, Roebuck sold for nearly $100 less in 1927.

The change to mass manufacturing occurred at the same time that modernist furniture designs appeared on the market. New materials, such as steel, aluminum, and plastics, were ideally suited to assembly-line production. The automobile had stimulated the light steel industry and furniture manufacturing became a new outlet for this product.

New metal "modernist" furniture developed first for the commercial market. During the 1920s, more modernist school and office furniture was produced in the United States than anywhere else in the world. The household market, however, did not follow so fast. In 1935, the author of a *Business Week* article titled "We Go Modern" claimed that the typical homeowner was not "ready to throw out its old colonial in favor of functionalism in chromium. Furniture makers and retailers, however, were beginning to see a shift toward modern design. There was a lack, however, of "well-designed modern furniture at anything approaching a popular price" (Pursell 1995, 139).

Sears, Roebuck did not offer any modernist style furniture in 1927, but by 1932 they had a section in the catalog announcing "America Goes Modern." The advertisements suggested that, "those who take pleasure in furnishing their homes with the very latest in style will find these pieces instantly appealing." The furniture included a "streamlined chrome-plated" davenport "upholstered with washable fabrikoid" (artificial leather). The "chromium plated" steel couch frame with "ebony color wood arms" cost $49.95. Modern chairs and bedrooms sets followed. The copy informed the reader that these modern styles brought "a new kind of comfort—a new smartness that reflects the architecture of Chicago's Century of Progress Exposition" (Sears, Roebuck 1932, 646).

In 1935 and 1936, Sears did not showcase any additional modernist styles. In fact, the catalog offered a limited selection of furniture. Though throughout the 1930s modernist styles flourished in design magazines, in the high-end market, and architectural circles, on the mass-consumer end of the market furniture sales slumped. People moving out of apartments and doubling up with other family members certainly were not buying new furniture. Others made due with the older furniture that they had already acquired. People did buy radios all through the Depression. But many postponed major furniture purchases during the height of the Depression from 1932–1936.

In 1937, the inside cover of the spring issue of the Sears, Roebuck catalog read in a bold statement, "Things really are better." The president of the company provided a statement saying, "since 1932 there has been a great change in the income of all Americans—particularly the wage earners and farmers. Gross farm income has risen from a low of five and a quarter billion in 1932 to an estimate of slightly over nine billion dollars in 1936. Our customers' position has improved, and so has that of this company, for our income rises and falls with that of our customers" (Sears, Roebuck 1937, inside cover).

The catalog contained a wide assortment of furniture and various furniture styles. The furniture section led with two different two-page spreads, the first read "Designed for Houses of Today," under which it read "decorated in perfect harmony of color." The pages included several images of modernist-style furniture along with an image of an International Style house with plain white facades, corner windows, and a flat roof. The second spread read, "Tradition Furnishings with Character," under which read, "in color schemes of ever lasting beauty." The catalog contained a lively mix of both modern and traditional styles of furniture. More than 20 couches reflected the influence of modernist designs (Sears, Roebuck 1937, 394–397).

Modernist style incubated during the Depression of the 1930s. Though purchased by offices and schools and wealthy homeowners at the high end of the market, prices did not fall into the range of the larger mass-market until late into the decade. When the economy picked up after 1937, as the United States began to prepare for World War Two, modernist styles of furniture were on par with traditional styles in the mass market. Modernism possibly succeeded in the consumer market because, in part, it offered an escape from the past, even if just the near past.

Arts and Crafts Styles

In the 1920s through the 1940s, Arts and Crafts, Craftsman, and Mission furniture all referred to the same category of Arts and Crafts styles. The actual Arts and Crafts style came from the philosophies of John Ruskin and William Morris in England. They believed that a use of simple and honest materials and a return to individual craftsmanship offered an alternative to the disruption of the modern industrial society at the turn of the century. The Arts and Crafts movement was the most active between 1895 and 1910.

Gustav Stickley, of upstate New York, dominated the American Arts and Crafts movement. He published *The Craftsman* magazine from 1901 to 1916, which promoted the Arts and Crafts lifestyle and offered design plans for Craftsman homes. Stickley operated the Stickley Brothers Furniture Company and produced a very successful line of furniture. In 1902, Gustav Stickley's brothers started their own furniture business incorporating as L. and J. G. Stickley, Inc. Gustav Stickley went bankrupt in 1917; L. and J. G. Stickley, Inc. is still in business today. Discussions of the furniture and advertisements often referred to the pieces as being "mission-style." Because of the success of the Stickley empire, Arts and Crafts, Craftsman, and Mission became synonymous in talking about the style.

Arts and Crafts furniture was heavy and blocky, based on rectilinear forms. Characteristically, pieces were constructed from quartersawn oak. Construction details, such as mortise and tenon connections, were designed to be expressions of craftsmanship. Vertical slats often added a vertical emphasis to the forms.

The Arts and Crafts style sought to integrate the home into a natural setting. Frank Lloyd Wright designed furniture for his houses with a very similar philosophy and a very similar look. Though the style is concentrated within the first two decades of the twentieth century, the furniture persisted throughout the 1920s and 1930s. Design advocates continued to call for its use in small cottages and bungalows.

Colonial Revival

In housing, the Colonial Revival styles lent themselves to traditional styles of furniture. Often, furniture was not sold as a particular style, but was marketed as having "late Georgian or Adam influence," or as being "suited to a room of Georgian influence." In these cases, the furniture was mass manufactured to provide the idea of a style.

This created an interesting juxtaposition where older styles associated with colonial America embraced a traditional artisan philosophy, and high styles associated with modernism embraced the machine age. Traditional furniture, copied or designed in the spirit of actual old styles, however, was successful because it could be factory produced and inexpensively shipped. The modernist designs associated with the new machine age were heralded as being designed for the times. But by looking at what was sold through popular outlets, such as newspapers and Sears, Roebuck catalogs, it is clear what style dominated most homes of the mid-twentieth century.

The Georgian Style

The Georgian style was popular from around 1720 to 1840. Named for King George I, who came to the throne in 1711, George II, who ascended in 1727, and George III who ruled during the American Revolution, the architectural style was imported into the American colonies from England. Houses dominated by proportion and symmetry were the hallmarks of the style.

Neo-Georgian interiors of the twentieth century also emphasized proportion and symmetry. Rooms were typically large and focused on light and air. The color palette of the rooms contained creams, rose, pea green, or beige. Delicate wood furniture in walnut and mahogany predominated, with carved Hepplewhite chairs, Chippendale highboys, and damask-upholstered Queen Anne wing chairs being typical. A large wooden fireplace surround with carved pillars on either side was the focal point of many rooms.

Decorative objects created focal points on the mantel and tables. Chinoiserie, Oriental-styled motifs, added color and interest to a Georgian room. Ming-style blue and white porcelain table lamps became very popular. Upholstery and curtains often had matching fabric.

The Adam Style

The Adams style is named for Robert Adam, one of the most famous British architects of the eighteenth century. Adam revolutionized neoclassical design by creating fluid interiors that recalled Roman gracefulness and extravagance at the same time. Where Georgian design was angular and rigid, the Adam style was graceful and curvilinear. Oval shapes appeared in abundance from entire rooms to intricate drawer pulls and handles. The style was eclectic, taking decorative elements from Byzantine, Italian Baroque, and Greek traditions.

Adamesque interiors in the twentieth century were decorated with swags, garlands, vines, medallions, scrolls, and ribbons. Vibrant colors balanced the classical proportions of the interior spaces. Delicately proportioned furniture in the style of Hepplewhite, Chippendale, or Thomas Sheraton could be found in every room. Classical motifs carved on or applied to furniture, doors, fireplace surrounds, and other decorative elements were common.

Federal Style

The actual Federal style in America occurred between 1780–1830. The style combined the Georgian style with Adam-style elements. The neo-Federal style interior of the twentieth century used a mix of vernacular American colonial furniture, such as Windsor chairs, and more refined Adamesque pieces of furniture, such as Hepplewhite, Sheraton, and Chippendale. Polished wood floors with oriental carpets were common. Paint and wallpaper colors were light powder blue, cream, yellow, soft pink, and muted rose.

Hepplewhite

George Hepplewhite, a cabinet and chair maker, produced furniture during the late 1700s. One of the "big three" English furniture makers of the eighteenth century, Hepplewhite gave his name to a distinctive style of light, elegant furniture that was fashionable between about 1775 and 1800. Cabinetmakers in both England and the American colonies reproduced his designs for many decades. A distinguishable characteristic of Hepplewhite furniture was a shield-shaped chair back. On the back of the chair, an expansive shield appeared instead of a narrower splat design.

In 1788, two years after Hepplewhite's death, his wife published *The Cabinet Maker and Upholsterers Guide,* a book with 300 of his furniture designs. Cabinetmakers and furniture companies used the book to design similar pieces for several generations. The work of these cabinetmakers, in turn, was copied in their original designs, or variants, throughout the nineteenth and twentieth centuries.

Sheraton

Thomas Sheraton was an English furniture designer working at the end of the eighteenth century. His furniture designs became influential through his manuals, especially the *Cabinet-Maker and Upholsterer's Drawing-Book,* published in 1791. The book contained 111 copper-plate engravings of furniture pieces. The delicate styles were marked by simplicity, by straight, vertical lines, and by an intricate decorative inlay. Reeded legs and classical motifs are very noticeable characteristics.

Sheraton did not physically produce his own furniture. He may have contracted with other cabinetmakers to produce his designs, but he mainly intended his books to be purchased and used as copybooks. In his work, he referenced the work of Thomas Chippendale as being antiquated and out of favor. In 1803, he authored another book, *The Cabinet Dictionary.* This work contained drawings of 88 furniture pieces as well as a listing of 252 master cabinetmakers working in London.

Chippendale

Thomas Chippendale was a London cabinetmaker and furniture designer working in the Georgian and neoclassical styles. In 1754, he published a book of his designs, *The Gentleman and Cabinet Maker's Director: being a large collection of the most elegant and useful designs of household furniture in the Gothic, Chinese and modern taste.* This was the first book of designs ever published by a cabinetmaker. A revised and enlarged third edition was published in 1762. This edition showed the influence of the architect Robert Adam and included more pieces of a neoclassical design.

Chippendale provided advice on furnishings and room color much like an interior designer. He worked in partnership with upholsters to complete ornate bedding and other large pieces of furniture. The Chippendale highboy is characteristic of the style with a large broken pediment, a classical motif, and cabriole legs. The cabriole leg with a claw and ball foot was very typical of Chippendale furniture with the claw and ball stemming from the Gothic and Chinese influence. This followed the Queen Anne style, also popular at the time, which had delicate cabriole legs.

MODERNISM AS AN AESTHETIC

By 1910, the idea of the *modern* had already begun to be the antithesis to the Victorian aesthetic ideal. Modern, however, was more than an aesthetic; it implied a particular set of technologies. As has already been shown, interior decoration did not necessarily match what would be considered a modern aesthetic. It is clear that as late as 1910 patterns of interior finishes still retained Victorian aesthetics, and yet the interiors of housing had begun to move into the modern.

The modern style was available to interior designers. A writer in the *Wallpaper News and Interior Decorator* reported in 1915, "The Modern style which has developed in Europe has been seen in this country in photographs of interiors which have come to the attention of decorators and designers from time to time and at the St. Louis Exposition. Many interiors of this character have been illustrated in this magazine during the past twelve years or so. These photographs have exerted some small influence upon the decoration in this country, but the style was not represented by actual work in American interiors until recently" ("American Interiors in the Modern Style" 1915, 19).

Modernism is a term given to forward-looking architects, designers, and artisans who, in their work, moved away from design ideas based on historicism and embraced principles, ideas, and methods that were new and diverse. Often in art circles practitioners of modernism were also called the avant-garde. Beginning in the late nineteenth century and flourishing in the early years of the twentieth-century movements, such as the art nouveau, de stijl, or art deco, all provided new experimentation in design that drove the cutting edge. Artists and architects self-consciously desired to create something new. They worked with new innovative forms; abstract ideas incorporated the "machine" aesthetics of the new industrial age. In housing, the "machine for living in" became a catch phrase for imbuing the house with the characteristics of industrial progress.

Art Nouveau

Art nouveau became the first modern design style when it broke with history and tradition and blended the fine arts and the decorative arts. Art nouveau artists and architects working at the turn of the century, like Antonio Gaudi and Gustav Klimt, took inspiration from the curvilinear forms of nature, developing new highly stylized natural forms and flowing shapes.

Art nouveau designs focused on ornament. Beauty could be found in any object. Design elements based on peacock feathers, poppies, thistles, and dragonflies could be found on patterns in wallpaper, textiles, and furniture. Japanese-inspired compositions often found their way into art nouveau interiors. Colors ranged from muted colors such as mustard, to dramatic colors such as lilac, gold, salmon, and robin's egg blue. Furniture fabric may have been brocade, damask, leather, linen, mohair, tapestry, or velvet. Louis Comfort Tiffany designed windows, lamp shades, and other elements with similar colors and forms in stained glass.

De Stijl

During the early 1920s, a small group of artists and architects in Holland, including Theo van Doesburg, Gerrit Rietveld, and Piet Mondrian, formed a movement called de stijl, the Dutch word for "style." They presented their ideas and designs in a publication of the same name. Their philosophical approach to aesthetics was based on functionalism. Only color was used as an applied decoration on forms limited to rectilinear planer elements. Planes slid past one another to make form and space, both in art and architecture. The planes operated in a manner that the architectural historian Colin Rowe referred to as "phenomenal transparency."

The de stijl artists and architects actually built very few of their designs. Gerrit Rietveld's Schroeder House (1924) was the major work completed in Utrecht. Here, the house and all of the furniture was designed and installed as well. The success of the de stijl practitioners lay in the distribution of their ideas. Though the output was small, the design philosophies influenced many of the modernist architects who came after them.

The de stijl movement had been influenced by the work of the cubists and the work of Frank Lloyd Wright, which had been published widely in Europe during the first two decades of the twentieth century. The work and writings of the de stijl group had a heavy influence on architects in Germany. This was especially true of Walter Gropius and Mies Van der Rohe and their work at the Bauhause. Both Gropius and Van der Rohe immigrated to the United States in the 1930s to practice and teach architecture.

Art Deco

With the advent of the machine age, the art nouveau style (1890–1914), which took inspiration from the curvilinear forms of nature, developing new highly stylized natural forms, lost all interest to the machined and streamlined forms of art deco.

Art deco was an eclectic style with roots in a machine aesthetic. Bauhaus architecture, industrial machinery, cubist painting, and even the discovery of King Tut's tomb in 1922 all served as diverse sources from which the movement drew forms and influences. Art deco forms varied from the aerodynamic curves of new airplanes to zigzag shapes to pyramids and sphinxes. During the 1930s, everything from cars to toasters received the machine aesthetic and curvilinear forms of art deco. Very typical forms of furniture included black leather chairs with chrome legs or rectangular leather couches with rosewood sides and arms.

Modernist

From 1920 to 1950, modernist architects and artists explored forms and materials of mass production and industrialization. The machine age, it was thought, needed unique forms, furniture, interiors, and fashion that were functional and beautiful on their own, without added ornament or embellishment. The modern movement and the International Style all referred to the primary idea of the simplicity of the machine aesthetic. Plain geometric shapes and neutral-colored walls, streamlined space-saving modular furniture, and new materials, such as glass, metal, concrete, and steel, all characterized the style.

In the 1930s, the architecture of the German Bauhaus, designed by Walter Gropius, focused on functionality and transparent space. The buildings at the Bauhaus lacked any ornament, had an austere expression of materials, and used ribbon windows to create a sense of the flow of space. At the Bauhaus school, mass production was seen as a way to get quality hand-crafted products into the hands of as many consumers as possible. Students and teachers at the Bauhaus worked to create furniture and commercial products that stressed these ideals.

In 1926, Marcel Breuer, a design instructor at the Bauhaus, designed a steel tube chair that revolutionized the concept of the chair. The chair was made from a single, chrome-plated steel tube that wound up the front, around the side, and up the back. A woven cane seat and back attached to the steel frame. Breuer based the support of the chair on a cantilever. The steel tube under the seat held the chair structurally so that no rear supports came from the back to the ground. Studies for the chair showed people sitting in mid-air, the concept being that the people could sit on a resilient column of air. Breuer's work revolutionized the chair because almost every architect working in the modernist style thereafter experimented with the idea of the chair.

On into the 1930s, modern furniture designs spread into the mass-consumer market. In the spring of 1933, Sears, Roebuck advertised an entire "living room in the Modern manner." The room contained a "rich rust color davenport," a "lounge chair and ottoman in Almond green," and a "gracefully proportioned guest chair in gold." The furniture had very clean lines with no embellishments and was covered with a heavy mohair. A combination tea table/occasional table veneered in a highly polished Oriental Walnut rounded out the set (Sears, Roebuck 1933, 528).

Gerrit Rietveld wrote: "every chair seems to be a stylization of an attitude to life." The chair is a piece of furniture that is dictated in its size and shape by its function. The chair is designed for the human body. In looking at the various differences in design styles, this makes the chair a great form to investigate.

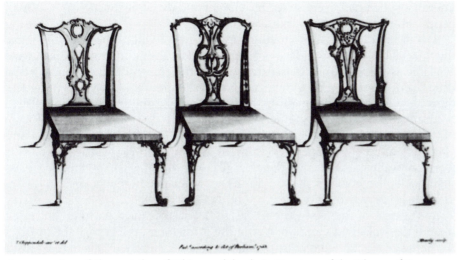

An engraving of three styles of Chippendale chair. Courtesy of the Library of Congress.

PAINT COLOR AND WALLPAPER

By the late 1920s and 1930s, color schemes inside the house began to change to neutral backgrounds that eliminated the multitude of color and pattern found in the Victorian home. Designers began to stress the importance of interior schemes that used color harmony. If walls were planned in a plain color, then the draperies should be patterned "for the sake of contrast." If the walls were papered with masses of colors, then the curtains should be a plain shade "in harmony with certain colors in the paper." Furniture covers and even lampshades were bought to match. Of concern was the use of figural Oriental rugs in the room, in which case the furniture "should be of plain colors, with perhaps one or two exceptions" (Stewart and Gerald 1935, 58–59).

Emily Post, in her book *The Personality of a House,* suggested that when thinking about colors in the house, the homeowner should create their own actual chromatic color chart by mixing the three primary colors and the three secondary colors together. This small color chart, of which she provided a sample, would show the homeowner how colors harmonized together. According to Post, "a complementary accent is to harmonious color arrangement what salt is to food. If there is none of this ingredient, the composition lacks flavor, but too much of it is a violent emetic!" (Post 1930,165).

For the idea of color harmony to work, the majority of colors in the room had to be neutral. As one design team wrote, "the color must be of a more of less subdued value so that it will not exact more attention than does the furniture displayed in front of it . . . A subdued color is a neutral or grayed color. A rule that we can safely follow with regard to wall color or to any quality of color is that the larger the area, the more neutral the color should be" (Stewart and Gerald 1935, 57).

Neutral colors offered a backdrop for the activities of the home. The popularity of neutral paints and wallpapers arose as activities became disassociated with the parlor and more associated with the automobile. When family entertainment, such as movies, provided visual stimulus outside of the home, interiors, which had been incredibly vibrant and dynamic during the Victorian period, moved toward beige, gray, and off white.

The mechanical mass production of wallpapers reduced the price and made them available to the middle-class market. Machine printed wallpapers were available as early as the 1840s. Advances in efficient production continued to drop the prices. By the turn of the century, wallpapers could be bought for less than the price of paint in many cases. Wallpaper became an inexpensive way to redecorate or freshen up an interior.

Wallpaper designs changed every season. In 1921, Sears, Roebuck and Company offered wallpapers for as low as 10 cents per double roll, or 16 yards worth, of wallpaper. Papering the average room with this paper would cost less than one dollar in materials. In many cases, wallpapers were changed in homes as often as every 7 to 10 years.

In the case of the living room, design advocates suggested that "the more neutral the walls and the more restful the furnishings, the greater the beauty." An advocate in a building journal stated that in a living room it is best to have a good plain paper "in a warm light-giving tone," suggesting that "a striped paper in the self-tone, with a frieze in some harmonizing color is good." Above all, the homeowner should "avoid figured wallpaper," which had been used heavily for decades. Another design advocate stated that the living room "could stand a stronger color" than some other rooms, but "as a rule, it is best to have plain walls and plain upholstery for the furniture, leaving the decoration to the hangings." These were all suggestions aimed at changing Victorian design sensibilities ("Suggested Treatment of Wall Spaces in Suburban Homes" 1912; Wright 1917, 114–115).

The color of the living room, suggested Emily Post, "should be soothing rather than exciting in tone, since it must be restful and sympathetic whether you are glad or sad, well or ill." If the homeowner papered the walls, Post was clear that the design should not be "one so decided in pattern that it unceasingly interrupts." Another advocate suggested that "if the dining-room and living-room are connected by a small door, the walls may be in some light, cloudy landscape paper, or in a small all-over pattern in alight cream, buff, gray, or tan" (Post 1930, 342; Better Homes in America 1923, 38).

In the case of modernist housing, interiors were often painted white, which was thought to appear sanitary, clean, and healthy. The de stijl artists argued for the use of white, black, and primary colors only. White interiors offered a backdrop that provided a canvas for the masses and colors of the furniture placed in the modernist house.

Not all houses designed by signature architects had unadorned white walls. The interior at Wingspread, a house designed by Frank Lloyd Wright for Herbert Fisk Johnson, the president of S. C. Johnson and Son, Inc., had a very different finish than other houses. Located in Wisconsin and built in 1938, the year after Fallingwater had been completed, the interior walls of the house were covered with a rough-plaster finish with a sand texture.

Wright had the plaster painted with a wax paint supplied by Johnson Wax. Painters melted and thinned the wax, added tinting pigments, and painted while the mixture was still hot. The walls all received a ground coat of an orange–yellow paint and were then were overpainted with a moderate red, grayish blue, or light green depending on the room.

The technique left the plaster walls and ceilings of the house with a mottled appearance. The orange–yellow paint slightly showed through the top coats, creating a harmony of coloration, but also a real depth not found in normal house paints. Wright achieved a very organic, soft natural interplay of colors, one using chiefly natural materials.

FURNISHING THE ROOMS IN THE HOUSE

Throughout the history of housing, public rooms have been located on the first floor. Renaissance villas elevated public rooms to the piano nobile, the principal story of a house sitting on a half basement. This placement allowed circulation of air and openness to breezes and kept the aristocratic occupants slightly above the filth and smells generated by the process of daily living. Many country houses and town houses of the eighteenth century followed a similar pattern.

The Victorian dwellings of the nineteenth century established a house type for an emerging business elite in medium and small towns all over the United States. Though substantially flexible in plan and elevation, owing to the new balloon framing techniques from the early nineteenth century, these dwellings had elements of traditionally aristocratic housing. This included the elevation of the principal floor with public rooms set aside for formal entertaining.

During the same time, the bungalow developed as a form of English military housing. A one-story residential structure, the bungalow was characterized by a large front porch and sweeping overhanging rooflines. Designed to protect residents from the unrelenting climate of the Caribbean and Indian colonies, the bungalow became a fashionable small house type by the late nineteenth century.

The Victorian house had developed several specialized rooms, many with specific rituals. By the turn of the twentieth century, many of these rooms still served specific functions, but mainly in large, stately, architect-designed homes. These minor rooms included tea rooms, billiard rooms, smoking rooms, and libraries.

As late as 1923, L. Eugene Robinson, a housing advocate and architect, had written an architectural textbook suggesting that a parlor or a tea room should be located near the entry hall. Likewise, he wrote that an architect should locate a billiard or smoking room near the dining room. He noted that when designed into houses, these rooms needed to be isolated from the living areas of the house but within proximity in order to receive visitors. The library should be isolated because only one person at a time used this room, however, the room needed to be located near the entry in case the occupants of the house used the room to receive callers here as well. Music rooms, dens, offices, and art rooms were all similar to the library and therefore should be set "a little aside from the regular rooms" (Robinson 1923, 62).

In contrast to these seemingly Victorian standards, by the early twentieth century the functions and use of residential spaces had been transformed to a typological form still present today. The front door opened inward to the first room, the living room. This room became a multifunctional room replacing many of the rooms in the Victorian home. This new concept in living arrangement and attitude altered the foremost room of the house; the transformation from hall and parlor to living room had a dramatic effect on the social institution of the house.

FURNISHING THE MODERN LIVING ROOM

In 1911, one design advocate wrote in *House Beautiful* magazine that a "well-designed wood trim, a side wall of good proportions, windows and doors that fit and balance, a simple fireplace, sunshine and ventilation—these are usually embodied in the modern living room" (Wentworth 1911a, 50). This description left out ideas of procession, entry sequence, furnishing, and multiuse nature of the living room.

When the front room or living room was located off the main entrance of the house, the room transitioned both the family and the visitor to the rest of the house. The central role as a "living" room necessitated the room to serve as entry hall, parlor, library, den, and music room. Robinson's textbook confirmed that "in the ordinary house" the living room took the place of all the above named rooms. As designed, the room combined features of all the other specialized rooms. The author continued:

> If in the house there is no library, a certain portion of the living room should be set aside in a cozy fashion containing bookcases where one may read comfortably. If in the house there is no music room, then an inside wall of the living room should be especially designed and reserved for a piano, and music cabinet. Since the living room is occupied for a large part of the day by the woman of the house,

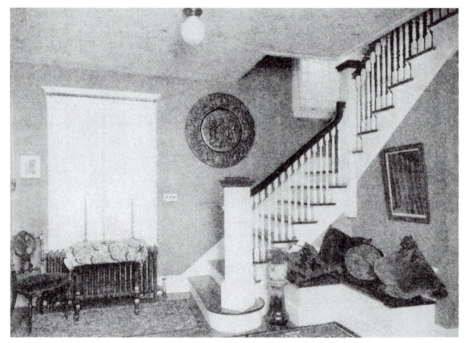

Living Room, Sears, Roebuck and Company, 1923. Ads like this showed prospective customers how the living room should be furnished. Sears, Roebuck, and Co., Chicago and Philadelphia, 1923.

it may be well to fit a particular part of that room with the paraphernalia needed in ordinary sewing work, so that the room also becomes a sewing room. Sometimes a writing desk, or secretary, is desirable in a living room. (Robinson 1923, 62–64)

At the heart of Robinson's argument was his conclusion that "the living room should be a room in which to live in every sense of the word, the variations in its arrangement depending upon the other rooms in the house, and the habits of the family" (Robinson 1923, 62–64).

The same argument applied to interior decorating and furniture. Agnes Foster Wright, a housing advocate who published books and articles on interior design, suggested in 1917 that "above all else, the furniture in the living room should make it livable." In breaking with the Victorian tradition of bric-a-brac, modern decorators preached that "where the living-room serves the purpose of library, drawing-room, and a general family room, it should be simply treated as to furnishings and decorations." The author even made a plea that the room would be as "free as possible from the purely useless things" (Wright 1917, 108). In an article titled "The Big Problem of the Little House," Margaret U. Barton implored readers to "not tolerate quantities of meaningless knickknacks, but let every vase and candlestick have for its purpose in being, real beauty or use" (Barton 1921, 34).

The family hearth maintained a presence in the home and often became the central feature in the living room. In many houses, the fireplace and mantel, with built-in cabinets or bookshelves on either side, was the one stylistically designed area of the house. Even in the high-style modernist works such as Wright's Fallingwater and Neutra's Lovell Health House, the hearth is the focal point of the living room.

The typical living room in the "small house" contained a grouping of furniture considered the main essentials. At the minimum, the room included "a comfortable divan, a table large enough to hold books, magazines and lamps, and at least two comfortable, upholstered chairs and a smaller table." This grouping of furniture was not necessarily exclusive, but these were the "certain pieces that [made] the living-room livable in any house" (Wright 1917, 112–113).

Costs of Living Room Furniture

Furnishing the small house could cost as much as $1,000 to $3,000 for a home costing $5,000. Many homeowners, however, spent less than $500.00. An inexpensive, complete living room set consisting of an arm rocker, a library table, a large armchair, a sewing rocker and chair (without arms), a taboret, and book ends for the table could be purchased from Sears, Roebuck and Company for $27.85. Local furniture dealers sold higher quality at a much higher price. Advertisements for furniture stores can be found in almost any local newspaper. In 1926, a three-piece Jaquard Velour living room suite consisting of an overstuffed couch and two armchairs sold in Marion, Ohio, for $230.00. Likewise, an eight-piece walnut dining room set, including a buffet, a table, and six chairs, cost $254.00. A quality dining room table from Sears, Roebuck, on the other hand, cost $39.50.

The extension of credit into the consumer goods market came to define the twentieth century. By the 1920s, it also made it possible for many families and young couples to purchase an entire set of furniture at one time. These sets included everything necessary for a new homeowner to furnish a new home and were often marketed to young couples who were first-time homebuyers.

Robert Lynd and Helen Lynd, in a second study of Muncie, Indiana, in 1937 noted that couples were getting married at younger ages in towns in the Midwest during the 1920s and 1930s. In Muncie, Indiana, for instance, 46.2 percent of females between the age of 15 and 24 were married in 1935. Furniture stores catered to this market by extending liberal consumer credit (Lynd and Lynd 1937, 147–149).

In Indianapolis, "young people" who were "planning for a new home" could "fit the home complete" at a store called Hoosier Outfitting. In Wheeling, West Virginia, another store offered both cash and credit prices for furniture offering to "aid and co-operate with the young couples starting out in life" by offering to extend credit on "complete home outfits for a period of eighteen months." Yet another store offered everything needed for a house consisting of a living room, dining room, kitchen, and bedroom. At another store a couple could get everything they needed to furnish a "4 room home," including carpets and oil paintings, for under $1,000, all on account. In May, of 1921, a *Washington Post* advertisement proclaimed that "June brides will find our low prices and liberal credit terms a great help when furnishing a new house." A whole 10-piece dining room set could be purchased for $3.75 a week (Hoosier Outfitting 1924; Cooey-Bentz Co. 1924; Palace Furniture Company 1924; Phillip and Levy 1921).

Homeowners filled their new homes with new suites of living room and dining room furniture. In 1939, 5,870 households were inventoried in Cleveland, Ohio, by the Cleveland Council of Parent-Teachers Associations. Of these families, 77 percent had purchased living room furniture between 1920 and 1939. Of those, 67.6 percent had purchased an entire suite. More than half of the families had also purchased an entire dining room suite (*Cleveland Home Inventory* 1939).

The primary piece of furniture in the living room was a sofa. This piece could also be called a *divan,* a *davenport,* or a *couch.* Interior designers preferred striped patterns, asserting that "a six foot sofa with a seat and back divided into three separate cushions, upholstered in a strie or wide striped velour is better than a sofa plainly upholstered." The second most important piece of furniture in the room was a "long, narrow table—3 × 6 feet." Often called a library table, this piece of furniture took the place of Victorian center tables. Like the living room itself, the long table answered "the modern need" and served multiple uses. The table could be used as a desk to write and study, for games, or "three or four people could sit on one side of it." The table also held "two lamps beautifully" that could shed "adjacent light on two groups." In 1908, the Sears, Roebuck catalog did not contain long tables. By 1927, this type of table commanded an entire page showing 16 different styles, listed as both "library" tables and "davenport" tables (Wright 1917, 115; Mirken 1970, 900–901).

Housing experts were consistent on the placement and use of furniture in the living room. Decorators promoted interiors that were meant to bestow "restfulness, peace and comfort, but with life and individuality." Housing experts believed that these ideas could be achieved by correct furniture placement. In 1922, one suggested that "in order to produce an impression of restfulness and space, the larger pieces of furniture should be placed parallel to the walls of the room" (Holloway 1920; Fales 1922).

Living rooms were set up and furnished specifically designed for a variety of interactions. Designers suggested positioning furniture in "a series of well-related groups, each designed for the utmost comfort and convenience." The groups would be complete by themselves but also "rhythmically co-ordinated so as to form one unified group." These groups formed around the chief points of interest in the room, "the fireplace, a bay window, a desk, or around an interesting picture" (Stewart and Gerald 1935, 87).

In their book *Home Decoration: Its Problems and Solutions,* Ross Stewart and John Gerald describe the design transformation of a living room. The first living room was an actual living room in a home costing $15,000.00. The owners had decorated the room themselves. The walls were putty in color and the sofa and two chairs were covered in blue tapestry. Rose damask curtains hung in front of the windows. A broadloom sand-colored carpet covered the floor. The professional decorators redesigned and changed the room dramatically in furniture placement and color. The walls were painted light gray–green, the chairs were covered with slips of English chintz in rose, green, and yellow on a beige background. The rose in the chairs matched the rose of the existing curtains. The sofa was recovered in a dark green rep. Oriental overcarpets tied the new groupings together (Stewart and Gerald 1935, 90–91, plans on 89).

The "typical American family" only uses the drawing room for company and "lives in the library, the living-room, the book-room, the study (or den), or the sitting room." In this case, the drawing room of a large suburban house acted in the same way as a Victorian parlor. The typical family used a living room with "easy going characteristics." According to Emily Post, the perfect living room had windows on the long wall filling the room with light, a "welcoming log fire," books, a "table spread like a small news-stand with magazines," a much-used desk, and chairs that were constantly sat in (Post 1930, 339, 341).

The Radio as Furniture

The culmination of radio technology occurred in the mid-1920s when the A-C tube was invented, allowing the radio to run on electricity. A cheap and practical A-C tube began to be produced by RCA in 1927, and the radio became a home appliance permanently placed in one room. After electrification, companies began to design large console sets made out of fine wood and resembling furniture. Companies such as RCA, Magnavox, Zenith, and Philco designed and marketed radios specifically to be placed in the living room.

The early consoles competed with the piano and the phonograph for the musical dominance of the living room. Before the production of Armstrong's Radiola Superheterodyne, the sound quality of the phonograph was much higher than the "tinny" sounds coming from the radio. After the introduction of the new set, however, sound came out of the radio loud and clear. Better, in some cases, than sound from the phonograph. The phonograph industry immediately began to decline.

The radio quickly became a fixture in American living rooms. During the 1930s, manufacturers increasingly marketed the radio as a piece of furniture.

The units became larger and were designed in the various styles to match other furniture in a given room. Every one of the 5,873 families inventoried in Cleveland in 1939 had a radio. Thirty percent of the radios had been purchased before 1931. Slightly more, 32 percent, had been purchased within the last three years, between 1936 and 1939 (*Cleveland Home Inventory* 1939).

Flooring in Living and Dining Rooms

Solid oak flooring, placed in two-inch strips and naturally finished, covered the floors throughout the living and dining areas of most houses. This was very typical from the beginning of the century through mid-century. One builder suggested that, "in practically every modern dwelling of the present day, a feature of the principal rooms is the finish flooring, usually of thin oak strips laid over a substantial under-floor and having a polished waxed surface." Carpenters applied finish to the floor after the floor was planed and sanded. Typically, a Stanley No. 12 1/2 steel scraper gave the best results for preparing the oak for sanding. Until the invention of the electric sander, sanding the oak floor was one of the hardest jobs on a construction site. After sanding, the painting contractor typically finished the floor with two coats of white alcohol shellac and a finish coat of well-polished wax ("Sanitary Flooring" 1910).

By the 1920s, floor coverings were widely available. All manner of carpeting and linoleum had come down in price. Many outlets sold both wall-to-wall carpets and area rugs. The area rug, however, was a very popular floor covering widely used in many rooms of the house.

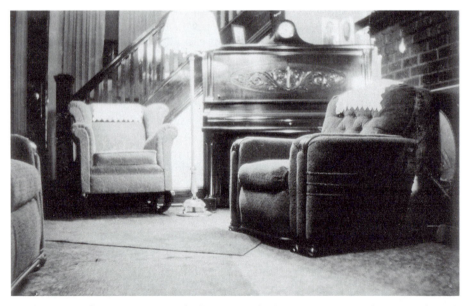

By the 1940s floor coverings of all manner had come into popular use. Though experts suggested the standard placement of furnitures, here, ca. 1940, the homeowners are using overcarpets and placing furniture as they needed, including an overstuffed chair in front of the fireplace. Sears, Roebuck, and Co., Chicago and Philadelphia, 1940.

Wool rugs came in many varieties. Jute tapestry or Brussels seamless rugs came in typical sizes of 6 × 9, 4 × 7, and 9 × 12 feet. These carpets consisted of dyed wool fibers looped through a jute backing. The different colors of fibers created designs in floral and geometric designs. These mass produced carpets were ubiquitous in houses and replaced the traditional Oriental carpet. In 1926, the industrialist Marshall Field modified a traditional powered loom to create a machine-made rug woven through the back, simulating a handmade Oriental carpet. Marketed as Karastan rugs, the faux Oriental carpets were offered to the public in 1928.

Seamless velvet rugs or Wilton velvet rugs came in a variety of styles. Wilton rugs and carpets had the tops of the loops cut; today, this would be called a cut-pile carpet. Wiltons could have an "openwork design on the plain ground" or could be a reproduction of a pattern "of Chinese origin and typical of the high development of rug art in the Orient." In 1927, the newest styles had "swung to the use of plain hued floor coverings" and were "recognized as a mark of excellent taste in any room" (Mirken 1970, 835).

In 1927, the Sears, Roebuck Company advertised that "the vogue for plain floor coverings has gained great popularity with in the last year, because of its practicality, its effectiveness as a setting for any color scheme, and its economy" (Mirken 1970, 835). Manufacturers produced broadloom carpets on large looms of 12 or 15 feet, hence the name broadloom. Loomed sections were sewn together to make wall-to-wall carpets. Sears, Roebuck offered to cut and sew carpets to order, based on room diagrams that customers sent in. Full-room carpets also could be used in combination with area rugs. Typical of nineteenth-century practices, one design team suggested that "if the floor is covered with a broadloom carpet," another simple means of strengthening the interrelation of a group is to use as a foundation a small Oriental rug on top of the carpet" (Stewart and Gerald 1935, 89).

Chinese grass matting was still being sold in 1927. Grass matting had been an inexpensive alternative or a summer floor covering since the end of the eighteenth century. In the late twentieth century, advertisers could say, "nothing quite takes the place of neat fresh matting for its pretty, serviceability and easy to keep clean." Grass matting, by nature of the material, was reversible, and when one side had worn, the mats could be flipped over and reused (Mirken 1970, 841).

Ingrain carpeting was also a reversible material that could be flipped over when worn out. Occasionally called Kidderminster carpet for where it originated in England, ingrain carpeting was a woven carpet with reverse figures on opposite sides. In the nineteenth century, over half of the carpets sold in the United States were ingrain carpets. Still sold in the 1920s, ingrain was "a truly practical carpet at the lowest possible price" (Mirken 1970, 841).

The cost of area rugs and carpets depended on their manufacture. In 1921, the Maxwell Furniture Company in Washington, D.C. sold a 9 × 12 grass rug for $6.45. A 9 × 12 Brussels rug sold for $16.50. At the top of the list, a 9 × 12 velvet rug sold for $27.50.

Linoleum flooring was very typical for use in kitchens, bathrooms, and bedrooms. This flooring material was made from solidified linseed oil mixed with wood flour or cork dust attached to a burlap backing. Manufacturers sold the fact that, "design and colorings go through to the burlap back, which assures years of hard service." Sears, Roebuck marketed linoleum "rugs." Designs in linoleum replicated carpet designs. Designs could be inlaid or printed. Inlaid linoleum was made of many small solid pieces, cut and molded into intricate designs. In 1932, Sears, Roebuck offered a line they called "Floor-o-leum." This flooring offered "authentic reproduction of quality carpet." Styles also came in faux stone, marble, and modern designs that looked like cubist paintings (Mirken 1970, 829; Sears, Roebuck 1932, 705).

THE DINING ROOM FURNITURE

The dining room came into existence in America during the first half of the eighteenth century. As the hall became an area dedicated to the reception of guests, the dining room became the heart of the room. The room, always located on the first floor, served the multipurpose function of storage, eating, and sleeping.

In the mid-nineteenth century, the Victorian dining room lost the sleeping function and held furniture and decorations associated with imagery of hunting and gathering of food. Nothing symbolized this better than the overly ornate sideboards that began to be the most prominent piece of furniture in the room. The iconographic display of dogs and dead animals pointed to the masculinity of the room.

The dining room served as a multipurpose space in many households. Families did everything from homework to dressmaking on the dining room table. The dining room also served, however, as the setting where the family defined the roll of etiquette and social behavior and established a set pattern

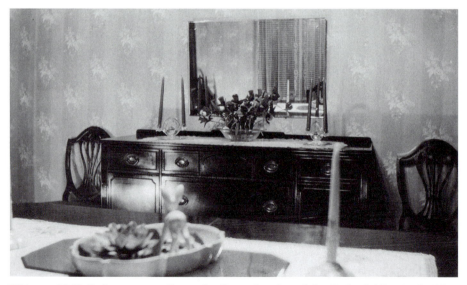

This ca. 1940 dining room reflects the formal order of the Colonial Revival with a centrally placed sideboard and symmetrical Hepplewhite style chairs. Sears, Roebuck, and Co., Chicago and Philadelphia, 1940.

of social standards. By the mid-twentieth century, silverplate flatware became a standard possession of the middle class, and the standard way of eating with the same utensils became a defining characteristic of the community. In this way, the dining room had replaced the parlor for the ritualized instruction of etiquette.

The dining room also functioned as the setting for family rituals such as holidays. In this sense, the dining room served as a forum for cultural consumption. Here, many families embraced a mass consumer culture that during the 1920s ever increasingly marketed holidays such as Christmas and Thanksgiving (Pleck 2000).

Owning to this formality, often the dining room was furnished with traditional style furnishings. The Better Homes in America, New Haven Prize house of 1922 contained a dining room with Windsor chairs accompanied by "an early American type drop-leaf dining table" and "Sheraton sideboard, serving table, china cupboard. An Oriental carpet completed the room (Better Homes in America 1923, 39).

In a *Better Homes and Gardens* article, Hazel T. Becker, discussed four houses that had been built without dining rooms. Her findings offer an insightful look into changing dining culture in the home. She states that, "one of the most striking departures from old customs in small house planning is the advent of the dining-room-less house. The house without a dining room has had ready acceptance and popularity with home builders-so much so that outlived the freak or fad stage and is now a recognized institution." She reasons that "the dining room is in use during the day fewer hours than any other room in the house," and that "busy housewives find it helpful to serve hurried breakfasts in the cozy kitchen or dining alcove." People who could barely afford a home could do well without the expense of a room that did not get continuous use. She continued to say, "even that relic of barbarism, the old style Sunday dinner, is replaced in many homes nowadays by a weekly meal at a hotel or restaurant, so that for the housewife too, the Sabbath may be a day of rest." Becker's analysis sheds light, in part, on why houses in the 1930s began to become smaller and smaller (Becker 1926, 14).

FOR THE MAN OF THE HOUSE: THE DEN

Historians have made the argument that the domestic reform movement divided the home into male and female spheres. Nowhere is this argument clearer than in the case of the room known as a den. Cheryl Robertson has discussed the bungalow style as an example to show that in space planning, the den became the masculine area of the house. By the late nineteenth century, the male resentment of the feminine parlor created a backlash of private male spaces in the domicile, and this occurred in a small room, usually located off of the living room (Robertson 1991).

Though the den appeared in several housing plans during the 1920s, the room was more suited for earlier Arts and Crafts homes. By the second decade of the twentieth century, the den was on the wane as a fundamental room in the modern house. As early as 1911, Ann Wentworth, a domestic advocate, had published an article in *House Beautiful* titled "The Passing of the Den." She stated that few floor plans contained the "once-popular room." By removing the den, "the gain in space makes possible a larger living room." Wentworth suggested, however, that the den had served a useful purpose: a means to escape the "over-feminine parlors and reception rooms" (Wentworth 1911b, 127–128).

In 1915, the *Wallpaper News and Interior Decorator* discussed the passing of the den, a small room "set apart as a place where the man temperament could have full expression, where colored curtains were not affected by tobacco smoke." In 1917, another expert, Agnes Foster Wright, wrote that "what used to be called the 'den' is now called a smoking room." Here, as in the den, men escaped to participate in traditional masculine pleasures. Within this room, the man of the house indulged in hobbies as well as smoking. Wright suggested that the room was directly related to the library, only for men who didn't like to read. ("The Passing of the Den" 1915, 21; Wright 1917, 132–133).

The den returned somewhat during the second half of the twentieth century. In a national survey of houses costing $7,500 or more in 1938, architects and designers argued that "when the man of the family has good use for it, a den should be included off the living room." Again, though it held a very small place in the design of the small house during the 1920s, the den served as a male dominated space in the 1940s and 1950s ("Colonial Home is Most Popular" 1938).

BEDROOM FURNITURE

> Bedsteads should be as simple as possible in design and construction . . . many of them are ornamented in the most tasteless manner.
>
> —Schell

In some houses, bedrooms were highly designed spaces with whole sets of matching furniture. On the whole, however, the bedroom was a room of necessity not seen by anyone but the family. Design advocates often suggested simplicity and plainness in both finish and furnishings. Mass production techniques brought the cost of bedroom furnishings down, however, the high end market still relied on the production of colonial revival styles just like the main public rooms of the house.

The adult bedroom recommended for a 1923 bungalow demonstration house had walls painted gray, ivory, or sand. The room also had a floor covered with linoleum. The recommended furnishings included an enameled iron bed with a mattress and pillows, an enameled chiffonier, and an enameled or painted chest of drawers. Experts suggested that "the first requisite in furnishing a room is that it appear crisp and clean. The walls light in color, must be restful and simple in design" (Better Homes 1923, 40).

Painted furniture was very popular for bedrooms. In 1920, a furniture company in Ohio marketed a "light and airy ivory suite" in an "Adam period design." Design consultants suggested that painted furniture had a "dainty appearance." But "dull finished mahogany or walnut in four-post or Colonial design" also made a "charming bedroom" ("Shop at the Home and Save" 1920; Better Homes 1923, 40).

During the 1920s, mass manufacturing and new industrial processes resulted in the manufacture and popularity of the steel bed. The Simmons steel bed was a signature piece of furniture during this time. In 1923, the Simmons Company manufactured nine separate suites of steel bedroom furniture. Simmons produced beds from seamless tubing electrically welded together. Manufacturers understood that an important feature of steel construction was that the cheapest bedroom set did not differ at all in strength or durability from the most expensive set. To compensate for this, Simmons painted higher priced suites with faux graining to resemble wood. This work was completed by skilled craftsmen all by hand so that work "did not have an artificial appearance of a printed or stenciled grain" (Pursell 1995, 137).

Sears, Roebuck sold similar steel beds in the 1932 catalog. At this time, there were multiple styles, many with faux graining. One, made from "all steel and moulded tubing," had head and foot panels with "exact reproductions of butt walnut and curly maple." The all-steel bed with "two-tone finish" sold for $21.98 (Sears, Roebuck 1932, 667).

Wooden bedroom furniture continued to be marketed and sold as well. In traditional styles, Sears, Roebuck offered full "Queen Anne Period Sets" for the bedroom. These sets included a dresser, bow end bed, chest of drawers, vanity dresser, chiffonrobe, a night table, and two chairs. In 1932, Sears, Roebuck offered their "contribution to the modern trend." This set was built on massive lines with "expensive inlays" of walnut and zebra wood veneers making "V-shaped inlays and matching diagonal graining." Advertisers claimed the furniture was "truly a classic among today's modern designs" (Mirken 1970, 864; Sears, Roebuck 1932, 660).

Throughout the 1920s and 1930s, closets in bedrooms were very small. In the nineteenth century they had been smaller, but closet dimensions began to change after the wire hanger was invented in 1903. People living in middle-class housing did not have excessive amounts of clothing, and closets were not excessive. The average closet was approximately 32 inches wide and 14 to 18 inches deep. Often the closet in a bedroom would be set into the space to the side of the chimney so that the interior wall remained flat.

SLEEPING PORCH FURNITURE

A sleeping porch, with wrap-around windows off a back bedroom or sometimes protruding over the back porch, added a space for open-air sleeping. Many cultural authorities held that sleeping in the open air was important for one's health. The standard personal hygiene text of the early twentieth century assured readers that outdoor sleeping increased the body's power to resist disease. Advertisements popularized this idea suggesting that "everybody knows now-a-days that the more fresh air we get into our lungs day and night the better off we are." One author writing in *House Beautiful* magazine suggested that outdoor sleeping could provide a relaxing "communion" with stars and nature, in general, and that there could "be no pleasanter, saner, more wholesome, and more efficacious remedy for insomnia than a bed out-of-doors" (Allen 1919, 220).

By the 1920s, the value of sleeping on a sleeping porch had come to be widely recognized. A valid selling point was the fact that the well-ventilated sleeping porch was cooler than the bedroom during the summer. For health, the sleeping porch was used all year round, but builders and designers also recognized that few would "deny their desirability in summer at least, whatever his views

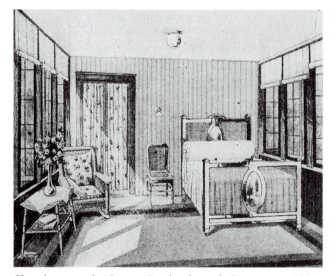

Sleeping porch, Sears, Roebuck and Company, 1919. Sleeping porches were thought to promote healthy sleeping, but they also provided comfort on hot nights. Sears, Roebuck, and Co., Chicago and Philadelphia, 1919.

on year-round outdoor sleeping" (Riley 1917, 136). Sears, Roebuck and Company building plans noted that on hot, stuffy summer nights a sleeping porch would make sleeping more pleasant.

The porch could come in many varieties. It could be located on a veranda over a porch, tucked under a dormer, in a gable, or off of a bedroom within the body of the house or on the corner. Often, sleeping porches had configurations of windows, which could be opened to allow in fresh air or closed to keep out bad weather. The real design solution was to incorporate the porch into the "characteristic features" of the house to "ensure good outward appearance, as well as comfort." The ideal sleeping porch was constructed on the second floor at the back of the house. This provided the most privacy, as sleeping porches on the first floor were "too hard to screen from neighbors and passers-by" and were "too open to dogs, chickens, and small boys" (Moore 1912, 173).

Optimally, the porch would be placed on the southern or western exposure to avoid morning sunlight that might wake sleepers. In most cases, the floor of the porch was painted wood flooring. Some advocates suggested that the floor should "slant slightly, making of it a natural drain" (Tachau 1921, 63).

Advocates suggested that the sleeping porch furnishings be "simplified" as far as was "consistent with convenience." This entailed a bed, a chair, a box for holding extra bedding, and a stand. The furniture needed to be "of a sort that rain [would] not harm." The one "really essential piece of furniture" was a "cot, day-bed, or couch," whichever the homeowner preferred. One lumberyard advertisement showed an iron day bed. The illustration for the Sears, Roebuck and Company Osborn house, published in the 1919 *Honor Bilt Homes Catalog*, showed a picture of the sleeping porch furnished with a wicker rocker, wicker side table, a small chair, and a wooden bed with woven head and foot boards (Moore 1912, 173; Tachau 1921, 63).

THE BREAKFAST NOOK

The breakfast nook was one of the rooms added to the small house to combat "the servant problem." A typical breakfast nook was a "tiny room, usually built off the kitchen" with a "built-in table, flanked by built-in benches or settles, either of painted wood or treated in some suitable informal style" (Whitton 1927, 38). The nook provided a space where the homemaker could prepare and serve small meals quickly and efficiently. Serving and cleaning up the meal became informal and easily accomplished by one individual.

Designed for practicality and the new speed of modern lifestyle, the breakfast room found a place in the new business culture of America. "Liberally lighted with windows and decorated and furnished in a bright and airy style," the room offered a setting where the "unconventional meal" could be eaten informally. The table could be "kept set without inconvenience, in case the family's breakfasting [was] irregular" ("The Breakfast Room in its Variety" 1920, 64).

Some breakfast rooms were large with multiple windows. These could be independent of other rooms. Experts suggested that the room "have a place in the sun." If the homeowner removed and concealed "china and table linen," the room could "be used between meals as a sun-room." In some cases, the room could actually take the place of a regular-dining room (Northend 1922, 50; "The Breakfast Room in its Variety" 1920, 64).

Breakfast rooms were often finished in very bright colors, offering a "welcoming cheeriness to the morning meal." One such room, described in *House and Garden* magazine, had plaster walls tinted yellow orange and a floor covered with a black rug. The room contained green–blue painted furniture against a backdrop of black cretonne curtains with green–blue and orange stripes (Northend 1922, 58).

Reference List

Allen, Francis H. 1919. "The Joy of Sleeping Out-of-Doors." *House Beautiful* 45: 220.

"American Interiors in the Modern Style." 1915. *The Wallpaper News and Interior Decorator* (January): 19.

Barton, Margaret U. 1921. "The Big Problem of the Little House." *Good Housekeeping* (November): 34.

Becker, Hazel T. 1926. "Four Dining-room-less Houses." *Better Homes and Gardens* 4 (June):14–15.

Better Homes in America Advisory Council. 1923. *Better Homes in America: Plan book prepared for the guidance of local committees in conducting better home demonstrations.* New York: The Delineator.

"The Breakfast Room in its Variety." 1920. *Sunset* (February): 64–65.

Cleveland Home Inventory: Seventh. 1939. Cleveland, OH: Cleveland Press.

"Colonial Home is Most Popular: Country-Wide Survey Brings Much Information." 1938. *The Cleveland Plain Dealer* (26 June).

Cooey-Bentz Co. 1924. Advertisement. *The Wheeling Register* (9 March).

Douglas, George H. 1987. *The Early Days of Radio Broadcasting.* Jefferson, NC: McFarland and Company, Inc.

Emmet, Boris, and John E. Jeuck. 1950. *Catalogues and Counters: A History of Sears, Roebuck and Company.* Chicago: The University of Chicago Press.

Fales, Winnifred. 1922. "A Simple Course in Home Decorating." *Good Housekeeping* (July): 43.

Greig, James Ashton. 1921. "Make Yourself a Home!" *The Bucyrus Evening Telegraph* (2 August).

Holloway, Edward Draton. 1920. "Furnishing the Small House." *House Beautiful* 48 (November): 374.

Hoosier Outfitting. 1924. Advertisement. *The Indianapolis Star* (8 June).

Lockwood, Sarah M. 1935. *Decoration: Past, Present, and Future.* Garden City, NY: Doubleday, Doran and Company, Inc.

Lynd, Robert, and Helen Lynd. 1937. *Middletown in Transition: A Study in Cultural Conflicts.* New York: Harcourt, Brace and Company.

Mirken, Alan. 1970. *1927 Edition of the Sears, Roebuck Catalog.* 900–901.

Moore, Elizabeth Conover. 1912. "How to Plan an Ideal Sleeping Porch." *House Beautiful* 31: 173.

National Resources Committee. 1937. *Technological Trends and National Policy: Including the Social Implications of New Inventions.* Washington, D.C.: National Resources Committee.

Nickels, Shelley. 2002. "Preserving Women:' Refrigerator Design as a Social Process in the 1930s," *Technology and Culture* 43 (October): 693–727

Northend, Mary H. 1922. "Assuring Better Breakfasts." *House and Garden* 41: 50.

Palace Furniture Company. 1924. Advertisement. *The Wheeling Register* (9 March).

"The Passing of the Den." 1915. *The Wallpaper News and Interior Decorator* (February): 21.

Phillip and Levy. 1921. Advertisement. *Washington Post* (15 May).

Pleck, Elizabeth H. 2000. *Celebrating Family: Ethnicity, Consumer Culture, and Family Rituals,* Cambridge, MA: Harvard University Press.

Post, Emily. 1930. *The Personality of a House: The Blue Book of Home Design and Decoration.* New York: Funk and Wagnalls.

Pursell, Caroll. 1995. "Variations on Mass Production: The Case of Furniture Manufacture in the United States to 1940." *History of Technology* 17: 131–141.

Riley, Phil M. 1917. "The Sleeping-Porch Problem." *House Beautiful* 41: 136.

Robertson, Cheryl. 1991. "Male and Female Agendas for Domestic Reform: The Middle-Class Bungalow in Gendered Perspective." *Winterthur Portfolio* 26: 123–141.

Robinson, L. Eugene. 1923. *Domestic Architecture.* New York: The McMillan Company.

"Sanitary Flooring." 1910. *The Building Age* 32: 132.

Sears, Roebuck and Company. 1932. *Sears, Roebuck Catalogue.* Chigago: Sears, Roebuck Company.

———. 1933. *Sears, Roebuck Catalogue.* Chigago: Sears, Roebuck Company.

———. 1937. *Sears, Roebuck Catalogue.* Chigago: Sears, Roebuck Company.

"Shop at the Home and Save." 1920. Advertisement. *Columbus Citizen Journal* (2 July).

Stewart, Ross, and John Gerald. 1935. *Home Decoration: Its Problems and Solutions.* New York: Julian Messner, Inc.

"Suggested Treatment of Wall Spaces in Suburban Homes: When Paper is Preferable for Use and When it is Better to Make Use of Tinting." 1912. *Building Age* 34: 413.

Tachau, Hanna. 1921. "A New Room in the House." *Country Life* (November): 63.

Wentworth, Ann. 1911a. "The Living Room: How to Decorate and Furnish It." *House Beautiful* 23: 50.

Wentworth, Ann. 1911b. "The Passing of the Den." *House Beautiful* 29: 127–128.

Whitton, Mary Ormsbee. 1927. *The New Servant: Electricity in the Home.* New York: Doubleday.

Wright, Agnes Foster. 1917. *Interior Decorations for Modern Needs.* New York: Frederick A. Stokes Company.

Landscaping and Outbuildings

During the decades between 1920 and 1945, housing production moved from being controlled by small local builders to being part of a housing delivery system. This system included the construction of large residential subdivision and neighborhoods, down to the individual house sitting on an individual lot. Throughout the building process, the landscape around the house was treated as part of the living area. In the twentieth century, the house required connection to the street and to the surrounding community. For many service functions of the residence, the house also needed the yard.

When the house was completed and the builder gone, the homeowner occupied the house and landscape. Beyond the walls of the building, what the homeowners received was in reality a blank canvas on which to create outdoor spaces of their own. Typically, images of newly constructed homes show no plantings in the yard or around the house. The builder constructed the basic elements that connected the home into a larger landscape of the neighborhood. The house typically had a porch, a sidewalk, a garage, and a driveway. All of the yard elements that softened the house or provided outdoor amenities were up to the resident.

The house itself was connected to the yard. The porch, the basement, and the garage all served functions that connected the house and yard together as working elements. The basement especially served as a service area that included food storage and laundry, elements that in previous centuries may have been relegated to outbuildings. In this sense, the yard served as the conduit between the community and the service areas of the house. This worked in the twentieth-century house because the houses were constructed as part of the community and contained the elements that linked the community and the home.

COMMUNITY BUILDERS

During the 1920s, the development of housing was increasingly controlled by a professionalized real estate industry. Community builders specialized in dividing large tracts of land into individual lots. These specialized businesses designed, engineered, developed, often financed, and then sold housing lots. This real estate activity is known as platting and provides the legal way in which individual house lots are registered with a county auditor (Weiss 1987, 1).

Single-family residential subdivisions, carved from the agrarian landscape, represented the first phase of modern transformation of urban land by private real estate developers. This phase reached maturity during the 1920s. Mark Weiss, in his book *The Rise of the Community Builders,* refers to this as "changes at the high end." During the second phase in the 1940s, "changes at the moderate end," land developers became suburban housing developers (Weiss 1987, 2).

Development companies provided everything. They planned, platted, built, and even sold the final product: the small suburban house. Here, builders like the Levitts built not just thousands of housing units, but schools, churches, and stores as well. Housing like this was an attractive investment for moderate-income families, exactly because each unit was part of a full community with amenities.

An important goal of the community builder was to professionalize the buying and selling of real estate and put controls on the mania of land speculation that had characterized the 1920s. Land speculation fueled some sectors of the market, but by the late 1920s, private debt, taxes, and assessment programs left many unimproved lots heavily encumbered. Both the success of the 1920s housing boom, and the subsequent decline caused builders, planners, architects, and developers to evaluate and rethink the housing development process.

Utopian Plans and Developments

Community developers operated with real world solutions to build, market, and sell housing. The houses that were built followed very closely the types of houses that people had always lived in. Neither the market nor banks encouraged dramatic new housing prototypes. Architects working in the realm of theory and design, however, brought ideas to the development of housing that were truly forward thinking. These ideas were often revolutionary at the time, although in looking at them through a historical lens, they appear prophetic. Famous architects designed ideal development proposals that were almost utopian in vision. On examination, what one finds is that utopia functioned around the life of the automobile and technology.

In 1922, he French modernist architect Le Corbusier published his "Contemporary City" for three million people. Here, 60-story steel and glass skyscrapers dominated the central core of the city. The cruciform-shaped buildings sat in rectangular parks and housed both offices and apartments. Business owners and wealthy citizens lived in the skyscrapers, and the working classes lived further out in smaller multistoried housing blocks. A large transportation depot at the center of the city provided connections to highways, trains, and airplanes. An admirer of Ford's industrial efficiency, Le Corbusier's city worked like a machine, just like the house he envisioned, the machine for living. The automobile served as the primary means of circulation. This may sound much like a city today, but at the time it was revolutionary. Le Corbusier was using what he saw as the developing American model to reorganize society.

Frank Lloyd Wright introduced the Broadacre City in 1932. In this utopian planning scheme, every citizen received a one-acre plot of ground. This was very different than Le Corbusier's dense urban utopia. Wright's vision of the decentralized city was based on an agrarian vision of America, much like Thomas Jefferson's. In Wright's model residential pattern, however, technology connected people together and promoted democratic beliefs. In Broadacre City, every family lived on a separate one-acre building lot in a Usonian house. The 761 houses in each four-mile square "city" were zoned around community institutions, such as churches and schools. Transportation by car dominated the development and ruled the landscape. In addition, individuals were all connected by telecommunications, in this case the telephone.

THE TYPICAL DEVELOPMENT OF A BUILDING LOT

Large housing developments often dominate the typical histories of suburbanization. The platting of near-urban and suburban residential developments followed patterns first demonstrated in the late nineteenth century that have been well documented. This is only the beginning of the story, however. Every individual house has a separate story of development as well. Houses were constructed on every manner of building lot, farmland, rural acreage, and urban infill. Certainly, in the cases of houses such as the Lowell Health House and Fallingwater, the context of the site the owner had purchased prior to hiring an architect had much to do with the ultimate design of the building. With speculative residential construction, such as a housing addition or a residential subdivision, this was not so much the case. The dense fabric of detached residential housing that began to surround American cities in the early twentieth century followed a discernable pattern. By looking at one building lot and its subsequent development, the idea of how land turned into a house and yard during the 1920s can be illustrated.

The Heed and Holton company developed the Broadview Addition in Columbus, Ohio, on 67.5 acres that had been a farm owned by David Binns, who had owned the farm since 1875. Binns died on December 15, 1920, and left the farm to his widow, Medora E. Binns, "absolutely and in fee simple." Heed and Holton did not purchase the land from Medora E Binns, but they developed it for her by hiring an engineer and laying out both streets and building lots on paper. These drawings were then submitted to the county Recorder's office, where they were accepted and recorded as house lots annexed into the City of Columbus and available for sale.

By spring 1923, the value of lot 21 was $140.00. The deed for the property carried restrictions to its sale. Houses on the first block could not cost less than $5,000. All other houses could not cost less than $4,000. Another stipulation was that no outbuilding would be used for habitation prior to completion of a main dwelling.

Other building lots in the development carried further restrictions. These deed covenants forbade the sale of intoxicating liquors, obnoxious business, and no dwelling could cost less than $2,000. A house built on lot 21 could not have less than a "30 ft. Court Yard." This allowed the developer to set a consistent depth off the lot line so that every house sat the same distance from the street. The court yard was the front yard with a lawn. These covenants were attached to the sale of the land and were to be in effect until July 1, 1938.

Medora Binns sold the property known as lot 21 to Charles T. Woodruff on May 31, 1923. This sale was filed and finalized on June 29, 1923. The same day, Charles Woodruff and Evelyn Woodruff received a mortgage on the property from the Columbian Building and Loan Company for $3,250.00. The mortgage was to be repaid in monthly installments of $32.50. This was a construction loan.

Charles Woodruff worked as a carpentry foreman for the E. J. Scarlett Company, a construction company specializing in residential construction. In 1920, he was renting a home in an older Victorian working-class neighborhood, living with his wife and 19-year-old son. By 1923, he was 53, had been promoted to a construction superintendent, and had begun to build his own home in an up-and-coming neighborhood.

The first operation in the construction of the house was the excavation of a "cellar." A specialized contractor performed the excavation. Typically, a large steel scoop pulled by two horses provided the power. In at least one case, this work employed three people, one guiding the horse and two setting the scoop. Each scoop of soil would be removed from the basement and dumped outside of the building area, one scoop about every two or three minutes. Rocks dug up in this process had to broken up by hand. In this way, excavation of the basement took the first week of construction. During this time, the sewage pipes would also be installed. By the end of the second week, the concrete block foundation and the poured concrete floor were completed.

The Woodruff house was constructed with dimensional lumber cut to length with a handsaw. Typically, the framing of a house required two to three competent carpenters who cut all of the framing lumber by hand. Usually the builder employed the carpentry crew directly. In 1924, the average general contractor in Columbus employed 10.6 men. It is unknown if Woodruff employed others or if he did all the work himself.

After the house had been dried in and all of the exterior walls and roof had been completed, the carpenters started installing subfloors while subcontractors installed mechanical and electrical systems. A plumbing subcontractor roughed in water pipes and drains at this time. And the electrical contractor ran wires in the framed walls.

After the completion of the electrical work, a separate plastering subcontractor returned to install wood lath. In the Woodruff house, the plasterer applied two coats of plaster to the lath, a scratch coat, and a finish coat. The plaster required two weeks of dry time, during which time the hardwood floors were installed. Woodruff installed interior oak trim in a style typical of other houses on the street.

Once a house had been completed by a builder, lawns and plantings had to be established. Occasionally the developer completed this work. In this case, however, the use of quick growing plants aided in the marketing of the development but was a detriment to the homeowner. One landscape expert suggested that the "real estate developer" plant specific plants in order to get "immediate effects by planting masses of young specimens of big-growing varieties." These would quickly become over-scaled for the house. "Transplant them as soon as seasonal conditions permit," the expert advised new homebuyers (Carhart 1936, 20).

In developments such as Broadview, the homeowner completed the landscaping on their own. In this case, the lawn was seen as an amenity to adapt and personalize both the house and landscape to the individual homeowner's lifestyle. Plenty of landscape design books and magazines existed to instruct the curious owner how to best accomplish this.

THE YARD: LAWNS AND SIDEWALKS

The yard was an integral part of the idea of the home. Today, we have the conception that the suburban American Dream was a house with a white picket fence. The fence enclosed a lawn, and the lawn was a surface that supported many other functions. These functions often serviced the house or connected the house to the larger community. This connection started with the sidewalk, the lawn, and the foundation plantings that tied the house to the building site.

A lawn in the 1920s and 1930s may sound very familiar to homeowners of a much later time. Chesla Sherlock, in *City and Suburban Gardening*, pointed out to readers in 1928 that good lawns were built, and the process of building them went on all the time. "A lawn, like every other integral part of a good garden, is never finished," she stated (Sherlock 1928, 32). The key to a successful lawn was good topsoil. This could be brought in or developed by spreading humus on top of the yard after construction.

In cases where quick results were desired, sod could be placed on the top soil. In most cases however, new lawns were developed from seed. Homeowners and builders purchased grass seed premixed with a variety of blends to be thrown on the yard. In central and northern climates, the best time to plant seed was in late August or September, and this often coincided with the end of the building season. Grass sown in the spring did not have time to become established before suffering from summer heat. Yearly treatment with ready-mixed fertilizers helped the lawn fully develop. Sherlock recommended yearly overseeding and the occasional addition of compost or humus to the lawn.

Lawns were kept short and smooth by mowing. The typical lawn mower, known as a reel-mower with rotary blades, consisted of two wheels with several blades in between. Pushed around the lawn, the blades spun and cut the grass at a consistent height. Sherlock suggested that keeping the lawn velvety smooth required two to three cuttings per week.

Sidewalks linked houses to community services in many neighborhoods. In near-urban neighborhoods built just outside of the traditional walking city, sidewalks connected residential neighborhoods to grocery stores, restaurants, and streetcars. Toward 1930, neighborhoods developed within driving distance instead of walking distance from many cities and towns. In these neighborhoods developers eliminated sidewalks. Here, curved streets and driveways dominated the front of the house.

Along the street and in front yards, trees played a big role in softening the streetscape. Trees created skylines around houses. As one landscape designer noted, "the 'roof' over our home landscape is the sky." Trees around the house produced a rhythm that framed "the sky vistas" (Carhart 1936, 15).

Plantings for almost all new housing began after the house was built. Today, older neighborhoods are filled with large shade trees. When the houses were new, so were all the trees. The placement of trees was not haphazard. According to advice books and experts, they needed to be carefully planned.

In planning the yard of a small home, scale was of primary importance. One designer noted, "the scale established by the groupings of woody plants in a home landscape almost fixes the scale of the whole composition." Too often the homeowner used quick growing trees to "get an immediate effect." When the homeowner planted these varieties of trees and shrubs, they quickly grew too large to maintain proper scale of the property (Carhart 1936, 19).

Trees planted in the front yard governed the scale of all woody plants throughout the building lot. Homeowners who selected medium and small trees achieved a roomier effect around their house. Medium trees used in the yard included the Wild Crabapple, the Wild Plum, Hawthorns, and Russian-olives. Small trees included the Japanese Maple, White Dogwood, Alder, and Redbud.

When approaching the house from the street, the trees in the front lawn were the first thing seen. A single tree planted in the front yard added "form, mass, and line emphasis" to the house front. A tree planted near the front walk could provide a "pleasing enframement of the front doorway" as someone approached. Small trees planted in this way could make the house appear larger. One expert suggested that the perfect trees for this use were "mountain-ash, the tree-like alders, flowering crab, and where the house is extremely informal in style, the Russian-olive" (Carhart 1936, 29–30).

Street trees were also part of the landscape of the house. There was a tendency to plant trees that were too large for the ordinary residential street. Trees that worked well for the narrow street included "hard maples, ashes, English elms, American linden or basswood, and laurel willow." A big elm gave the effect that many people desired for the residential street. The high overarching head had a "tendency to 'snuggle down' a small house by enframing the view seen under rather than between the heads of the street trees" (Carhart 1936, 29).

Almost unknown by the twenty-first century, the American Elm was ubiquitous throughout neighborhoods in cities both large and small. Millions of the trees were planted along streets and in front yards in developing neighborhoods during the early twentieth century. The trees could grow nearly 100 feet tall and had very nice oval canopies that provided shade. Perfect for an urban environment, the American elm grew quickly, was tolerant of air pollution, and grew in compacted soil. They were also very hardy and could survive the harsh winters of the American North and Northwest.

In 1930, Dutch Elm Disease was introduced to the American Elm through logs shipped from France. The disease is a fungus that keeps water from moving up through tree. Millions of trees have died in the last several decades. St. Paul, Minnesota, provides a typical example. There were over 100,000 elms in St. Paul, most planted at the turn of the century. By 1988, the city had lost 58,000 trees to the disease. Elm trees lined residential streets so heavily that there are over 5,000 Elm Streets across America. Luckily, the elm was not the only shade tree planted in neighborhoods during the 1920s and 1930s. There are also over 6,000 Maple Streets and almost 7,000 Oak Streets.

PORCHES

One of the distinctive architectural characteristics of the house during the 1920s was the front porch. The porch has a long history in domestic architecture. During the early twentieth century, the porch became an extension of the living area of the home. The workable area of the first floor of the average home contained an area of 24 feet by 28 feet with an additional 8 feet of exterior space on the porch. It was in this way that the porch extended the living area of the house.

Much like the hall in Victorian culture, the porch served as a transitional zone between familial and communal life. The porch acted as the catalyst for community involvement. Strolling along the street, residents could see all of their neighbors sitting on their porches. Although the porch was a prominent feature of many residential streets, by the late 1930s, porches had already started to go out of style. Robert and Helen Lynd had found that some residents viewed the porch as old fashioned even by 1925. At least one of the people interviewed by the Lynds in Muncie, Indiana, made reference to the fact that housewives no longer sat on their front porches "visiting" after getting "dressed up" (Lynd and Lynd, 1929, 95).

The Lynds documented how people used the porch for community visitation. One Muncie resident recalled that in the 1890s, her family brought chairs and cushions out into the yard and sat during the evenings. The family also placed a carpet and cushions on the porch steps to "take care of the unlimited overflow of neighbors that dropped by." Younger couples would go off from time to time to get a soda. The family and neighbors sat all evening singing informally or listening to someone play the guitar or mandolin. The woman being interviewed suggested that her neighbors "were all much more together" before the automobile (Lynd and Lynd 1929, 257).

FOUNDATION PLANTINGS

By the turn of the century, foundation plantings began to appear around porches and the sides of houses. Today the idea of "curb appeal" is discussed as a desirable aspect of new homes and subdivisions. Foundation plantings during the 1920s achieved this same aim. Denise Wiles Adams, in her book *Restoring American Gardens* (2004), explains that plantings around the house became a significant part of the transition from nature to structure. Craftsman and Prairie style houses gave new appreciation for outdoor space. These house types used natural materials and integrated the interior and exterior of the house. The design and use of exterior natural materials, gardens, and planting beds followed suit. Foundation plants, and especially vines, worked as a transition between ground and wall. The Colonial style house used rigid and linear systems emphasizing straight lines and a central axis. A combination of perennials, shrubs, and vines seamlessly integrated the house into the yard.

A gardening expert suggested that "architectural, one might say structural plant effects, are more logical than naturalistic groupings or purely horticultural displays on the front lawn." On the newly developed suburban house site, the builder did not leave much else other than "a concrete curb and sidewalk and probably signs of the nature of the 'rough fill' on the lot." Experts suggested that the plantings on the front lawn should be seen as "complimentary to the architecture of the house" (Johnson 1927, xvi). Many specialists wrote directions of how the homeowner could accomplish this.

On the small house, the plantings achieved this architectural aim, but were often simple affairs. "A simple structure looks best accompanied by a simple planting," wrote one author. Described was a small grouping of five plants on either side of the steps leading up to the porch. All of the plants were low growth, with rose bushes anchoring the outer edges (Johnson 1927, 106). Two very effective shrubs used at the foundation were Spirea and Barberry. These plants would be staggered. Here, the plants rose to triangular form on either side of the steps of the porch and were used specifically to create a controlled architectural form.

Evergreens often played this role in the front of the house as well. Again, the experts stated, "the very nature of architectural planting calls for the free use in foundation plantings of evergreen trees and shrubs because of their year-around effect and the endless variety of types, heights and outlines available among them" (Johnson 1927, xvii). *The Seattle Bungalow* by Janet Ore shows several images of bungalows and two-story houses all taken in 1937. Almost every one of the houses has evergreens planted along the foundation either at the sides of the porch or at the corner of the house. Another expert suggested that "evergreens should be restricted to the foundation planting." They were not to be mixed, however, with other flowers or deciduous shrubs. The author warned that a "foundation planting serves a very definite purpose," and the front of the house "should not be made into a flower garden" (Sherlock 1928, 51).

Denise Adams has written, "if we could designate any specific plant type as symbolic of historic American gardening style, it would have to be the vine or climbing shrub" (Adams 2004, 133). One contemporary gardening advocate wrote that vines should be planted immediately after the builder left, independently from the rest of the garden or planting plan. Climbing vines "could transform a cold, bare house into a livable home." Used at corners, chimneys, or porches, Virginia creeper, climbing rose Dorothy Perkins, or sweet autumn clematis could be attached to trellis or grown on string or chicken wire (Johnson 1927, 102).

THE GARAGE AND THE AUTOMOBILE

In housing of the 1920s and 1930s, the one outbuilding that was ubiquitous was the garage. The garage was made for the automobile. The over 17 million automobiles registered in the United States by the mid-1920s required a lot of garages. In 1929, there were 5,337,087 cars produced by American manufacturers. This was a new production record. During the same year, 509,000 houses were constructed. Typically the builder supplied a garage with the house, but, for many new car owners, the purchase of a car also meant the purchase of a garage.

Sanborn insurance maps are maps of cities showing every building and every building lot so that insurance companies could assess the potential for a fire in any particular structure. They are excellent documents to study the history of what was built in urban areas. It is evident when looking at the maps from the 1920s that a staggering number of garages were built in existing neighborhoods. A 1910 map will show a few structures in the alleys of new neighborhoods, but a map of the same neighborhood in the 1920s shows a garage at almost every house.

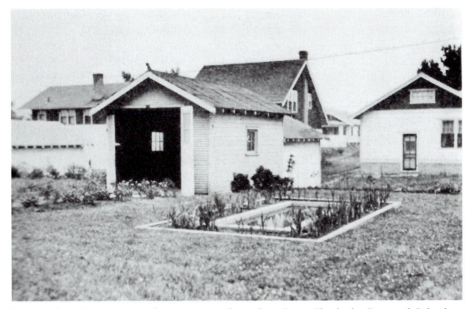

Image showing rear yard, garage, and garden. From Sherlock, City and Suburban Gardening, p. 25.

It was not unusual for a homeowner to use a second mortgage to pay for a new car. In this case, financing tied the automobile directly into the ownership of a house. The desire to own an automobile helped to create the acceptance of a smaller house during the 1920s. The Lynds suggested that by the 1920s, lawns had given way to driveways extending back to garages. By the end of the decade, the author of an architectural textbook recognized that the "lessened desire for a large house" came because the new "sign of distinction [was] a high-priced car" (Allen 1930, 145).

The 1918 catalog of Aladdin Homes offered five garages for sale. Each was named after a specific brand of car, the Buick, Peerless, Winton, Maxwell, and Packard. Aladdin advertised that they had led the market in precut garages for the last 10 years. The Buick, a wood framed and sided garage with no windows, came in two sizes, 8 × 14 feet and 10 × 16 feet. The smaller garage was designed specifically for Ford touring cars, which would fit with the top either up or down. The Wilton was 12 × 20 feet and designed to hold the largest car on the market "with ample room at the sides for working about the car and for supplies" (The Aladdin Company 1918, 113). Many catalog home companies offered garages. The garages offered by the Montgomery Ward Company in 1924 looked almost identical to the garages offered by Aladdin, though the Wardway garages were offered in several sizes within two-foot increments. They were named for cities that manufactured cars: the Flint and the Detroit.

The garage was typically built at the rear of the lot. Access could be directly from the alley, in which case the doors would face the alley. If the garage was accessed from the street, the building tended to sit further up on the lot. The driveway of newer houses usually consisted of two concrete strips spaced as far as the typical wheel base of the car.

The garage served the needs of the automobile. Garages were not just for storage, but they also served as an area in which to work on the car. Often people referred to this as "tinkering." The Lynds, for instance, attribute the decline of gardening in 1925 to "riding and tinkering on the car" (Lynd and Lynd 1929, 95).

For one family, working on the car in their garage was nearly tragic. Edward Eagan lived in the Broadview addition mentioned previously. In 1935, he lived in a two-story frame house with his wife, her father, and their eldest son and his wife. Though unemployed during the height of the Depression, he worked three days a week on the Columbus relief rolls. The young couple, both of whom had steady employment, supported the family. In January, Edward became asphyxiated while working on the family car in the garage at the rear of their property. He would have died except that he was found and rescued by his wife's father, who was also home during the day. Doctors worked on him for an hour before he was revived.

The garage was a service element at the rear of the house, just like the stable before it. The rear corner of the lot was an ideal location for the stable, and often the garage was placed here as well. In many cases, however, the garage was moved up closer to the house and accessed from a drive off the street instead of off of the alley. The garbage receptacle and compost heap could be grouped with the ash pit at the far end of the service walk adjacent to the garage.

The garage required landscape treatments like any other part of the home. Experts suggested that, designed for utility instead of beauty, the garage should receive "shrub and tree plantings that blend with the residence." If screening the garage was desired, this was best accomplished with good-sized flowering shrubs. Tall shrubs of narrow growth worked very well because they did not intrude into the yard. Tall perennials, such as Hollyhocks or Sunflowers, could also be used to provide color. Another possible effect "tending to make the outbuilding less conspicuous" was to plant low growing trees behind the garage so that as they grew they would show foliage above the roof line "softening the view as well as giving an appearance of greater depth to the grounds" (Johnson 1927, 165).

BACKYARDS

Between 1925 and 1935, the Lynds noted four specific changes in the backyard. The development of backyard grills for cookouts and picnics in the 1930s, backyard furniture that made the yard like a living room, revival of vegetable gardens to augment food, and a mania for flower gardens all extended life out from the house and into the yard.

The backyard garden, especially on densely placed small house lots, served multiple purposes. The garden provided a pleasant backdrop for outside leisure activities. Larger plantings also provided screening for the neighboring outbuildings, or the neighbor's outside activities. As is clear from the countless publications, gardening was also seen as a therapeutic activity. The gardens in Muncie were not just beans and tomatoes, but "flowers in startling variety, some of them painstakingly gathered from remote places, and familiarly identified by their scientific names" (Lynd and Lynd 1937, 251).

Expert Chesla Sherlock gave suggestions on how the owner of a newly built home should begin a garden in the yard. Usually, large amounts of clay existed in the soil from the basement excavation. Modern means of removing this soil in the 1920s and 1930s did not exist, and therefore treating the yard was left up the owner. Sherlock explained that preparing areas for future planting was a priority in the yard, because "more failures in gardening are due to a lack of adequate preparation of soil than anything else." She suggested that in newer residential sections the entire first season should be devoted to vegetable gardening. In this way, the soil could be worked over before the "more intricate business of flower gardening is undertaken" (Sherlock 1928, 16–17).

In the rear yard with exceptionally hard basement clay, during the first autumn of occupancy the whole rear yard would be spaded up and left in the biggest chunks possible. In the spring, straw and manure would be spread and forked under. The freezing and thawing of the spaded dirt broke it down, and the humus changed the consistency of the soil. Coal ashes, from the heater, could also be added to the stubborn soils, as well as yearly treatments of compost, made from clippings, grass, and vegetable refuse collected and stored in the yard. Whether this was standard practice for the average homeowner is unclear, but almost everyone buying a new home had to prepare the yard for planting in some way.

A backyard garden planted at a Colonial revival styled house, according to design experts, would include linear elements and balance. Linear elements came in the form of lines and shapes. Balance could be achieved through symmetry, or by creating groupings that were triangular or circular in form. An example of this would be radiating lines in garden planning, such as the spokes of a wheel. In many cases gardens would be designed around a focal point such as a pool or a sundial.

Sherlock described a specific garden on a 50 × 150 foot lot. This lot contained a two-story house with a two-car garage at the rear accessed by a drive from the street. A small vegetable garden at the very rear of the lot had been screened off from the rest of the yard with a lattice fence built by the homeowner. This fence continued around the perimeter of the yard. The garden was laid out in borders all the way around the back yard. Inexpensive perennials filled the beds. Most of them had been grown from seeds. Turf filled the rest of the yard, with a sundial placed directly in the center. A large bed of Iris bordered the driveway. This entire garden layout, including the fence and sundial, cost the homeowner $25.00. The author included the garden as an example of what could be tastefully achieved on a reasonable budget.

The garden was only half of the backyard in the early twentieth century. The other half of the yard was needed as a service area. The service area included a garage, an ash pit, a clothesline, a garbage receptacle, a dog run, a compost heap, and a utility vegetable garden. Many of the service elements in the yard related directly to the technological improvements that came with the twentieth century. Appliances, whether the refrigerator, the washing machine, or the furnace, required servicing with some kind of exterior area.

The coal-fired furnace used to heat the house required both fuel to be brought into the house and waste cinders and ashes to be brought out. Coal was often purchased once a year and delivered to the house. In the yard, arrangements had to be made to transport a pile of coal to the coal chute where it could be loaded into the basement through a chute placed on the side of the house. Very often this chute was placed under the front porch, where the coal storage room was located. A house with a driveway off of the street was positioned to easily access the

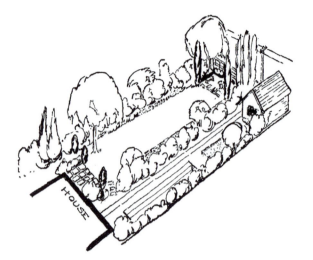

Carhart drawing of rear yard. This image shows the proposed layout of how the typical rear yard of the 1920s small house should look, pleasure garden on the left, clothesline and garage on the right. Carhart, Arthur H. 1935. *How to Plan the Home Landscape.* New York: Doubleday, Doran and Company, Inc.

coal chute. If the garage was accessed from the alley, then the route became somewhat more difficult. The alternative was to install a service walk through the backyard. One expert suggested that wooden planks could be laid over the yard "if the service walk does not reach all the way to the coal hole" (Carhart 1936, 49).

The ash pit was usually at the very back of the yard. This was a hole dug to collect the ashes that had to be removed from the coal furnace. Here, someone from the house, usually one of the children, would have the chore of cleaning out the ashes from inside the furnace and running them out to the ash pit to be buried. This was a ubiquitous service element of every house with a coal furnace. In St. Louis, in a neighborhood known as Dogtown, the Vezeau family lived in a small house with two parents and nine children. One of the sons, John, recorded this very typical situation in the family history: "We had to feed the furnace from the coal bin with irregular chunks of raw coal and later carry out the ashes to the ash pit by the back fence. It was always dirty and inconvenient. Then, we converted to oil heat. The best thing: no more ashes to carry out in the cold of winter" (Vezeau 2006).

The clothesline was also an essential part of the backyard service area. After the wide acceptance of the electric washing machine, laundry became somewhat easier, but clothes still had to be hung to dry in the sun. This occurred all year. Clotheslines needed to be located near a service entrance, in many houses one located with direct access to the basement, where laundry was completed. Though washing was generally completed only once a week, the clotheslines could be used for rinsing, airing, and dusting. Many times, therefore, the lines were hung on metal poles set in the ground along one side of the rear service walk. John Vezeau again recollected that "All year round, people throughout the neighborhood hung their wash out to dry in the sunlight . . . Our back yard always had a sea of diapers flapping in the wind" (Vezeau 2006).

LAUNDRY WORK AND THE HOME

The first labor-saving electrical devices to be accepted and used in the home helped housewives with laundry. Laundry was the most tedious and dangerous work activity in the home and the first to be alleviated by electrification. Susan Strasser, in her book *Never Done,* offers one of the best discussions of the history of domestic laundry work. The process of doing laundry, a task usually completed by a servant in the nineteenth century, changed in the twentieth century owing to technological innovations. But, throughout the twentieth century, laundry still required the backyard as an integral workspace.

New technology solved problems within existing established patterns of work. The electric flatiron relieved the person doing laundry from having to use a cast-iron clothes iron. For several decades, the cast-iron clothes irons had been heated over the stove and used to press fabrics. Most homes utilized several irons of different shapes and sizes for different fabrics. Ironing with these items was hard and dangerous.

Though it seems like a simple device, the hand-held electric iron revolutionized the most difficult aspect of the homemaker's week. Most households could afford the appliance, and large numbers of consumers soon viewed an iron as indispensable. In giving advice on the selection of "electrical equipment" for the home, one domestic housing expert suggested that the homemaker "buy an electric flatiron first." This, he stated, was not just his advice but was "the verdict of the entire country." In Muncie, Indiana, for instance, nearly 90 percent of the homes had electric irons by 1923 (Whitehorne 1918, 372; Lynd and Lynd 1929, 172).

Likewise, the electric washing machine became a standard "labor saving device" in the small house. In an article aimed at a "bride" checking off her "laundry bill," the author argued that the new bride should "persuade her husband to invest in an electrical washing machine." Because of the savings associated with the decreased stress on fabrics washed in a machine, the young couple "sensibly regarded the electrical laundry equipment in their new home as a necessity, rather than a luxury." Although the article was depicting a fictitious couple, the message was one understood by many couples buying new houses—the new house brought new technology to the laundry area (Hollis 1920, 70).

In the middle-class home, the washing machine became one of the most common appliances. In Cleveland, an electric washing machine was the second most purchased electrical device after the radio, and the electric iron was third. Technological systems made home laundry an irresistible option for most residents. Water and sewer systems, electrification of the home, and cheap washing machines all worked together to allow the processes of commercial laundries to be packaged in sizes that could be fitted into the home.

New washing machines may have appeared to bring economic savings, but they did not necessarily save on the labor necessary to do laundry. In fact, the first electric machines still required hand labor to operate. Some electrical advocates suggested that new appliances reduced the typical Monday work to an hour-a-week wash day. Historian Ruth Swartz Cowan suggests, however, that electrical appliances did not lessen the amount of work but actually lengthened the workday in the home. In part, the increased amount of time devoted to housework resulted from the rising expectations of middle-class women. During the same time that labor-saving devices entered the home, women began to prepare more meals, sweep more carpets, maintain larger wardrobes, do more laundry, and spend more time with children. The electric washing machine, however, replaced the grueling regiment of the traditional Monday washday and the physically demanding use of the washboard (Cowan 1983, 199). Susan Strasser argues that because of the washing machine, middle-class women did laundry in the "isolated privacy of their own homes" and lost the community interaction of the hydrant and clothesline (Strasser 1982, 121–122).

THE ELECTRIC WASHING MACHINE AND THE BASEMENT

The electric washing machine consisted of a steel tub with a motor attached to the bottom and a wringer with a pair of wooden or rubber rollers attached to the top. The machine did not fill or run automatically. The operator filled the tub with heated water from a hose or bucket. Soap flakes were then added and mixed. Clothes and linens placed in the tub were washed by the agitation of the motor. The operator then manually lifted each article and ran it through the ringer and into rinse water in the tub where the clothes were moved around the water with a stick. Clothes, once rinsed, were fed back through the wringer and collected into a basket to be taken outdoors to the clothesline.

Contractors built homes with planned space for the new machines in the basement. Plumbers placed water lines and a soapstone double sink along an exterior wall. The washing machine was placed next to this sink where it could be easily filled with water and where clothes could be rinsed. Plumbing for the machine also required coordination with the electrical system. In many small houses, the laundry area was in proximity to the stairs. Often, an exterior door allowed easy ground level access to the rear yard and laundry lines.

THE YARD AND MIDDLETOWN

Robert and Helen Lynd, in their books on Middletown, offer an excellent example of the transformations of the yard in their 1925 study of Muncie, Indiana, and their follow up comparison in 1935. They noted that the average lot size in the 1880s was 62.5 feet wide by 125 feet deep. But the standard building lot in 1925 was 40 feet in width. Decreasing the size of the lot allowed the density of houses to increase. In Muncie, the typical block of houses contained 12 to 14 houses in 1925, whereas the nineteenth-century block of houses contained just 8.

The decline in the size of yards, according to the Lynds, resulted in less room for children, leisure activities, family privacy, and pride in the appearance of one's yard. They attributed part of these issues to the automobile. The driveway and garage took up room on the lot, especially if the driveway came through the front yard off of the street. The family spent less time in the yard since "the advent of the automobile and the movies" (Lynd and Lynd 1929, 95).

Changes in foodways also affected the yard. Again the Lynds noted that fewer back yards had the fruit trees and grape arbors of previous generations. The housewife no longer sat in the yard peeling potatoes for dinner or cutting up fruit for canning. The backyard vegetable garden also began to decline. Advances in food storage and shipping made the canning and putting up of food not nearly as important as it had been before. By the first decades of the twentieth century, many fruits and vegetables could be purchased at the grocery store more cheaply and easily than the process of home canning.

The Lynds attributed many of the changes in the yard to the design of the small house and bungalow. The lack of storage space and a "modern basement" in the house meant less room to store foods during the winter. Because of this, and the availability of local groceries, people began to "substitute the corner grocery for the family storage of food in quantities in the cellar and attic." Where in the past people had bought "potatoes and apples by the barrel," the new tendency became to "purchase potatoes by the peck and fruit by the dozen or by the pound" (Lynd and Lynd 1929, 97).

Returning in 1935, the Lynds understood the yard to have undergone a transformation. In 1925, planned parties and outings in the car had replaced the old habits of "dropping in." The Depression had then brought a new set of circumstances. While cutting expenses on clothes and the car, more business-class families spent less on leisure activities as well. Dinner parties became less formal. Instead of sit down meals, food was served buffet style and BBQ grills began to appear in the back yard. Screened in porches became the "rendezvous for many social gatherings," and many families set "their tables under shade trees on their lawns or near their pools and flower gardens" (Lynd and Lynd 1937, 250).

BARBECUE AND THE BACKYARD

Grilling may have its tradition in the pork barbecue of the nineteenth century, but it was during the 1930s that it became a backyard institution. When the first Europeans arrived in the New World the native peoples already were smoking meat over charcoal fires as a way of preserving food. They called this "barbarcoa." In Spanish, the word still refers to a slow-cooked beef. The word barbecue is a logical colonial American derivative of the native practice.

In the eighteenth and nineteenth centuries, the roasting of a whole hog became a staple of southern social gatherings. The barbecue was very often a community activity reserved for special occasions. This tradition was very strong throughout the twentieth century, moving into southern barbecue restaurants serving pulled pork.

The first backyard grills were large masonry structures with brazier-type metal grill tops. In the 1930s, these types of grills were constructed in many state and national parks around the country. Automobile day trips to these locations resulted in a family outing where picnicking and grilling were part of the activity.

The new automobile, responsible for many changes in leisure, was also responsible for the development of charcoal briquettes. The production of the Model-T Ford resulted in a great deal of scrap wood. Utilizing a new patented charcoal-making process, by 1921, Henry Ford had constructed a charcoal plant to process scrap wood. The wood scraps were baked in a vacuum, ground into a fine powder, and then compressed into pillow-shaped briquettes. E. G. Kingsford, a distant relative of Ford, ran the plant. The charcoal was originally marketed for light commercial uses such as foundries. The growing trend of backyard barbecuing and grilling throughout the 1930s and 1940s resulted in a marketing shift. In 1950, Kingsford took over controlling interest in the plant, which was renamed the Kingsford Charcoal Company.

Also noticing the trend toward backyard grilling was a Chicago suburbanite named George Stephen. A metalworker for the Weber Bros. Metal Spinning Co., a company that made spun-metal harbor buoys, Stephen experimented and modified the metal buoy bodies into a workable grill. He cut the large metal balls in half, added a grate, cut vents into the top to act as a temperature-controlled lid, and placed the cooker on a three-legged stand. In 1952, Stephen inherited a controlling interest in the company, and the Weber grill was born.

The magazine *Better Homes and Gardens* was established by the Meredith Company in 1924. The company was founded in 1902 with the introduction of a magazine titled *Successful Farming.* The founder, Edwin Moses, was appointed Secretary of Agriculture under Wilson in 1920 and 1921. In 1922 the title changed to *Fruit, Garden, and Home,* and in keeping with the times, this was changed to *Better Homes and Gardens* in 1924.

The large metal grill was portable, could hold a whole pork shoulder, and could smoke, grill, and barbecue. The movement toward backyard social entertaining, owing directly to the economic downturn of the Depression, resulted in backyard grilling as we know it today.

REAR RESIDENCE

The phenomenon of owner building has a rich history in the housing markets of North America. The architectural historian Richard Harris has suggested that the owner–builder is an often-overlooked component of suburban housing development. He states that as late as 1945, 69 percent of all builders constructing housing were possibly owner–builders, people constructing their own homes (Harris 1997). Historians looking at the owner–builder phenomenon, such as Harris and Oliver Zunz (1982), often place this construction in areas outside of controlled metropolitan developments where the working class and immigrants were building their own communities.

It was not uncommon for an owner–builder to construct a small temporary dwelling at the rear of the building lot to live while building a larger house. Sometimes this house became a garage; sometimes this house became a small rental unit. One example of this type of residential structure comes from the story of a printer who built his own home. This printer earned $100 a month and had steady employment. He bought a $450 lot in order to build a large house for himself and his family. After acquiring the building lot, he constructed a small two-room house at the back of the lot, paying for the lumber and labor using money he had been paying for rent. A couple of years later, he financed an addition on this house through a savings and loan. After completing a comfortable place to stay, he paid the first mortgage off and then financed a construction loan through a savings and loan company to build a 10-room house at the front of the lot. Sixteen years after building his first home, he moved into a large "attractive bungalow," which he then sold two years later for $7,500. "Considerable work on both places was done by himself on his own time" (Creviston 1925, 5–6).

A chapter by Harris in *Exploring Everyday Landscapes: Perspectives in Vernacular Architecture, VII* documents the practice of building garages as temporary residences in Flint, Michigan (1997, 259, 262). A Canadian advertisement for a residential development showed that one could build a small house on a lot in order to live while building a bigger house. This was stated in the copy of the ad: "build a little place until you are able (with saved rent money) to enlarge it. If you can't build, put up a tent for the summer. What you save in rent builds you a little home in the fall" (Harris 1997; Patterson 1989, 126).

Reference List

Adams, Denise Wiles. 2004. *Restoring American Gardens: An Encyclopedia of Heirloom Ornamental Plants, 1640–1940.* Portland: Timber Press.

The Aladdin Company. 1918. *Aladdin Homes.* Bay City, MI: The Aladdin Company.

Allen, Edith. 1930. *American Housing: As Affected by Social and Economic Conditions.* Peoria, IL: The Manual Arts Press.

Carhart, Arthur H. 1936. *Trees and Shrubs: For the Small Place.* New York: Doubleday, Doran and Company, Inc.

Cowan, Ruth Schwartz. 1983. *More Work for Mother: The Ironies of Household Technology from the Open Hearth to the Microwave.* New York: Basic Books.

Creviston, Harry J. 1925. "First Steps in Owning Your Own Home." *Better Homes and Gardens.* (November): 5–6.

Harris, Richard. 1997. "Reading Sanborns for the Spoor of the Owner-Builder, 1890–1950." In *Exploring Everyday Landscapes: Perspectives in Vernacular Architecture, VII,* ed. Annmarie Adams and Sally McMurry, 251–267. Knoxville: University of Tennessee Press.

Hollis, Elaine. 1920. "Electrifying the Home," *Sunset* 45, (October) 70, 72.

Johnson, Leonard. 1927. *Foundation Planting.* New York: A.T. Delmare Company, Inc.

Lynd, Robert, and Helen Merrell Lynd. 1937. *Middletown in Transition: A Study in Cultural Conflicts.* New York: Harcourt, Brace and Company.

———. 1929. *Middletown: A Study in Modern American Culture.* New York: Harcourt, Brace and World, Inc.

Ore, Janet. 2007. *The Seattle Bungalow: People and Houses, 1900–1940.* Seattle: University of Washington Press.

Patterson, Ross. 1989. "Creating the Packaged Suburb." In *Suburbia Re-examined,* ed. Barbara M. Kelly, 123–127. Westport, CT: Greenwood Press.

Sherlock, Chesla C. 1928. *City and Suburban Gardening.* New York: A.T. De La Mare Company.

Strasser, Susan. 1982. *Never Done: The History of American Housework.* New York: Henry Holt and Company.

Vezeau, John. 2006. *Vezeau Family—Waldo, Rosalie and children, 6464 Lloyd Avenue, February 23.* Available at: http://www.webster.edu/~corbetre/dogtown/people/vezeau-waldo.html. Accessed June 1, 2007.

Weiss, Marc. 1987. *The Rise of the Community Builders: the American Real Estate Industry and Urban Land Planning.* New York: Columbia University Press.

Whitehorne, Earl E. 1918. "Electricity in the Home: Which Shall We Buy First?" *House Beautiful* 43: 372.

Zunz, Oliver. 1982. *The Changing Face of Inequality: Urbanization, Industrial Development, and Immigrants in Detroit, 1880–1920.* Chicago: University of Chicago Press.

Glossary

Adamesque: Interior designs related to the work of Robert Adams, an English architect working in the Neoclassical style in the late sixteenth century. Characteristics are swags, garlands, vines, medallions, scrolls, and ribbons in vibrant colors placed within interior spaces of classical proportions. Delicately proportioned furniture in the style of Hepplewhite, Chippendale, or Thomas Sheraton decorated the rooms. In the twentieth century, the style referred to the use of designed neoclassical–revival homes.

American foursquare: A two-and-one-half-story house structured on simplicity. Developed at the turn of the century to oppose ornate Victorian housing. Layout often featured four rooms per floor.

art deco: A style of decorative art and architecture that was widely popular in Europe and the United States during the 1920s and 1930s. Characteristics include simple, clean shapes, with a "streamlined" look. Art deco ornament was often geometric or stylized from representational forms. Materials included man-made substances such as plastics, bakelite, vita-glass, and ferroconcrete. The style was influenced by art nouveau, Bauhaus, and cubism. French in origin, art deco has become a blanket term for a wide variety of works produced between the two world wars.

art moderne: Streamlined industrial design for ships, airplanes, and automobiles inspired the art moderne style. The style was sleek and plain and characterized by smooth surfaces, curved corners, and horizontal orientation.

art nouveau: A style focused on flowing ornament. Practitioners found beauty in natural, often organic, objects. Stylized design elements could be based on such objects as peacock feathers, poppies, thistles, and dragonflies.

avant-garde: Art or architecture that pushes the known boundaries of popularly acceptable design. The art and artist was imbued with revolutionary, cultural, or political implications. In the 1930s it was an accepted fact that there was an avant-garde community.

Bauhaus: A German school of art and architecture that operated from 1919 to 1933. The modernist approach to design that was taught at the school had a profound influence on Modern architecture in Europe and the United States.

Bolshevism: A socialist movement, advocating the violent overthrow of capitalism. The Bolshevist party was led by Lenin and eventually overtook the government and formed the USSR during the October revolution of 1917.

British Admiralty Board: A defunct department responsible for overseeing the Royal Navy. The position was founded in the fifteenth century.

Brussels carpet: A level loop carpet where the wool not exposed as pile is woven through a heavy jute backing.

Byzantine: The eastern Roman Empire. Constantine moved the capital of Rome from Italy to Constantinople in 330. Eastern Orthodox Christianity reached its golden age during the Empire's stay. The Ottoman Turks finally overthrew the country in 1452. As an architectural style, combines classical, Romanesque, and Middle Eastern influences.

cabriole: A furniture leg that curves outward and then narrows downward into an ornamental foot. The leg is typical of Queen Anne and Chippendale furniture.

chiffonier: A small clothes cabinet with doors. Very similar to a small armoire.

chiffonrobe: A clothes cabinet with a combination of drawers and a wardrobe for hanging clothes. Many times the cabinet also had a mirror.

Department of Commerce: A Cabinet department in the U.S. federal government established in 1903. The center of the federal government's programs to promote the economy and encourage business, often through the encouragement of technological advances.

De Stijl: The Dutch word for "style." De Stijl was more of a movement than a style, but practitioners held a philosophical approach to aesthetics based on functionalism. Characteristics included flat, rectangular areas and only straight, horizontal, and vertical lines with components of the primary colors. The movement heavily influenced the development of modernism in architecture.

dormer: Windows added to the half-floor above the main house to utilize space.

English Hall House: Vernacular housing in England built in 1200–1800. The two-room dwelling was a yeoman's imitation of a manor house. The house contained a hall and a parlor. The hall was a utilitarian room containing all of the necessary functions of the house. The parlor was the "best room" but was also used as a bedroom.

Federal Housing Administration (FHA): Government agency established by the Housing Act of 1934 to administer federal housing policy.

Ford Motor Company: Incorporated in 1903 by Henry Ford. Notable for the industrial assembly line. Introduced the Model T in 1908. Introduced the Model A in 1928.

galena: Mineral derived from lead ore. The mineral is a superconductor, making it perfect for early radios.

Great Migration: Large populations of African Americans moved north after the Emancipation Proclamation due to racial tensions and job opportunities. A large surge occurred due to World War I when a lack of immigration from Europe opened northern factory jobs.

Gustav Klimt: 1862–1918. Known for his powerful portraits of women. Many of his most famous paintings feature gold paint. His painting "Portrait of Adele Bloch-Bauer I" was sold in 2006 for $135 million.

ingrain carpet or Kidderminster carpets: A reversible woven carpet popular from the eighteenth century to the mid-twentieth century. The woven pattern is shown on each side in opposing colors.

magneto: Self-contained source of electricity for early phones. Often used as an igniter in small engines. The use of a magneto was phased out of cars with the advent of higher voltage batteries.

modernism: An early twentieth-century philosophy stating that new inventions and discoveries had rendered earlier methods obsolete. Term applies to many facets of human growth including art, architecture, and politics. Design during this period was based around mechanic, scientific, and sanitary developments.

New International Style: One architectural arm of modernism popular in the 1920s and 1930s. The architect's goal was to create simplicity through the removal of architectural ornamentation. International Style was mimicked in skyscraper construction throughout the latter twentieth century.

Progressivism: Ideology based on the belief that society, culture, and the majority of the world was constantly improving. Political progressivism allowed for numerous national changes, such as woman's suffrage, laissez-faire economy, National parks, and prohibition. Multiple presidents ran on progressive platforms. Progressivism died out during World War I.

Queen Anne: Eclectic Victorian style in the United States and England in the 1870s and 1880s. Houses generally characterized by asymmetrical facades, emphasis on the vertical, round corner towers, brackets, and gingerbread trim. Furniture was a blend of older styles but was characterized by the use of the cabriole leg similar to the Chippendale style. In the 1920s, Queen Anne styled furniture referred to pieces that were designed to resemble early Victorian styles.

quoin: A decorative stone element forming the external corner of a wall, often a different color or texture than the rest of the building.

Ribbon window: Strips of horizontal windows that ran along an entire facade of a building. The steel construction of modernist buildings made the windows possible because the exterior wall was not structural.

sewer gasses: Gasses released from open interior plumbing. First generation indoor plumbing owners were worried that the smells were dangerous, so piping was left exposed to give homeowners quick access to any problems.

tabouret: A low stand or stool without a back or arms.

vernacular: Houses and other buildings built for functional use with the materials, methods, and forms common to a particular location without reference to a stylistic design.

Victorian culture: A culture based on the mixture of modern developments and dogmatic societal practices. A highly conservative society allowed for sheltered sexuality and the desire to spread Christendom as the dominant moral virtue. Domestic design was based around lavish and ornate architecture and collections.

vitreous ceramics: Glassy ceramic with extremely low permeability, making it perfect for modern sinks and toilets.

Wilton carpet: A carpet with the same structure as Brussels but the pile was cut and sheared, producing a velvet-like quality. Wilton was roughly double the cost of Brussels.

Resource Guide

PRINTED SOURCES

Adams, Denise Wiles. 2004. *Restoring American Gardens: An Encyclopedia of Heirloom Ornamental Plants, 1640–1940.* Portland: Timber Press.

Allen, Frederick Lewis. 1931. *Only Yesterday.* New York: Bantam Books.

Atkinson, Ronald. 1965. *The People of New England.* Boston: Hutchinson.

Baily, Beth. 1988. *From Front Porch to Back Seat: Courtship in Twentieth Century America.* Baltimore: John Hopkins University Press.

Banham, Reyner. 1980. *Theory and Design in the First Machine Age.* Cambridge: MIT Press.

Baritz, Loren. 1989. *The Good Life: The Meaning of Success for the American Middle Class.* New York: Alfred A. Knopf.

Bauman, John F., Roger Biles, and Kristin M. Szylvian, eds. 2000. *From Tenements to Taylor Homes: In Search of an Urban Housing Policy in Twentieth-Century America.* University Park: Pennsylvania State University Press.

Baxandall, Rosalyn, and Elizabeth Ewen. 2000. *Picture Windows: How the Suburbs Happened.* New York: Basic Books.

Beck, Marjorie. 1999. "Food in the Hudson Valley." *Food USA* 24: 9–30.

Bennett, Michael. 1996. *When Dreams Came True: The GI Bill and the Making of Modern America.* Washington: Brassey's.

Berger, Michael. 2001. *The Automobile in American History and Culture: A Reference Guide.* Westport, CT: Greenwood Press.

Note: This is the resource guide for Part II of the volume (1901–1945). For the resource guide to Part I (1901–1920), see page 161.

Beuka, Robert. 2004. *SuburbiaNation: Reading Suburban Landscape in Twentieth Century American Fiction and Film.* New York: Palgrave Macmillan.

Biggot, Joseph C. 2001. *From Cottage to Bungalow: Houses and the Working Class in Metropolitan Chicago, 1869–1929.* Chicago: University of Chicago Press.

Bix, Amy Sue. 2002. "Equipped for Life: Gendered Technical Training and Consumerism in Home Economics, 1920–1980." *Technology and Culture* 43: 728–254.

Bledstein, Burton J., and Robert D. Johnston, eds. 2001. *The Middling Sorts: Explorations in the History of the American Middle Class.* New York: Routledge.

Brady, John Edson. 1934. *National Housing Act of 1934; Amendments to the Federal Home Loan Bank Act of 1932 and the Home Owners' Loan Act of 1933.* Cambridge, MA: The Banking Law Journal.

Burgess, Patricia. 1988. "Deed Restrictions and Subdivision Development in Columbus, Ohio 1900–1970." *Journal of Urban History* 15: 42–68.

Calder, Lendol. 1999. *Financing the American Dream: A Cultural History of Consumer Credit.* Princeton: Princeton University Press.

Carrol, Michael Thomas. 2000. *Popular Modernity in America: Experience, Technology, Mythohistory.* New York: State University of New York Press.

Clark, Clifford Edward, Jr. 1986. *The American Family Home: 1800–1960.* Chapel Hill: University of North Carolina Press.

Clark, S. D. 1966. *The Suburban Society.* Toronto: University of Toronto Press.

Clements, Kendrick A. 2000. *Hoover, Conservation, and Consumerism: Engineering the Good Life.* Lawrence: University Press of Kansas.

Cooper, Gail. 1998. *Air-Conditioning America: Engineers and the Controlled Environment, 1900–1960.* Baltimore: John Hopkins University Press.

Cowan, Ruth Schwartz. 1983. *More Work for Mother: The Ironies of Household Technology from the Open Hearth to the Microwave.* New York: Basic Books.

Curtis, William J. R. 1986. *Le Corbusier: Ideas and Forms.* New York: Rizzoli International Publications.

Davis, Clark. 2000. *Company Men: White Collar Life and Corporate Cultures in Los Angeles, 1892–1941.* Baltimore: John Hopkins University Press.

Doucet, Michael, and John Weaver. 1991. *Housing the North American City.* Montreal: McGill-Queen's University Press.

Douglas, George H. 1987. *The Early Days of Radio Broadcasting.* Jefferson, NC: McFarland and Company.

Douglas, Harlan Paul. 1925. *The Suburban Trend.* New York: Century Co.

Douglas, Susan. 1987. *Inventing American Broadcasting.* Baltimore: John Hopkins University Press.

Duany, Andres, Elizabeth Plater-Zyberk, and Jeff Speck. 2000. *Suburban Nation: The Rise of Sprawl and the Decline of the American Dream.* New York: North Point Press.

Dunn-Haley, Karen. 1995. "The House that Uncle Sam Built: The Political Culture of Federal Housing Policy, 1919–1932." PhD dissertation, Stanford University.

Eccles, Marriner S. 1951. *Beckoning Frontiers: Public and Personal Recollections.* New York: Alfred A. Knopf.

Eichler, Ned. 1982. *The Merchant Builders.* Cambridge, MA: MIT Press.

Emmet, Boris, and John E. Jeuck. 1950. *Catalogues and Counters: A History of Sears, Roebuck and Company.* Chicago: The University of Chicago Press.

Ewen, Stuart. 1988. *All Consuming Images: The Politics of Style in Contemporary Culture.* New York: Basic Books.

Fish, Gertrude Sipperly. 1979. *The Story of Housing.* New York: Macmillan Publishing Co.

Fishman, Robert. 1987. *Bourgeois Utopias: The Rise and Fall of Suburbia.* New York: Basic Books.

Foner, Eric. 1990. *The New American History.* Philadelphia: Temple University Press.

Foster, Mark. 1981. *From Streetcar to Superhighway: American City Planners and Urban Transportation, 1900–1940.* Philadelphia: Temple University Press.

Fox, Richard, and T. J. Jackson Lears, eds. 1983. *The Culture of Consumption.* New York: Pantheon Books.

Glickman, Lawence B., ed. 1999. *Consumer Society in American History: A Reader.* Ithaca, NY: Cornell University Press.

Goldstein, Carolyn. 1997. "From Service to Sales: Home Economics in Light and Power, 1920–1940." *Technology and Culture* 38: 121–152.

Gordon, Jean, and Jan McArthur. 1989. "Popular Culture, Magazines and American Domestic Interiors, 1898–1940." *Journal of Popular Culture* 22: 35–60.

Gordon-Van Tine Co. 1992 [1923]. *117 House Designs of the Twenties.* New York: Dover Publications and The Athenaeum of Philadelphia (republished plan book).

Gotham, Kevin Fox. 2000. "Urban Space, Restrictive Covenants, and the Origin of Racial Residential Segregation in a U.S. City, 1900–1950." *International Journal of Urban and Regional Research* 24: 616–633.

Gowans, Alan. 1986. *The Comfortable House: North American Suburban Architecture, 1890–1930.* Cambridge, MA: MIT Press.

Grier, Katherine C. 1988. *Culture and Comfort: Parlor Making and Middle-Class Identity, 1850–1930.* Washington, D.C.: Smithsonian Institution Press.

Gries, John, and James S. Taylor. 1925. *How to Own Your Own Home: A Handbook for Prospective Owners.* Washington, D.C.: Government Printing Office.

Harris, Richard. 1991. "Self-Building in the Urban Housing Market." *Economic Geography* 67: 1–21.

Harris, Richard, and Michael Buzzelli. 2005. "House Building in the Machine Age, 1920–1970s: Realities and Perceptions of Modernization in North America and Australia." *Business History* 47.

Harris, Richard, and P. Larkham, eds. 1999. *Changing Suburbs: Foundation, Form, and Function.* New York: Routledge.

Hayden, Dolores. 1984. *Redesigning the American Dream: The Future of Housing, Work, and Family Life.* New York: W. W. Norton.

Hayden, Dolores. 2003. *Building Suburbia: Greenfields and Suburban Growth, 1820–2000.* New York: Vintage Books.

Hines, Thomas S. 2005. *Richard Neutra: and the Search for Modern Architecture.* New York: Rizzoli.

Hise, Greg. 1993. "Home Building and Industrial Decentralization in Los Angeles: The Roots of the Postwar Urban Region." *Journal of Urban History* 19: 95–125.

Hise, Greg. 1997. *Magnetic Los Angeles: Planning the Twentieth-Century Metropolis.* Baltimore: John Hopkins University Press.

Hoffman, Steven J. 1992. " 'A Plan of Quality': The Development of Mt. Lebanon, a 1920s Automobile Suburb." *Journal of Urban History* 18: 141–181.

Hollis, Elaine. 1920. "Electrifying the Home." *Sunset* 45: 70,72.

Hopkins, Harry. 1936. *Spending to Save: The Complete Story of Relief.* New York: W. W. Norton.

Horowitz, Roger, and Arwen Mohun, eds. 1998. *His and Hers: Gender, Consumption, and Technology.* Charlottesville: University Press of Virginia.

Hovinen, Gary R. 1985. "Suburbanization in Greater Philadelphia 1880–1941." *Journal of Historical Geography* 11: 174–195.

Hughes, Thomas P. 1983. *Networks of Power: Electrification in Western Society, 1880–1930.* Baltimore: John Hopkins University Press.

Hutchison, Janet. 1997. "Building for Babbitt: The State and the Suburban Home Ideal." *Journal of Policy History* 9: 184–210.

Ierley, Merritt. 1999. *The Comforts of Home: The American House and the Evolution of Modern Convenience.* New York: Clarkson Potter Publishers.

Jackson, Kenneth. 1985. *Crabgrass Frontier: The Suburbanization of the United States.* New York: Oxford University Press.

Jacobs, Jane. 1961. *The Death and Life of Great American Cities.* New York: Random House.

Jandl, H. Ward, John A. Burns, and Michael J. Auer. 1991. *Yesterday's Houses of Tomorrow: Innovative American Homes 1850–1950.* Washington, D.C.: The Preservation Press.

Jennings, Jan, ed. 1990. *Roadside America: The Automobile in Design and Culture.* Ames: Iowa State University for the Society for Commercial Archeology.

Keating, Ann Durkin. 1988. *Building Chicago: Suburban Developers and the Creation of a Divided Metropolis.* Columbus: Ohio State University Press.

Keith, Nathaniel S. 1973. *Politics and the Housing Crisis Since 1930.* New York: Universe Books.

Keller-Harris, Alice. 1980. *Out to Work: A History of Wage Earning Women in the United States.* New York: Oxford University Press.

Kimball, Fiske. 1922. *Domestic Architecture of the American Colonies and of the Early Republic.* New York: Scribner's Sons.

Kline, Ronald. 2000. *Consumers in the Country: Technology and Social Change in Rural America.* Baltimore: John Hopkins University Press.

Kline, Ronald, and Trevor Pinch. 1996. "Users and Agents of Technological Change: The Social Construction of the Automobile in the Rural United States." *Technology and Culture* 37: 763–795.

Krabbendam, Hans. 2001. *The Model Man: A Life of Edward William Bok, 1863–1930.* Amsterdam: Rodopi.

Kruse, Kevin, and Thomas Sugrue. 2006. *The New Suburban History.* Chicago: University of Chicago Press.

Leicester, A. 1921. "Furnishing a Little House for the Cost of a Little Car." *House Beautiful* 50: 268–269.

Leuchtenburg, William E. 1963. *Franklin D. Roosevelt and the New Deal, 1932–1940.* New York: Harper & Row.

Lewis, David L., and Laurence Goldstein, eds. 1983. *The Automobile and American Culture.* Ann Arbor: University of Michigan Press.

Loeb, Carolyn S. 2001. *Entrepreneurial Vernacular: Developers' Subdivisions in the 1920s.* Baltimore: The John Hopkins University Press.

Longstreth, Richard. 1986. "J.C. Nichols, The Country Club Plaza, and Notions of Modernity." *Harvard Architectural Review* 5: 120–135.

Lynd, Robert, and Helen Merrell Lynd. 1929. *Middletown: A Study in Modern American Culture.* New York: Harcourt, Brace and World, Inc.

Lynd, Robert, and Helen Merrell Lynd. 1937. *Middletown in Transition: A Study in Cultural Conflicts.* New York: Harcourt, Brace and Company.

MacDonald, J. Fred. 1979. *Don't Touch that Dial: Radio Programming in American Life, 1920–1960*. Chicago: Nelson-Hall.

Mack, Arien, ed. 1997. *Technology and the Rest of Culture*. Columbus: The Ohio State University Press.

Mackenzie, Donald, and Judy Wajcman. 1986. *The Social Shaping of Technology: How the Refrigerator Got Its Hum*. Philadelphia: Open University Press.

Marchand, Roland. 1986. *Advertising the American Dream: Making Way for Modernity, 1920–1940*. Berkeley: University of California Press.

Martinez, Katharine, and Kenneth L. Ames, 1997. *The Material Culture of Gender: The Gender of Material Culture*. Winterthur, DE: Henry Francis du Pont Winterthur Museum.

Mason, David L. 2004. *From Buildings and Loans to Bail- Outs: A History of the American Savings and Loan Industry, 1831–1995*. New York: Cambridge University Press.

Mathews, Glenna. 1987. *"Just a Housewife:" The Rise and Fall of Domesticity in America*. New York: Oxford University Press.

Mattingly, Paul H. 2001. *Suburban Landscape: Culture and Politics in a New York Metropolitan Community*. Baltimore: John Hopkins University Press.

McCarter, Robert, ed. 2005. *On and By Frank Lloyd Wright: A Primer on Architectural Principles*. New York: Phaidon Press.

McShane, Clay. 1994. *Down the Asphalt Path: The Automobile and the American City*. New York: Columbia University Press.

McShane, Clay, and Stanley K. Schultz. 1978. "To Engineer the Metropolis: Sewers, Sanitation, and City Planning in Late 19th Century America." *Journal of American History* 65: 389–411.

Melosi, Martin. 2000. *The Sanitary City: Urban Infrastructure from Colonial Times to Present*. Baltimore: John Hopkins University Press.

Meyerowitz, Joanne. 1988. *Women Adrift: Independent Wage Earners in Chicago, 1880–1930*. Chicago: University of Chicago Press.

Miller, Zane. 1981. *Suburb: Neighborhood and Community in Forest Park, Ohio, 1935–1976*. Knoxville: The University of Tennessee Press.

Mills, C. Wright. 1956. *White Collar: The American Middle Classes*. New York: Oxford University Press.

Mirken, Alan, ed. 1970. *1927 Edition of the Sears, Roebuck Catalog*. New York: Bounty Books.

Mohun, Arwen. 1999. *Steam Laundries: Gender, Technology, and Work in the United States and Great Britain, 1880–1940*. Baltimore: John Hopkins University Press.

Morris, Earl W., and Mary Winter. 1978. *Housing, Family, and Society*. New York: John Wiley and Sons.

Mumford, Lewis. 1961. *The City in History: Its Origins, Its Transformations, and Its Prospects*. New York: Harcourt Brace Jovanovich.

Nickels, Shelley. 2002. " 'Preserving Women:' Refrigerator Design as a Social Process in the 1930s." *Technology and Culture* 42: 693–727.

Nye, David E. 1997. *Electrifying America: Social Meanings of a New Technology, 1880–1940*. Cambridge, MA: MIT Press.

Ogburn, William F. 1930. *Social Changes in 1929*. Chicago: University of Chicago Press.

Ogle, Maureen. 1996. *All the Modern Conveniences: American Household Plumbing, 1840–1990*. Baltimore: John Hopkins University Press.

Olney, Martha. 1991. *Buy Now Pay Later: Advertising, Credit, and Consumer Durables in the 1920s*. Chapel Hill: University of North Carolina Press.

Ore, Janet. 1981. "Jud Yoho, 'the Bungalow Craftsman,' and the Development of Seattle Suburbs." *Perspective in Vernacular Architecture VI.*

Ore, Janet. 2007. *The Seattle Bungalow: People and Houses, 1900–1940.* Seattle: University of Washington Press.

Patnode, Randall. 2004. "What These People Need is a Radio: New Technology, the Press, and Otherness in 1920s America." *Technology and Culture* 45: 396–405.

Pegg, Mark. 1983. *Broadcasting and Society 1918–1939.* London: Croom Helm.

Perin, Constance. 1978. *Everything in its Place: The Social Order of Land Use in America.* Princeton: Princeton University Press.

Petro, Sylvester. 1961. *The Kohler Strike: Union Violence and Administrative Law.* Chicago: H. Regnery Co.

Peyser, Ethel R. 1932. "The Electrically Equipped Home." *House and Garden* 43: 37–39.

Pleck, Elizabeth H. 2000. *Celebrating Family: Ethnicity, Consumer Culture, and Family Rituals.* Cambridge, MA: Harvard University Press.

Potter, David. 1954. *People of Plenty: Economic Abundance and the American Character.* Chicago: University of Chicago Press.

Prosser, Daniel. 1981. "Chicago and the Bungalow Boom of the Late 1920s." *Chicago History* (Summer): 86–96.

Radford, Gail. 1996. *Modern Housing for America: Policy Struggles in the New Deal Era.* Chicago: University of Chicago Press.

Reiff, Daniel D. 2000. *Houses from Books: Treatises, Pattern Books, and Catalogs in American Architecture, 1738–1950: A History and Guide.* University Park: Pennsylvania State University Press.

Rhoads, William B. 1976. "The Colonial Revival and American Nationalism." *Journal of the Society of Architectural Historians* (December): 239–254.

Robertson, Cheryl. 1991. "Male and Female Agendas for Domestic Reform: The Middle-Class Bungalow in Gendered Perspective." *Winterthur Portfolio* 26: 123–141.

Roell, Craig H. 1989. *The Piano in America, 1890–1940.* Chapel Hill: University of North Carolina Press.

Roland Reisley, 2001. *Usonia, New York: Building a Community with Frank Lloyd Wright.* New York: Princeton Architectural Press.

Rose, Mark. 1990. *Interstate Express: Highway Politics, 1939–1989.* Knoxville: The University of Tennessee Press.

Rose, Mark. 1995. *Cities of Light and Heat: Domesticating Gas and Electricity in Urban America.* University Park: Pennsylvania State University Press.

Salomonsky, Verna Cook. 1923. "Furnishing the Small House: IV. Practical Suggestions for the Living-Room." *House Beautiful* 54: 226–227.

Sandweiss, Eric. 2001. *St. Louis: The Evolution of the American Urban Landscape.* Philadelphia: Temple University Press.

Schartz, Barry, ed. 1976. *The Changing Face of the Suburbs.* Chicago: University of Chicago Press.

Schweitzer, Robert, and Michael W. R. Davis. 1990. *America's Favorite Homes: Mail Order Catalogs as a Guide to Popular Early 20th Century Houses.* Detroit: Wayne State University Press.

Sears, Roebuck and Co. 1991 [1926]. *Small Houses of the Twenties: The Sears, Roebuck 1926 House Catalog.* New York: Dover Publications and The Athenaeum of Philadelphia.

Sharp, Dennis. 1991. *Twentieth Century Architecture: A Visual History.* New York: Facts on File.

Sivulka, Juliann. 2001. *Stronger Than Dirt: A Cultural History of Advertising Personal Hygiene in America, 1875 to 1940.* New York: Humanity Books.

Smeins, Linda E. 1999. *Building An American Identity: Pattern Book Homes and Communities.* Walnut Creek, CA: Alta Mira Press.

Smulyan, Susan. 1994. *Selling Radio: The Commercialization of American Broadcasting, 1920–1934.* Washington, D.C.: Smithsonian Press.

Spiegel, Lynn. 2001. *Welcome to the Dreamhouse: Popular Media and Postwar Suburbs.* Durham, NC: Duke University Press.

Stage, Sarah, and Virginia B. Vincenti, eds. 1997. *Rethinking Home Economics: Women and the History of a Profession.* Ithaca, NY: Cornell University Press.

Steinberg, Salme Harju. 1979. *Reformer in the Marketplace: Edward W. Bok and the Ladies' Home Journal.* Baton Rouge: Louisiana State University Press.

Stevenson, Katherine Cole, and H. Ward Jandl. 1986. *Houses by Mail: A Guide to Houses from Sears, Roebuck and Company.* Washington, D.C.: Preservation Press.

Stewart, Ross, and John Gerald. 1935. *Home Decoration: Its Problems and Solutions.* New York: Julian Messner, Inc.

Stilgoe, John R. 1988. *Borderland: Origins of the American Suburb, 1820–1939.* New Haven, CT: Yale University Press.

St. John, F. J. 1925. "Artificial Refrigeration: Ice without the Iceman." *House Beautiful* 57: 404, 433.

Storrer, William Allin. 1993. *The Frank Lloyd Wright Companion.* Chicago: University of Chicago Press.

Strasser, Susan. 1982. *Never Done: The History of American Housework.* New York: Henry Holt and Company.

Sugrue, Thomas. 1996. *The Origins of the Urban Crisis: Race and Inequality in Postwar Detroit.* Princeton: Princeton University Press.

Susman, Warren. 1984. *Culture as History: The Transformation of American Society in the Twentieth Century.* New York: Pantheon Books.

Swisher, Jacob A. 1940. "The Evolution of Wash Day." *Iowa Journal of History and Politics* 38: 3–49.

Tarr, Joel A. 1996. *The Search for the Ultimate Sink: Urban Pollution in Historical Perspective.* Akron, OH: University of Akron Press.

Taylor, Henry Louis. 1979. "The Building of a Black Industrial Suburb: The Lincoln Heights, Ohio, Story." PhD dissertation, State University of New York at Buffalo.

Taylor, Ronald D., and Margaret C. Wang, eds. 2000. *Resilience Across Contexts: Family, Work, Culture, and Community.* Mahwah, NJ: Lawrence Erlbaum.

Thornton, Rosemary. 2002. *The Houses That Sears Built: Everything You Ever Wanted to Know About Sears Catalog Homes.* Alton, IL: Gentle Beam Publications.

Tobey, Ronald. 1996. *Technology as Freedom: The New Deal and the Electrical Modernization of the American Home.* Berkeley: University of California Press.

Vale, Lawrence J. 2000. *From the Puritans to the Projects: Public Housing and Public Neighbors.* Cambridge, MA: Harvard University Press.

Verhoff, Andrew John. 1996. "A Steady Demand for the Usual: The Federal Housing Administration's Effect on the Design of Houses in Suburban Indianapolis, 1949–1955." Master's thesis, Indiana University.

Volti, Rudi. 2004. "William F. Ogburn: Social Change with Respect to Culture and Original Nature." *Technology and Culture* 45: 396–405.

Wachs, Martin, and Margaret Crawford. 1996. *The Car and the City: The Automobile, the Built Environment, Daily Urban Life.* Ann Arbor: University of Michigan Press.

Walch, Timothy, ed. 2003. *Uncommon Americans: The Lives and Legacies of Herbert and Lou Henry Hoover.* Westport, CT: Praeger.

Weiss, Marc. 1987. *The Rise of the Community Builders: the American Real Estate Industry and Urban Land Planning.* New York: Columbia University Press.

Weiss, Marc. 1991. *Own Your Own Home: Housing Policy and Home Ownership in America.* New York: Columbia University Press.

West, Patricia. 1976. "The Rise and Fall of the American Porch." *Landscape* 20: 42–47.

Whitton, Mary Ormsbee. 1927. *The New Servant: Electricity in the Home.* New York: Doubleday.

Wiese, Andrew. 2004. *Places of Their Own: African American Suburbanization in the Twentieth Century.* Chicago: University of Chicago Press.

Wilson, Kristina. 2004. *Livable Modernism: Interior Decorating and Design During the Great Depression.* New Haven, CT: Yale University Press.

Wilson, Richard Guy. 1979. "Idealism and the Origin of the First American Suburb: Llewellyn Park, New Jersey." *The American Art Journal* (October): 79–90.

Wright, Gwendolyn. 1975. "Sweet and Clean: The Domestic Landscape in the Progressive Era." *Landscape* (October): 38–43.

Wright, Gwendolyn. 1980. *Moralism and the Model Home: Domestic Architecture and Cultural Conflict in Chicago.* Chicago: University of Chicago Press.

Wright, Gwendolyn. 1981. *Building the Dream: A Social History of Housing in America.* Cambridge, MA: MIT Press.

Yukio Futagawa and Bruce Brooks Pfeiffer. 2002. *Frank Lloyd Wright: Usonian Houses.* Tokyo: A.D.A. Edita.

Yukio Futagawa and Bruce Brooks Pfeiffer. 2002. *Frank Lloyd Wright: Prairie Houses.* Tokyo: A.D.A. Edita.

Zunz, Olivier. 1982. *The Changing Face of Inequality: Urbanization, Industrial Development, and Immigrants in Detroit, 1880–1920.* Chicago: University of Chicago Press.

MUSEUMS, ORGANIZATIONS, SPECIAL COLLECTIONS, AND USEFUL WEB SITES

Modernism: Designing a New World, 1914–1939. Critically acclaimed exhibition. Corcoran Gallery, Washington, D.C. Exhibition site. http://www.corcoran.org/modernism/index.htm. V&A, London. Exhibition site. http://www.vam.ac.uk/vastatic/microsites/1331_modernism/home.html. Exhibition catalog. Wilk, Christopher, ed. 2006. *Modernism: Designing a New World, 1914–1939.* London: V&A Publications. The largest and most comprehensive exhibition to be staged on modernism was originally organized by London's Victoria and Albert Museum in 2006 and hosted by the Corcoran Gallery of Art in 2007.

Art Deco Welcome Center
Miami Design Preservation League
1001 Ocean Drive
Miami Beach, FL 33139
http://www.mdpl.org/

The largest twentieth-century National Register Historic District in the United States, the art deco area in South Beach contains over 800 historic buildings erected during the 1920s and 1930s. Flat roofs, smooth stucco walls, and a distinctly modern design characterize the art deco buildings. Guided and self-guided walking tours are available.

Fallingwater
Western Pennsylvania Conservancy
Fallingwater PO Box R
Mill Run, PA 15464
http://www.paconserve.org/index-fw1.asp

Frank Lloyd Wright's masterpiece Fallingwater is located on PA Route 381 between the villages of Mill Run and Ohiopyle.

Greenbelt Museum
15 Crescent Road
Greenbelt, MD. 20770
http://www.greenbeltmuseum.org/

Greenbelt, Maryland is a New Deal planned community built in 1937 and now registered as a National Historic Landmark. Designed as a cooperative garden suburb, Greenbelt was a model of modern town planning. Visitors experience Greenbelt's history through walking tours, exhibits, and tours of a historic art deco house museum.

Pope-Leighey House
P.O. Box 37
Mount Vernon, VA 22309
http://www.nationaltrust.org/woodlawn/

This Frank Lloyd Wright designed Usonian house was originally planned and built in Falls Church, Virginia, in 1938–1939. The house was given to the National Trust for Historic Preservation and moved to the Woodlawn Plantation grounds when threatened with demolition in 1964 during the construction of Interstate 66. It is now open to the public and visitors can explore both the interior and exterior of the house.

Warren G. Harding Home
380 Mt. Vernon Avenue
Marion, OH 43302
http://www.ohiohistory.org/places/harding/

Warren G. Harding was elected president in the wake of his famous 1920 "front porch" campaign conducted from his Victorian home in Marion, Ohio. The restored house was built in 1891 and contains almost all original furnishings owned by President Harding and his wife, Florence. In preparation for the campaign, Harding renovated his house with the latest in interior furnishings and modern decoration. Beginning in 2005, the museum began a room-by-room restoration of the 1920 interiors. Adjacent to the Harding

Home is a press house used during the 1920 campaign that now serves as a museum dedicated to President and Mrs. Harding's lives.

Woodrow Wilson House Museum
2340 S Street, N.W.
Washington, D.C. 20008
http://www.woodrowwilsonhouse.org/

A museum property of the National Trust for Historic Preservation, the house was purchased by the President in 1920. Wilson lived in the house until his death in 1924. The house is a textbook of modern American life in the 1920s filled with the furniture, clothing, and artifacts from the period. The house underwent an award winning $1 million interior and exterior restoration completed in 2005.

National Register Bulletin: Historic Residential Suburbs. National Register, History and Education. http://www.nps.gov/history/nr/publications/bulletins/suburbs/part3.htm. U.S. Department of the Interior, National Park Service.

Richman, Joe. "Conrad's Garage," Lost and Found Sound series. http://www.npr.org/programs/lnfsound/stories/011130.garage.html. National Public Radio. Nov. 30, 2001. Radio program about Frank Conrad "replaying the earliest days of radio." Available in Real Audio format.

VIDEOS/FILMS

It's a Wonderful Life. Dir. Frank Capra. James Stewart, Donna Reed, and Lionel Barrymore. Paramount. 1946. 60th anniversary DVD release 2006.

A timeless classic, but one where the savings and loan is central to the development of a small town. It also shows a number of houses, including a subdivision of new houses in the 1940s.

The Awful Truth. Dir. Leo McCarey. Cary Grant and Irene Dunne. Sony Pictures. 1937. DVD release 2003.

As their divorce becomes final, a couple tries to ruin each others plans for remarriage, one to a socialite and one to an oil-rich country bumpkin. A superb comedy that showcases the country's infatuation with wealth and high society at the height of the Depression.

Index

Mount Vernon house (Washington), 56
Mount Wilson observatory, 75, 76
Movie industry, 189–90
Muir, John, 133
Multiple-family dwellings, 46
Mumford, Lewis, 110
Murphy, Paul, 266
Museum of Fine Arts (Boston), 114
Museums
  Beaux-Arts mansions as, 31–33
  Frick Museum and Library, 31–32
  Isabella Stewart Gardner Museum, 32
  La Jolla Museum of Contemporary Art, 33, 74
  Metropolitan Museum of Art, 31, 118, 207
  Museum of Fine Arts (Boston), 114
  Smithsonian National Design Museum, 31

Nantucket Cape homes, 98
National Association of Real Estate Boards, 197
National Board of Realtors, 181
National Builder journal, 248
National Federation of Construction Industries, 266
National Origins Act (1924), 184
National Park Service Organic Act (1916), 136
National parks/urban parks, 135–36
National Playground Association, 130
National Register of Historic Places, 134
National Retail Lumber Dealers Association, 197
Native American Revivals, in Southwest, 59–60, 116, 117
Nativism, in U.S., 184
Natural materials, in home construction
  adobe and stucco, 89
  bricks and mortar, 87–89
  masonry, 89
  in New England, 85
  roofs and roofing materials, 87
  wood, wood framing, 86–87
  wood siding and shingles, 87
  See also Woods Hole Oceanographic Institute
Near-urban neighborhoods, 203–4
Necessity of outbuildings, 127–28
Neff, Wallace, 116
Neutra, Richard, 216–17

New Deal programs, 183, 196–97, 268–69
New York, 18
  Fifth Avenue mansions and garden, 31–32, 53
  Greenwich Village art studios, 35
  neoclassical facades for libraries, 52
  New York Public Library, 16, 21, 40
  revival houses and estates, 51
  Roosevelt's Sagamore Hill home, 22;
  Set-Back Law (NYC), 90
  skyscrapers of, 36
  subway construction, 20
New York Times, 19, 23, 27–28, 29, 91
Nichols, J. C., 202–3
Nickels, Shelley, 232

Observatories
  homes for, 75
  Lamont Earth Observatory, 33
  Mount Palomar observatory, 75, 76
  Mount Wilson observatory, 75, 76
  in Southern California, 74
Oceanography
  homes by the sea, 76–77
  Woods Hole Oceanographic Institute, 86
Ogburn, W. F., 190
Olmstead, Frederick Law, 133, 136, 145, 149
Olmstead Brothers, 135, 136
  See also Frederick Law Olmsted National Historic Site
Orbaugh, William, 233
Orders of architecture
  See Classical Orders of architecture; Corinthian Order; Doric Order; Ionic Order
Ore, Janet, 209
Organic and geometric homes, 77–79
  See also Gill, Irving; Wright, Frank Lloyd
Organizational society *vs.* specialization, in U.S., 180–81
Oriental carpets, 281, 291, 293, 295
The Origins of the Urban Crisis: Race and Inequality in Postwar Detroit (Sugrue), 271
Outbuildings
  carports, 218, 219, 261–62
  front yards/back yards, 130
  garages, 308–10
  for leisure and sport, 128–29
  for necessity and labor, 127–28
  playhouses, 129–30
  porches, 307

About the Editor and Authors

LESLIE HUMM CORMIER, historian and critic of modern architecture, received her doctorate and masters' degrees in architectural history and theory from Brown University, where she was a Samuel H. Kress Fellow. She holds a professional MCRP degree in urban planning and has been named De Montequin Fellow of the Society of Architectural Historians. Having taught modern art and architecture at Radcliffe and Harvard University Extension, Cormier is currently on the visual arts faculty of Emerson College, Boston.

NEAL V. HITCH is a historian, preservation architect, and a museum specialist. He holds a master's degree in architecture and a doctorate in history from The Ohio State University. He specializes in nineteenth- and twentieth-century life, culture, and architecture. His current work includes research and implementation for the restoration of authentic twentieth-century domestic interiors.

Since 1997, Dr. Hitch has worked for the Ohio Historical Society, a nonprofit corporation providing historical services for the State of Ohio. He is a historic housing specialist and has worked on some of the Society's premier restoration projects. In 2005, his restoration of the Paul Laurence Dunbar House, in Dayton, Ohio, received preservation awards from the Victorian Society in America and from the American Association of State and Local History.

THOMAS W. PARADIS is Director, Office of Academic Assessment, and Associate Professor of Geography and Planning at Northern Arizona University. He has taught and written on historic preservation, cultural geography, urban design, and assessment of student learning.